Neuromorphic Computing Principles and Organization

Abderazek Ben Abdallah • Khanh N. Dang

Neuromorphic Computing Principles and Organization

Second Edition

Springer

Abderazek Ben Abdallah
School of Computer Science and Engineering
The Aizu University
Aizu-Wakamatsu, Fukushima, Japan

Khanh N. Dang
School of Computer Science and Engineering
The Aizu University
Aizu-Wakamatsu, Fukushima, Japan

ISBN 978-3-031-83091-4 ISBN 978-3-031-83089-1 (eBook)
https://doi.org/10.1007/978-3-031-83089-1

This Springer imprint is published by the registered company Springer Nature Switzerland AG
The registered company address is: Gewerbestrasse 11, 6330 Cham, Switzerland

ABA – To my parents, wife sonia, daughter Tesnim, and son Beyram

KND – To my parents, wife Trang, and son Bach

Foreword

The second edition of *Neuromorphic Computing Principles and Organization* by Professor Ben Abdallah and Associate Professor Khanh N. Dang is a remarkable contribution to the rapidly evolving field of neuromorphic computing. These two luminaries, renowned for their expertise in 3D-ICs, embedded systems, and neuromorphic system design, have once again provided an authoritative and comprehensive resource for researchers, practitioners, and students alike.

My journey with Professor Ben Abdallah's work began many years ago when I first encountered his seminal publications. Over time, my admiration for his groundbreaking contributions deepened as I had the privilege of attending the prestigious IEEE Symposium on Embedded Multicore/Many-core Systems-on-Chip (MCSoC) multiple times, a forum initiated and led by Professor Ben Abdallah himself. These forums have been a crucible of innovation, bringing together leading experts and fostering critical discussions that shape the future of computing. His ability to inspire and educate, through both his written work and his leadership at these events, is unparalleled.

This book, co-authored with Associate Professor Khanh N. Dang, exemplifies their dedication to advancing the frontiers of neuromorphic computing. The second edition is not merely an update of the original text, it is a comprehensive expansion and refinement. Each chapter has been meticulously revised to reflect the latest advancements, and the inclusion of a new chapter on advanced neuromorphic prosthesis design is particularly noteworthy. This chapter provides an in-depth case study demonstrating the transformative potential of neuromorphic principles in addressing real-world challenges, particularly in healthcare and assistive technologies.

The book is structured to provide a logical and accessible pathway for readers. It begins with an overview of neuromorphic systems and fundamental concepts of artificial neural networks, ensuring readers build a strong foundation before progressing to more complex topics. The discussions on artificial neurons, neuron models, and inter-neuron communication are detailed and insightful, offering readers a clear understanding of the intricate mechanisms underlying spiking neural networks.

One of the standout features of this edition is its exploration of emerging memory technologies and their integration into neuromorphic systems. Memory has long been a critical bottleneck in computing systems, and the book addresses this challenge head-on. From photonic interconnects to Address Event Representation (AER) protocols, the authors provide innovative solutions and forward-looking insights that are both timely and impactful.

The chapter dedicated to circuits and architectures is another highlight. The discussions on Network-on-Chip (NoC) fabric, memory access methods, and fault tolerance are particularly relevant in building scalable and reliable neuromorphic systems. These concepts are theoretically sound and rooted in practical implementation, reflecting the authors' deep understanding of the interplay between hardware and software in neuromorphic design.

Reliability and scalability are recurring themes throughout the book. The emphasis on recovery methods for multicore systems and reconfigurable designs capable of supporting multiple applications is especially significant. These features are essential for building systems adapting to the dynamic demands of modern computing environments. The book's exploration of a three-dimensional neuromorphic processor is a testament to this adaptability. By focusing on high integration density, minimal spike delay, and scalability, the authors provide a roadmap for future innovations in neuromorphic hardware.

Another remarkable aspect of this book is its accessibility. Recognizing the diverse audience it serves, the authors have included exercises at the end of each chapter to reinforce understanding and encourage hands-on learning. Furthermore, the book is accompanied by a dedicated website where readers can access supplementary materials, including slides for each chapter, laboratory exercises, and tutorials. This online resource significantly enhances the learning experience, making it an invaluable tool for educators and self-learners alike.

As a fellow academic and researcher, I am deeply impressed by the depth and breadth of this book. Professor Ben Abdallah and Associate Professor Khanh N. Dang have masterfully synthesized complex ideas into a cohesive narrative that is both informative and engaging. The concluding chapter, which provides a comprehensive review of neuromorphic systems, ties together the key concepts discussed throughout the text and offers a holistic understanding of the field.

For those new to neuromorphic computing, this book is an excellent introduction. For seasoned professionals, it offers fresh insights and a wealth of advanced knowledge. It is a resource that will undoubtedly inspire and educate generations of researchers and practitioners.

As Professor Kiat Seng Yeo, an IEEE Fellow and someone deeply committed to advancing low-power integrated circuit design, I have always appreciated the importance of interdisciplinary collaboration and innovation. This book exemplifies both. It is a privilege to commend this work to you, and I am confident that it will serve as a cornerstone in the ongoing development of neuromorphic computing.

Professor Ben Abdallah and Associate Professor Khanh N. Dang remind us that the future of computing lies not only in faster processors or larger storage capacities but also in systems that emulate the extraordinary capabilities of the human brain. This book is a step toward that future, and it is an honor to endorse it.

Prof. Kiat Seng Yeo, a Singaporean Academic and an IEEE Fellow known for his contributions to low-power integrated circuit design *Singapore University of Technology and Design (SUTD), Singapore*.

Preface

As technology advances at an extraordinary pace, the need for intelligent, efficient, and adaptive computing solutions is becoming increasingly apparent. Neuromorphic computing has emerged as a transformative approach inspired by the architecture and functioning of the human brain. The landscape of neuromorphic computing has evolved significantly since the first edition of this book, driven by an increasing demand for systems that mimic human cognitive processes. With advancements in artificial intelligence, machine learning, robotics, and IoT technologies, the exploration of brain-inspired computing systems has become more pertinent.

The roots of neuromorphic computing can be traced back several decades, with significant contributions from pioneers such as Carver Mead, who envisioned systems that could replicate the brain's capabilities. The field has matured into a vibrant interdisciplinary study area, combining insights from neuroscience, computer engineering, and cognitive science. As research progresses, neuromorphic systems are beginning to demonstrate their potential in real-world applications, from autonomous machines to advanced data processing techniques.

The first edition of this book has provided a comprehensive exploration of this innovative field, and it is with great excitement that we present this second edition, which includes updates and expansions on key topics initially covered, as well as new advancements and challenges faced in this fast-evolving discipline. This edition reflects contemporary trends in the field, addressing the latest developments in neuromorphic architecture, computational models, learning mechanisms, and emerging technologies. By revisiting the chapters, readers will recognize the continuity of ideas while appreciating the emerging insights and knowledge landscapes. In addition, this second edition includes exercises at the end of each chapter. These exercises reinforce the concepts, helping readers deepen their understanding and apply their knowledge practically. By working through these exercises, readers can enhance their learning experience and gain valuable hands-on practice in the fascinating field of neuromorphic computing. This new edition aims to build upon the solid foundation established in the first, incorporating new research findings, technological advancements, and practical applications that have emerged since its initial publication.

This book is structured into ten independent chapters. Each chapter is designed to be self-contained, ensuring you can fully understand the material without referring to other sections.

Chapter 1 introduces the fundamental concepts of neuromorphic computing systems, framing the current state of research and applications in a broader context. A key focus is placed on the motivations behind developing brain-inspired systems and their potential impact across various domains. We first discuss biological neurons and the dynamics that are abstracted from them to model artificial neurons. Next, we discuss artificial neurons and how they have evolved in their representation of biological neuronal dynamics. Afterward, we discuss implementing these neural networks in terms of neuron models, storage technologies, inter-neuron communication networks, learning, and various design approaches.

In **Chap. 2**, the book delves into the essential principles of designing neuromorphic systems. It provides an updated exploration of neuron models, synaptic structures, architectural considerations, design challenges, and hardware-software integration in the design process. The challenges that need to be solved in building a spiking neural network architecture with many synapses in hardware include building a small-sized massively parallel architecture with low power consumption, an efficient neuron coding scheme, and a lightweight on-chip learning algorithm. The other significant challenges are the on-chip communication and routing network, which allows data to be communicated between neurocores and off-chip data to be transferred to the cores. The revised content aims to give readers a holistic understanding of the underlying principles guiding effective neuromorphic designs.

Chapter 3 presents how learning in neuromorphic computing systems is conducted. Neuromorphic hardware aims to emulate brain-like neural networks to solve real-world problems. However, training on neuromorphic systems is challenging to the required non-local computations of gradient-based learning algorithms. Spiking neural networks gained popularity by incorporating learning. In these neural networks, there are two fundamental modes: inference and learning. The learning phase, which minimizes a particular cost (loss) function, is a complex process of acquiring the parameters to output the correct inference results. In contrast, inference is computing the output values based on the input and the network parameters. This edition highlights novel learning algorithms and their efficacy in enhancing the performance of neuromorphic systems, accompanied by practical examples of their application.

Chapter 4 discusses the major emerging memory technologies that promise neuromorphic computing and highlights recent significant progress in device studies. To design a neuromorphic system on hardware, it is imperative to develop artificial neurons that mimic biological neurons and artificial synapses that emulate biological synapses. Recently, numerous efforts have been made to realize artificial synapses using post-CMOS devices, including resistive random access memory (ReRAM), ferroelectric field-effect transistor (FeFET), phase change memory devices, magnetoresistive random access memory (MRAM), etc. A CMOS neuron based on emerging devices has also been investigated.

Chapter 5 presents the circuits and architectures used for communication in neuromorphic systems. In particular, the Network-on-Chip fabric is introduced for receiving and transmitting spikes following the Address Event Representation (AER) protocol and the memory accessing method. Since each neuron is connected to many others, high bandwidth and low communication latency are needed. Therefore, effective communication protocols are fundamental for ensuring the efficiency of neuromorphic systems. First, the chapter describes the interconnect method for inter-neuron communication. Second, the interconnect design principle is covered to help understand the overall concept of on-chip and off-chip communication. The remaining parts cover advanced on-chip interconnect technologies, including si-photonic three-dimensional interconnects. The updated content addresses the challenges of scaling and managing communication in increasingly complex systems.

In response to the growing complexity of neuromorphic systems, **Chap. 6** has been expanded to discuss advanced methodologies for ensuring reliability and robustness. It examines fault-tolerant techniques that draw inspiration from biological systems and presents novel strategies to enhance the resilience of neuromorphic architectures against component failures and environmental variability.

In **Chap. 7**, we explore the concept of reconfigurability in neuromorphic systems in greater depth. We highlight cutting-edge hardware and software innovations that facilitate dynamic adjustments in system architecture, providing readers with valuable insights into how reconfigurable designs can enhance performance across various applications. This chapter introduces the architecture and hardware design of a reconfigurable spiking neuromorphic system that features a reconfigurable Multi-Layer Perceptron. This system can recover from faults using practical methods that leverage field programmable gate array (FPGA) technology while avoiding reliance on proprietary FPGA intellectual property. This strategy enables implementation in application-specific integrated circuits (ASICs). Traditional spiking neuromorphic designs typically prioritize fixed functionality using off-the-shelf components, which limits their adaptability to diverse computing environments. In contrast, a reconfigurable design approach promotes support for multiple target applications through dynamic reconfigurability, independence from specific network topologies, and enhanced network expandability.

Chapter 8 introduces a hardware-software design for a reliable three-dimensional digital neuromorphic processor specifically tailored to mimic the biological brain's three-dimensional structure found in 3D integrated circuits (3D-ICs). This platform boasts high integration density, minimal spike delays within spiking networks, and a scalable architecture. The design utilizes through-silicon-via (TSV) technology, enabling the implementation of spiking neural networks on clustered neurons through a network-on-chip (NoC) framework. Additionally, the system includes a memory interface with the host CPU, facilitating online training and inference for spiking neural networks. Notably, the system incorporates fault detection and recovery mechanisms, allowing for graceful performance degradation under adverse conditions.

Chapter 9 provides an in-depth exploration of cutting-edge approaches to prosthetic technology, serving as a compelling case study for Neuromorphic AI-chip applications. It begins by examining 3D printing techniques developed explicitly for the AIzuHand prosthetic, showcasing significant advancements in customization and accessibility. The chapter then delves into artificial neural network-based control systems that improve prosthetic performance and presents various neural network architectures optimized for accurate gesture classification. Furthermore, it investigates spiking neural network (SNN) methods for prosthetic control, highlighting their superior processing capabilities and responsiveness. The chapter also introduces a user-friendly mobile app that allows direct control of the prosthetic system, promoting enhanced user engagement and convenience. To illustrate the real-world applicability of these technologies, it concludes with interactive virtual scenarios set in kitchen and workbench environments, demonstrating how these innovations can facilitate everyday tasks and elevate the overall user experience.

Chapter 10 offers a thorough survey of the research landscape in neuromorphic computing systems. It begins by outlining the motivations behind neuromorphic computing, highlighting its significance and potential benefits. The chapter then explores vital research contributions in this domain, categorizing them into three main approaches: software emulation, digital hardware, and analog/mixed-signal hardware. This chapter aims to comprehensively review existing research in neuromorphic computing while identifying critical gaps that present opportunities for future investigation and innovation.

Acknowledgments

Completing this book has been a nearly three-year journey rooted in our research and educational experiences in adaptive computing and the design of neuromorphic systems. The neuromorphic computing paradigm has provided exceptional opportunities to investigate the performance of cognitive AI systems while presenting numerous design challenges that engineers must address. To propel the field of neuromorphic computing forward, it is essential to explore innovative materials and devices that enhance power efficiency and scalability beyond current CMOS solutions. This pursuit requires continuous innovation in algorithms and techniques to tackle these challenges effectively. Additionally, it is crucial to educate future computer science and computer engineering students in both neuromorphic computing and engineering principles.

As we strive to improve the quality and relevance of our content continuously, we would be immensely grateful for your feedback on these exercises and other aspects of the book. Your insights will help us refine our approach, address gaps, and develop a more comprehensive third edition tailored to the needs of our readers. By collaborating with students, educators, researchers, and industry professionals, we can ensure that the book remains current and addresses the challenges and advancements in this fast-growing and emerging computing paradigm. Thank you for your contributions to this endeavor; your input is invaluable in shaping the future editions of the book.

We extend our deepest gratitude to Dr. Mark Ogbodo, Dr. Zhishang Wang, and Dr. Wang Jiangkun from the University of Aizu and Dr. Vu for their invaluable insights and unwavering support throughout this endeavor. Special thanks to the University of Aizu for providing the essential software and hardware tools for several experiments.

This book on neuromorphic computing principles and organization is an essential resource for researchers, scientists, graduate students, and hardware-software engineers grappling with the increasing demands for fault tolerance, scalability, and energy efficiency in computational systems. It also provides a robust foundation for instructing advanced undergraduate and graduate students on the core concepts, organizational frameworks, and practical hardware-software designs of reliable neuromorphic systems that incorporate learning and fault-tolerance mechanisms. By effectively bridging theory and application, this book empowers readers with the knowledge and skills to navigate the complexities of neuromorphic computing, enabling them to make meaningful contributions to this cutting-edge field. To enhance the learning experience further, each chapter includes a set of exercises designed to reinforce key concepts and promote the practical application of the material. These exercises encourage deeper engagement with the topics and facilitate a more comprehensive understanding, ensuring readers can effectively apply their knowledge in real-world scenarios.

Aizu-Wakamatsu, Japan

Abderazek Ben Abdallah
Khanh N. Dang

Contents

About the Authors

Dr. Abderazek Ben Abdallah received his Ph.D. in computer engineering from the University of Electro-Communications in Tokyo in 2002. From April 2014 to March 2022, he served as the Head of the Computer Engineering Division at the University of Aizu, Japan. Since April 2022, he has held the position of Dean at the School of Computer Science and Engineering at the University of Aizu. Currently, Dr. Ben Abdallah is a Full Professor at the University of Aizu. He is the author of four books and holds six registered and eight provisional Japanese patents. Additionally, he has published over 150 peer-reviewed journal articles and conference papers. His research interests span adaptive and self-organizing systems, neuromorphic computing, interconnection networks, and AI-powered cyber-physical systems. Dr. Ben Abdallah is a Senior Member of both the IEEE and ACM, reflecting his significant contributions to computer engineering.

Dr. Khanh N. Dang currently serves as an Associate Professor in the Department of Computer Science and Engineering at the University of Aizu. He earned his Ph.D. from the University of Aizu and his M.Sc. from the University of Paris XI. Dr. Dang has published numerous peer-reviewed journal articles and presented his work at various conferences. He is also the author of one book and holds several provisional patents in Japan. Dr. Dang's research areas include Network-on-Chips (NoC), 3D Integrated Circuits (3D-ICs), neuromorphic computing, and fault-tolerant systems. Within these fields, he focuses on developing efficient communication architectures and enhancing the reliability and performance of multi-core processors. In neuromorphic computing, he explores the implementation of brain-inspired algorithms to create more efficient and intelligent systems. He is a member of IEEE.

Acronyms

AAAI	American Association for Artificial Intelligence
ACK	Acknowledgment
ACM	Association for Computing Machinery
ADC	Analog-to-Digital Converter
ADM	Approximate Derivative Method
AER	Address Event Representation
AHB	Advanced High-performance Bus
AI	Artificial Intelligence
AMBA	Advanced Microcontroller Bus Architecture
AMD	Advanced Micro Devices
ANN	Artificial Neural Network
API	Application Programming Interface
ARM	Advanced RISC Machines
ASIC	Application-Specific Integrated Circuit
ASID	Anti-Counterfeiting, Security and Identification
BCM	Building Cube Method
BE	Best Effort
BL	Bit Line
BP	Backpropagation
BW	Buffer Writing
BWCCA	Broadband and Wireless Computing, Communication and Applications
CAD	Computer-Aided Design
CAM	Content-Access-Memory
CASES	Conference on Compilers, Architecture and Synthesis for Embedded Systems
CD	Compact Disc
CICC	Custom Integrated Circuits Conference
CIFAR	Canadian Institute For Advanced Research
CLEO	Conference on Lasers and Electro-Optics
CMD	Command

CMOS	Complementary Metal-Oxide Semiconductor
CNN	Convolution Neural Network
CP	Configuration Packet
CPU	Central Processing Unit
CRC	Cyclic Redundancy Code
CS	Computer Science
CS	Chip Select
CSUR	Computing Surveys
CT	Crossbar Traversal
DAC	Digital-to-Analog Converter
DBN	Deep Belief Network
DMA	Direct Memory Access
DNN	Deep Neural Network
DOR	Dimension Order Routing
DRAM	Dynamic Random Access Memory
DTCM	Data Tightly Coupled Memory
DVD	Digital Versatile Disk
DWDM	Dense Wavelength Division Multiplexing
DWM	Domain Wall Memory
EC	Electronic Controller
ECC	Error Correction Code
ECN	Electronic Control Network
ECTC	Electronic Components and Technology Conference
EDRAM	Embedded Dynamic Random Access Memory
EMCSI	Electromagnetic Compatibility Signal/Power Integrity
ESD	ElectroStatic Discharge
ETE	End-To-End
FeFET	Ferroelectric Field-Effect Transistor
FIFO	First In, First Out
FPGA	Field Programmable Gate Array
FPNA	Field Programmable Neural Array
FT-PHENIC	Fault-Tolerant Photonic Network-on-Chip
FTMC-3DR	Fault-Tolerant Multicast 3D Routers
FTPP	Fault-Tolerant Photonic Path-configuration algorithm
FTSP-KMCR	Fault-Tolerant Shortest Path K-means-based MultiCast Routing algorithm
FTSPKMCR	Fault-Tolerant MultiCast Routing algorithm
GA	Genetic Algorithm
GPU	Graphic Processing Units
GPGPU	General Purpose Graphic Processing Units
GS	Greedy Search
GUI	Graphical User Interface
HAL	Hardware Abstraction Layer
HDD	Hard Disk Drive
HiPC	High Performance Computing

HPCA	High Performance Computer Architecture
HRS	High Resistive State
IBM	International Business Machines
IC	Integrated Circuit
ID	Identification
IEEE	Institute of Electrical and Electronics Engineers
IF	Integrate and Fire
ILP	Integer Linear Programming
i-PACT	Innovations in Power and Advanced Computing Technologies
IP	Intellectual Property
ISBN	International Standard Book Number
ISCA	International Symposium on Computer Architecture
ISCAS	International Symposium on Circuits and Systems
ISI	Inter-Spike-Interval
ITCM	Instruction Tightly Coupled Memory
JPEG	Joint Photographic Experts Group
KB	Kilobyte
KL	Kernighan-Lin
LA-XYZ	Look-Ahead XYZ
LIF	Leaky Integrate-and-Fire
LRS	Low-Resistive State
LRU	Least Recently Used
LTD	Long-Term Depression
LTP	Long-Term Potentiation
LUT	Look-Up-Table
MB	Mega Bytes
MCSoC	Multicore/Many-core Systems-on-Chip
MFMC	Max-Flow Min-Cut
MIVs	Monolithic Intertier Vias
MJT	Multi Junction Technology
MLP	Multi-Layer Perceptron
MNIST	Modified National Institute of Standards and Technology database
MPI	Message Passing Interface
MR	Microring Resonator
MRAM	Magnetoresistive Random-Access Memory
MRCT	Micro Ring Configuration Table
MRPR	Microring fault-Resilient Photonic Router
MRST	Micro Ring State Table
MTBF	Mean Time Between Failures
MTJ	Magnetic Tunneling Junction
MTTF	Mean Time to Failures
MTTR	Mean Time to Repair
NACK	Negative Acknowledgement
NAND	Not And
NASH	Neuro-inspired ArchitectureS in Hardware

NEWS	North-East-West-South
NI	Network Interface
NP-hard	Non-deterministic Polynomial-time hard
NSEW	North South East West
NVM	Non-volatile Memories
OE	Output Enable
OSI	Open Systems Interconnection Model
OSI	Open Systems Interconnection
PB	Path_Blocked
PCB	Process Control Block
PCM	Phase Change Memory
PCN	Photonic Communication Network
PE	Processing Element
PJ	Picojoule
PNoC	Photonic Network-on-Chip
PS	Photonic Switch
PSCP	Path-Setup-Control Packet
PSO	Particle Swarm Optimization
PSP	Post-Synaptic Potential
PV	Process Variation
RAM	Random-Access Memory
RBL	Resistance Between Layers
RC	Routing Calculation
RE	Read Enable
RELU	Rectified Linear Unit
RISC	Reduced Instruction Set Computing
RMP	Residual Membrane Potential
R-NASH	Reconfigurable Neuro-inspired ArchitectureS in Hardware
RNN	Recurrent Neural Network
ROM	Read-Only Memory
RPM	Randomized Partially Minimal
RRAM	Resistive Random-Access Memory
RSP	Rapid System Prototyping
RTL	Register-Transfer Level
SA	Switch Allocation
SAF	Store-And-Forward
SDRAM	Synchronous Dynamic Random Access Memory
SDSP	Spike-Driven Synaptic Plasticity
SECDED	Single Error Correction, Double Error Detection
SEQ	Sequencer
SET	Single-Event Transients
SEU	Single-Event Upsets
SMC	Systems, Man and Cybernetics
SNN	Spiking Neural Network
SNPC	Spiking Neuron Processing Core

SoC	System On a Chip
SP	Shortest Path
SRAM	Static Random Access Memory
SRDS	Symposium on Reliable Distributed Systems
STA	Sciences and Techniques of Automatic Control and Computer Engineering
STDP	Spike Timing Synaptic Plasticity
STPD	Spike-Timing-Dependent Plasticity
STT-RAM	Spin-Transfer Torque RAM
TDM	Time-Division Multiplexing
TDMA	Time-Division-Multiple-Access
TECS	Transactions on Embedded Computing Systems
TMR	Triple Modular Redundancy
TODAES	Transactions on Design Automation of Electronic Systems
TSVs	Through Silicon Vias
TTFS	Time-To-First-Spike
TV	Thermal Variations
UI	User Interface
USA	United States of America
USB	Universal Serial Bus
VCSEL	Vertically Cavity Surface Emitting Laser
VGG	Visual Geometry Group Network
VLSI	Very-Large-Scale Integration
VTS	VLSI Test Symposium
WDM	Wavelength Division Multiplexing
WE	Write Enable
WL	Word Line
WL	Worst Loss
WTA	Winner-Take-All
XOR	Exclusive OR

Chapter 1
Foundations of Neuromorphic Computing

Abstract The chapter thoroughly investigates neuromorphic engineering, providing readers with a solid foundation. It opens with an introduction that establishes the basic principles of neuromorphic computing and underscores its importance in modern technology. The neuromorphic systems design challenges section addresses technical and conceptual hurdles in creating effective and scalable neuromorphic systems, emphasizing the intricacies involved in their development. Next, Neural Network Models are explored in depth, shedding light on the various architectures that emulate brain-like functions and their respective roles. The chapter also presents Learning in Spiking Neural Networks and synapse memory technologies, focusing on innovative learning algorithms and memory technologies that enhance the system's adaptability and performance. These discussions are enriched with examples and case studies that illustrate practical applications. Concluding with Exercises, the chapter offers practical tasks designed to reinforce the concepts covered, allowing readers to apply their knowledge and gain a deeper understanding of neuromorphic computing principles and their applications. This comprehensive approach ensures that readers are well-equipped to navigate and contribute to the evolving field of neuromorphic engineering.

1.1 Introduction

The human nervous system comprises more than 100 billion cells, known as neurons. The neurons perceive changes in the environment, convey these changes to other neurons, and direct body responses to these perceptions. It has received so much attention because these neurons can rapidly process information in a fast, parallel, fault-tolerant, and energy-efficient manner. This chapter introduces the fundamentals of neuromorphic computing systems by discussing biological neurons and the dynamics abstracted from them to model artificial neurons.

Neuromorphic computing brain-inspired computing paradigm takes inspiration from the brain to develop energy-efficient circuits and systems for future information processing, capable of highly complicated tasks. Such computing promises to drastically improve the efficiency of critical computational tasks, such as decision-

A. Ben Abdallah, K. N. Dang, *Neuromorphic Computing Principles and Organization*, https://doi.org/10.1007/978-3-031-83089-1_1

making and perception. Unlike the typical artificial neural networks (ANNs), where neurons fire (output) at each propagation cycle, the neurons in a brain-inspired neural network model, named spiking neural networks (SNNs), fire only when a membrane potential crosses a threshold value. Spiking neurons are only activated when sufficient signals are integrated from other neurons, which leads to sparse neural activities at the network level.

A general description of a biological neuron is presented in Fig. 1.1: A neuron comprises several parts: dendrites, axon, and soma. Dendrites serve as the input channels, while the axon is the output channel. Neurons receive electrochemical signals from other neurons at their dendrites. If the cumulative inputs are strong enough, the neuron becomes activated and sends an electrochemical signal through its axon to other neurons connected to its axon terminals via dendrites. These connections are facilitated through synapses. The neuro-biological system is highly interconnected, with a typical cortical neuron having up to 10,000 inputs and some cerebellar neurons having up to a quarter of a million inputs. Hence, artificial neurons are designed to mimic the operational mechanisms of biological neurons. Figure 1.1b shows a computational neuron model. The input signals (e.g., x_0) received from the axon of other neurons are multiplied by the weight of the synapse

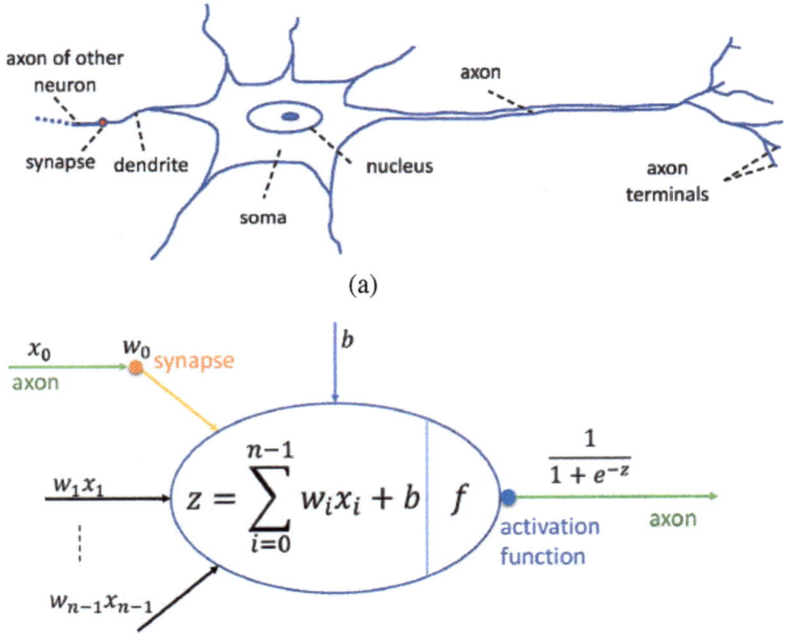

(b)

Fig. 1.1 Neuron organization: (**a**) Biological neuron, (**b**) Corresponding mathematical model. The mathematical model of a biological neuron translates the complex biophysical processes of a neuron into a set of mathematical rules, enabling the study and simulation of neural behavior in both normal and pathological conditions

that connects them (e.g., w_0). The dendrite then transports weighted inputs (e.g., w_0x_0) to the soma of the receiving neuron. The weighted inputs are summed up as the neuron membrane potential and passed through an activation function that maps it to the neuron's output.

Over the years, several neural network modeling approaches have been proposed, differing in topology and features, to capture the dynamics of neural computation. These modeling approaches have evolved through three generations, keeping in mind the computational principles of the biological brain. Figure 1.2 shows the three neural network generation. In the first generation, the neurons were referred to as perceptrons. These perceptrons process only digital signals using a single layer. The sum of weighted inputs of this neuron is mapped to the neuron output using a binary threshold. Some examples of perceptrons include Hopfield networks and Boltzmann machines. The second generation, neurons, are called a conventional artificial neural network. It maps the sum of weighted inputs to the neuron output using activation functions such as sigmoid, exponential, and polynomial, which have a continuous set of possible outputs. Also, this second-generation network employs learning algorithms based on gradient descent. Examples of this generation of the neural network include feedforward, radial basis function units, and recurrent sigmoid neural networks. The third generation, referred to as the Spiking Neural Network (SNN), is modeled more analogous to the dynamics of biological neurons than previous generations. It is event-driven and operates by accumulating input spikes at its membrane potential. The neuron fires, and output spikes only when its membrane potential exceeds a certain threshold. Like their biological counterparts, artificial neurons must be connected to perform tasks. How neurons are connected determines their topology. A summary of some neural network topologies is illustrated in Fig. 1.3.

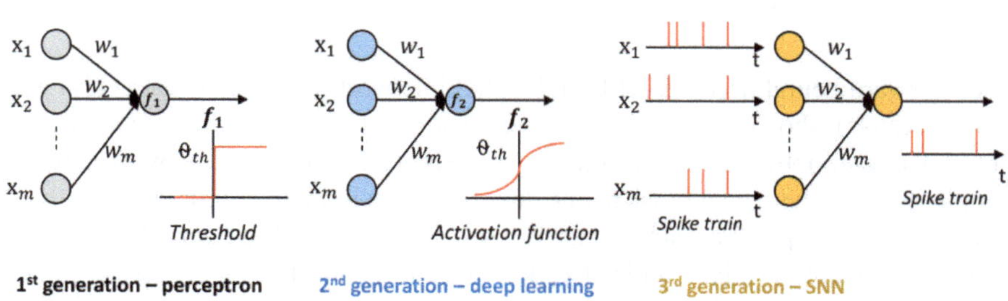

Fig. 1.2 Neural network generations. Neural networks have evolved through three primary generations. The first generation comprises Artificial Neural Networks (ANN) inspired by the human brain's interconnected neurons, excelling in pattern recognition tasks. The second generation introduced deep learning (i.e., Convolution Neural Networks (CNN)). The latest third-generation features Spiking Neural Networks (SNN), mimicking biological neurons more closely with event-driven processing, achieving superior energy efficiency and real-time adaptability

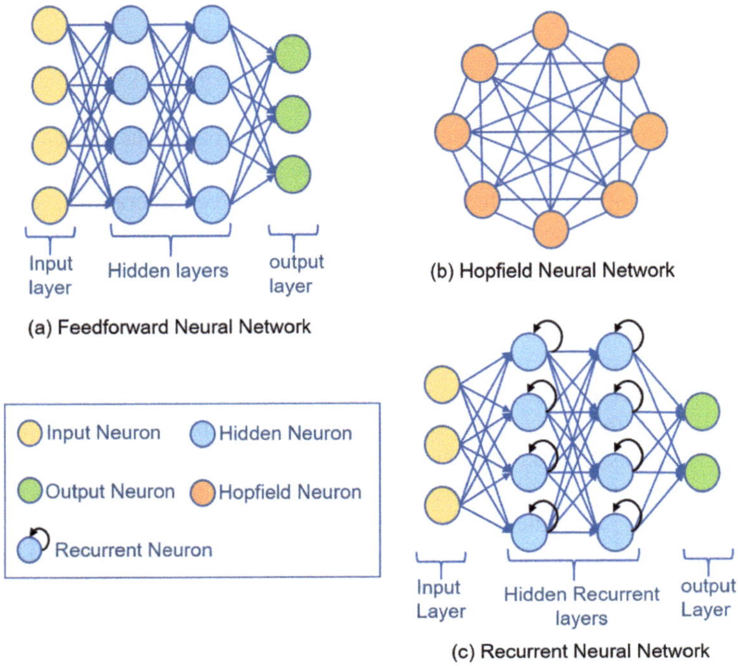

Fig. 1.3 Some prevalent neural network topologies. Feedforward Neural Networks (FNN) are the simplest type. Hopfield Networks are recurrent networks with all neurons connected. Recurrent Neural Networks (RNNs) excel at processing sequential data and capturing temporal dependencies, making them ideal for tasks like language modeling and time-series prediction

1.1.1 Neural Network Topologies

Feed-forward neural networks (FFN), Hopfield networks, and recurrent neural networks (RNNs), shown in Fig. 1.3, represent distinct architectures in artificial neural networks, each optimized for different tasks. Feed-forward neural networks are the simplest form, where data flows in one direction from input to output layers without any cycles or loops; they are primarily used for tasks such as classification and regression. In contrast, Hopfield networks, a type of recurrent network, are designed explicitly for associative memory and optimization problems; they utilize symmetric connections among neurons to store patterns that can be recalled even from partial or noisy inputs, functioning by converging to stable states that represent these stored memories. RNNs, on the other hand, are explicitly constructed to handle sequential data, featuring loops that allow information to be retained over time, which makes them ideal for applications such as natural language processing and time series analysis. While RNNs can learn from past inputs to inform future outputs, they can be more complex and are subject to challenges like vanishing gradients. Together, these three types of networks showcase the diversity of approaches in tackling various problems in machine learning and artificial intelligence.

Spiking feed-forward neural networks, spiking Hopfield networks, and spiking recurrent neural networks (RNNs) are specialized architectures within the domain of spiking neural networks (SNNs), each designed to leverage the temporal dynamics of neuron firing for enhanced information processing.

1.1.1.1 Feed-Forward Neural Networks

The Feed-forward neural network (FNN) topology described in Fig. 1.3a is organized into three categories of layers: input, hidden, and output layers. The connections between neurons in this network are made across layers and not within a layer. Information flows forward from the input layer, through the hidden layer(s), and finally to the output layer. The backpropagation learning method is usually employed in training this network.

The input layer consists of neurons that receive external data and pass it on to the subsequent layer. These neurons act as the initial processing nodes, preparing the raw input data for deeper analysis. The hidden layers, which can be multiple and vary in size, perform the core computations. They extract and transform features through learned weights and activation functions, enabling the network to capture complex patterns within the data. Each hidden layer refines the information further, progressively distilling relevant features. The output layer consists of neurons that produce the final predictions or classifications based on the processed information from the hidden layers. The number of neurons in the output layer typically corresponds to the number of classes or outputs the network is designed to predict.

The backpropagation learning method, an essential component in FNN training, involves propagating the error gradient backward through the network. This process adjusts the weights of the connections between neurons iteratively, minimizing the error between predicted and actual outcomes. The network fine-tunes its weights through multiple training iterations, improving its predictive accuracy.

Spiking feed-forward networks extend traditional architectures by incorporating time-dependent spike events. This allows them to process inputs in a way that more closely mimics biological neural behavior. By encoding information in the timing of spikes, they excel at tasks such as pattern recognition and classification.

1.1.1.2 Hopfield Neural Networks

The Hopfield neural network, shown in Fig. 1.3b, is a recurrent artificial neural network primarily used for associative memory and optimization problems. Introduced by John Hopfield in 1982, this network consists of interconnected neurons that collectively function as a dynamic system. Each neuron in the network is binary, producing either 0 or 1 outputs, and operates on the energy minimization principle. The interconnections between neurons are established with symmetric weights, meaning the connection strength from neuron A to neuron B is the same as from B to A. This allows the network to exhibit a stable state or memory pattern.

When presented with an input pattern, the Hopfield network iteratively updates its neurons, moving toward a lower energy state corresponding to a stored memory pattern. The network can retrieve the closest stored pattern even from incomplete or noisy data, making it particularly effective for applications like pattern recognition, optimization, and solving NP-complete problems. However, its performance can be limited by local minima and a finite memory capacity dictated by the number of neurons and connections.

Spiking Hopfield networks serve as memory systems, utilizing spike-based communication between neurons to retrieve stored patterns from incomplete or noisy data, thus providing robust associative memory capabilities.

1.1.1.3 Recurrent Neural Networks

A recurrent neural network (RNN), shown in Fig. 1.3c, is a class of artificial neural networks designed to recognize patterns in sequences of data, making it particularly well-suited for tasks involving time series or sequential inputs, such as natural language processing and speech recognition. Unlike traditional feedforward neural networks, RNNs include connections that loop back on themselves, allowing information to persist across time steps. This architecture enables RNNs to maintain a hidden state that carries information from previous inputs, effectively capturing temporal dependencies and context within the sequence. RNNs process inputs one at a time and updates their hidden state with each new input, making them capable of modeling sequences of variable lengths. Although RNNs can learn complex patterns, they often face challenges like vanishing and exploding gradient problems, hindering their training over long sequences. To address these issues, more advanced architectures, such as Long Short-Term Memory (LSTM) networks and Gated Recurrent Units (GRUs), have been developed, incorporating mechanisms that regulate the flow of information and improve the network's ability to learn long-range dependencies.

Spiking RNNs add the ability to maintain temporal context through recurrent connections, enabling them to model complex sequences and dependencies over time; they are particularly effective for applications like speech recognition and temporal prediction. Combining the advantages of spiking dynamics with the unique features of feed-forward, associative memory, and recurrent interactions, these spiking architectures offer powerful tools for advancing our understanding of neural computation and developing bio-inspired computational models.

1.2 Neuromorphic Systems Design Challenges

With the increasing demand for computing machines that emulate the biological brain, neuro-inspired computing has advanced toward developing architectures that address the limitations of traditional computer systems. Based on the Von

Neumann architecture, conventional computer systems starkly contrast with the biological brain regarding structure, power consumption, and computational power. Therefore, utilizing densely connected neurons, a biologically inspired approach enables modeling neuroscience theories and solving machine learning problems.

Recent advances in artificial neural networks (ANN), particularly convolutional neural networks (CNN), have propelled machine learning tasks such as visual and auditory recognition and classification to a large scale [25, 31, 34]. However, as the complexity of tasks increases, ANNs require more layers, escalating the demand for hardware resources (power consumption and processing power) to simulate them. The spiking neural network (SNN) approach was proposed to mitigate these costs. By mimicking the behavior of biological neurons more closely, SNNs can achieve low-power consumption at picojoules (pJ) compared to ANNs [19].

Despite being an efficient method for exploring neuronal behavior, simulating large-scale SNNs in software is slow and does not fully exploit their energy efficiency. Scalable hardware multicore neuromorphic architectures that support many neurons and synapses and leverage the parallelism and spike sparsity inherent in SNNs are crucial for rapid, low-power processing.

Realizing such neuromorphic architectures necessitates developing small-sized spiking neuron cores with low power consumption, efficient neuron coding schemes, and lightweight learning algorithms. Additionally, these neurocores require a scalable inter-neuron communication architecture to manage the substantial traffic generated by the numerous neurons. Traditional communication architectures, such as shared buses, perform poorly with an increased number of neurons, and two-dimensional packet-switched network-on-chip designs struggle to achieve high parallelism. Moving to 3D integrated circuits (3D-ICs) provides a scalable solution with high parallelism, shorter connections, and lower power consumption.

However, dense neuromorphic architectures face reliability issues, where a single point of failure can impact overall operation. Neuromorphic systems rely heavily on precise spike communication, and any interruption or timing violation can negatively affect their performance and accuracy. Therefore, neuromorphic systems must be adaptive to mitigate the effects of faults.

1.3 Neural Network Models

1.3.1 Artificial Neural Networks

In conventional ANN, input signals and weights are represented with actual values, and the implementation methods can be categorized as analog or digital. Analog implementations offer rapid processing, power efficiency, and low area cost. However, they are susceptible to noise, which makes the representation of natural numbers complex and limits accuracy. Digital implementation, on the other hand, provides programmability, high precision, and reliability, but compared to analog performance, they suffer from high area cost and latency.

Learning in neural networks finds the best synaptic weights to maximize a neural network's accuracy. Implementing on-chip or off-chip learning has been a significant challenge in designing neural network systems. The choice of implementation approach is made on many factors, including the neural network model and hardware resources. Two of the notable neural network learning approaches are supervised and unsupervised learning. This subsection reviews those approaches and learning rules employed in training conventional artificial neural networks.

The learning approach entails training a neural network based on input-output pairs, where the network learns by example. One of the prevalent learning rules used in training conventional ANN is the backpropagation (BP) learning rule. This learning rule trains an ANN by modifying its synaptic weights based on the error rate obtained in its previous training stage. It can be employed in training neural network topologies such as feed-forward, recurrent, and convolution. The BP learning rule is usually implemented off-chip [24, 45] on a traditional host machine. There, it is used to train ANN weights, and after the training, the trained weights are mapped to the neuromorphic chip. This learning rule has demonstrated high precision in its training, taking advantage of the software platform.

In contrast to the supervised learning approach, the unsupervised learning approach has no input-output pair and has no example to learn from. This learning approach is quite unpopular, and there have been some unsupervised learning rules based on self-organizing maps [5, 32, 43] that have been implemented on neuromorphic chips.

1.3.2 Spiking Neural Networks

Spiking neural networks (SNNs) are artificial models that more closely mimic biological neural networks. In addition to neuronal and synaptic states, SNNs incorporate variant time scales into their computational model. Since each neuron in these networks is connected to thousands of others, high bandwidth is required [46, 47]. Moreover, since the spike times encode information in SNN, very low communication latency is also needed.

Figure 1.4a shows the biological neuron model where dendrites receive inputs from upstream neurons via the synapses. Incoming spikes are integrated into soma as its membrane potential. If the membrane potential crosses the threshold, the neuron issues an outgoing spike to an axon. The axon sends the spike to the downstream neurons via synapses. Figure 1.4b shows an example of a spiking neuron. The input spikes (memory reading) are multiplied with the corresponding weights to have weighted inputs. The membrane potential is accumulated from the weighted inputs and creates an outgoing spike if it is higher than the threshold. In the spiking neuron models, there are three significant parameters for being stored:

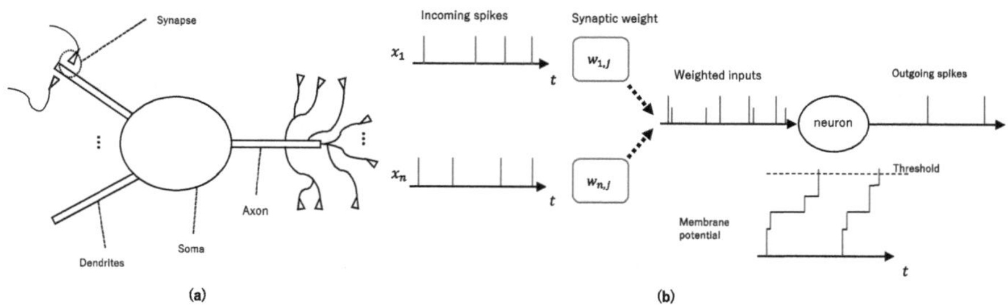

Fig. 1.4 Biological (**a**) and spiking (**b**) neuron components: The Biological neuron consists of several key components: the cell body (soma), which contains the nucleus and maintains the cell; dendrites, which receive signals from other neurons; and the axon, which transmits electrical impulses to other neurons or muscles. The axon terminals, or synaptic, release neurotransmitters to communicate with other neurons across synapses. These components work together to process and transmit information throughout the nervous system

(1) incoming spikes; *(2)* synaptic weights, and *(3)* neuron's internal parameters (membrane potential, threshold, etc.).

In SNN, biological neurons communicate information via short electrical pulses called spikes. Neural coding focuses on how this information is represented with electrical activity at the neuron level and in networks of neurons. Efforts have been made over the years to determine how these spikes can be encoded to contain information. Some coding schemes that have been proposed are presented in [21]. The rate coding scheme, sometimes called frequency coding, conveys information based on a neuron's firing rate, proportional to the stimulus level. Several studies have shown that the temporal resolution of neural code is on a scale of milliseconds. Therefore, in temporal coding, information is represented in the precise timing of spikes. As described in previous sections, SNN, unlike its predecessors, mimics the brain's behavior more closely, and several spiking neuron models have been proposed over the years. These spiking neuron models [28] differ in the level of detail they abstract from biological neurons. In this subsection, we describe some of the prevalent models.

The Hodgkin-Huxley neuron model, proposed in the early 1950s [26], is a mathematical representation of neuron dynamics. It presents a mathematical description of the electric current through the membrane potential, giving the details of spike generation. The Hodgkin-Huxley model is the most biologically plausible; however, its complexity with many parameters consumes tremendous hardware resources, making it costly for large-scale implementations. Compared to Hodgkin-Huxley, a less complex model was proposed by Izhikevich [27]. This model computes a broad range of neuron spiking patterns using mathematical equations.

In summary, among the existing spiking models, Hodgkin-Huxley [26], Izhikevich [27], and Leaky Integrate-and-Fire (LIF) [9] are often used. The Hodgkin-Huxley model is the best when measurable physiological parameters are highly considered. However, it consists of many coefficients, which leads to high costs when implementing large SNNs. In contrast, the LIF neural model can simulate hundreds of thousands of neurons, but it cannot produce rich spiking patterns. Finally, Izhikevich exhibits a good compromise regarding biophysical similarity and computational cost. It is close to the Hodgkin-Huxley model in biological plausibility while analogous to the LIF in computational complexity.

1.3.3 Artificial Neural Networks vs Spiking Neural Networks

Artificial Neural Networks (ANN) and Spiking Neural Networks (SNN) represent two branches of neural network architectures, each with unique features, advantages, and limitations. ANN, inspired by the structure and function of the human brain, comprises layers of interconnected neurons that process input data through weighted connections. This architecture is highly effective for image recognition, natural language processing, and other machine-learning applications. ANNs, intense learning models, can achieve high accuracy and performance by leveraging massive amounts of training data and computational power. However, their continuous activation of neurons leads to substantial power consumption, making them less efficient for energy-sensitive applications.

In contrast, SNNs are designed to emulate the more intricate workings of biological neurons, incorporating the concept of spikes or discrete events. This event-based processing allows SNNs to operate with significantly lower power consumption, as neurons only activate when a specific threshold is reached. This approach mimics how information is processed in the human brain more closely than ANN. SNNs' temporal dynamics enable them to handle time-dependent data more naturally, making them particularly suitable for robotics, real-time signal processing, and neuromorphic engineering applications. Despite their advantages in power efficiency and temporal processing, SNNs are more challenging to train and implement due to the complexity of their spiking behavior and the need for specialized hardware.

In summary, while ANNs excel in accuracy and performance for many applications, their high energy consumption can be a drawback. On the other hand, SNNs offer a more energy-efficient alternative with superior temporal dynamics but face challenges in training and practical implementation. The choice between ANN and SNN depends on the application's specific requirements, including factors such as computational resources, power constraints, and the nature of the data being processed.

1.4 Learning in Spiking Neural Networks

Learning in Spiking Neural Networks (SNNs) poses several challenges due to their event-driven nature and the need for precise timing. One significant difficulty is designing practical learning algorithms, such as Spike-Timing-Dependent Plasticity

(STDP), that can handle the intricate timing of spikes to modify synaptic weights accurately. Additionally, the lack of well-established frameworks and tools for training SNNs compared to traditional neural networks adds to the complexity. These challenges are further compounded by the need for efficient hardware implementations to leverage the low-power benefits of SNNs, necessitating specialized neuromorphic chips and architectures.

Figure 1.5 illustrates the architecture of Spike-Timing-Dependent Plasticity (STDP), a fundamental mechanism underlying synaptic learning in Spiking Neural Networks (SNNs). In this architecture, the synaptic weights are adjusted based on the precise timing of spikes between pre-synaptic and post-synaptic neurons. The figure showcases how the timing of spikes influences the strength of synaptic connections, promoting learning and memory formation. When a pre-synaptic neuron fires shortly before a post-synaptic neuron, the synapse is strengthened, known as long-term potentiation (LTP). Conversely, if the pre-synaptic neuron fires after the post-synaptic neuron, the synapse is weakened, referred to as long-term depression (LTD). The STDP mechanism is essential for the dynamic adjustment of synaptic strengths, allowing SNNs to adapt and learn from their environment effectively. This architecture is pivotal in replicating the biological processes of learning and memory in artificial neural systems, enabling the development of more efficient and brain-like computational models. Spike timing-dependent plasticity (STDP), a widely adopted learning rule in neuromorphic systems [13, 29, 48], is based on Hebbian learning principles observed in the biological brain [41].

Apart from the predominant use of Spike-Timing-Dependent Plasticity (STDP), spiking neuromorphic systems have also incorporated supervised learning rules. These systems use a *teacher* signal during training to guide learning. Other learning methods, such as [18], successfully implemented the Spike-Driven Synaptic Plasticity (SDSP) learning rule. Unlike STDP, SDSP induces an update each time a pre-synaptic spike occurs. Furthermore, backpropagation has also been adopted for spiking systems [49]. In [16], the ANN is first trained using backpropagation

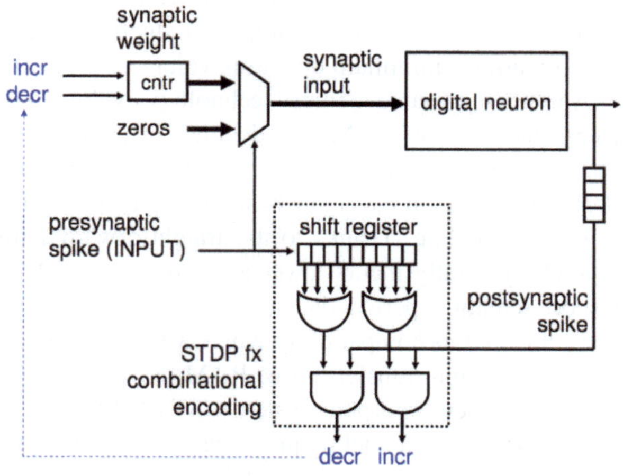

Fig. 1.5 STDP Architecture. Key elements include the pre-synaptic neuron, which sends spike signals to the post-synaptic neuron. The timing detection mechanism measures the relative timing of these spikes. The synaptic weight storage holds the current strength of the connection, and the plasticity rule implementation adjusts this weight based on the spike timing

(BP) and then converted into an SNN by mapping real-valued inputs and activations to the average firing rates of Poisson spikes. This conversion mechanism can be implemented on spiking hardware as an off-chip learning method.

1.5 Synapse Memory Technologies

In traditional Von Neumann computers, CPUs and memory units are distinct and separate entities. However, neurons and synapses in neuromorphic computing systems handle processing and memory tasks. Spiking neurons operate based on events, communicating at rates around 10 Hz, in stark contrast to traditional processors that function and communicate in the megahertz to gigahertz range. This significant difference in speed allows neuromorphic processors to utilize time multiplexing effectively, enhancing their efficiency and mimicking the parallel processing capabilities of the human brain.

In Spiking Neural Networks (SNNs), storing and reading synaptic weights are crucial. Designing a large SNN with many synapses demands significant memory bandwidth. While communication speed is not a primary concern in neuromorphic systems, overcoming memory bandwidth limitations is essential. Researchers have explored various memory technologies to implement these synapses in CMOS, one of which is static random-access memory (SRAM), a widely used memory technology in semiconductor design. In [40], a neuromorphic chip with 256 neurons employs a transposable 8-transistor SRAM-based crossbar, enabling both row and column access. A typical SRAM comprises six transistors (6-T) and offers multiple read and write capabilities despite its high leakage current and low density. SRAM is notably advantageous in speed and reliability compared to other memory technologies [7].

Adding two extra transistors in the 8-T SRAM configuration provides access to the word and bit lines in a transposed arrangement, differing from the conventional 6-T design. To mitigate the chip's overall leakage power, the authors utilized ultra-high-Vt devices, achieving a threefold reduction, albeit at the expense of raising the memory array's minimum operating voltage.

Another innovative memory technology explored is embedded dynamic random-access memory (eDRAM), as detailed in [30]. This technology creates a high-density memory suitable for a programmable digital neuromorphic architecture. eDRAM features a capacitor-based memory structure integrated within the same multi-chip module. Thanks to its straightforward 1-transistor, 1-capacitor design, eDRAM generally incurs lower area costs than SRAM. However, it suffers from a short retention period due to the gradual leakage of its stored charge during operation, and its compatibility with CMOS technology is limited.

In [44], a spin-transfer torque RAM (STT-RAM) was proposed as a memristive synapse for neuromorphic systems. STT-RAM is a type of magnetic RAM that employs magnetic tunneling junctions (MTJs) within its cells, resulting in a smaller area footprint than SRAM and eDRAM. Following the approach outlined in [42], the authors structured the STT-RAM MTJs into a crossbar configuration linking input and output neurons. However, the inherent magnetization in STT-RAM leads to slower writing processes and higher energy consumption.

Resistive random-access memory (RRAM or ReRAM) is another significant memory technology employed in the design of neuromorphic chips. The memristor, known for its nonvolatility and ability to adjust resistance continuously, is a promising component for neuromorphic architectures. It operates on the principle of ion migration, which enables the storage and retrieval of electrical charges. Recognized as the fourth fundamental electronic element, alongside the resistor, capacitor, and inductor, the memristor is crucial in advancing memory technology [11].

Memristors can be classified into two categories based on their terminal configurations: two-terminal and three-terminal devices. The two-terminal memristor closely resembles biological synapses, making it suitable for emulating neural functions. In contrast, the three-terminal memristor features an additional modulation port, offering enhanced control over its operation. This differentiation allows for greater flexibility in designing neuromorphic systems that mimic the behavior of biological neural networks.

Numerous FPGA-based hardware emulators have been developed for neuromorphic chips utilizing RRAM-based crossbar architectures. RRAM presents advantages such as reduced area, low power consumption, and seamless integration with CMOS technology. However, it is prone to stuck-at faults (SAF) [51], which can result in short-circuiting, increased power consumption, and significant fluctuations in the dynamic switching resistance of the memory. In addition to RRAM, other memory technologies such as Phase Change Memory (PCM) also hold potential for neuromorphic applications. PCM provides unique characteristics that can complement the functionalities offered by RRAM and contribute to advancements in neuromorphic computing.

1.6 Neurons Communication

Communication architectures for spiking neuromorphic systems enable the transmission of spikes between neurocores or tiles and are categorized as either intra-chip or inter-chip. Address Event Representation (AER) is commonly used for inter-chip communication [8, 36]. In the AER protocol, each neuron is assigned a unique address, allowing it to send its address to post-synaptic neurons when it generates a spike. This communication occurs via a high-speed digital bus, enhancing efficiency by activating the communication infrastructure only when neurons fire. AER can be structured hierarchically in a tree configuration to accommodate more extensive systems, improving scalability and efficient communication across multiple neurocores. This hierarchical approach optimizes bandwidth utilization and supports the complex connectivity patterns inherent in spiking neural networks (SNNs). Additionally, AER significantly reduces data transmission volume by sending only the addresses of firing neurons rather than continuous spike data. This method minimizes communication latency, ensuring the precise timing of spikes is maintained, which is crucial for accurate neural processing.

Network-on-Chip (NoC) architectures are widely utilized for on-chip communication in neuromorphic systems [1–3]. Initially, some early implementations of neuromorphic systems relied on bus-based communication[37]. However, a comparative analysis of bus, tree, point-to-point, and mesh-based systems indicates that mesh configurations with multicast capabilities deliver the best performance for spiking neural network (SNN) implementations. As a result, later designs increasingly embraced mesh-based interconnects as the standard NoC topology [4, 14].

Integrating Address Event Representation (AER) and Network-on-Chip (NoC) in neuromorphic chip communication networks enhances scalability and efficiency. AER efficiently encodes and transmits the addresses of firing neurons, reducing data volume and communication latency. The system can handle complex connectivity patterns and high data throughput when combined with NoC, which provides a robust and scalable communication infrastructure. This integration ensures that spikes are transmitted accurately and promptly across multiple neurocores, maintaining the precise timing crucial for neural processing. The hierarchical structure of NoC further optimizes bandwidth utilization, making it ideal for large-scale neuromorphic systems.

For instance, the SpiNNaker architecture employs a toroidal NoC that integrates both on-chip and off-chip communication systems [20]. Address Event Representation (AER) is also utilized for on-chip communication in various architectures [4, 14, 15, 20].

1.7 Neuromorphic System Design Domains

Full-custom digital ASICs have become a widely adopted platform for spiking neuromorphic implementations, with notable examples including TrueNorth [4] and SpiNNaker [20]. TrueNorth is specifically designed to support the leaky integrate-and-fire neuron model but lacks on-chip learning capabilities. In contrast, SpiNNaker provides exceptional flexibility across neuron models, synaptic configurations, and learning algorithms. However, TrueNorth stands out for its energy efficiency, consuming only 25 pJ per connection, whereas SpiNNaker consumes 10 nJ per connection, as noted in [19].

Field Programmable Gate Arrays (FPGAs) are also frequently utilized in spiking neuromorphic systems [12, 22, 35]. These devices can be integrated into both the system architecture and final implementations. While FPGAs are praised for their ability to accelerate software simulations, they are typically not optimized for low-power operation.

Analog platforms possess several vital characteristics suitable for spiking neural system implementations, such as charge conservation, amplification, thresholding, and integration. These features contribute to a wide range of successful applications in neuromorphic computing [38]. Additionally, analog platforms can be designed to operate in both subthreshold [50] and superthreshold modes, facilitating performance improvements by optimizing speed [39]. Field-programmable analog Arrays (FPAAs) are an essential category of analog platforms, offering customization for neural network implementations. Examples include the Field Programmable Neural Array (FPNA) [17] and Neuro FPAA [33], both of which provide programmable components such as neurons and synapses. Moreover, mixed-signal designs have become common in neuromorphic systems [23], harnessing the strengths of both analog and digital platforms. In these systems, weights and other parameters are stored in digital memories, enhancing reliability and reducing noise. Digital architectures are also employed for inter-chip and intra-chip communication [10], while neurons are typically realized in analog form. Notable implementations exemplifying this hybrid approach include Neurogrid [6] and BrainScales [39].

1.8 Chapter Summary

This chapter provided a comprehensive overview of artificial neural networks (ANNs), specifically focusing on spiking neural networks (SNNs) as the most advanced generation. It digs into the implementation of SNNs, highlighting their ability to closely mimic biological neural networks through event-based operations and reduce computational demands, which resulted in exceptional energy efficiency. The discussion underscored the innovative nature of SNNs, making them a powerful tool for applications requiring high efficiency and low power consumption.

Additionally, the chapter covered the fundamental principles and architecture of SNNs, explaining how they leverage the inherent dynamics of biological neurons to process information more naturally and efficiently. It explored the mechanisms behind event-based processing, where spikes—short bursts of electrical activity—trigger computations only when necessary, thereby conserving energy. This approach contrasts sharply with the continuous operation of traditional ANNs, emphasizing the unique advantages of SNNs in energy-sensitive applications.

Furthermore, the chapter set the stage for the following discussion by introducing the concept of interconnection networks and their critical role in neuromorphic systems. It highlighted the challenges posed by the many connections required in SNNs, which can lead to significant communication overhead and inefficiencies. The chapter teased the forthcoming exploration of how advanced interconnection networks are designed to address these challenges, enabling efficient communication between neurons in large-scale spiking neuromorphic systems.

In summary, this chapter provided a detailed introduction to ANNs and SNNs and paved the way for understanding the sophisticated network architectures that facilitate their implementation. The following chapter promises to analyze these interconnection networks further, offering insights into how they overcome the hurdles associated with neuron communication in SNNs, ultimately contributing to neuromorphic computing systems' overall efficiency and scalability.

1.9 Exercises

1.9.1 Exercise 1

Consider a Leaky Integrate-and-Fire (LIF) neuron described by the following differential equation:

$$\tau \frac{dV(t)}{dt} = -V(t) + RI(t)$$

where:

- $V(t)$ is the membrane potential at time t,
- τ is the membrane time constant ($\tau = 20$ ms),
- R is the membrane resistance ($R = 1$ MΩ),
- $I(t)$ is the input current ($I(t) = 1.5$ nA).

Given the initial membrane potential $V(0) = 0$ mV, calculate the following: Determine the steady-state membrane potential V_∞. Calculate the membrane potential $V(t)$ at $t = 10$ ms and $t = 50$ ms. If the neuron fires a spike when $V(t)$ reaches 10 mV, determine if the neuron will fire a spike with the given input current. Use the solution to the differential equation:

$$V(t) = V_\infty \left(1 - e^{-t/\tau}\right)$$

1.9.2 Exercise 2

Neuromorphic engineering holds immense promise for revolutionizing various fields. Beyond the well-known applications in artificial intelligence and machine learning, what are some critical, yet potentially less-explored, areas where neuromorphic chips and systems could significantly impact in the coming years?

1.9.3 Exercise 3

Consider a neuromorphic chip that uses the Address Event Representation (AER) protocol for communication between neurons.

1. Explain the basic working principle of the AER protocol. How does it differ from traditional continuous signal communication?
2. Suppose a neuron in an AER-based system fires and sends an event to its post-synaptic neurons. Describe the steps involved in the transmission of this event.

3. Discuss the advantages and potential challenges of using AER in large-scale neuromorphic systems. Provide examples to support your arguments.
4. How can the AER protocol be organized hierarchically to support scalability in neuromorphic systems? Illustrate with a diagram if necessary.

1.9.4 Exercise 4

Neuromorphic computing aims to mimic the structure and function of the brain using specialized hardware. Compared to traditional computing architectures, what are some key considerations and steps specific to the design process of a neuromorphic system for a real-world application (e.g., pattern recognition, robotic control)?

1.9.5 Exercise 5

Synapse Memory Technologies focuses on developing memory solutions inspired by the brain's synaptic connections. How could these advancements in memory technologies potentially benefit the design and performance of neuromorphic computing systems, particularly in areas like low-power operation and efficient information processing?

1.9.6 Exercise 6

The following differential equation describes the membrane voltage dynamics of an LIF neuron:

$$\tau_m \frac{dV}{dt} = -(V - E_L) + I g_L$$

Where: (V) represents the membrane potential; (τ_m) is the membrane time constant; (E_L) is the resting potential (the membrane potential when no external input is applied); (I) represents the external input current; and (g_L) is the leak conductance. What is the significance of the leak conductance in the LIF neuron model?

1.9.7 Exercise 7

In a spiking neural network (SNN), communication between neurons relies on the transmission of spikes rather than continuous signals. Compared to traditional artificial neural network (ANN) communication protocols, what are the advantages and disadvantages of using Address-Event Representation (AER) for spiking neuron communication, particularly in large-scale SNN simulations on neuromorphic hardware?

1.9.8 Exercise 8

While recurrent neural networks (RNNs) excel at capturing temporal dependencies in data, training them for very long sequences can be challenging due to the vanishing/exploding gradient problem. How does this problem manifest differently in spiking recurrent neural networks (SRNNs) compared to traditional RNNs, and what are some potential strategies to address this challenge and enable SRNNs to learn long-term dependencies effectively?

1.9.9 Exercise 9

Traditional Hopfield networks utilize binary neurons with continuous updates. However, researchers have explored building spiking Hopfield networks with integrate-and-fire neurons. How does introducing spiking dynamics and the resulting temporal coding affect a Hopfield network's memory storage and retrieval capabilities?

1.9.10 Exercise 10

The evolution of Artificial Neural Networks (ANNs) can be broadly categorized into three generations. While the first generation focused on mimicking simple biological neurons (perceptrons) and the second leveraged deep learning architectures, the third generation explores spiking neural networks (SNNs) inspired by the biological nervous system's spiking behavior. Considering the computational efficiency and potential for low-power applications, what are the key challenges hindering the broader adoption of spiking neural networks compared to deep learning models, and how might future advancements bridge this gap?

1.9.11 Exercise 11

Consider a Hopfield network with four neurons. The symmetric weight matrix for the connections between the neurons is given by:

$$W = \begin{pmatrix} 0 & -1 & 1 & 0 \\ -1 & 0 & -1 & 1 \\ 1 & -1 & 0 & -1 \\ 0 & 1 & -1 & 0 \end{pmatrix}$$

Given the initial state vector of the network as $\mathbf{s} = (1, -1, 1, -1)$: Calculate the energy of the network using the formula:

$$E = -\frac{1}{2}\sum_{i}\sum_{j} W_{ij}s_i s_j$$

Substitute the given state vector and weight matrix into the formula to find the numerical value of the energy. If neuron 3 receives an input that flips its state, update the state vector and recalculate the energy. Compare the energy before and after the state update to determine if the network has moved to a lower energy state. Calculate the initial energy, perform the state update, and determine the new energy of the system.

References

1. Abdallah AB (2017) Advanced multicore systems-on-chip: architecture on-chip network, design. Springer, Berlin
2. Ahmed AB, Abdallah AB (2013) Architecture and design of high-throughput, low-latency, and fault-tolerant routing algorithm for 3D-network-on-chip (3D-NoC). J Supercomput 66(3):1507–1532
3. Ahmed AB, Abdallah AB (2014) Graceful deadlock-free fault-tolerant routing algorithm for 3D network-on-chip architectures. J Parallel Distrib Comput 74(4):2229–2240
4. Akopyan F, Sawada J, Cassidy A, Alvarez-Icaza R, Arthur J, Merolla P, Imam N, Nakamura Y, Datta P, Nam G, Taba B, Beakes M, Brezzo B, Kuang JB, Manohar R, Risk WP, Jackson B, Modha DS (2015) Truenorth: design and tool flow of a 65 mW 1 million neuron programmable neurosynaptic chip. IEEE Trans Comput Aid Des Integr Circuits Syst 34(10):1537–1557
5. Ben Khalifa K, Girau B, Alexandre F, Bedoui MH (2004) Parallel FPGA implementation of self-organizing maps. In: Proceedings. The 16th international conference on microelectronics (ICM 2004), pp 709–712
6. Benjamin BV, Gao P, McQuinn E, Choudhary S, Chandrasekaran AR, Bussat JM, Alvarez-Icaza R, Arthur JV, Merolla PA, Boahen K (2014) Neurogrid: a mixed-analog-digital multichip system for large-scale neural simulations. Proc IEEE 102(5):699–716
7. Bhaskar A (2017) Design and analysis of low power sram cells. In: 2017 innovations in power and advanced computing technologies (i-PACT), pp 1–5
8. Boahen KA (1998) Communicating neuronal ensembles between neuromorphic chips. Springer, Berlin, pp 229–259
9. Burkitt, N (2006) A review of the integrate-and-fire neuron model: I. Homogeneous synaptic input. Biol Cybern 95(1):1–19
10. Charles G, Gordon C, Alexander WE (2008) An implementation of a biological neural model using analog-digital integrated circuits. In: 2008 IEEE international behavioral modeling and simulation workshop, pp 78–83

11. Chen L, Zhou W, Li C, Huang J (2021) Forgetting memristors and memristor bridge synapses with long- and short-term memories. Neurocomputing 456:126–135
12. Cheung K, Schultz SR, Luk W (2012) A large-scale spiking neural network accelerator for FPGA systems. In: International conference on artificial neural networks. Springer, Berlin, pp 113–120
13. Dan Y, Poo MM (2004) Spike timing-dependent plasticity of neural circuits. Neuron 44(1):23–30
14. Davies M, et al (2018) Loihi: a neuromorphic manycore processor with on-chip learning. IEEE Micro 38(1):82–99
15. Deiss SR, Douglas RJ, Whatley AM (1999) A pulse-coded communications infrastructure for neuromorphic systems. In: Maass W, Bishop CM (eds) Pulsed neural networks. MIT Press, Cambridge, pp 157–178
16. Diehl PU, Neil D, Binas J, Cook M, Liu S, Pfeiffer M (2015) Fast-classifying, high-accuracy spiking deep networks through weight and threshold balancing. In: 2015 international joint conference on neural networks (IJCNN), pp 1–8
17. Farquhar E, Gordon C, Hasler P (2006) A field programmable neural array. In: 2006 IEEE international symposium on circuits and systems, p 4117
18. Frenkel C, Lefebvre M, Legat J, Bol D (2019) A 0.086-mm^2 12.7-pj/sop 64k-synapse 256-neuron online-learning digital spiking neuromorphic processor in 28-nm cmos. IEEE Trans Biomed Circuits Syst 13(1):145–158
19. Furber, S (2016) Large-scale neuromorphic computing systems. J Neural Eng 13(5):051001
20. Furber SB, Galluppi F, Temple S, Plana LA (2014) The spinnaker project. Proc IEEE 102(5):652–665
21. Gerstner W, Kistler W (2002) Spiking neuron models: single neurons, populations, plasticity. Cambridge University Press, Cambridge
22. Glackin B, McGinnity TM, Maguire LP, Wu Q, Belatreche A (2005) A novel approach for the implementation of large-scale spiking neural networks on FPGA hardware. In: International work-conference on artificial neural networks. Springer, Berlin, pp 552–563
23. Hahnloser RHR, Sarpeshkar R, Mahowald MA, Douglas RJ, Seung HS (2000) Digital selection and analog amplification coexist in a cortex-inspired silicon circuit. Nature 405(6789):947–951
24. Haykin S (1998) Neural networks: a comprehensive foundation, 2nd edn. Prentice Hall, Upper Saddle River
25. He K, Zhang X, Ren S, Sun J (2016) Deep residual learning for image recognition. In: Proceedings of the IEEE conference on computer vision and pattern recognition, pp 770–778
26. Hodgkin A, Huxley A (1952) A quantitative description of membrane current and its application to conduction and excitation in nerve. J Physiol 117:500–544
27. Izhikevich EM (2003) Simple model of spiking neurons. IEEE Trans Neural Netw 14(6):1569–1572
28. Izhikevich EM (2004) Which model to use for cortical spiking neurons? IEEE Trans Neural Netw 15(5):1063–1070
29. Jin X, Rast A, Galluppi F, Davies S, Furber S (2010) Implementing spike-timing-dependent plasticity on spinnaker neuromorphic hardware. In: The 2010 international joint conference on neural networks (IJCNN), pp 1–8
30. Kim D, Kung J, Chai S, Yalamanchili S, Mukhopadhyay S (2016) Neurocube: a programmable digital neuromorphic architecture with high-density 3D memory. In: 2016 ACM/IEEE 43rd annual international symposium on computer architecture (ISCA), pp 380–392
31. Krizhevsky A, Sutskever I, Hinton GE (2012) Imagenet classification with deep convolutional neural networks. Adv Neural Inf Process Syst 25:1097–1105
32. Kumar S, Forward K, Palaniswami M (1996) Performance evaluation of a risc neuro-processor for neural networks. In: Proceedings of 3rd international conference on high performance computing (HiPC), pp 351–356
33. Liu M, Yu H, Wang W (2009) FPAA based on integration of cmos and nanojunction devices for neuromorphic applications. In: Cheng M (ed) Nano-net. Springer, Berlin, pp 44–48

34. Liu W, Anguelov D, Erhan D, Szegedy C, Reed S, Fu CY, Berg, AC (2016) Ssd: single shot multibox detector. In: European conference on computer vision. Springer, Berlin, pp 21–37
35. Maguire LP, McGinnity TM, Glackin B, Ghani A, Belatreche A, Harkin, J (2007) Challenges for large-scale implementations of spiking neural networks on FPGAs. Neurocomputing 71(1–3):13–29
36. Merolla P, Arthur J, Alvarez R, Bussat J, Boahen K (2014) A multicast tree router for multichip neuromorphic systems. IEEE Trans Circuits Syst I Regular Pap 61(3):820–833
37. Mortara A, Vittoz EA, Venier P (1995) A communication scheme for analog VLSI perceptive systems. IEEE J Solid-State Circuits 30(6):660–669
38. Nawrocki RA, Shaheen SE, Voyles RM (2011) A neuromorphic architecture from single transistor neurons with organic bistable devices for weights. In: The 2011 international joint conference on neural networks, pp 450–456
39. Schemmel J, Grübl A, Hartmann S, Kononov A, Mayr C, Meier K, Millner S, Partzsch J, Schiefer S, Scholze S, Schüffny R, Schwartz M (2012) Live demonstration: a scaled-down version of the brainscales wafer-scale neuromorphic system. In: 2012 IEEE international symposium on circuits and systems, pp 702–702
40. Seo J, Brezzo B, Liu Y, Parker BD, Esser SK, Montoye RK, Rajendran B, Tierno JA, Chang L, Modha DS, Friedman DJ (2011) A 45nm CMOS neuromorphic chip with a scalable architecture for learning in networks of spiking neurons. In: 2011 IEEE custom integrated circuits conference (CICC), pp 1–4
41. Song S, Miller KD, Abbott LF (2000) Competitive hebbian learning through spike-timing-dependent synapticplasticity. Nat Neurosci 3(9):919–926
42. Suri M, Bichler O, Querlioz D, Cueto O, Perniola L, Sousa V, Vuillaume D, Gamrat C, DeSalvo B (2011) Phase change memory as synapse for ultra-dense neuromorphic systems: application to complex visual pattern extraction. In: 2011 International electron devices meeting, pp 4.4.1–4.4.4
43. Tamukoh H, Sekine M (2010) A dynamically reconfigurable platform for self-organizing neural network hardware. In: Wong KW, Mendis BSU, Bouzerdoum A (eds) Neural information processing. Models and applications. Springer, Berlin, pp 439–446
44. Vincent AF, Larroque J, Locatelli N, Ben Romdhane N, Bichler O, Gamrat C, Zhao WS, Klein J, Galdin-Retailleau S, Querlioz D (2015) Spin-transfer torque magnetic memory as a stochastic memristive synapse for neuromorphic systems. IEEE Trans Biomed Circuits Syst 9(2):166–174
45. Vu TH, Murakami R, Okuyama Y, Abdallah AB (2018) Efficient optimization and hardware acceleration of CNNs towards the design of a scalable neuro-inspired architecture in hardware. In: 2018 IEEE international conference on big data and smart computing (BigComp), pp 326–332
46. Vu TH, Ikechukwu OM, Ben Abdallah A (2019) Fault-tolerant spike routing algorithm and architecture for three dimensional NoC-based neuromorphic systems. IEEE Access 7:90436–90452
47. Vu TH, Okuyama Y, Abdallah AB (2019) Comprehensive analytic performance assessment and k-means based multicast routing algorithm and architecture for 3D-NoC of spiking neurons. ACM J Emerg Technol Comput Syst 15(4):1–28
48. Yang Z, Murray A, Worgotter F, Cameron K, Boonsobhak V (2006) A neuromorphic depth-from-motion vision model with STDP adaptation. IEEE Trans Neural Netw 17(2):482–495
49. Yin, S, Venkataramanaiah SK, Chen GK, Krishnamurthy R, Cao Y, Chakrabarti C, Seo J (2017) Algorithm and hardware design of discrete-time spiking neural networks based on back propagation with binary activations (2017). CoRR, abs/1709.06206
50. Yu T, Cauwenberghs G (2009) Analog VLSI neuromorphic network with programmable membrane channel kinetics. In: 2009 IEEE international symposium on circuits and systems, pp 349–352
51. Yu S, Wu Y, Wong HSP (2011) Investigating the switching dynamics and multilevel capability of bipolar metal oxide resistive switching memory. Appl Phys Lett 98(10):103514

Chapter 2
Neuromorphic System Design Fundamentals

Abstract This chapter provides an in-depth exploration of the core principles and methodologies underlying the development of neuromorphic systems, which emulate the structure and functionality of biological neural networks. It begins by presenting the biological inspiration for neuromorphic designs, examining key characteristics of neuronal behavior and synaptic plasticity that inform system architecture. The chapter outlines various neuron models, including Leaky Integrate-and-Fire, Izhikevich, and Hodgkin-Huxley, highlighting their advantages regarding computational efficiency and biological realism. It emphasizes the importance of efficient communication protocols, such as Address-Event Representation (AER), in facilitating robust information processing and integrates discussions on memory components, including SRAM and memristors, that support the dynamic nature of these systems. Furthermore, the chapter addresses the challenges of designing scalable and adaptable neuromorphic architectures capable of learning from diverse inputs. This chapter provides a comprehensive resource for researchers and practitioners aiming to expand the boundaries of artificial intelligence and cognitive computing by providing a foundational understanding of the design principles and technological considerations necessary for constructing effective neuromorphic systems.

2.1 Introduction

Neuromorphic engineering, a concept introduced by Carver Mead [23] in the late 1980s, involves using VLSI systems with analog electronic circuits to mimic the neuro-biological structures found in the nervous system. Recently, interest in neuromorphic systems has grown as we gain a deeper understanding of the brain and neural operations in structures like the retina, hippocampus, brainstem, and cerebral cortex. Current neuromorphic systems are hybrid analog-digital electronic systems fabricated using CMOS VLSI technology. Thus, the neuromorphic paradigm opens up computing prospects beyond the traditional approach.

SNNs can potentially provide essential gains in energy efficiency and throughput for specific machine-learning tasks. Additionally, SNNs can trade off classification

A. Ben Abdallah, K. N. Dang, *Neuromorphic Computing Principles and Organization*, https://doi.org/10.1007/978-3-031-83089-1_2

error rates against the number of available operations. In contrast, continuous-valued artificial neural networks require a fixed number of functions to achieve their classification error rate. With an increase in error rate of a few percentage points, SNNs can achieve more than 2× reductions in operations when compared to the original ANNs (CNNs) for LeNet and MNIST, and BinaryNet CIFAR-10 [32]. This clearly shows the potential of SNNs, mainly when they are deployed on power-efficient embedded neuromorphic devices. Also, SNNs can generate results (fast inference) after the first output spike is produced, unlike ANNs, where the output is available only after all layers have been completely processed [10]. Moreover, SNNs are naturally suited to process event-based sensor data. Still, even in classical frame-based machine vision applications, they are accurate, fast, and efficient, primarily when implemented on neuromorphic hardware. However, SNNs have limitations, such as tradeoffs between performance, sparsity, and inference latency [38].

Several neuromorphic processors have been designed for applications ranging from vision systems for object recognition (i.e., in drones) or simulation of some part of the brain to running clustering algorithms that detect trade patterns.

Unlike ANN, where neurons communicate using tensors, communication between neurons in an SNN is performed via spikes. The operations of an SNN are generally grouped into learning and inference. Therefore, a typical neuromorphic system is evaluated for efficiency while targeted towards maintaining low power, small footprint, and scalability. For a neuromorphic processor to efficiently carry out learning and inference, factors like learning rules and neuron models that significantly determine the performance of an SNN must be carefully considered.

Years of research in learning methods and inference in neuromorphic systems have narrowed it down to three approaches. The first involves training and inference on high-end servers and then exporting the result. The second requires training on high-end servers and inference on an autonomous agent, while the third requires conducting both training and inference on an autonomous agent. However, the first approach requires a network connection that utilizes more resources and poses security challenges. The second approach presents the possibility of conserving energy, but with increasing demand for real-time adaptation in a dynamic environment from autonomous agents, the third approach is imperative.

2.1.1 *Spiking Neural Networks*

Unlike the typical artificial neural networks, where neurons fire at each propagation cycle, the neurons in a spiking neural network model (SNN) fire only when their membrane potential reaches a certain threshold. Spiking neurons are only activated when sufficient signals are integrated from other neurons, which leads to sparse neural activities at the network level. Furthermore, their asynchronous event-driven operations, distributed memory, and massive parallelism significantly accelerate information processing and reduce energy consumption in many applications (i.e., pattern recognition, object detection, navigation, motor control, and so on).

Neuroscience research has significantly advanced our understanding of neuron structure and function in recent years. Medical tools have also provided insights into neural activity in various brain regions in response to sensory stimuli [12]. Meanwhile, significant advancements in artificial intelligence (AI) have brought us closer to building brain-like devices that overcome traditional computing limitations. The critical difference between neuromorphic and conventional systems lies in their memory structures [16]. While von Neumann systems use centralized processing units separate from memory, spiking neural networks feature distributed, co-localized memory and computation.

Neuromorphic systems utilizing spiking neural networks (SNNs) are increasingly recognized for their potential to deepen our understanding of brain function and to inspire new biologically driven computational methods [46–48]. SNNs have shown effectiveness in visual recognition and classification, and the development of neuromorphic hardware has enabled the real-time operation of large-scale networks, an essential feature for embedded applications.

SNNs aim to replicate the information processing observed in the mammalian brain, using networks of neurons that communicate through spike-based events. In contrast to traditional multi-layer perceptron networks, where neurons activate at every propagation cycle, neurons in SNNs emit spikes only when their membrane potential reaches a specific threshold.

In an SNN, neurons produce spikes or pulses that travel along neural pathways when sufficient stimuli from other neurons or external factors are present. These pulses, typically lasting 1–2 ms, may differ in amplitude, shape, or duration but are treated as discrete events. SNNs utilize different schemes to encode information, including coincidence, rate, and temporal encoding. Communication between neurons occurs at junctions known as synapses, which can be either chemical or electrical. Most synapses are chemical, relying on neurotransmitters, while electrical synapses allow ions to pass directly between neurons. Figure 2.1 illustrates a pre-synaptic neuron transmitting a signal across a synapse to a post-synaptic neuron.

Simulating spiking neural networks (SNNs) in software offers flexibility for exploring the characteristics and dynamics of neuronal models. Despite this, large-

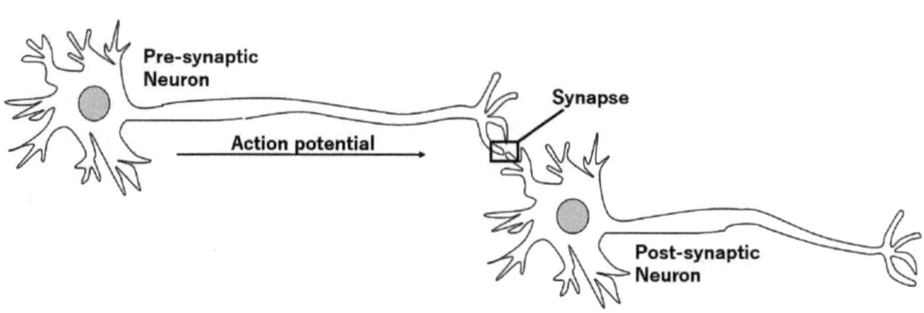

Fig. 2.1 Two neurons communicating via a synapse. Two neurons communicate through a synapse, a junction where information transfers from one neuron to another. This communication typically involves the release and reception of neurotransmitters, chemical messengers that convey signals across the synaptic gap or synaptic cleft

scale SNN simulations can be slow and computationally intensive, often short of delivering the performance and scalability required for real-world applications.

To address these limitations, hardware implementations provide an alternative capable of generating precise spikes and outputting them in real time. Hardware-based approaches not only offer significant computational speed gains but also fully leverage the parallel processing capabilities inherent in SNNs. By employing specialized architectures with multiple neurocores, hardware implementations can achieve high processing speeds and maintain low power consumption, making them ideal for embedded neuromorphic systems and control-related applications. Some simulation frameworks now also incorporate hardware acceleration to boost performance further [2].

Modern artificial neural networks (ANNs), particularly deep neural networks (DNNs), are characterized by multiple interconnected layers. In applications such as image recognition, these layers typically form a 2D arrangement, creating a complex 3D network structure. However, mapping this 3D architecture onto conventional 2D hardware presents challenges, especially with the need for extended inter-layer wiring.

2.1.2 Neural Coding Schemes

Spiking neurons propagate signals rapidly over long distances by generating electrical pulses called action potentials that can travel down axons. Sensory neurons change their activities by firing sequences of action potentials, known as spike-train, in various temporal patterns, with external sensory stimuli, such as light, sound, etc. In a small area of the cortex, thousands of spikes are emitted in every millisecond. This raises the question of how the spikes can be encoded into information. Some other specialized neurons can communicate more information through so-called graded potentials. However, contrary to the action potential of spiking neurons, the signal in graded potential neurons decays much faster, necessitating high neuronal density and short inter-neuron distances. Graded potential neurons have higher information rates capable of encoding more states than spiking neurons [33].

A spike train may contain information based on different coding schemes. For example, in motor neurons, the strength at which a muscle is contracted depends on the average number of spikes per unit of time (firing rate). On the other hand, a complex temporal code is based on the precise timing of single spikes. This section describes the most common coding schemes used in spiking neuromorphic systems.

2.1.2.1 Rate Coding

The rate coding scheme, also known as frequency coding, is a simple traditional coding scheme. It states that the action potentials rate increases as a stimulus's intensity increases. Since the sequence of action potentials generated by a given stimulus varies from trial to trial, the firing rates are used for decoding brain activity instead of specific spike sequences. Consequently, rate coding is inefficient but highly robust due to ISI (Inter-Spike-Interference) noise [37]. This approach also neglects all the information possibly contained in the exact timing of the spikes.

In rate coding, precisely calculating the firing rate is essential. There are different rate averaging methods used in rate codings, such as an average over time (rate as a single-neuron spike count) or several repetitions:

Spike Count Rate This method is determined by the average number of spikes in an interval time as shown in Eq. (2.1).

$$v_{sc} = \frac{n_{spike}}{\Delta t} \tag{2.1}$$

where n_{spike} is the spike number, Δt is the interval (time window) and v_{sc} is the value. The length of Δt depends on the neural models used. This coding method has been successfully used for sensory and motor systems experiments.

Spike Density Rate In this coding method, the same stimulation sequence is repeated K times, then the number of spikes n_K is summed over all repetitions. The rate coding method is expressed in Eq. (2.2) as:

$$v_{sd} = \frac{n_K}{K\Delta t} \tag{2.2}$$

Where Δt is the period of repetition, although biological neurons do not use this method, it is valuable for evaluating neuron activity.

Population Activity Rate Many neurons have the same characteristics and interact with the same stimuli. Population activity rate is proposed to measure the firing rate of a population of neurons as shown in Eq. (2.3):

$$v_{pa} = \frac{n_p}{N\Delta t} \tag{2.3}$$

Where n_p is the total number of spikes generated by N neurons, Δt is the time window.

2.1.2.2 Temporal Coding

In temporal coding, the information about stimulus or action is contained in the relative timing of spikes, not just in the rate of those spikes. Temporal code is generally divided into the following coding schemes:

- *Time-to-first-spike:* The idea is to encode the latency information of the first spike event given a stream of spikes, where the precise timing of the spikes indicates the strength of the stimulation [13, 29, 35]. The first spike is generally

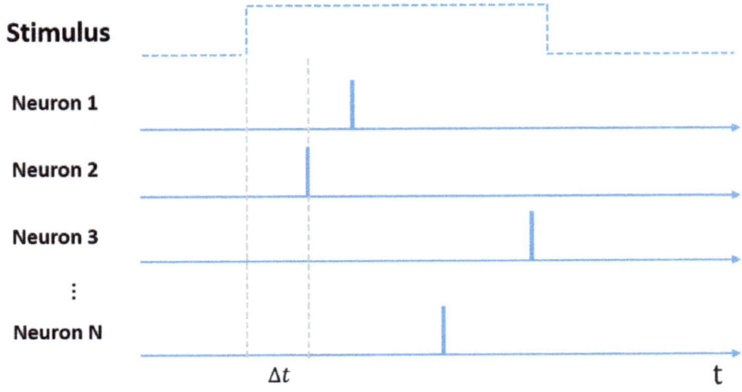

Fig. 2.2 Time to first spike (TTFS). The TTFS coding is a neural coding scheme that emphasizes the significance of the timing of the first action potential (or spike) in response to a stimulus. This coding method focuses on how quickly a neuron responds to a given input, with the time elapsed from the onset of the stimulus to the generation of the first spike serving as a critical signal for encoding information

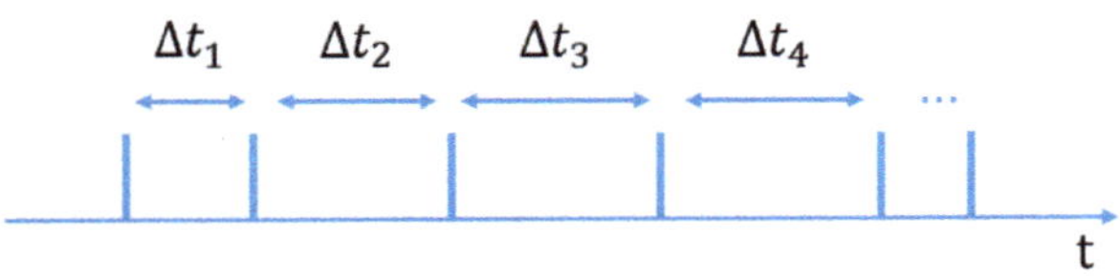

Fig. 2.3 Inter-spike-interval (ISI). The ISI coding is a neural coding scheme that focuses on the timing between a neuron's consecutive action potentials (or spikes) rather than solely relying on the average firing rate. In this approach, the specific intervals—how long one spike occurs after another—encode information about a stimulus or event

interpreted to carry a more robust stimulus feature, and the following spikes are ignored [12, 27]. Figure 2.2 illustrates the Time-to-first-spike coding scheme. Figure 2.3 illustrates the Time-to-first-spike coding scheme.

- *Inter-spike-interval:* The inter-spike-interval (ISI) refers to the internal time correlation between spikes rather than the absolute time concerning stimulus onset [52, 53]. Also, the merit of the ISI approach, compared to time-to-first-spike (TTFS), relies on the internal reference frames. Thus, more messages can be conveyed during the same sampling period in this coding approach [1].
- *Phase coding:* The neural oscillations are intrinsically rhythmic and are prevalent in many brain areas with different frequency bands. When the activity of a cluster of neurons is periodic, the neurons can create rhythmic electrical patterns [3, 14]. The oscillations could serve as time inference signals, and the phase could be encoded into neuronal spike trains to convey relevant information. Figure 2.4 illustrates the Phase coding scheme.
- *Rank order coding:* The rank order neural coding (shown in Fig. 2.5) is a type of neural encoding where the representation of stimuli in a neural population is determined by the relative firing rates of individual neurons, often organized

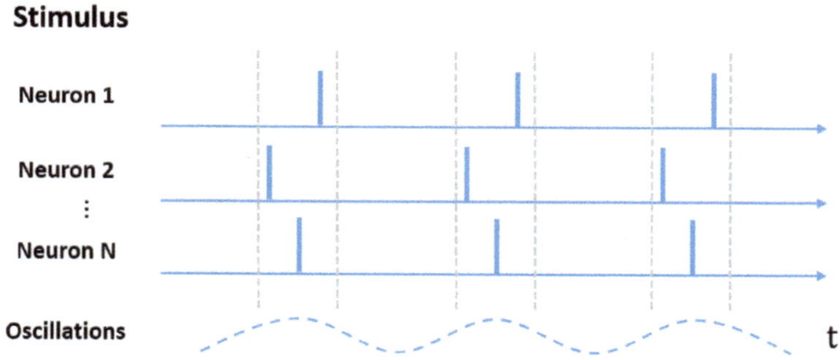

Fig. 2.4 Phase coding. In phase coding, individual spikes occur at precise phases of an ongoing oscillatory cycle. For example, a spike might occur at a specific point in the sine wave of an oscillating signal. By varying the phase at which spikes occur, the brain can encode different properties of sensory input, such as the features of a sound or the characteristics of a visual stimulus. This means that even if two neurons fire at the same average rate, the relative timing of their spikes concerning the oscillatory phase can convey distinct information

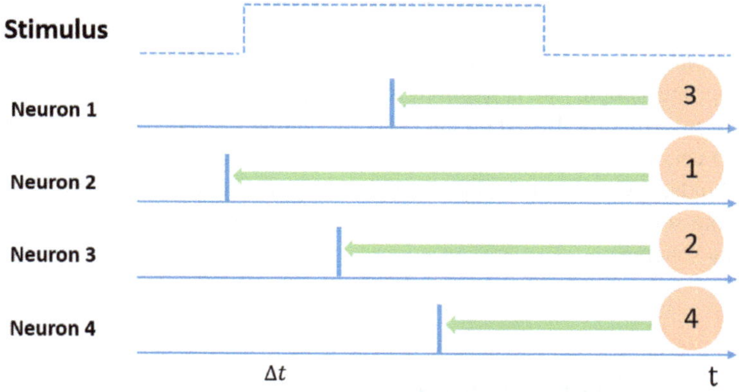

Fig. 2.5 Rank order coding. This approach can enhance the robustness of neural representations, as the precise firing rates of individual neurons may vary due to noise or other factors, but the relative ranking of their activity remains stable

in ranked order according to their activity level. In this coding scheme, neurons encode information based on rank rather than absolute firing rates. For instance, the neuron with the highest firing rate in response to a particular stimulus is assigned the top rank, the second highest the next rank, and so on. The idea is to omit the precise timing information by using only the order in which the spikes arrive [39, 40]. This coding strategy relies on the observation that the first-spike latency jitter between two trials is less than 1 ms (median value) in all cases and thus is believed to be highly reliable [44]. An example is its robustness against image degradations like intensity and contrast change [39].

- *Correlation and synchrony:* Consider a pair or a group of neurons that are nearly synchronous. Such synchrony might imply some additional or specific

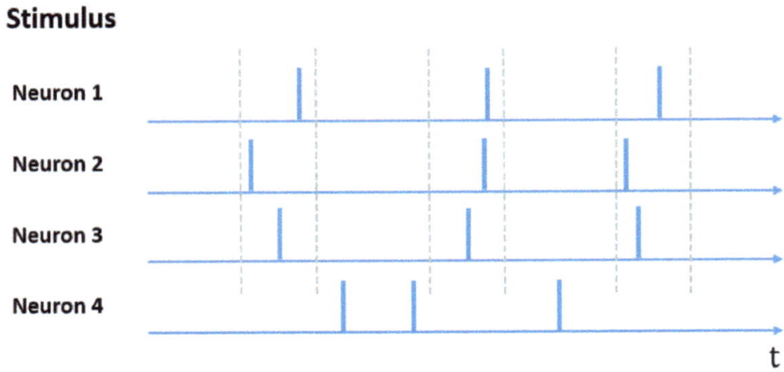

Fig. 2.6 Correlation and synchrony. Correlation and synchrony refer to how the activity patterns of group neurons can be coordinated and interpreted to enhance information processing and representation in neural networks

information that cannot be represented using the simple firing rate of neurons [12] (Fig. 2.6).

- *Threshold coding:* Generally, when processing a continuous audio signal, an appropriate sample rate is required for ideal preservation and perfect reconstruction of information. Based on the observation that the interval of sampling is the key to encoding the stimuli, the sound intensity can be divided into a group of thresholds, and onset and offset neurons are used to encode the information each time the sound waves cross a threshold [27]. Figure 2.7 illustrates the threshold coding scheme.

2.2 Spiking Neuron Models

Spiking neuron models vary significantly in implementation cost and biological plausibility, each offering different trade-offs that make them suitable for various applications in computational neuroscience and neuromorphic engineering.

Among the most prominent models is the Leaky Integrate-and-Fire (LIF) model, which simulates the integration of synaptic inputs and the gradual decay of membrane potential, culminating in spike generation when a threshold is reached. The Izhikevich model expands on this by incorporating a more complex set of equations, enabling it to reproduce various neuronal firing patterns, including spiking, bursting, and oscillatory behaviors, while maintaining computational efficiency. The Hodgkin-Huxley model offers a highly detailed representation of neuronal dynamics by modeling multiple ionic currents and their interactions. It provides high biological fidelity, albeit at a more significant computational cost. Another notable model is the Fitzhugh-Nagumo model, a simplified version of the Hodgkin-Huxley framework, capturing essential excitability features while being more accessible

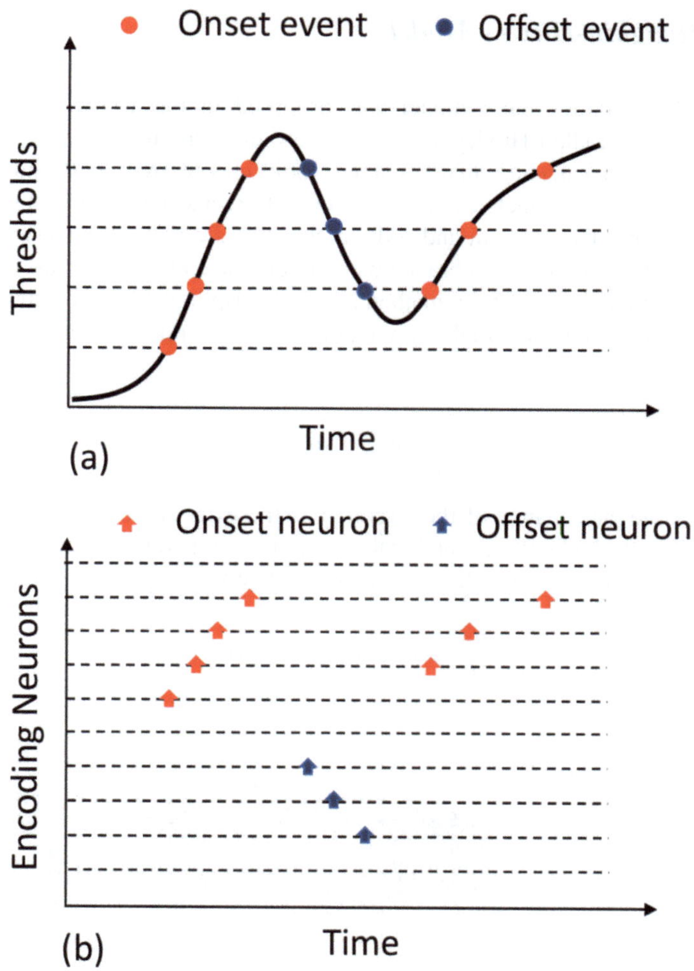

Fig. 2.7 Threshold coding: the threshold temporal coding is a neural coding scheme that emphasizes the timing of action potentials (or spikes) in conveying information within neural circuits. Unlike rate coding, where information is encoded primarily in the frequency of spikes over a given period, temporal coding focuses on the precise timing of individual spikes relative to one another and to external stimuli

to implement. Each of these models presents unique advantages and challenges, balancing biological plausibility with computational efficiency, and they are selected based on specific research goals, whether for simulating large neural networks or studying the intricacies of neuronal dynamics. Together, these spiking neuron models form the foundation for understanding neural computation and inform the development of neuromorphic systems.

2.2.1 Hodgkin-Huxley Model

The Hodgkin-Huxley neural model was proposed in the 1950s. As described in Fig. 2.8, the Hodkin-Huxley neuron models in a circuit, the cell membrane of a neuron as a capacitor that separates ionic charge from both sides of the membrane, the ion channels as conductors/resistors, and the membrane potential as a battery [26]. The calcium and sodium channels are voltage-gated and change connectivity based on the membrane potential, but the leak channels are not gated. This neuron model presents a mathematical description of the electric current through the membrane potential v, giving the details of spike generation, as shown in Eq. (2.4):

$$\frac{dv}{dt} = (\frac{1}{C})I - g_k n^4(V - V_k) - g_{Na} m^3 h(V - V_{Na}) - g_L(V - V_L) \tag{2.4}$$

where C is the capacitance of the circuit, I is the external current, conductances are potassium g_k, sodium g_{Na}, and leakage g_L. Gating parameters n, m, and h are determined by Eqs. (2.5), (2.6), and (2.7), respectively

$$\frac{dn}{dt} = (n_\infty(v) - n)/\tau_n(v) \tag{2.5}$$

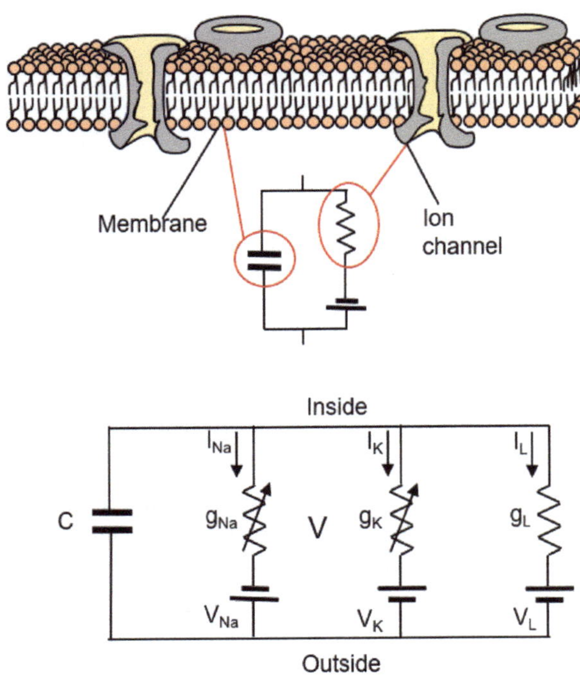

Fig. 2.8 The Hodgkin-Huxley model

$$\frac{dm}{dt} = (m_{\infty}(v) - m)/\tau_m(v) \tag{2.6}$$

$$\frac{dh}{dt} = (h_{\infty}(v) - h)/\tau_h(v) \tag{2.7}$$

As shown in Fig. 2.8, the Hodgkin-Huxley model is the most biologically plausible. However, its complexity and many features consume many hardware resources. It, therefore, is costly for large-scale implementations.

2.2.2 Izhikevich Model

The Izhikevich model [18] is a prominent mathematical framework used to simulate the dynamic behavior of biological neurons, combining the simplicity of integrate-and-fire models with the richness of Hodgkin-Huxley dynamics. It is characterized by a set of differential equations that describe the membrane potential and recovery dynamics of the neuron, allowing it to reproduce a wide variety of spiking and bursting behaviors found in different types of neurons. The model incorporates two key variables: the membrane potential, which integrates incoming synaptic currents, and a recovery variable that accounts for the neuron's adaptation to input over time. It features several parameters that can be adjusted to mimic various neuronal firing patterns, such as regular spiking, bursting, and fast spiking. The following equations describe the model:

$$\frac{dv}{dt} = 0.04v^2 + 5v + 140 - u + I \tag{2.8}$$

$$\frac{du}{dt} = a(bv - u) \tag{2.9}$$

$$\begin{cases} v \leftarrow c \\ u \leftarrow u + d \end{cases} \quad if\ v \geq 30mV \tag{2.10}$$

Where v is the membrane potential of the neuron, u is a membrane recovery variable, I is the neuron current, and a, b, c, d are parameters of the models, in which the various values of these parameters result in different types of neuron characteristics. When membrane potential v exceeds the threshold (30 mV), the membrane potential v and recovery variable v are reset as Eq. (2.10). The Izhikevich model reproduces the spiking and bursting characteristics of known cortical neurons. These spiking characteristics include regular spiking (RS), intrinsically bursting (IB), chattering (CH), fast-spiking (FS), thalamocortical (TC), resonator(RZ), and low-threshold spiking (LTS).

2.2.3 Leaky Integrate and Fire Model

The Leaky Integrate-and-Fire (LIF) model is a simple yet powerful representation of neuronal dynamics characterized by several key components. First, it features a membrane potential that integrates incoming currents over time, representing synaptic inputs. The "leaky" aspect refers to the gradual decay of this potential toward a resting state due to a passive leakage of ions across the membrane. When the membrane potential reaches a specified threshold, the neuron produces an action potential (or spike), after which the potential is reset to a lower value. This model captures essential features of neuronal behavior, such as spiking, resting, and integration of synaptic inputs, making it a foundational tool in computational neuroscience.

The Leaky Integrate and Fire (LIF) model is one of the most commonly used models in SNN. It is described by Eqs. (2.11) and (2.12).

$$\frac{dv}{dt} = I + a - bv \tag{2.11}$$

$$v \leftarrow c, \; if \; v \geq v_{th} \tag{2.12}$$

v is the neuron's membrane potential, I is the neuron current, and a, b, and c are model parameters. When the membrane potential v exceeds a threshold v_{th}, it will be reset to c. The primary circuit presenting the LIF model is shown in Fig. 2.9. It consists of capacitor C and resistor R connected in parallel and driven by a current $I(t)$. In summary, among the existing spiking models, Hodgkin-Huxley, Izhikevich [18], and Leaky Integrate-and-Fire (LIF) [17] are often used. The Hodgkin-Huxley type is the best when measurable physiological parameters are highly considered. The model is based on many coefficients. This leads to challenges when implementing large SNNs because of the high hardware cost. In contrast, the LIF neural model can simulate hundreds of thousands of neurons but cannot produce rich spiking patterns. Finally, Izhikevich exhibits a good compromise regarding biophysical similarity and computational cost. It is close to the Hodgkin-Huxley model in biological plausibility while analogous to the LIF in computational complexity.

2.3 Learning Algorithms

Learning in SNN is based on modifying the strength of synaptic connections between neurons. Spiking Neural Networks (SNNs) utilize various learning algorithms that harness the temporal dynamics of spikes to enable learning and adaptation. Hebbian learning is another fundamental principle, encapsulated in the idea that "cells that fire together wire together", allowing neurons that activate simultaneously to develop stronger connections. By following that rule, one

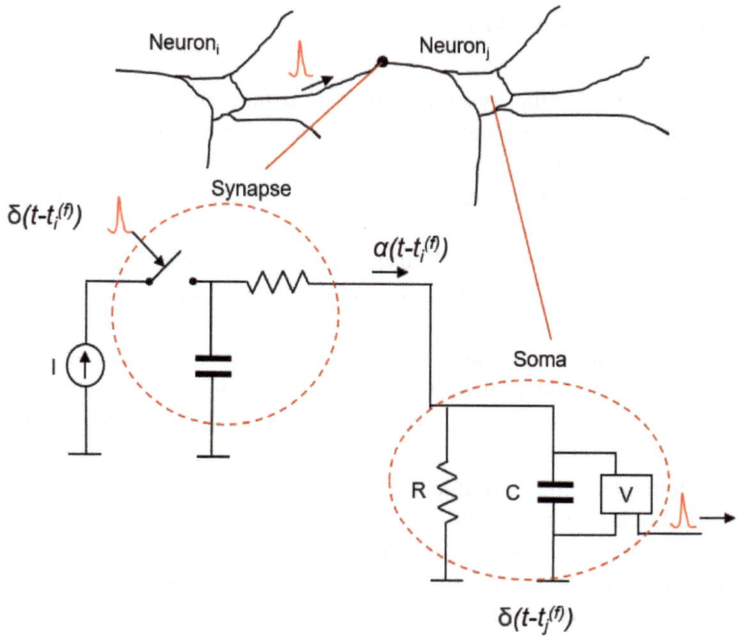

Fig. 2.9 Schematic diagram of the LIF model. The LIF neuron model serves as a foundational framework for understanding the principles of spiking neural networks and neuronal dynamics in computational neuroscience

prominent approach is Spike-Timing-Dependent Plasticity (STDP), which adjusts synaptic weights based on the precise timing of spikes between pre- and post-synaptic neurons, promoting synaptic strengthening when a pre-synaptic neuron fires before a post-synaptic one. Reinforcement learning techniques can also be incorporated, enabling SNNs to learn from feedback and rewards, thus adapting their responses to external stimuli based on past experiences. Competitive learning promotes distinct feature extraction by allowing neurons to compete for activation, where the winning neuron strengthens its weight while others may weaken theirs. Additionally, while adaptations of traditional backpropagation have been explored for SNNs, they face inherent challenges due to the non-differentiable nature of spike events.

Designing practical learning algorithms for SNNs also encounters several challenges, including balancing the complexity of biologically plausible rules with computational efficiency, establishing stable and robust learning dynamics, and the limited understanding of how best to represent and optimize temporal information within the spiking framework.

Learning in a neuromorphic system is based on supervised and unsupervised learning paradigms.

2.3.1 Supervised Learning

In supervised learning, the system is trained using labeled input-output pairs, allowing it to learn to associate specific input patterns with desired outcomes through error correction and feedback mechanisms. This approach enables the network to adjust its synaptic weights to minimize the difference between predicted and actual outputs.

Backpropagation (BP) is a widely used supervised learning algorithm in neuromorphic programming, applicable across various neural network models, such as feed-forward, recurrent, and convolutional neural networks. The most straightforward approach for implementing BP in hardware is through an off-chip method, where BP runs on an external host machine. Following training, the pre-trained parameters are transferred to the neuromorphic chip. This off-chip approach enables precise software-based BP and reduces hardware resource requirements but is less ideal for systems that require frequent retraining.

However, on-chip implementations of BP have also been explored in neuromorphic systems. Some of these adaptations use optimized or simplified versions of BP tailored for neuromorphic hardware. Various on-chip learning methods have also been implemented for convolutional neural networks, Boltzmann machines, restricted Boltzmann machines, and deep belief networks.

In a related approach, [11] introduces spike-driven synaptic plasticity (SDSP), a learning rule guided by a "teacher" signal. Unlike spike-timing-dependent plasticity (STDP), SDSP updates synaptic weights each time a presynaptic spike is detected. Backpropagation has also been adapted to spiking neural networks (SNNs) [51], where an artificial neural network (ANN) is initially trained using BP and then converted to an SNN. This conversion maps continuous activation values in the ANN to average firing rates represented by Poisson spikes in the SNN. This makes it suitable for spiking hardware as an off-chip learning method.

2.3.2 Unsupervised Learning

Unsupervised learning relies on the inherent structure of the input data without external labels, allowing the system to discover patterns, relationships, or clusters within the data autonomously. This dual approach enables neuromorphic systems to adaptively learn from explicit instructions and implicit structures in the environment, enhancing their ability to process complex information like biological neural networks.

Compared to supervised learning, implementations of unsupervised learning are less popular. Some on-chip ones have been implemented in neuromorphic systems. Most of them were based on self-organizing maps or self-organizing learning rules.The spike-timing-dependent plasticity (STDP), Hebbian-based learning, is a popular learning rule already implemented in several neuromorphic systems [16].

The operation of STDP depends on the firing time of presynaptic and postsynaptic neurons in which the synaptic weight will be increased when a spike arrives before a postsynaptic neuron "fires" and decreased when it comes after a postsynaptic neuron fires. STDP is an unsupervised learning rule and is generally implemented on-chip.

2.3.2.1 Spike Timing Dependent Plasticity (STDP)

Spike-Timing-Dependent Plasticity (STDP) is a biologically inspired learning mechanism that offers several merits and demerits in the context of neural network training. One of its key advantages is its ability to encode the temporal relationships between spikes, which allows for fine-tuning synaptic connections based on the timing of neuronal activity. This biologically plausible mechanism enhances the network's capacity for learning complex patterns and facilitating temporal coding, leading to more robust representations of input stimuli. Additionally, STDP promotes adaptive learning, enabling the neural network to respond dynamically to environmental changes and strengthen relevant connections while weakening less significant ones.

One drawback associated with STDP is the potential for instability in learning, as the continual adjustment of synaptic weights based purely on timing can lead to runaway potentiation or depression if not properly regulated. Furthermore, STDP can be slower than traditional gradient-based learning methods, as it relies on spike timing information rather than global error signals, which can impede its applicability in scenarios requiring rapid learning. Moreover, the implementation of STDP in artificial systems often necessitates fine-tuning parameters and careful consideration of network architecture to achieve desired learning outcomes, making it complex to integrate effectively in large-scale neural networks. While STDP offers exciting possibilities for emulating biological learning processes, its practical application involves navigating these inherent merits and demerits.

The STDP learning rule, as originally expressed in [15], is described by the following rule:

$$\Delta w = \begin{cases} \Delta w^{+} = A^{+} e^{\left(\frac{-\Delta t}{\tau_{+}}\right)}, & \text{if } \Delta t > 0 \\ \Delta w^{-} = -A^{-} e^{\left(\frac{\Delta t}{\tau_{-}}\right)}, & \text{if } \Delta t \leq 0 \end{cases} \tag{2.13}$$

Where Δw is the change in synaptic weight, if a presynaptic spike arrives at the postsynaptic neuron within a time window τ_{+} before the postsynaptic spike, the synaptic weight increases Δw^{+}. Still, if it arrives within a time window τ_{-}, after the postsynaptic spike, the synaptic weight decreases Δw^{-}. Δt is the time difference between the presynaptic and postsynaptic spike, which is expressed as $\Delta t = t_{post} - t_{pre}$, while A^{+} and A^{-} are potentiation and depression amplitude parameters respectively.

2.3.2.2 Spike Driven Synaptic Plasticity (SDSP)

Another SNN learning rule that has been employed in neuromorphic processors is spike-driven synaptic plasticity (SDSP) [7]. This approach extends beyond traditional plasticity models by considering the frequency, timing, and correlation of spikes from pre- and post-synaptic neurons. At the arrival of a presynaptic spike, if the postsynaptic membrane potential exceeds the threshold, the synaptic weight is increased and decreased otherwise, ensuring that the calcium absorption in the postsynaptic site C(t) is preserved within a boundary when the presynaptic spike arrives. The Spike-driven synaptic plasticity (SDSP) operation is described in [31] as:

$$\begin{cases} W = W + a, & \text{if } V_{\text{mem}}(t) > V_{\text{mth}} \text{ and } \theta_{\text{up}}^{l} < C(t) < \theta_{\text{up}}^{h} \\ W = W - b, & \text{if } V_{\text{mem}}(t) \le V_{\text{mth}} \text{ and } \theta_{dn}^{l} < C(t) < \theta_{dn}^{h} \end{cases} \tag{2.14}$$

where V_{mem} is the post synaptic membrane potential, V_{th} the threshold voltage, a and b the measure of potentiation and depression respectively. θ_{up}^{l}, θ_{up}^{h}, θ_{dn}^{l} and θ_{dn}^{h} are the boundaries for calcium absorption. In the absence of pre-synaptic spikes which determine potentiation and depression, the synaptic weights increase or decrease depending on their value, which could be higher or lower than a set threshold θ_W. This operation is described in [7] as:

$$\begin{cases} \dfrac{dW(t)}{dt} = \alpha, & \text{if } W(t) > \theta_W \\[2ex] \dfrac{dW(t)}{dt} = -\beta, & \text{if } W(t) \le \theta_W. \end{cases} \tag{2.15}$$

Other learning rules that have been implemented on neuromorphic processors include the BCM-like Local Correlation learning rule [22], Modified Ion Channel-based learning rule [36], and Stochastic gradient descent [30].

The primary merit of SDSP lies in its ability to adaptively reshape connectivity based on the specific firing patterns observed in dynamic environments, allowing for more nuanced learning that aligns closely with biological processes. However, like other synaptic plasticity mechanisms, SDSP can face challenges such as maintaining stability and avoiding overly rapid adaptations that might destabilize the network's performance over time. Overall, SDSP represents a promising avenue for developing more biologically realistic and practical learning algorithms in spiking neural networks.

In Chap. 3, we provide a comprehensive exploration of the various learning methods utilized in Spiking Neural Networks, discussing their underlying principles, advantages, limitations, and potential applications in neuromorphic computing.

2.4 Synapse Memory

Unlike traditional computer systems, which have memory and processing different, SNN-like biological neural networks combine both, having neurons as the processing elements and the synapses as memory. Efficiently replicating these synapses in neuromorphic processors has been challenging because a memory that behaves like synapses is required.

In traditional computer systems, memory speed is a bottleneck because processors have significantly improved over the years, surpassing memory speed and throughput, leaving processors idle while waiting for memory. However, SNN is different. These spiking neurons process events, and as opposed to traditional processors that operate and communicate in megahertz and gigahertz ranges, they communicate in around 10 Hz. This difference in speed enables neuromorphic processors to use time multiplexing to combine many events into a single communication channel.

In SNN, Storing and reading synaptic weights constitutes the primary operation, and designing a large SNN with an enormous number of synapses will require a large memory bandwidth. So while communication speed is not somewhat challenging in neuromorphic systems, memory bandwidth must be overcome. In addressing this challenge, researchers have taken several approaches to realize these synapses in CMOS by exploring various memory technologies. Some of these memory technologies include static random-access memory (SRAM), a prominent memory technology in semiconductor design. In [34], a neuromorphic chip with 256 neurons that implements a transposable 8-transistor SRAM-based crossbar, which grants row and column access, was employed.

In recent years, significant progress has been made toward creating artificial synapses using post-CMOS technologies. These efforts include various memory devices, such as resistive random-access memory (ReRAM), phase-change memory (PCM), magneto-resistive random-access memory (MRAM), and ferroelectric field-effect transistors (FeFET). Researchers have recently begun exploring non-CMOS neuron designs leveraging emerging memory technologies. In this section, we discuss the main emerging memory technologies with the potential to mimic synaptic behavior in neuromorphic systems. Each technology brings distinct advantages and limitations, making it suitable for specific applications. Depending on the target use, one type of memory device may be preferable over others due to scalability, energy efficiency, retention, switching speed, and integration compatibility.

2.4.1 SRAM

A typical SRAM contains six transistors (6-T), and although having high leakage current and low density, SRAM offers multiple read and write. Its significant advantages are speed and reliability compared to other memory technologies.

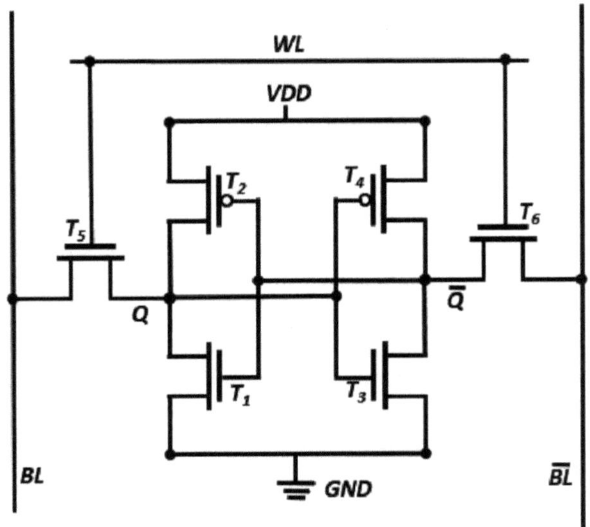

Fig. 2.10 Static Random Access Memory (SRAM) cell. SRAM plays a vital role in neuromorphic chips designed to emulate the architecture and functioning of biological neural networks. In these chips, SRAM is typically employed as a part of the memory architecture to store synaptic weights, neuron states, and other essential parameters required for processing and learning

Another SRAM utilized in neuromorphic systems is the eight-transistor (8-T) SRAM [5]. The two more transistors on the 8-T SRAM add access to the word and bit lines in transposed orientation to the typical 6-T design. To handle the general leakage power of the chip, the authors leveraged ultra-high-Vt devices, which reduced it by 3, at the cost of increasing the minimum operating voltage of the memory array (Fig. 2.10).

2.4.2 eDRAM

Another memory technology is embedded dynamic random-access memory (eDRAM), used in [8] to design a high-density 3D memory for a programmable digital neuromorphic architecture. eDRAM is a capacitor-based memory integrated into the same multi-chip module. Due to its simple conventional one 1-transistor 1-capacitor design, it is inclined to have less area cost when compared to SRAM. However, its retention period is low due to the gradual leakage of its storage charge during operation. Also, its design is not easily compatible with CMOS. In [45], a spin-transfer torque ram (STT-RAM) was proposed as a stochastic memristive synapse for neuromorphic systems. An STT-RAM is a magnetic RAM that uses magnetic tunneling junction (MTJ) in its cells, and its simple design has a small area compared to SRAM and eDRAM. By adopting a schema proposed in [21], the authors organized the STT-RAM MJT as a crossbar connecting input and output neurons. However, the magnetization of the STT-RAM makes the writing process slow and consumes more energy (Fig. 2.11).

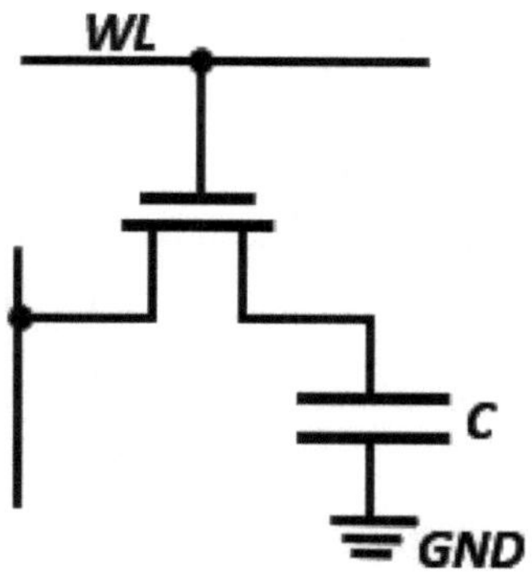

Fig. 2.11 Embedded Dynamic Random Access Memory (eDRAM) cell. eDRAM is a memory commonly used in neuromorphic chips to enhance their computational efficiency and capacity. Unlike traditional static RAM (SRAM), eDRAM utilizes a capacitor to store data, which allows it to achieve higher storage density, making it a more space-efficient solution for memory-intensive applications

2.4.3 Memristor

Resistive random-access memory (RRAM or ReRAM) relies on the resistance change of its cells to store information, and it has a similar architecture to eDRAM. In [20], the authors proposed an FPGA-based hardware emulator for a neuromorphic chip with an RRAM-based crossbar. RRAM offers low area, low power, and easy integration on CMOS. However, it suffers from stuck at faults (SAF) [50], which may cause short-circuiting and lead to increased power and dynamic switching variation, which leads to a significant variation in the resistance of the memory. Other memory technologies include Phase Change Memory (PCM). In Chap. 4, we comprehensively explore various memory technologies utilized in Spiking Neural Networks, highlighting their underlying principles, advantages, limitations, and potential applications in neuromorphic computing (Fig. 2.12).

2.5 Inter-Neuron Communication Schemes

Communication architectures for multicore spiking neuromorphic systems deliver spikes between neuro-cores/tiles. They can be classified as intra-chip and inter-chip. For inter-chip, address event presentation (AER) is commonly employed [4, 6, 24]. In AER, each neuron has a unique address. Whenever a neuron generates a spike, its address is sent to postsynaptic neurons by a high-speed digital bus. AER is suitable for SNN implementations since it only needs to be active whenever neurons fire. A hierarchical AER as a tree structure was implemented to scale up the system in [28].

On the other hand, network-on-chip (NoC) is commonly implemented for on-chip communication. In the early implementation stage, buses are employed in

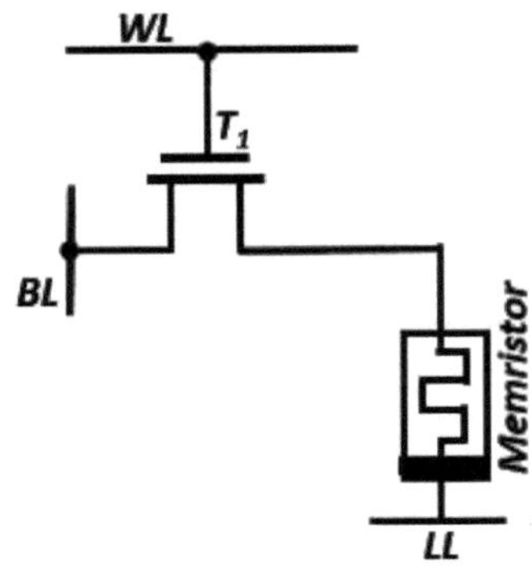

Fig. 2.12 RRAM cell. A memristor's resistance can be adjusted based on the history of voltage and current applied to it, allowing it to "remember" the amount of charge that has passed through. This property makes memristors particularly suitable for emulating synaptic behaviors, as they can store and modify synaptic weights dynamically based on the timing and frequency of voltage pulses, similar to how biological synapses strengthen or weaken in response to neuronal activity

some systems [25]. However, works in [41, 42] evaluated and compared four architectures: bus, tree, point-to-point, and mesh. The results show that mesh with multicast offers the highest performance for SNN implementations. Furthermore, AER also is used for on-chip communication [9, 43].

2.5.1 AER: Address Event Representation

A neuromorphic system consists of many neurons, axons, and synapses integrated into a 3D or 2D silicon substrate. Unlike standard digital logic, where the output of a gate is generally connected to the input of three to four other gates, a neuron is typically connected to thousands of other neurons. On the other hand, the spiking rate is shallow (tens of Hz) compared to the speed of digital electronics, which is in the range of GHz. The time-multiplexed communication protocol is often used to solve the speed difference between electronic and ionic transmissions. The circuits used to multiplex communication for a cluster of neurons into a single communication channel are known as AER [19]. AER is a neuromorphic inter-chip communication protocol that allows massive real-time connectivity between many neurons on different chips. Figure 2.13 shows the AER protocol. Address-event representation (AER) is a proposed communication protocol to communicate sparse neural events between neuromorphic chips.

Initially, inter-chip communication networks provided only simple unidirectional, point-to-point connectivity between arrays of neuromorphic on two neuromorphic chips. These communication schemes map spikes from output nodes in the sending chip to any appropriate input nodes in the receiving chip. The mapping occurs asynchronously and provides random access to the receiver nodes. The spikes

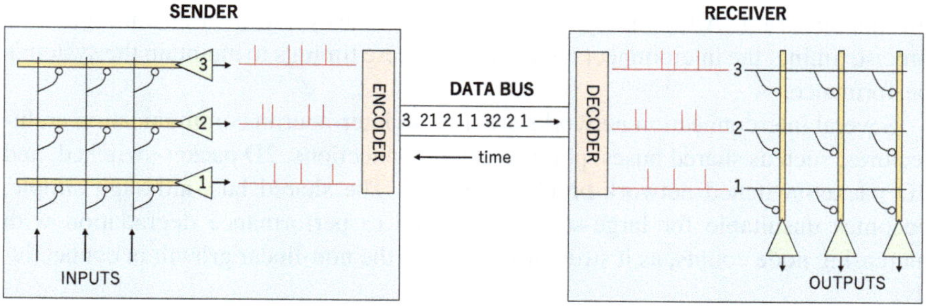

Fig. 2.13 The Address-Event Representation (AER) protocol is a widely used communication framework in neuromorphic computing. AER facilitates the asynchronous exchange of event-based information among neuromorphic systems or between different parts of the same system. It provides a scalable, low-power method for transmitting sparse, spike-like data while preserving temporal information

are represented as addresses. An address encoder at the output node generates a unique binary address identifying that node (neuron).

The output addresses are transmitted over a shared bus to the receiving chip, where an address decoder selects the appropriate receiver node (input) and activates it. Two versions of this random-access scheme have been proposed: a hard-wired version and an arbitered version Each spike is represented by its location (explicitly encoded as an address) and the time it occurs (implicitly encoded).

2.6 Interconnection Networks for Neuromorphic Systems

Inter-neuron communication networks are integral to the functioning of the nervous system, facilitating the transmission of signals between neurons and enabling complex processing. These networks utilize various synaptic connections, including excitatory and inhibitory interactions, which regulate neuronal activity and information flow. Different communication mechanisms, such as electrical synapses and chemical neurotransmission, play crucial roles in shaping network dynamics and influencing behaviors, learning processes, and responses to stimuli. The structural organization of these networks can vary widely, from local circuits that mediate reflex actions to larger-scale networks that integrate information across brain regions. Understanding these communication pathways is essential for unraveling the complexities of neural functions and can offer insights into developing neuromorphic systems that mimic biological processing.

Neuromorphic computing systems are typically designed using a tile-based architecture, where tiles communicate through a shared interconnect. Each neuron must multicast messages to multiple nodes within a single or manycore system-on-chip in these systems. A scalable interconnect architecture is essential for a neuromorphic system to support a substantial number of neurons akin to those in the human brain. Additionally, because spikes convey information through their precise timing, the interconnect must preserve these timings to maintain the system's performance.

Several interconnection networks are used in inter-neuron communication architectures, such as shared buses, point-to-point connections, 2D packet-switched, and 3D packet-switched network-on-chips (NoCs). The shared bus, although simple, becomes unsuitable for large-scale SNNs due to performance degradation with increasing node counts, as it struggles to handle the non-linear growth in connectivity.

The 2D packet-switched NoC (2D-NoC) is a promising scalability, latency, and speed option. However, due to communication constraints, 2D-NoCs may encounter power and performance issues at larger scales. By contrast, 3D packet-switched NoCs (3D-NoCs) integrate NoC architecture with 3D integrated circuits (3D-ICs) [49]. Through-silicon-Vias (TSVs) in 3D-NoCs enable vertical communication between layers, significantly reducing communication overheads.

Moreover, since the brain is inherently organized in a 3D structure, adopting 3D interconnects allows neuromorphic systems to mirror biological brains' spatial structure and connectivity. Figure 2.14 illustrates the various network architectures

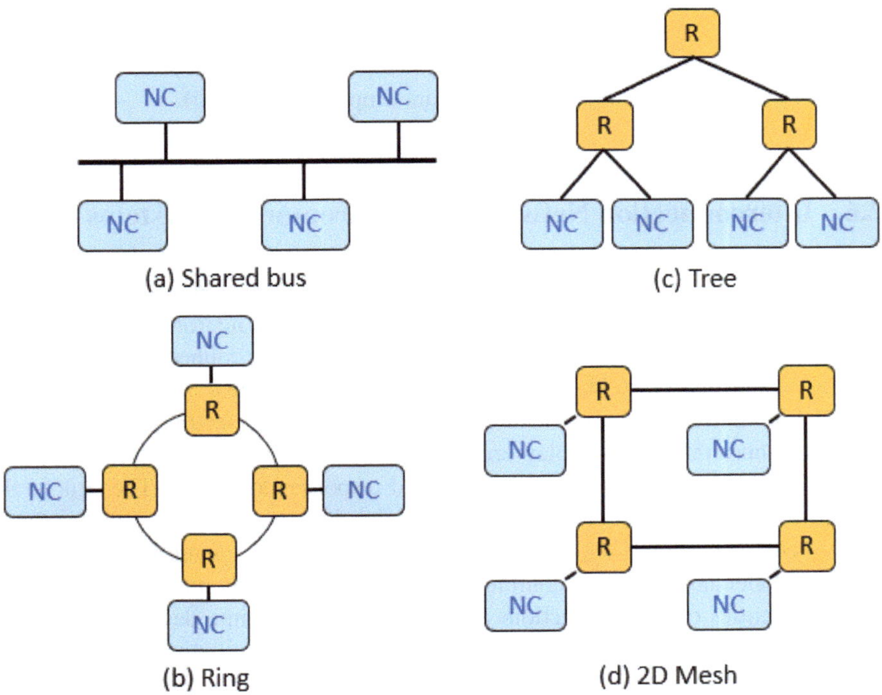

Fig. 2.14 Various inter-neuron communication network topologies: NC—neural core, R—Router. (**a**) Shared bus (**b**) Ring, (**c**) Tree, and (**d**) 2D Mesh. The network in a neuromorphic chip is designed to mimic the key aspects of biological neural circuits, including adaptability, efficiency, and robustness, which are crucial for implementing advanced cognitive functions, such as sensory processing and decision-making, in an energy-efficient and scalable way

available for connecting neurons in neuromorphic systems. In Chap. 5, we comprehensively explore various on-chip and off-chip interconnects used in Spiking Neural Networks, highlighting their underlying principles, advantages, limitations, and potential applications in neuromorphic computing.

2.6.1 Design Challenges

Designing inter-neuron communication networks presents many challenges stemming from the inherent complexity and variability of neuronal behavior and connectivity patterns. One of the primary challenges is accurately modeling the diverse range of neuron types and their specific roles within a network. Neurons exhibit varying firing rates, response properties, and synaptic dynamics, necessitating sophisticated models that can capture these differences while maintaining computational efficiency. Additionally, establishing effective communication pathways between neurons involves addressing the stochastic nature of neurotransmitter release and receptor sensitivity, which can lead to variability in signal transmission and processing.

Synaptic strength, or plasticity, is another critical factor that complicates network design; it is essential to account for how synapses strengthen or weaken in response to activity, which is fundamental for learning and memory but challenging to integrate into rigid architectural frameworks. Furthermore, the topology of neuronal networks—whether local, global, or hierarchical—plays a crucial role in determining the efficiency and robustness of communication; designing networks that can adapt dynamically to changes in connectivity or environmental conditions presents yet another layer of complexity. These challenges necessitate interdisciplinary approaches, drawing on insights from neuroscience, computation, and materials science to create reliable and efficient inter-neuron communication networks that emulate the versatility and adaptability of biological systems.

2.7 Chapter Summary

Neuromorphic computing technology has captivated researchers since the pioneering work of Carver Mead and his team at CalTech in the 1980s. This academic interest has recently transcended into the commercial realm, with significant industry players like IBM and Intel actively exploring the technology. Additionally, start-up companies commercialize neuromorphic solutions for various applications, ranging from inference in low-power edge systems to GPUs for large language models and deep learning.

This chapter presented the fundamental design principles essential for successfully implementing neuromorphic systems in hardware. By exploring key concepts such as neuron organization, circuit design, and efficient information representation, we have laid the groundwork for understanding how these systems can achieve superior energy efficiency and performance compared to traditional computing models.

Furthermore, the chapter emphasized the importance of developing robust and adaptable architectures to facilitate learning and evolution in real-time environments. This adaptability is crucial for applications in dynamic fields such as robotics, artificial intelligence, and data processing, where rapid responsiveness to changing conditions is paramount.

Designing a neuromorphic system presents several key challenges, including organizing individual neurons, circuits, applications, and the overall architecture to facilitate energy-efficient computations. Additional considerations involve how information is represented and how the system can adapt to local variations and evolutionary changes. A massively parallel neuromorphic architecture also necessitates the development of compact neuro-processing cores with low power consumption, efficient neuron coding schemes, and lightweight on-chip learning algorithms, adding to the complexity of the design. The chapter discussed the challenges of creating massively parallel architectures, which require innovations in low-power neuro-processing cores and sophisticated coding schemes to maximize efficiency without compromising functionality. As the field of neuromorphic computing continues to evolve, addressing these challenges will be vital for harnessing its full potential.

2.8 Exercises

2.8.1 Exercise 1

Unlike the typical artificial neural networks, where neurons fire at each propagation cycle, the neurons in a spiking neural network model (SNN) fire only when their membrane potential reaches a certain threshold. Explain the main benefits of this feature on the hardware complexity and inference time of a given neuromorphic system.

2.8.2 Exercise 2

Spiking Neural Networks (SNNs) rely on the timing and frequency of spikes to represent information, unlike traditional ANNs that use continuous activation values. This difference necessitates using specific coding schemes to convert input data into spike trains suitable for SNN processing. Discuss the two main categories of SNN coding schemes (rate coding and temporal coding) and their impact on the performance of SNNs.

2.8.3 Exercise 3

The membrane potential Vm of a neuron is given by the following differential equation:

$$\tau_m \frac{dV_m}{dt} = E_L - V_m + R_m I_e \tag{2.16}$$

Where:

- $\tau_m = R\text{m}C\text{m}$ is the membrane time constant
- E_L is the leak potential,
- R_m is the membrane resistance,
- I_e is the external current.

When the membrane potential $V\text{m}$ reaches a certain threshold $V\text{th}$, the neuron fires a spike and then resets its membrane potential to a reset potential reset.

$$if,\, V_{\text{m}} \geq V_{\text{th}},\, then \begin{cases} \text{Fire a spike} \\ V_{\text{m}} = V_{\text{reset}} \end{cases} \tag{2.17}$$

How does the membrane time constant τ_{m} influence the firing rate of a neuron in an SNN?

2.8.4 Exercise 4

Design a Spiking Neural Network (SNN) using the Leaky Integrate-and-Fire (LIF) neuron model to detect the presence of light. Imagine a robot equipped with a light sensor. You want to build an SNN that processes the sensor signal (representing light intensity) and outputs a spike when light is detected.

2.8.5 Exercise 5

While the Address-Event Representation (AER) protocol offers significant advantages for communication in large-scale spiking neural networks (SNNs), recent research suggests limitations in its scalability for ultra-large networks. Considering these limitations, discuss the potential trade-offs in using alternative communication protocols or modifying the AER protocol to achieve efficient information routing in future generations of ultra-large-scale SNNs implemented on neuromorphic hardware.

2.8.6 Exercise 6

Traditional Network-on-Chip (NoC) architectures designed for general-purpose computing may not be optimal for high-performance neuromorphic systems. Discuss the key challenges of using traditional NoCs in neuromorphic systems, focusing on communication patterns and energy efficiency. Furthermore, potential modifications or alternative interconnection network designs should be explicitly proposed and tailored for the communication needs of spiking neural networks on neuromorphic hardware.

2.8.7 Exercise 7

While Network-on-Chip (NoC) architectures are crucial for communication in large-scale neuromorphic systems, traditional NoCs designed for general-purpose processors might not be ideal for Spiking Neural Networks (SNNs). Discuss the specific challenges faced when adapting NoC designs for SNN hardware. Considering factors like communication patterns, real-time processing, and energy efficiency, how can these challenges be addressed to achieve efficient and scalable communication for SNNs?

2.8.8 Exercise 8

Memristor crossbar arrays hold immense promise for building energy-efficient neuromorphic computing systems due to their ability to mimic synaptic behavior. However, challenges exist in terms of device variability and sneak path currents. Discuss these challenges and propose potential solutions for mitigating their impact on the performance and reliability of memristor crossbar arrays in neuromorphic computing applications.

2.8.9 Exercise 9

Compared to traditional SRAM, Embedded Dynamic Random-Access Memory (EDRAM) offers advantages like high-speed data access and lower power consumption. This makes it an attractive candidate for in-memory computing applications. However, EDRAM might not be a perfect fit for all aspects of neuromorphic systems. Discuss the potential benefits and drawbacks of using EDRAM for in-memory computing within neuromorphic architectures, considering factors like synapse emulation, learning, and plasticity.

2.8.10 Exercise 10

Designing synapse memory for neuromorphic chips involves managing large numbers of synaptic weights and ensuring efficient, low-latency access to these values. Answer the following questions:

1. A neuromorphic chip consists of 256 neuromorphic cores, each equipped with 512 KB of SRAM to store synaptic weights. Calculate the total on-chip memory capacity dedicated to synaptic weights.
2. If each synaptic weight is represented using 8 bits, determine the total number of synaptic weights that can be stored in the chip's SRAM memory.
3. Assume that the average access latency for the SRAM is 2 ns. Calculate the total time required to read 10^6 synaptic weights from memory.
4. If each memory access consumes 5 picojoules of energy, determine the total energy consumed to read 10^6 synaptic weights.
5. Discuss the impact of potential memory faults on synaptic weight storage and retrieval and propose a method to enhance fault tolerance in synapse memory design.

References

1. Bai K, Yi Y (2019) Opening the "black box" of silicon chip design in neuromorphic computing. In: Bio-inspired technology. IntechOpen, London
2. Balaji A, Adiraju P, Kashyap HJ, Das A, Krichmar JL, Dutt ND, Catthoor F (2020) PyCARL: a PyNN interface for hardware-software co-simulation of spiking neural network (2020). arXiv:2003.09696
3. Başar E (2013) Brain oscillations in neuropsychiatric disease. Dial Clin Neurosci 15(3):291
4. Ben Abdallah A, Dang KN (2021) Toward robust cognitive 3D brain-inspired cross-paradigm system. Front Neurosci 15:795
5. Bhaskar A (2017) Design and analysis of low power SRAM cells. In: 2017 innovations in power and advanced computing technologies (i-PACT). IEEE, Piscataway, pp 1–5
6. Boahen KA (1998) Communicating neuronal ensembles between neuromorphic chips. In: Neuromorphic systems engineering. Springer, Berlin, pp 229–259
7. Brader JM, Senn W, Fusi S (2007) Learning real-world stimuli in a neural network with spike-driven synaptic dynamics. Neural Comput 19(11):2881–2912
8. Chang M, Rosenfeld P, Lu S, Jacob B (2013) Technology comparison for large last-level caches (L^3CS): low-leakage SRAM, low write-energy STT-RAM, and refresh-optimized eDRAM. In: 2013 IEEE 19th international symposium on high performance computer architecture (HPCA), pp 143–154
9. Deiss SR, Douglas RJ, Whatley AM, Maass W (1999) A pulse-coded communications infrastructure for neuromorphic systems. Pulsed Neural Netw 6:157–178
10. Diehl PU, Neil D, Binas J, Cook M, Liu S, Pfeiffer M (2015) Fast-classifying, high-accuracy spiking deep networks through weight and threshold balancing. In: 2015 international joint conference on neural networks (IJCNN), pp 1–8
11. Frenkel C, Legat J, Bol D (2019) Morphic: a 65-nm 738k-synapse/mm^2 quad-core binary-weight digital neuromorphic processor with stochastic spike-driven online learning. IEEE Trans Biomed Circuits Syst 13:999

12. Gerstner W, Kistler WM, Naud R, Paninski L (2014) Neuronal dynamics: from single neurons to networks and models of cognition. Cambridge University Press, Cambridge
13. Göltz J, Baumbach A, Billaudelle S, Breitwieser O, Dold D, Kriener L, Kungl AF, Senn W, Schemmel J, Meier K et al (2019) Fast and deep neuromorphic learning with time-to-first-spike coding. arXiv:1912.11443
14. Hakim N, Vogel EK (2018) Phase-coding memories in mind. PLoS Biol 16(8):e3000012
15. Iannella N, Launey T, Tanaka S (2010) Spike timing-dependent plasticity as the origin of the formation of clustered synaptic efficacy engrams. Front Comput Neurosci 4:21
16. Ikechukwu OM, Dang KN, Abdallah AB (2021) On the design of a fault-tolerant scalable three dimensional NOC-based digital neuromorphic system with on-chip learning. IEEE Access 9:64331–64345
17. Indiveri G, Chicca E, Douglas R (2006) A VLSI array of low-power spiking neurons and bistable synapses with spike-timing dependent plasticity. IEEE Trans Neural Netw 17(1):211–221
18. Izhikevich, E. (2003) Simple model of spiking neurons. IEEE Trans Neural Netw 14(6):1569–1572
19. Lazzaro J, Wawrzynek J, Mahowald M, Sivilotti M, Gillespie D (1993) Silicon auditory processors as computer peripherals. IEEE Trans Neural Netw 4(3):523–528
20. Luo T, Wang X, Qu C, Lee MKF, Tang WT, Wong WF, Goh RSM (2018) An FPGA-based hardware emulator for neuromorphic chip with RRAM. IEEE Trans Comput Aided Des Integr Circuits Syst 39(2):438–450
21. Majumder T, Suri M, Shekhar V (2015) NoC router using STT-MRAM based hybrid buffers with error correction and limited flit retransmission. In: 2015 IEEE international symposium on circuits and systems (ISCAS). IEEE, Piscataway, pp 2305–2308
22. Mayr CG, Partzsch J (2010) Rate and pulse based plasticity governed by local synaptic state variables. Front Synaptic Neurosci 2:33
23. Mead C (1990) Neuromorphic electronic systems. Proc IEEE 78(10):1629–1636
24. Merolla PA, Arthur JV, Alvarez-Icaza R, Cassidy AS, Sawada J, Akopyan F, Jackson BL, Imam N, Guo C, Nakamura Y et al (2014) A million spiking-neuron integrated circuit with a scalable communication network and interface. Science 345(6197):668–673
25. Mortara A, Vittoz EA, Venier P (1995) A communication scheme for analog VLSI perceptive systems. IEEE J Solid-State Circuits 30(6):660–669
26. Ogbodo M (2022) On the design of adaptive digital neuromorphic system. Ph.D. Thesis
27. Pan Z, Wu J, Zhang M, Li H, Chua Y (2019) Neural population coding for effective temporal classification. In: 2019 international joint conference on neural networks (IJCNN). IEEE, Piscataway, pp 1–8
28. Park J, Yu T, Joshi S, Maier C, Cauwenberghs G (2016) Hierarchical address event routing for reconfigurable large-scale neuromorphic systems. IEEE Trans Neural Netw Learn Syst 28(10):2408–2422
29. Park S, Kim S, Na B, Yoon S (2020) T2FSNN: deep spiking neural networks with time-to-first-spike coding. arXiv:2003.11741
30. Ponulak F, Kasiński A (2010) Supervised learning in spiking neural networks with resume: sequence learning, classification, and spike shifting. Neural Comput 22(2):467–510
31. Rahimi Azghadi M, Iannella N, Al-Sarawi SF, Indiveri G, Abbott D (2014) Spike-based synaptic plasticity in silicon: design, implementation, application, and challenges. Proc IEEE 102(5):717–737
32. Rueckauer B, Lungu IA, Hu Y, Pfeiffer M, Liu SC (2017) Conversion of continuous-valued deep networks to efficient event-driven networks for image classification. Front Neurosci 11:682
33. Sengupta B, Barry Laughlin S, Niven JE (2014) Consequences of converting graded to action potentials upon neural information coding and energy efficiency. PLOS Comput Biol 10(1):1–18
34. Seo JS, Brezzo B, Liu Y, Parker BD, Esser SK, Montoye RK, Rajendran B, Tierno JA, Chang L, Modha DS et al (2011) A 45nm CMOS neuromorphic chip with a scalable architecture for

learning in networks of spiking neurons. In: 2011 IEEE custom integrated circuits conference (CICC). IEEE, Piscataway, pp 1–4
35. Shoushun C, Bermak A (2005) A low power CMOS imager based on time-to-first-spike encoding and fair AER. In: 2005 IEEE international symposium on circuits and systems. IEEE, Piscataway, pp 5306–5309
36. Sjostrom PJ, Rancz EA, Roth A, Hausser M (2008) Dendritic excitability and synaptic plasticity. Physiol Rev 88(2):769–840
37. Stein RB, Gossen ER, Jones KE (2005) Neuronal variability: noise or part of the signal? Nat Rev Neurosci 6(5):389–397
38. The VH (2019) Algorithms and architectures for spiking neuromorphic systems. Ph.D. Thesis
39. Thorpe S, Gautrais J (1998) Rank order coding. In: Computational neuroscience. Springer, Berlin, pp 113–118
40. Thorpe S, Delorme A, Van Rullen R (2001) Spike-based strategies for rapid processing. Neural Netw 14(6–7):715–725
41. Vainbrand D, Ginosar R (2010) Comparing NoC architectures for neural networks. In: 2010 IEEE 26-th convention of electrical and electronics engineers in Israel. IEEE, Piscataway, pp 000660–000664
42. Vainbrand D, Ginosar R (2010) Network-on-chip architectures for neural networks. In: 2010 Fourth ACM/IEEE international symposium on networks-on-chip. IEEE, Piscataway, pp 135–144
43. van Schaik A, Liu SC (2005) AER ear: a matched silicon cochlea pair with address event representation interface. In: 2005 IEEE international symposium on circuits and systems. IEEE, Piscataway, pp 4213–4216
44. VanRullen R, Guyonneau R, Thorpe SJ (2005) Spike times make sense. Trends Neurosci 28(1):1–4
45. Vincent AF, Larroque J, Locatelli N, Romdhane NB, Bichler O, Gamrat C, Zhao WS, Klein JO, Galdin-Retailleau S, Querlioz D (2015) Spin-transfer torque magnetic memory as a stochastic memristive synapse for neuromorphic systems. IEEE Trans Biomed Circuits Syst 9(2):166–174
46. Vu TH, Ikechukwu OM, Abdallah AB (2019) Fault-tolerant spike routing algorithm and architecture for three dimensional NoC-based neuromorphic systems. IEEE Access 7:90436–90452
47. Vu TH, Murakami Y, Abdallah AB (2019) Graceful fault-tolerant on-chip spike routing algorithm for mesh-based spiking neural networks. In: 2019 2nd international conference on intelligent autonomous systems (ICoIAS), Singapore
48. Vu TH, Murakami Y, Abdallah AB (2019) A low-latency tree-based multicast spike routing for scalable multicore neuromorphic chips. In: ACM 5th international conference of computing for engineering and sciences, Hammamet, Tunisia
49. Vu TH, Okuyama Y, Abdallah AB (2019) Comprehensive analytic performance assessment and k-means based multicast routing algorithm and architecture for 3d-NoC of spiking neurons. ACM J Emerg Technol Comput Syst 15(4):1–28
50. Xia L, Huangfu W, Tang T, Yin X, Chakrabarty K, Xie Y, Wang Y, Yang H (2017) Stuck-at fault tolerance in RRAM computing systems. IEEE J Emerg Sel Top Circuits Syst 8(1):102–115
51. Yin S, Venkataramanaiah S, Chen G, Krishnamurthy R, Cao Y, Chakrabarti C, Seo JS (2018) Algorithm and hardware design of discrete-time spiking neural networks based on back propagation with binary activations. In: 2017 IEEE biomedical circuits and systems conference, BioCAS 2017 - proceedings, vol 2018. Institute of Electrical and Electronics Engineers, Piscataway, pp 1–4
52. Zhao, C, Wysocki BT, Thiem CD, McDonald NR, Li J, Liu L, Yi Y (2016) Energy efficient spiking temporal encoder design for neuromorphic computing systems. IEEE Trans Multi-Scale Comput Syst 2(4):265–276
53. Zhao C, Yi Y, Li J, Fu X, Liu L (2017) Interspike-interval-based analog spike-time-dependent encoder for neuromorphic processors. IEEE Trans Very Large Scale Integr Syst 25(8):2193–2205

Chapter 3
Learning in Neuromorphic Computing Systems

Abstract This chapter shows the various learning methodologies that underpin the development and optimization of neuromorphic systems, which mimic the learning processes observed in biological brains. It begins by examining the conversion from Artificial Neural Networks (ANNs) to Spiking Neural Networks (SNNs). It highlights the challenges and techniques in translating continuous-valued outputs into discrete spike events, thus preserving the temporal dynamics essential for effective information processing. The chapter categorizes learning methods into supervised and unsupervised learning paradigms. In the context of supervised learning, it explores techniques such as Spike-Timing-Dependent Plasticity (STDP) and backpropagation algorithms adapted for spiking neurons, detailing how these approaches facilitate the adjustment of synaptic weights based on labeled data to improve network performance. Conversely, the chapter discusses unsupervised learning strategies. By providing a comprehensive overview of these learning techniques, the chapter emphasizes the potential of neuromorphic computing systems to tackle complex tasks in cognitive computing, robotics, and sensory processing, ultimately advancing our understanding of artificial intelligence aligned with biological principles.

3.1 Learning Methods and Challenges

Spiking neural networks (SNNs) have gradually gained awareness because of their ability to process and communicate sparse binary signals (spikes) in a highly parallel and event-driven manner analogous to the biological brain [15–17]. However, simulating large-scale SNN in software is slow and does not fully harness the energy efficiency of SNN. As an alternative, scalable multicore spike-based neuromorphic architectures that can support many neurons and synapses and leverage the spike sparsity available in SNN to deliver rapid parallel processing with low power are being proposed. However, realizing such a neuromorphic architecture requires building small-sized spiking neuro-cores with low-power consumption, efficient neural coding schemes, and learning methods [12].

A. Ben Abdallah, K. N. Dang, *Neuromorphic Computing Principles and Organization*, https://doi.org/10.1007/978-3-031-83089-1_3

The learning phase, which minimizes a particular cost (loss) function, is a complex process of acquiring the parameters to output the correct inference results. The cost function optimization is performed with a gradient-descent-based optimization or other classical optimization methods, such as a genetic algorithm. In gradient-decent-based optimization, the basic idea is to find out the gradients of the cost function concerning each learning parameter. Various proposed training/learning algorithms exist for SNNs, such as supervised backpropagation through time, unsupervised STDP learning, and ANN to SNN conversion. The following will describe standard training rules and methods in neuromorphic systems.

Learning in neuromorphic chips presents several challenges that stem from the inherent complexities of replicating biological learning processes in a hardware environment. One major challenge is the integration of various learning algorithms that can effectively operate within the constraints of spiking neural networks (SNNs). Unlike traditional artificial neural networks, SNNs rely on discrete spikes for communication, making it challenging to apply conventional gradient-based learning methods directly due to the non-differentiable nature of spike events.

Another significant challenge is the representation and storage of synaptic weights. In neuromorphic systems, synapses are often implemented using non-volatile memory elements like memristors, which can introduce variability and noise in weight updates. This can lead to instability in learning, making it difficult to achieve robust performance in dynamic environments. Moreover, the need for efficient on-chip memory that can support real-time learning while minimizing power consumption adds another layer of complexity.

Temporal dynamics also pose challenges, as the timing of spikes is crucial for learning rules like Spike-Timing-Dependent Plasticity (STDP). Ensuring precise timing and synchronization among neurons can be difficult, especially as the network's scale increases. Additionally, hardware limitations, such as limited processing power and memory bandwidth, can hinder the ability to perform complex computations required for advanced learning tasks. Finally, developing effective evaluation metrics for learning performance in neuromorphic systems is challenging. Traditional metrics used in standard neural networks may not accurately reflect the capabilities of spiking networks, necessitating the creation of new benchmarks that account for the unique characteristics of neuromorphic computing.

3.2 Conversion from ANN to SNN

The conversion of Artificial Neural Networks (ANNs) to Spiking Neural Networks (SNNs) [3, 14] for implementation in neuromorphic chips is a complex yet essential process aimed at leveraging the advantages of spike-based computation to emulate biological neural function. This conversion begins with the need to translate the continuous-valued outputs of ANN activations into discrete spike events, often accomplished through encoding schemes like rate coding, where the firing rate of neurons reflects the strength of activation, or temporal coding, where the timing of spikes carries the information. The adaptation of weights from the ANN must also align with the dynamics of spiking neurons; for example, while ANN weights are typically represented as natural numbers, SNN weights may need to be conditioned based on the frequency and timing of spikes using mechanisms such as Spike-Timing-Dependent Plasticity (STDP). Here, the interplay between pre-synaptic and post-synaptic spike timings directly influences synaptic strengthening or weakening, necessitating re-evaluating how these weights are initialized and modified during the learning phase. Practical implementation challenges also arise; neuromorphic chips often operate with hardware constraints such as limited power budgets and the need for real-time processing.

Techniques such as quantization of weights and careful calibration of synaptic conductance are paramount, as they directly impact the stability and performance of the SNN during learning tasks. Additionally, the sparsity of connections in SNNs compared to more densely connected ANNs must be carefully designed to maintain effective communication among neurons, as evidenced in systems like Intel's Loihi chip, which aims to integrate STDP for on-chip learning. Further complicating the conversion are variability and noise inherent in the physical components of neuromorphic hardware, particularly in memristor-based systems, where variations can lead to inconsistencies in synaptic behavior. This biophysical variability necessitates robust learning algorithms that can adapt to changes and uncertainties in real time. Ultimately, while converting from ANN to SNN involves navigating intricate challenges, advancements in neuromorphic design and a deeper understanding of spiking dynamics hold promise for building more efficient, adaptable, and biologically inspired computational systems.

Converting an Artificial Neural Network (ANN) to a Spiking Neural Network (SNN) for implementation in neuromorphic chips involves several steps that require careful consideration of the differences in information representation and learning dynamics between the two types of networks. Here is an overview of the essential conversion steps:

1. **Encoding Continuous Values into Spikes:** The first step involves converting the continuous-valued outputs from the ANN into spike-based representations suitable for the SNN. Standard encoding methods include rate coding, where the firing rate of a neuron encodes the value of an input, and temporal coding, where the timing of spikes carries the information. The choice of encoding scheme must be aligned with the specific task to ensure that relevant information is preserved.
2. **Mapping ANN Architecture to SNN:** Once the encoding scheme is established, the architecture of the ANN must be adapted to the structure of the SNN. This involves defining the connectivity and topology of the spiking network. While ANN layers may be fully connected, SNNs can employ dense and sparse connections, depending on the application. Maintaining functional equivalence between the original ANN and the SNN during this mapping is crucial for performance.
3. **Weight Initialization:** After establishing connectivity, the initialization of synaptic weights is key. Weight values from the ANN can be used to initialize

the weights in the SNN. Still, it is necessary to consider the differences in activation functions and behaviors of spiking neurons. Techniques such as weight normalization or adjustment may be required to adapt the values appropriately for spiking dynamics.

4. **Adapting Learning Rules:** The next step involves selecting the appropriate learning rules for the SNN. While ANNs typically use backpropagation to update weights based on error gradients, SNNs often rely on STDP and other spike-based learning mechanisms. The learning rules must be redefined to make the weight updates depend on the timing of spikes rather than continuous error signals, requiring potentially new algorithms or adaptations of existing methods.
5. **Testing and Validation:** After conversion, the SNN must be thoroughly tested to validate its performance against the original ANN. This step involves running the SNN on the same datasets used to train the ANN and evaluating metrics such as accuracy, convergence speed, and robustness. Fine-tuning parameters like learning rates, encoding strategies, and connectivity patterns may be necessary to enhance performance following the conversion.
6. **Optimizing for Neuromorphic Hardware:** Finally, specific optimizations must ensure that the converted SNN can operate effectively on neuromorphic chips. This may include considerations for power efficiency, computing resource constraints, and real-time processing capabilities. Adjustments might involve simplifying the model structure to fit the hardware architecture, ensuring low-latency spike transmission, and developing appropriate protocols for communication among neurons.

By following these steps, practitioners can successfully convert ANNs to SNNs, enabling the deployment of efficient, biologically inspired neural networks on neuromorphic hardware.

3.2.1 Challenges of ANN to SNN Conversion

Converting Artificial Neural Networks (ANNs) to Spiking Neural Networks (SNNs) for implementation in neuromorphic chips presents many challenges stemming from the fundamental differences in operational principles and data representation. One primary challenge is the inherent disparity in processing information: ANNs output continuous values through activation functions. At the same time, SNNs rely on discrete spikes to communicate information, necessitating efficient encoding schemes to transform real-valued outputs from ANNs into spike trains without losing critical information. Techniques such as rate coding, where the firing rate correlates with the input strength, or temporal coding, where the precise timing of spikes conveys meaning, must be carefully implemented to ensure that the nuances of the ANN's learned parameters are preserved. Additionally, the weight mapping from ANNs to SNNs is not straightforward; the learning dynamics of SNNs employ mechanisms like Spike-Timing-Dependent Plasticity (STDP), which require the model to adjust synaptic strengths based on the timing of spikes, emphasizing the need for a thorough reassessment of how weights are articulated and modified post-conversion.

The process is further complicated by the temporal dynamics intrinsic to SNNs, which require precise timing often absent in traditional ANN training regimes. Moreover, practical hardware limitations in neuromorphic chips introduce another layer of difficulty; these systems usually have constraints on power efficiency and real-time processing capabilities, challenging the implementation of complex spike-based learning rules. Issues such as the variability of synaptic weights due to quantization, the potential noise in memristor-based storage devices, and the sparsity of connections in SNNs relative to ANNs can significantly impair the conversion process and degrade model performance. These factors can lead to instability in learning and a diminished ability to generalize across tasks. Furthermore, ensuring that the transformed SNN retains the robustness and accuracy of its ANN predecessor often requires iterative experimentation and fine-tuning of both the encoding strategies and the network architecture. As a result, the conversion from ANN to SNN necessitates advanced technical solutions and a deep understanding of the underlying biological processes that SNNs aim to emulate, making it a complex but vital endeavor in neuromorphic computing. Figure 3.1 shows a typical network architecture and connectivity of a spiking neural network.

3.3 Supervised Learning

Supervised learning methods are a machine learning technique category that involves training models on labeled datasets, where each input is associated with a corresponding target output. When these methods are implemented in neuromorphic chips, they introduce significant hardware complexity due to the unique

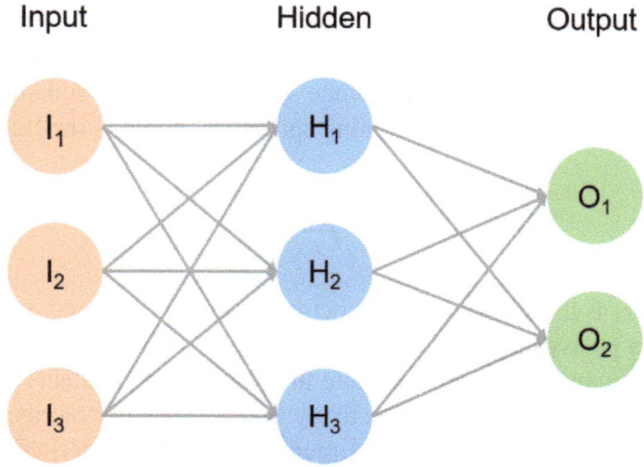

Fig. 3.1 Network architecture and connectivity of a spiking neural network. The network architecture and connectivity of a Spiking Neural Network (SNN) are fundamental aspects that determine its computational capabilities and overall performance in mimicking biological neural systems

requirements of spiking neural networks (SNNs). The hardware must be capable of performing rapid computations while accurately processing the temporal dynamics of spiking activity. For instance, neural networks trained using backpropagation face challenges translating the continuous gradients into discrete weight updates in a spiking context, necessitating specialized circuitry to handle this conversion. Additionally, the limit in the number of allowed connections, power consumption, and the need for precise timing in weight adjustments complicate the design of these systems. As a result, developing hardware that successfully integrates these supervised learning algorithms requires a careful balance of computational efficiency, energy management, and the capacity to maintain the retrospective nature of learning in a temporal domain, highlighting the intricate complexities involved in achieving effective supervised learning in neuromorphic chips.

3.3.1 Tempotron Learning

Tempotron learning [6] is a specific algorithm designed for spiking neural networks (SNNs) that address the unique challenges of learning in a temporal context, leveraging the inherent capabilities of spiking neurons to process information through the timing of their spikes. The Tempotron model mimics the behavior of biological neurons, particularly in how they respond to incoming stimuli over time. In this framework, each neuron integrates incoming spikes from pre-synaptic neurons and generates a spike only when a certain membrane potential threshold is reached. The critical innovation of Tempotron learning lies in its focus on using the precise timing of spikes to classify input patterns effectively.

The learning mechanism defines a target spiking pattern for each input class during the training phase. When the Tempotron neuron receives spikes, its effects accumulate over time, reflecting a gradual integration of the incoming signals. If the neuron successfully spikes in response to a desired input pattern, the associated synaptic weights are reinforced to encourage this behavior in subsequent training episodes. If the neuron fails to spike when expected or spikes incorrectly in response to a non-target pattern, the weights are adjusted to discourage this outcome. The subthreshold membrane voltage is a weighted sum of postsynaptic potentials contributed by all incoming spikes, as shown in the formula below:

$$V(t) = \sum_i w_i \sum_{t_i} V_0(e^{-\frac{t-t_i}{\tau}} - e^{-\frac{t-t_i}{\tau_s}}) + V_{rest} \tag{3.1}$$

w_i is the synaptic weight between neuron i and one of its postsynaptic neurons, and a postsynaptic potential is induced by an input spike from neuron i at time t_i. The parameters τ and τ_s denote the decay time constants of membrane integration and synaptic currents, respectively, and are used to describe the form of the postsynaptic potentials, where the maximum value of PSP is normalized to 1 with a factor V_0. For the *Tempotron* learning rule, each synaptic efficacy w_i follows the gradient descent updating mechanism:

$$\Delta w_i = \lambda \sum_{t_i < t_{max}} (e^{-\frac{t_{max} - t_i}{\tau}} - e^{-\frac{t_{max} - t_i}{\tau_s}}) \tag{3.2}$$

where t_{max} is when the postsynaptic potential reaches its maximum value without the neuron firing. Based on the learning rule, when the erroneous output spike occurs, the corresponding synaptic weight should be decreased to contribute less to the wrong pattern. When the neuron should fire but does not, the update scheme will increase weight w_i in the iteration.

When implemented on neuromorphic chips, Tempotron learning benefits from such hardware's low power consumption and efficient parallel processing capabilities. Neuromorphic systems are designed to support spike-based computations, making them inherently compatible with the temporal dynamics utilized in Tempotron learning. The challenges of implementing this learning algorithm include ensuring stability in weight updates and managing the effects of noise and variability in the hardware. Nonetheless, Tempotron learning represents a compelling approach to harnessing the power of spiking neural networks for temporal pattern recognition, emphasizing the importance of timing and adaptability in neuromorphic computing.

3.3.2 Reinforcement Spike-Timing-Dependent Plasticity

Reinforcement Spike-timing-dependent Plasticity (ReSuMe) for Spiking Neural Networks is a learning algorithm designed explicitly for spiking neural networks (SNNs) that combine elements of reinforcement learning with spike-timing-dependent plasticity (STDP) [4]. This method is particularly advantageous in neuromorphic chips, as it harnesses the advantages of biologically inspired learning principles while leveraging the unique characteristics of spiking neurons.

The *Tempotron* learning rule can be considered as a particular case of the remote supervised method (*ReSuMe*) [11]. Due to the relation between these two learning rules, a tempotron-like *ReSuMe* learning rule is proposed. In the proposed remote supervision, the synaptic efficacy between given pre- and postsynaptic neurons does not only depend on the correlated pair.

The change in synaptic weight Δw_{ij} for the connection from neuron i to neuron j in the ReSuMe learning rule can be expressed as:

$$\Delta w_{ij} = \eta \cdot R(t) \cdot \Delta t_{ij} \cdot \Theta(\Delta t_{ij})$$

Where:

- Δw_{ij} is the change in synaptic weight from neuron i to neuron j.
- η is the learning rate, determining the size of the weight update.

- $R(t)$ is the reinforcement signal at time t, indicating feedback from the performance of the network.
- $\Delta t_{ij} = t_{post} - t_{pre}$ is the time difference between the pre-synaptic spike from neuron i and the post-synaptic spike from neuron j.
- $\Theta(\Delta t_{ij})$ is a temporal gating function that applies an activation condition based on the time difference.

Implementing ReSuMe in neuromorphic chips also presents challenges, such as managing the stability of weight updates and ensuring effective feedback propagation in the presence of noise or hardware variability. Nonetheless, ReSuMe is an exciting advancement in neuromorphic computing. It combines principles of synaptic plasticity and reinforcement learning to create adaptive, resilient spiking neural networks capable of learning in real-time and handling complex tasks that mirror the learning processes of biological systems.

3.3.3 SpikeProp *Algorithm*

The SpikeProp learning algorithm is a specialized method designed for training spiking neural networks (SNNs) that emphasizes the importance of spike timing and network feedback in the learning process. This algorithm leverages Spike-Timing-Dependent Plasticity (STDP) principles, where spikes between pre-synaptic and post-synaptic neurons dictate how synaptic connections are strengthened or weakened. SpikePro dynamically adjusts learning rules based on overall network performance by incorporating a feedback mechanism. This allows the algorithm to refine synaptic weights according to how well the network achieves its objectives. This adaptation leads to more precise temporal learning, which is particularly beneficial for tasks requiring high temporal resolution, such as speech recognition and sensory processing. The weight updates in SpikePro are informed by local spike events and influenced by more considerable contextual feedback from network activity, enhancing stability and robustness in the learning process.

3.3.3.1 Mathematical Model of the SpikeProp Algorithm

The SpikeProp learning algorithm can be described mathematically through the following key components:

Error Signal The error signal δ_j for the output neuron j can be defined as:

$$\delta_j = y_j - \hat{y}_j$$

where y_j is the target output and $\hat{y}_j$ is the actual output of the neuron.

Weight Update Rule The change in weights from the pre-synaptic neuron i to the post-synaptic neuron j is given by:

$$\Delta w_{ij} = \eta \cdot \delta_j \cdot h_i \cdot \Theta(t_{post} - t_{pre})$$

where:

- w_{ij} is the weight from neuron i to neuron j,
- η is the learning rate,
- h_i is the firing rate or activity of the pre-synaptic neuron i,
- $\Theta(t_{post} - t_{pre})$ is the gating function that accounts for the time difference between pre-synaptic and post-synaptic spikes.

Spike Timing Factor The function $\Theta(t_{post} - t_{pre})$ can be defined using a piecewise function that indicates whether the update should occur based on the timing of spikes:

$$\Theta(t_{post} - t_{pre}) = \begin{cases} 1 & \text{if } t_{post} > t_{pre} \\ 0 & \text{otherwise} \end{cases}$$

Overall Weight Update The overall update rule combining cumulative adjustments for all training patterns can be expressed as:

$$w_{ij}(t+1) = w_{ij}(t) + \Delta w_{ij}$$

where $w_{ij}(t)$ is the weight at time step t and $w_{ij}(t+1)$ is the updated weight after considering all relevant spikes.

Implementing the SpikeProp algorithm in hardware for neuromorphic chips presents several challenges stemming from the algorithm's inherent complexities and the hardware environment's constraints. One significant difficulty is translating the continuous error signals used in traditional backpropagation methods into the discrete spike events characteristic of spiking neural networks (SNNs). This conversion demands accurate encoding strategies that can effectively represent error signals through spike timing and frequency, which can lead to information loss or misrepresentation during the training process. Additionally, the SpikeProp algorithm relies on precise timing and synchronization of spikes between neurons for effective weight updates, making it susceptible to issues arising from hardware variability, such as noise and inconsistencies in spike generation.

The physical limitations of neuromorphic chips also pose practical challenges, as these systems often have power consumption, memory bandwidth, and processing speed constraints. Implementing effective weight updates while maintaining low latency is crucial; however, the temporal dynamics involved in the SpikeProp learning process can exacerbate computational load, complicating the integration of the algorithm into a real-time learning framework. Moreover, the stability of weight updates is a significant concern, as the dynamic nature of spike-based learning can lead to instability and oscillations if not appropriately regulated. As a result, achieving reliable performance under these conditions requires careful calibration of learning parameters and robust mechanisms to ensure convergence and stability in the face of the inherent uncertainties of approximate spikes and timing in neuromorphic hardware.

3.3.4 Approximate Derivative Method

An alternative way to use spike-based backpropagation is to approximate the activation of IF neurons at the first step. This method is particularly advantageous in scenarios where computing exact gradients are complex or computationally expensive due to the discrete nature of spike-based signals.

The Approximate Derivative Learning Method uses finite difference approximations to estimate the derivatives of a given loss function concerning synaptic weights by evaluating the network output for small perturbations in the input or weights. Essentially, the method involves observing the change in the network's output in response to slight changes in the synaptic weights, allowing for the calculation of gradients that can guide weight updates in the direction that minimizes error. This approach aligns well with the intrinsic characteristics of SNNs, where learning is often driven by temporal dynamics and spike interactions rather than continuous activation functions.

By leveraging approximate numerical methods, the Approximate Derivative Learning Method provides a practical solution to implementing learning rules that can adapt online, effectively capturing the temporal aspects of data without requiring complex backpropagation algorithms typical of traditional neural networks. Implementing this method on neuromorphic hardware enhances learning efficiency and supports the design of robust networks capable of real-time adaptation in dynamic environments. However, carefully considering the choice of perturbation size and the balance between accuracy and computational efficiency is crucial to ensure that the learning process remains effective and stable. Overall, the Approximate Derivative Learning Method represents a valuable approach to achieving effective learning in hardware implementations of spiking neural networks, promoting the advancement of neuromorphic computing systems.

A leak factor is introduced to compensate for the leaky effect [8]. Figure 3.2 depicts the bidirectional backpropagation of this method.

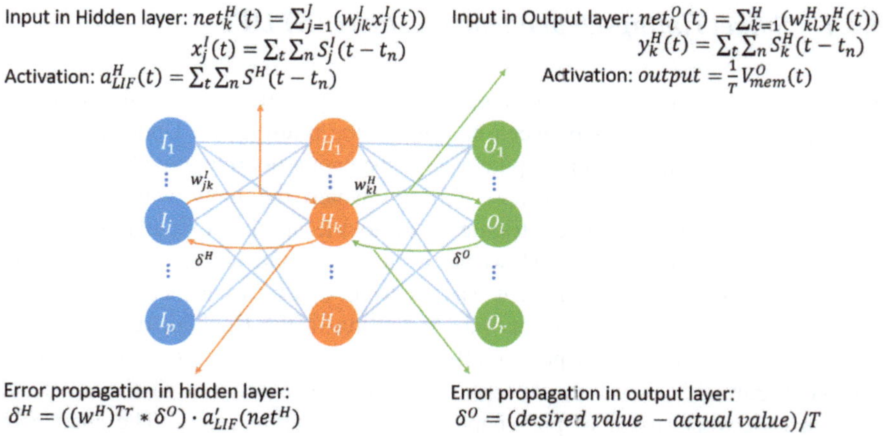

Fig. 3.2 Approximate derivative method. The Approximate Derivative Method involves using finite differences to approximate the derivative of a function. The basic idea is to evaluate the function at a set of discrete points and use these values to compute an approximate slope that represents the derivative at a specific point

3.4 Unsupervised Learning

Unsupervised in neuromorphic chips refers to a learning process in which the system is trained on input data without explicitly labeled outputs. This approach is particularly well-suited for spiking neural networks (SNNs) deployed in neuromorphic computing, which aim to emulate how biological systems learn from their environment by autonomously discovering patterns and structures in the data. Unlike supervised learning, which relies on labeled data to guide the learning process and adjust synaptic weights based on direct feedback, unsupervised learning focuses on extracting meaningful representations from the input.

In neuromorphic chips, unsupervised learning can involve various algorithms and mechanisms, such as clustering, self-organization, and feature extraction. Techniques such as Spike-Time-Dependent Plasticity (STDP) allow neurons to adjust their synaptic connections based on the timing and correlation of input spikes, effectively capturing the statistical properties of incoming data over time. This process enables the network to identify patterns, recognize correlations, and learn representations useful for classification or anomaly detection without requiring predefined categories or labels.

One typical application of unsupervised learning in neuromorphic systems is feature learning, where the network autonomously discovers salient features in the data, making it easier to process and classify future inputs. For example, in visual recognition tasks, a neuromorphic chip could learn to identify edges, shapes, or textures in images based on the spike patterns generated by different visual stimuli, allowing for more efficient processing and facilitating subsequent steps like classification or decision-making.

3.4.1 Spike-Timing-Dependent Plasticity (STDP)

STDP is a biological process that characterizes the synaptic plasticity for adjusting the strength of connections between neurons in the brain [5, 9]. Under the STDP learning mechanism, if an input spike to a postsynaptic neuron precedes an output spike from the neuron, the synapse through which the input was received is strengthened, enabling it to contribute more to the spiking of the postsynaptic neuron in the upcoming period. However, if the input spike arrives after the output spike, the synapse through which it was received will be weakened, reducing its contribution in the forthcoming period. According to the Hebbian rule, synapses increase their efficacy if they persistently participate in the firing of a postsynaptic neuron. Figure 3.3 shows the synaptic weight change relating to the temporal difference between a pair of presynaptic and postsynaptic spikes. The change in weight of a synapse can be expressed as:

$$\Delta w = \begin{cases} A_+ e^{+\Delta t/\tau_+}, & \Delta t < 0, A_+ > 0 \\ A_- e^{-\Delta t/\tau_-}, & \Delta t > 0, A_- < 0 \end{cases} \tag{3.3}$$

where $\Delta t = t_{pre} - t_{post}$, denoting the time difference between presynaptic and its postsynaptic spike, A_+ and A_- denote the learning rate depending on the synaptic weight. τ_+ and τ_- are the time constants [2].

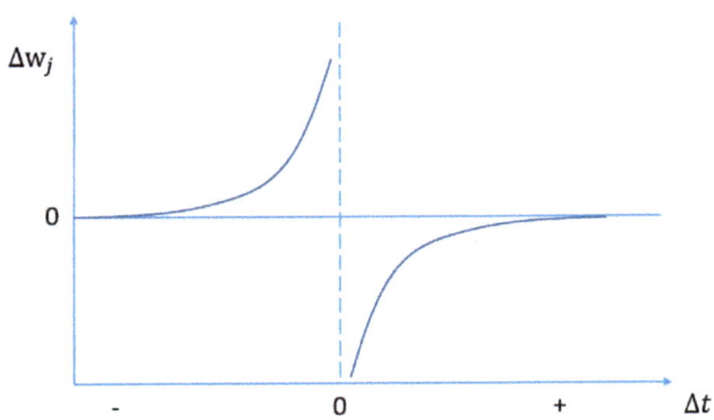

Fig. 3.3 Basic Spike-Timing-Dependent Plasticity (STDP) learning rule. The STDP is a fundamental learning mechanism in SNNs that adjusts the strength of synaptic connections based on the relative timing of spikes between pre-synaptic and post-synaptic neurons. The basic STDP learning rule is characterized by its operability on two primary principles: the temporal order of spikes and the magnitude of the time difference between spikes

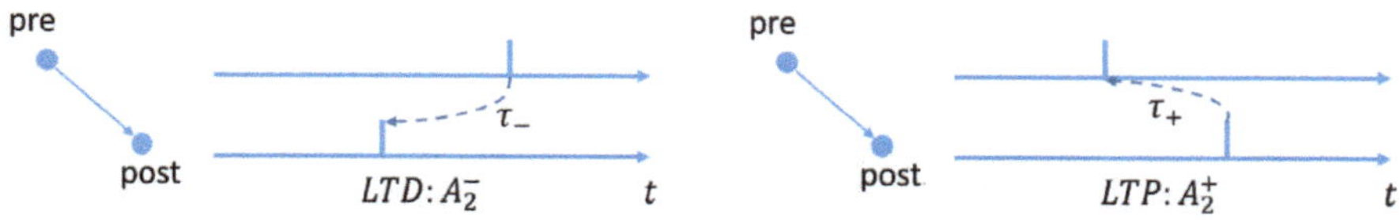

Fig. 3.4 Pair-based STDP learning rule. The Pair-based STDP learning rule provides a refined framework that emphasizes the important interplay between the timing of spike pairs in the adjustment of synaptic strengths. Focusing on these spikes' interactions enhances the model's capacity to learn and exhibit behaviors that closely resemble the plasticity seen in biological neural systems

3.4.2 Pair-Based STDP Learning Rule

The pair-based STDP rule (see Fig. 3.4) considers the time difference of a pair of pre-and post-synaptic spikes, in which a potentiation potential r_1 and a depression potential o_1 are updated iteratively w.r.t. the differential equations below:

$$\frac{dr_1(t)}{dt} = -\frac{r_1(t)}{\tau_+}, \text{ if } t = t_{pre}, \text{ then } r_1 \to r_1 + 1 \tag{3.4}$$

$$\frac{do_1(t)}{dt} = -\frac{o_1(t)}{\tau_-}, \text{ if } t = t_{post}, \text{ then } o_1 \to o_1 + 1 \tag{3.5}$$

The potentiating potential r_1 changes whenever a presynaptic spike occurs, and the depression potential o_1 updates whenever a postsynaptic spike occurs. The weight change at the time when either the pre- or post-synaptic spike arrives is then described as:

$$w(t) \to w(t) - A_2^- o_1(t), \text{ if } t = t_{pre} \tag{3.6}$$

$$w(t) \to w(t) + A_2^+ r_1(t), \text{ if } t = t_{post} \tag{3.7}$$

Where A_2^- and A_2^+ denote the amplitude of weight change controlling the long-term depression (LTD) and the long-term potentiation (LTP) term, respectively.

3.4.3 Triplet STDP Learning Rule

An observation is that in the pair-based rule, the potentiation is exhibited with pre-before-post or post-before-pre timing in the low-frequency limit without considering the interaction between the pair of pre-and postsynaptic spikes with others. However, with the increase in frequency, there might be an additional impact from the presynaptic spikes of the following couple on the postsynaptic spike of the previous pair. This property can not be captured by the standard pair-based model [10]. The

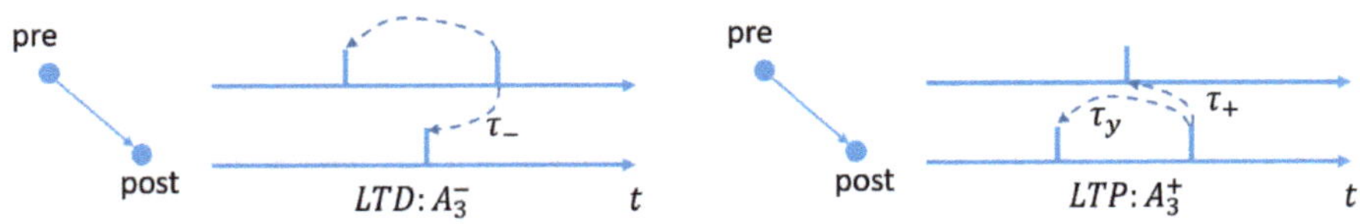

Fig. 3.5 Triplet-based STDP Learning Rule. The Triplet-based STDP learning rule enhances the conventional STDP framework by incorporating the interactions of spike triplets, allowing for a more intricate and context-sensitive approach to learning in spiking neural networks. By capturing the complexities of temporal dynamics in neuronal firing, this rule provides a powerful mechanism for synaptic plasticity that closely aligns with the behavior of biological neural circuits

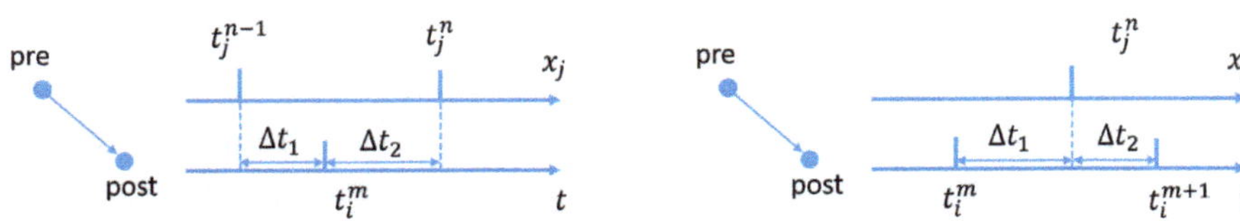

Fig. 3.6 Spike pairing scheme. All-to-All interaction and Nearest-Neighbor interaction scheme

pair-based model can be extended to triplet-based STDP, whereby either a pre-post-pre and post-pre-post scheme is formed (Fig. 3.5). The time constant τ_x and τ_y are introduced for the decaying potential between two presynaptic spikes. Accordingly, the update rule of two additional variables r_2 and o_2 can be written as:

$$\frac{dr_2(t)}{dt} = -\frac{r_2(t)}{\tau_x}, \text{ if } t = t_{pre}, \text{ then } r_2 \rightarrow r_2 + 1 \tag{3.8}$$

$$\frac{do_2(t)}{dt} = -\frac{o_2(t)}{\tau_y}, \text{ if } t = t_{post}, \text{ then } o_2 \rightarrow o_2 + 1 \tag{3.9}$$

Therefore, the weight change in the triplet STDP learning rule can be extended as follows:

$$w(t) \rightarrow w(t) - o_1(t)[A_2^- + A_3^- r_2(t - \varepsilon)], \text{ if } t = t_{pre} \tag{3.10}$$

$$w(t) \rightarrow w(t) + r_1(t)[A_2^+ + A_3^+ o_2(t - \varepsilon)], \text{ if } t = t_{post} \tag{3.11}$$

Where A_3^- and A_3^+ denote the amplitude of the weight change of post-successive pre-synaptic pairs and post-synaptic pairs, respectively. Note that the above triplet learning rule is associated with All-to-All interactions. In Nearest-spike interactions, where only the nearest spikes are considered, the update rule for synaptic weights will be modified accordingly (Fig. 3.6). Wang et al. [18] propose the Quadruplet protocol by further taking the interaction between a post-pre pair and a pre-post pair into consideration.

The spike Pairing scheme facilitates learning through the interactions of spike pairs, which is essential for synaptic plasticity in spiking neural networks. The All-to-All interaction scheme provides comprehensive connectivity, allowing for robust information sharing but with higher computational demands. In contrast, the Nearest-Neighbor interaction scheme promotes efficient local connectivity suited for large networks. The choice between these interaction schemes depends on the modeling task's specific goals, the network's scale, and the computational resources available, ultimately influencing the effectiveness and efficiency of spiking neural networks in processing information and learning.

3.4.4 Reward-Modulated STDP Learning

The reward-modulated STDP learning (R-STDP) rule extends the unsupervised STDP learning rule by adding sparse external reinforcement signals to modulate an SNN. To a great extent, the brain has been found in physiological experiments to exhibit a reward system using a neuromodulator called dopamine (DA) [13]. Dopaminergic neurons in the brain show behaviors akin to rewards by inflecting synaptic plasticity at corticostriatal synapses [7]. This reward mechanism depends on the modulation of dopamine during synaptic adaptation by STDP. Using the equation, the work in [19] shows how the weight changes are determined for R-STDP.

$$\dot{w} = e \times (d - b) \tag{3.12}$$

where w is the synaptic weight change, e is the eligibility trace, d is the reward function, and b is the baseline. The eligibility traces and reward function can be computed as

$$\dot{e} = -\frac{e}{\tau_e} + \mathrm{STDP}(\Delta t)\delta(t - t_{pre/post}) \tag{3.13}$$

$$\dot{d} = -\frac{d}{\tau_d} + \frac{\delta(t - t_n)}{\tau_d} \tag{3.14}$$

where τ_e is the synaptic eligibility time constant, δ the dirac delta function, and τ_d the neuromodulator concentration time constant.

3.4.5 Other Variants of STDP Learning Rule

An alternative is proposed to model the STDP scheme using only one dynamic variable instead of measuring the time difference in the pair-based model [1]. The idea is to consider only the voltage dependence of the single postsynaptic neuron of membrane $V(t)$ with an integrate-and-fire neuron model. In this model, updating the synaptic weight depends on the membrane voltage threshold and a function of postsynaptic spiking activity, which is referred to as the Calcium concentration of a neuron.

3.4.6 Hardware Design Challenges of Unsupervised Learning

The design challenges of implementing unsupervised learning in neuromorphic chips are multifaceted and significant, primarily due to the intricate interplay between biological inspiration and computational efficiency.

The hardware design challenges of implementing unsupervised learning in neuromorphic chips are complex and multifaceted, arising from the need to emulate biological neural processes effectively while simultaneously addressing computational and physical constraints. One of the primary challenges is achieving a suitable level of synaptic plasticity that can accurately capture the learning dynamics typical of biological systems. Unsupervised learning, mainly when relying on mechanisms like Spike-Timing-Dependent Plasticity (STDP), demands precise tuning of synaptic strength, which can be challenging to implement in hardware due to variations in component characteristics, temperature fluctuations, and noise in physical circuitry. Additionally, the data representation within spiking neural networks is inherently sparse and time-dependent, which can complicate the flow of information and lead to inefficient learning if not designed correctly. This sparsity requires the hardware to manage event-driven processing effectively, necessitating architectures that can handle the quick bursts of activity typical in neuromorphic systems while avoiding bottlenecks that can slow down the learning process or hinder real-time decision-making.

Moreover, integrating learning algorithms into hardware must consider power consumption, as neuromorphic chips are often deployed in energy-critical applications where performance efficiency is paramount. Designing circuits that can execute unsupervised learning tasks with low power requirements poses additional challenges, especially when dealing with complex functions such as clustering or feature extraction, which require considerable computational resources. Furthermore, the need for robust inter-neuronal communication protocols, such as those leveraging Address-Event Representation (AER), becomes more pronounced as the accuracy and timing of spike transmissions must remain precise to achieve desired learning outcomes. Finally, the adaptability of the hardware to accommodate various learning conditions and input dynamics adds further complexity, as the design must allow for fine-tuning and reconfiguration based on changing environments or tasks. Overall, successfully addressing these hardware design challenges is crucial for realizing effective unsupervised learning capabilities in neuromorphic chips, necessitating ongoing collaboration between neuroscience, engineering, and computer science to create systems that can learn and adapt to real-world applications.

3.5 Supervised vs Unsupervised Learning Algorithms

The hardware implementation of supervised and unsupervised learning algorithms in neuromorphic chips poses distinct challenges and opportunities, driven by the unique characteristics of spiking neural networks (SNNs) and the underlying principles of each learning paradigm. While supervised and unsupervised learning algorithms can be effectively adapted for implementation on neuromorphic chips, they each present unique hardware challenges that necessitate innovative design strategies to optimize performance, stability, and energy efficiency in spiking neural networks for real-world applications.

For supervised learning, neuromorphic hardware must be designed to handle fixed input-output mappings, where labeled training data guides the adjustment of synaptic weights through learning rules, such as Spike-Timing-Dependent Plasticity (STDP) or modified backpropagation. This implementation demands precision in both the quantization of weights and the timing of spikes, as the network must effectively minimize discrepancies between predicted outputs and target labels. The challenge arises from the need for high-throughput processing capabilities to manage the flow of error signals and timely weight updates, often necessitating specialized circuits that can accommodate the event-driven nature of spiking computations while ensuring low power consumption and efficient data handling.

In contrast, implementing unsupervised learning algorithms in neuromorphic chips allows for greater flexibility, as these algorithms can operate without labeled data, focusing instead on discovering intrinsic patterns and structures within the input space. However, this adaptability comes with its technical hurdles; the hardware must be able to support dynamic weight adjustments based on local spike interactions and global network statistics, requiring robust mechanisms to enable learning based on the statistical properties of incoming data. This often necessitates an efficient integration of local learning rules and mechanisms for clustering or representation learning, which can be computationally demanding in terms of processing power and memory. Furthermore, while unsupervised learning may allow for more straightforward training data preparation, it requires careful calibration of synaptic plasticity rules to ensure that the learned representations are meaningful and generalizable.

3.6 Chapter Summary

This chapter comprehensively overviews the various learning methodologies employed in neuromorphic systems that mimic biological neural networks' learning processes. It begins by discussing the different learning methods utilized within these systems, including supervised and unsupervised learning paradigms, and highlights the unique challenges of implementing these techniques in spiking neural networks (SNNs). The complexities of converting from traditional Artificial Neural Networks (ANNs) to SNNs are explored, detailing the necessary adaptations in representation and learning rules to accommodate the temporal nature of spike-based communication.

The chapter details unsupervised learning algorithms such as Spike-Timing-Dependent Plasticity (STDP). These algorithms are crucial in neural networks because they enable systems to learn and adapt without needing labeled data, enhancing their capability to detect patterns and make decisions based on input data. Additionally, the chapter highlights the significance of precise gradient estimation in this context.

The chapter highlights the interplay between learning methods and the unique characteristics of neuromorphic computing, addressing the significant opportunities and challenges involved in developing systems that can efficiently learn and adapt in a way that emulates biological cognition. By integrating insights from traditional learning paradigms and innovations specific to neuromorphic architectures, this chapter provides valuable knowledge for researchers and practitioners aiming to advance the field of neuromorphic computing and its applications.

3.7 Exercises

3.7.1 Exercise 1

In a spiking neural network utilizing Spike-Timing-Dependent Plasticity (STDP), consider the following scenario:

A pre-synaptic neuron fires a spike at time $t_{pre} = 15$ ms, and a post-synaptic neuron fires a spike at time $t_{post} = 10$ ms. According to the given STDP rules:

- If the post-synaptic spike occurs before the pre-synaptic spike, the change in synaptic weight is given by:

$$\Delta w_- = A_- e^{\frac{\Delta t}{\tau_-}}$$

  where $A_- = 0.4$ and $\tau_- = 15$ ms.
- If the pre-synaptic spike occurs before the post-synaptic spike, the change in synaptic weight is given by:

$$\Delta w_+ = A_+ e^{-\frac{\Delta t}{\tau_+}}$$

  where $A_+ = 0.4$ and $\tau_+ = 15$ ms.

Questions

(a) Calculate the time difference Δt between the spikes.

(b) Determine whether the synaptic weight will increase or decrease based on the timing of the spikes.

(c) Using the appropriate formula, calculate the change in synaptic strength Δw due to the interaction of these spikes.

Note For this question, assume any required constants (e.g., A, τ) are given as above and focus only on the calculations related to the provided spikes.

3.7.2 Exercise 2

Suppose you are designing a neuromorphic system using spiking neural networks (SNNs) for real-time gesture recognition. The system's task is to recognize hand gestures from input spike trains generated by sensors. Answer the following questions:

1. How would you encode sensor data (e.g., accelerometers, gyroscopes) into spike trains? Explain your choice.
2. What type of SNN architecture would you choose (e.g., feedforward, recurrent, etc.)?
3. Which learning rule(s) would you use to train the SNN? Explain why?
4. How would you evaluate the performance of your neuromorphic system?

3.7.3 Exercise 3

Explain how a neural network's architecture impacts individual neurons' learning process. Explain the differences in learning behavior between recurrent and spiking neural networks (SNNs). Consider factors such as activation functions, temporal dynamics, and weight updates.

3.7.4 Exercise 4

How do different learning mechanisms impact the performance and efficiency of spiking neuromorphic computing systems? Consider mechanisms like Spike Time Dependent Plasticity (STDP), unsupervised learning, and backpropagation. Discuss their merits, demists, and potential applications in neuromorphic hardware.

3.7.5 Exercise 5

How does choosing a spike coding scheme impact the learning process and performance of neuromorphic computing systems? Consider different coding mechanisms like rate, burst coding, and time-to-first spike (TTFS). Discuss their advantages, limitations, and suitability for specific tasks in the context of neuromorphic hardware.

3.7.6 Exercise 6

What are the key differences in learning mechanisms between ANNs and SNNs? How does the notion of time impact the learning process in SNNs when compared to the continuous-valued inputs used in ANNs? Provide an example to illustrate these differences.

3.7.7 Exercise 7

How does the choice of memory technology impact the learning process and overall performance of neuromorphic computing systems? Consider factors such as access speed, energy efficiency, scalability, and compatibility with spiking neural networks (SNNs). Please provide examples of memory technologies commonly used in neuromorphic systems and discuss their pros and cons.

3.7.8 Exercise 8

Consider a pre-trained Artificial Neural Network (ANN) that consists of one hidden layer with three neurons. The output layer has two neurons. The weights from the hidden layer to the output layer are given as follows:

$$W_{hidden\_to\_output} = \begin{bmatrix} 0.5 & 0.2 \\ 0.3 & 0.8 \\ 0.1 & 0.4 \end{bmatrix}$$

Where the rows correspond to the hidden layer neurons and the columns correspond to the output layer neurons.

When converting this ANN to a Spiking Neural Network (SNN), assume the following:

1. Each output neuron will fire a spike if its input exceeds a specific threshold. The threshold for both output neurons is set to $\theta = 0.6$. 2. The output of each neuron in the hidden layer after applying a sigmoid activation function is given by: $h_1 = 0.7; h_2 = 0.4; h_3 = 0.9$

Questions

(a) Compute the total input to each output neuron from the hidden layer using the weights provided.

(b) Determine whether each output neuron will fire a spike based on the computed inputs and threshold.

(c) Explain how the outputs from the ANN can be converted into spike representations for the SNN.

Note You can use the following formulas for your calculations:

– Total input to an output neuron o_j is given by:

$$I_j = \sum_{i=1}^{3} W_{ij} \times h_i$$

– Where I_j is the total input to the jth output neuron, W_{ij} is the weight from hidden neuron i to output neuron j, and h_i is the output of hidden neuron i.

3.7.9 *Exercise 9*

The Tempotron is a supervised learning algorithm designed explicitly for SNNs. It offers advantages like learning based on spike timing and potentially achieving high computational efficiency. However, the Tempotron might not be suitable for all SNN tasks. Discuss the key strengths and limitations of Tempotron learning in the context of SNN training. How does Tempotron learning compare to popular learning rules for SNNs like Spike-Timing-Dependent Plasticity (STDP)? Discuss the strengths and weaknesses of each approach.

3.7.10 *Exercise 10*

SpikeProp is a pioneering algorithm that introduced the concept of backpropagation-like techniques for training SNNs. However, it has limitations compared to more recent learning algorithms. Discuss the role of SpikeProp in developing SNN training and its key features. Furthermore, elaborate on the limitations of SpikeProp and how more recent learning algorithms address these limitations.

References

1. Brader JM, Senn W, Fusi S (2007) Learning real-world stimuli in a neural network with spike-driven synaptic dynamics. Neural Comput 19(11):2881–2912
2. Cai W, Ellinger F, Tetzlaff R (2014) Neuronal synapse as a memristor: modeling pair-and triplet-based STDP rule. IEEE Trans Biomed Circuits Syst 9(1):87–95
3. Cao Y, Chen Y, Khosla D (2015) Spiking deep convolutional neural networks for energy-efficient object recognition. Int J Comput Vis 113(1):54–66
4. Florian RV (2008) Tempotron-like learning with resume. In: International conference on artificial neural networks. Springer, Berlin, pp 368–375
5. Gerstner W, Kempter R, Van Hemmen JL, Wagner H (1996) A neuronal learning rule for sub-millisecond temporal coding. Nature 383(6595):76–78
6. Gütig R, Sompolinsky H (2006) The tempotron: a neuron that learns spike timing–based decisions. Nat Neurosci 9(3):420–428
7. Izhikevich EM (2007) Solving the distal reward problem through linkage of STDP and dopamine signaling. Cerebral Cortex 17(10):2443–2452
8. Lee C, Sarwar SS, Panda P, Srinivasan G, Roy K (2020) Enabling spike-based backpropagation for training deep neural network architectures. Front Neurosci 14:1–22
9. Morrison A, Diesmann M, Gerstner W (2008) Phenomenological models of synaptic plasticity based on spike timing. Biol Cybern 98(6):459–478
10. Pfister JP, Gerstner W (2006) Triplets of spikes in a model of spike timing-dependent plasticity. J Neurosci 26(38):9673–9682
11. Ponulak F (2006) Supervised learning in spiking neural networks with resume method. Phd, Poznan University of Technology, 46:47
12. Roy K, Jaiswal A, Panda P (2019) Towards spike-based machine intelligence with neuromorphic computing. Nature 575(7784):607–617
13. Schultz W (1998) Predictive reward signal of dopamine neurons. J Neurophysiol 80(1):1–27
14. Tang J, Yuan F, Shen X, Wang Z, Rao M, He Y, Sun Y, Li X, Zhang W, Li Y, et al (2019) Bridging biological and artificial neural networks with emerging neuromorphic devices: fundamentals, progress, and challenges. Adv Mater 31(49):1902761
15. Vu TH, Ikechukwu OM, Abdallah AB (2019) Fault-tolerant spike routing algorithm and architecture for three dimensional NoC-based neuromorphic systems. IEEE Access 7:90436–90452
16. Vu TH, Murakami Y, Abdallah AB (2019) A low-latency tree-based multicast spike routing for scalable multicore neuromorphic chips. In: ACM 5th international conference of computing for engineering and sciences, Hammamet, Tunisia
17. Vu TH, Okuyama Y, Abdallah AB (2019) Comprehensive analytic performance assessment and k-means based multicast routing algorithm and architecture for 3D-NoC of spiking neurons. ACM J Emerg Technol Comput Syst 15(4):1–28
18. Wang HX, Gerkin RC, Nauen DW, Bi GQ (2005) Coactivation and timing-dependent integration of synaptic potentiation and depression. Nat Neurosci 8(2):187–193
19. Yan H, Liu X, Huo H, Fang T (2019) Mechanisms of reward-modulated STDP and winner-take-all in Bayesian spiking decision-making circuit. In: Neural information processing. Springer, Berlin, pp 162–172

Chapter 4
Emerging Memory Devices for Neuromorphic Systems

Abstract To design a neuromorphic hardware system, it is essential to develop artificial neurons that replicate the behavior of biological neurons, together with artificial synapses that emulate the function of biological synapses. This chapter thoroughly examines crucial memory technologies for developing neuromorphic computing systems. Beginning with an overview of general memory technology, the chapter provides the specific applications and requirements of memory for neuromorphic systems. Then, it explores various memory types, including static RAM (SRAM) synapse memory and non-volatile synapse memory, emphasizing their roles and performance characteristics. The chapter also discusses Non Volatile Memory (NVM) in-memory computing, highlighting its potential to revolutionize the efficiency and functionality of neuromorphic hardware. In addition, it investigates how learning can be integrated with these advanced memory technologies to enhance system capabilities. The chapter concludes with exercises designed to apply and reinforce the discussed concepts to consolidate understanding.

4.1 Introduction

Neuromorphic computing systems typically comprise thousands or even millions of neurons [2, 12]. As a result, the vast array of parameters and temporal values required for these systems significantly exceed the local storage capacities found in conventional *von Neumann* architectures. Efficiently accessing this extensive data is crucial for enabling inference, learning, and debugging functionalities. However, the sheer volume of data and the necessity for efficient, low-latency access pose significant design challenges in current neuromorphic systems.

To replicate the rapid response times observed in biological neural networks, many state-of-the-art neuromorphic designs adopt a serial processing mode that operates at high clock speeds [1, 7, 11]. In this approach, neuron parameters must be continuously loaded from memory for each computation cycle; therefore, robust and high-speed memory systems are needed to handle frequent data access. This requirement places substantial pressure on memory selection, as different memory technologies' area costs, power consumption, and speed constraints directly

A. Ben Abdallah, K. N. Dang, *Neuromorphic Computing Principles and Organization*, https://doi.org/10.1007/978-3-031-83089-1_4

impact neuromorphic system performance. Over the past several decades, various memory technologies have emerged, each offering distinct trade-offs regarding area efficiency, power usage, read/write speed, endurance, and data retention, which are critical to neuromorphic applications.

In conventional von Neumann systems, memory is typically separated from the central processing unit (CPU), as illustrated in Fig. 4.1 (left). Only a small amount of static memory (SRAM), known as registers or caches, is available within the processor. This memory offers high-speed but limited storage capacity, providing rapid access with nanosecond-level latency enabled by D-flip-flops. However, its limited capacity is necessary for efficient read/write operations and cache utilization. Consequently, the need to transfer data between memory and processing units creates the von Neumann bottleneck, where data bandwidth limitations and latency slow overall processing speed. This limitation is particularly pronounced in applications requiring frequent memory access, such as neuromorphic systems.

In contrast, neuromorphic computing, as illustrated in Fig. 4.1 (right), integrates computing units (neurons) and memory units (synapses), creating architectures where memory is tightly coupled with computation. This integration allows neurons to access memory immediately, significantly reducing latency and eliminating the memory bottlenecks typically seen in von Neumann systems. This memory-near-compute approach reduces data transfer delays and enables more energy-efficient processing. For instance, advances in emerging memory technologies, such as Resistive RAM (RRAM) and Phase-Change Memory (PCM), allow for in-memory and near-memory computing, where data processing can occur directly within the memory infrastructure rather than solely within a dedicated CPU or processing unit. This shift has shown promise in enhancing the scalability and speed of neuromorphic systems.

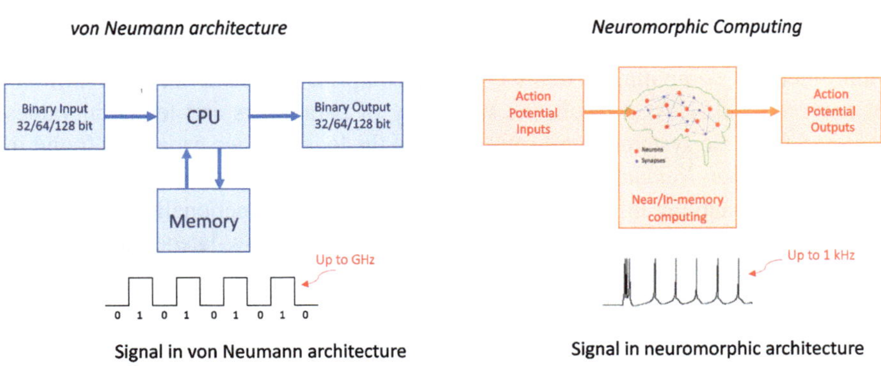

Fig. 4.1 Comparison of the von Neumann and neuromorphic architectures. The von Neumann model uses scalar inputs and outputs (e.g., 32/64/128-bit) synchronized with high-frequency clocks (GHz) with separate memory and processing units, leading to data transfer bottlenecks and higher energy consumption. Neuromorphic system architecture closely integrates memory and processing units, mimicking the human brain's neural networks to achieve efficient and adaptive computational performance

Recent advancements in memory technology have significantly contributed to the integrated approach of neuromorphic computing. Non-volatile memory technologies, for instance, retain data even when powered off, enabling persistent states and reducing the need for continuous refreshing. This feature mainly benefits neuromorphic applications requiring frequent state updates and low power consumption. Emerging technologies like magnetoresistive RAM (MRAM) and ferroelectric RAM (FeRAM) offer the advantages of non-volatility and high-speed access, addressing some limitations of traditional dynamic and static RAM. Additionally, ongoing research into 3D-stacked memory architectures aims to reduce latency by layering memory components in a compact structure, bringing neurons and synapses closer together within the hardware.

Advancements in memory technologies and their integration within neuromorphic computing systems are revolutionizing how we process and store information. By minimizing reliance on traditional memory hierarchies and embracing in-memory computing principles, neuromorphic systems are beginning to overcome the data bandwidth and latency challenges that have previously impeded their performance. The future of neuromorphic systems holds the promise of even closer approximations to biological neural processing, with significantly lower power consumption and faster response times than conventional computing models.

Figure 4.2a depicts the biological neuron model, where dendrites receive inputs from upstream neurons via synapses. These incoming spikes are integrated into the soma, accumulating to its membrane potential. When the membrane potential surpasses a certain threshold, the neuron generates an outgoing spike through its axon, which transmits to downstream neurons via synapses. On the other hand, Fig. 4.2b illustrates an example of a spiking neuron model in neuromorphic computing. In this model, input spikes (originating from memory reads) are weighted and integrated to form the membrane potential. If this potential exceeds the predefined threshold, an

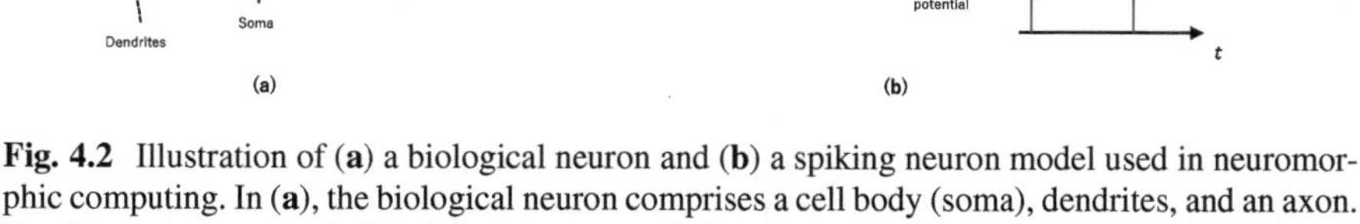

Fig. 4.2 Illustration of (**a**) a biological neuron and (**b**) a spiking neuron model used in neuromorphic computing. In (**a**), the biological neuron comprises a cell body (soma), dendrites, and an axon. Dendrites receive signals from other neurons, which are processed in the soma. When these signals accumulate and reach a threshold, the neuron generates an action potential (spike) that travels along the axon to communicate with other neurons. In (**b**), the spiking neuron model replicates these processes by generating discrete spikes when membrane potentials surpass a threshold. The axon-synapse-dendrite structure is simplified into a single-point model, represented as a synaptic weight, to streamline signal processing in neuromorphic hardware

outgoing spike is generated. In spiking neuron models, three key parameters must be stored to simulate neuronal behavior accurately:

1. **Incoming Spikes:** These represent the discrete events received from other neurons, indicating the transmission of information through synaptic connections.
2. **Synaptic Weights:** These weights determine the strength and influence of incoming spikes on the neuron's membrane potential, effectively modulating the impact of each input.
3. **Internal Parameters:** This includes the neuron's membrane potential, threshold values, and other dynamic properties that govern the neuron's firing behavior and temporal dynamics.

Efficiently managing and storing these parameters is crucial for the performance and scalability of neuromorphic systems. As discussed earlier, integrating memory and computation is vital in rapidly accessing and modifying these parameters, facilitating the system's real-time inference, learning, and debugging processes.

4.2 Memory Technology

Memory is a foundational component of computing systems. This section reviews the major storage technologies used in neuromorphic computing systems. The basic building block of semiconductor memory is the memory cell. Although memory technologies vary widely, all semiconductor memory cells share the following essential properties:

- They operate in distinct states or levels, typically representing two binary values: 0 and 1. Some multi-level cell technologies can represent more than two levels, allowing denser data storage.
- They support both write operations, to set the cell's state, and read operations, to sense the cell's current state.
- A typical memory cell includes two control inputs: *select* and *control*, along with two data inputs/outputs (or a single I/O line in duplex mode). The *control* input signals the data direction, indicating whether data should be read from or written to the cell. The *select* input specifies whether the *control* operation applies to the current cell. Figure 4.3 illustrates the organization and operation of a typical memory system.

Table 4.1 presents a taxonomy of memory technologies. Among these, registers are commonly used as local memory within processing engines due to their high-speed access times (on the order of nanoseconds) and compatibility with CMOS technology. Registers enable digital neurons to quickly access critical data, such as membrane potential, threshold, and input weights, essential for emulating neuron functions. This speed advantage places registers at the top of the memory hierarchy in neuromorphic systems. However, the high area cost of registers limits the memory capacity allocated within neuromorphic architectures.

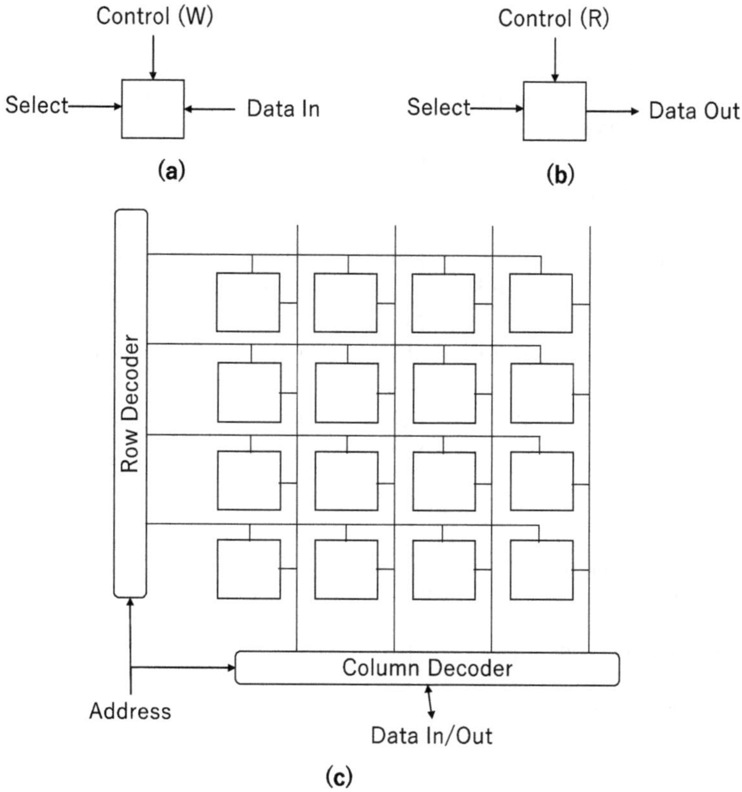

Fig. 4.3 An organization of memory operations and structure: (**a**) Writing to a memory cell, where data is stored by altering the state of the cell through electrical signals (select, control as write (W), and data in). (**b**) Reading a memory cell involves retrieving stored data by sensing its state without altering it. (**c**) A 2D array of memory cells is a common organization in a memory architecture, where cells are arranged in rows and columns to enable efficient data storage and access

For instance, with F representing the feature size of the technology, a typical register cell can occupy around 2200–3500 F^2, which is 15–20× the size of an SRAM cell. This makes registers the largest in cell size compared to other memory technologies. Due to this constraint, memory technologies with smaller cell sizes, such as SRAM, are often used to balance capacity and performance at the second level of the memory hierarchy. In most cases, memory cells are arranged in a two-dimensional (2D) array, where the accessing address is divided into a row address and a column address. When a row is selected, the values within that row can be read or written based on the provided control and data signals. This 2D organization is commonly used in embedded memory due to its efficiency in accessing and managing data.

In contrast, other storage technologies, such as hard disk drives (HDD), compact discs (CD), and digital versatile discs (DVD), employ serial organization and require

Table 4.1 The taxonomy of memory technologies with key design parameters

Technology	Cell size (F^2)	Write endurance	Speed (R/W)	Leakage power	Dynamic energy (R/W)	Retention period
Register	2200–3500	10^{16}	Extremely fast	Very high	Low	Voltage applied
SRAM	120–200	10^{16}	Very fast	High	Low	Voltage applied
eDRAM	60–100	10^{16}	Fast	Medium	Medium	30–100 μs
STT-RAM	6–50	4×10^{12}	Fast/slow	Low	Low/high	Years
RRAM	4–10	10^{11}	Fast/slow	Low	Low/high	Years
PCM	4–12	10^{8}–10^{9}	Slow/very slow	Low	Medium/high	Years
DWM	≥2	10^{16}	Fast/slow	Low	Low/high	Years
Flash (NAND)	1–4	10^{4}	Very slow	Very low	Low	Years

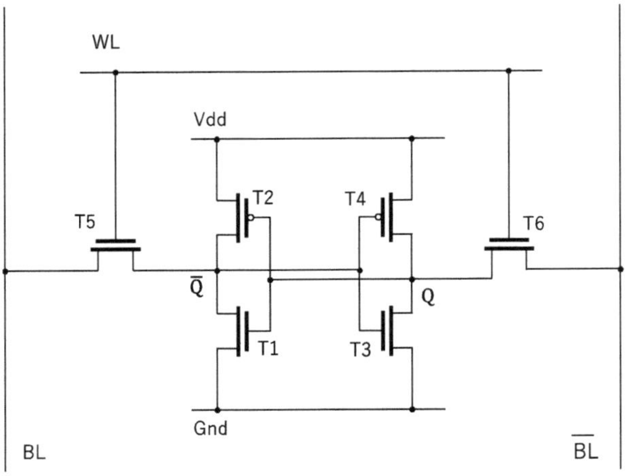

Fig. 4.4 A six-transistor (6T) SRAM cell, a fundamental building block for static random-access memory. The 6T SRAM cell consists of two cross-coupled inverters (T1&T2, T3&T4) and two access transistors (T5, T6), providing a storage bit. The cross-coupled inverters maintain the stored value as long as power is supplied. The two access transistors connect the cell to bit lines during the read and write processes

different access methods. These technologies typically access data sequentially, which can impact access speed and is better suited to applications with large, continuous data streams. For neuromorphic computing, it is unlikely these technologies will be helpful.

4.2.1 SRAM

Static random-access memory (SRAM) is one of the most widely used memory technologies in semiconductor applications. A typical embedded SRAM cell consists of six transistors, as illustrated in Fig. 4.4. SRAM cells are built entirely from transistors, with the arbitration logic using the same gates as those in standard digital designs. This makes SRAM fully compatible with CMOS technology. An SRAM cell retains its stored value as long as power is supplied, making it a volatile memory type.

Figure 4.4 shows a standard 6T SRAM cell. Four transistors (T1, T2, T3, and T4) form a bistable circuit with a stable logic state, represented by Q and $\overline{Q}$. If the logic state Q is high (1), then $\overline{Q}$ is low (0), and vice versa. In the state where Q is high, transistors T1 and T4 are on, while T2 and T3 are off. Conversely, when Q is low, T1 and T4 are off, and T2 and T3 are on. These transistors maintain their logic level as long as power is supplied to the cell.

SRAM cells also support read-and-write operations using two additional transistors, T5 and T6. To read the cell's value, the word line (WL) is activated (set to 1), turning on T5 and T6. This action allows either bit line (BL) or its complement ($\overline{BL}$) to be pulled to zero, depending on the states of Q and $\overline{Q}$. The stored value can be read from the cell by sensing the BL or $\overline{BL}$ voltage.

During a write operation, WL is also set to 1, and the bit lines BL and $\overline{BL}$ are driven with the desired values to change the state of the cell. This action forces the bistable circuit of transistors T1 through T4 to adopt the new state, thereby updating the stored value. SRAM implementation is fully compatible with CMOS design and is supported by most modern CAD tools. Compared to register files, SRAM offers higher density (requiring only six transistors) and lower power consumption (as it operates without a clock, relying solely on the power supply).

The main advantages of SRAM are its speed and reliability. The primary source of delay in SRAM is the connected wiring, while its mature CMOS design ensures reliability, typically enduring around 10^{16} accesses. However, SRAM has notable drawbacks, including high leakage current and relatively low density compared to other memory technologies. Despite these limitations, SRAM remains the most compatible memory design with CMOS processes, making it easy to integrate into systems without requiring significant modifications.

In [19], an 8T SRAM design is proposed that allows both row and column access, which enhances efficiency for learning in neuromorphic systems. Typical SRAM cells can only be accessed for reading and writing in rows. Still, by adding two additional transistors for transpose reading and writing, the 8T SRAM design enables column access. This modification emulates the operation of a crossbar network for connecting presynaptic to postsynaptic neurons, with each SRAM cell functioning as a binary weight synapse.

4.2.2 eDRAM

Embedded dynamic random-access memory (eDRAM) is a capacitor-based dynamic RAM that can be integrated into CMOS technology. The eDRAM cell can be designed as a conventional 1T1C (1-transistor 1-capacitor) configuration or as a gain cell, as shown in Fig. 4.5.

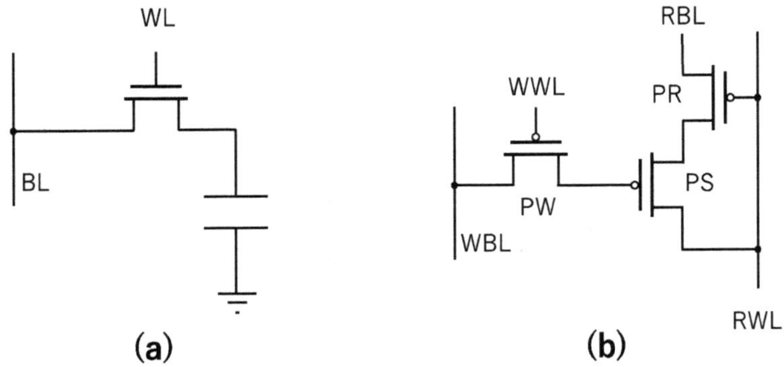

Fig. 4.5 eDRAM cell designs: (**a**) The 1T1C (one-transistor, one-capacitor) cell, a common structure in embedded dynamic random-access memory (eDRAM), where data is stored as a charge in a capacitor and accessed via a single transistor. The 1T1C design is compact and provides higher density than SRAM (see Fig. 4.4), though it requires periodic refresh cycles to maintain data integrity. (**b**) The gain cell is an alternative eDRAM design that uses two transistors to control data storage and amplification. Gain cells offer the advantage of reduced refresh requirements compared to 1T1C cells, enhancing retention time, though they typically have a larger area footprint

A 1T1C eDRAM cell stores its state in a capacitor, C, as illustrated in Fig. 4.5a. The capacitor's presence or absence of charge represents the value stored in the eDRAM cell. The word line (WL) is activated to read the value, and the transistor is turned on. The voltage stored in the capacitor is then transferred to a sense amplifier, which compares the voltage to a threshold to determine the stored value. For writing, the WL turns on the transistor, and the bit line (BL) is connected to either ground or a high voltage to set the cell's value.

Due to the inherent charge leakage from the capacitor, eDRAM requires periodic refreshing to maintain the stored data. A standard retention method for eDRAM involves reading the entire row, capturing its values, and then writing them back to the same row. The gain cell design shown in Fig. 4.5b eliminates the need for a capacitor. Instead, the transistor itself holds the value of the cell. This design enhances the compatibility of eDRAM with CMOS technology, as no capacitor is required. However, it comes at the cost of increased cell size, as three transistors are needed instead of one.

Although eDRAM offers a more straightforward cell design and is expected to have lower area costs than SRAM, it has some notable drawbacks. Due to charge leakage, eDRAM requires a retention period to preserve its stored value. Furthermore, the 1T1C eDRAM design is not fully compatible with standard CMOS processes, requiring additional steps in fabrication. Another challenge is that reading the eDRAM cell can cause a loss of high-value charge. Additionally, the refreshing mechanism for eDRAM is more complex than for SRAM, as it involves managing high fan-out and addressing skewing issues, similar to challenges encountered in clock distribution.

4.2.3 STT-RAM

Spin-transfer torque RAM (STT-RAM) [4] is a type of magnetic RAM that utilizes a magnetic tunneling junction (MTJ) in each memory cell. The MTJ comprises two ferromagnetic layers, fixed and free, separated by a thin insulating layer. This insulator is thin enough to permit quantum tunneling, allowing electrons to pass through it.

The operation of STT-RAM is based on the relative magnetization directions of the two ferromagnetic layers. When the magnetizations are aligned in the same direction (parallel), the MTJ is in a low-resistance state. Conversely, when the magnetizations are aligned in opposite directions (anti-parallel), the MTJ is in a high-resistance state. This resistance variation enables STT-RAM to function as a non-volatile memory device.

In the high-resistance (anti-parallel) state, the voltage of the bit line (BL) is close to 0 V due to the high resistance of the MTJ. When the MTJ is in the low-resistance (parallel) state, the current can flow through the junction, driving the bit line closer to the supply voltage. Figure 4.6 shows a Spin-Transfer Torque Random Access Memory cell architecture. Due to its simple design, STT-RAM occupies a smaller area than SRAM or eDRAM, making it a compact memory option. However, the time required to switch the magnetization direction in STT-RAM is relatively long, which slows down the writing process and increases power consumption. Consequently, although STT-RAM is an efficient non-volatile memory (NVM), its write latency and energy usage present challenges for specific applications.

This chapter categorizes STT-RAM as a non-volatile memory (NVM). In addition to SRAM, resistive NVMs are extensively utilized in neuromorphic systems due to their small cell size and capability for in-memory computing. These attributes make resistive NVMs ideal for applications requiring high-density storage and direct data processing within memory, as in neuromorphic systems.

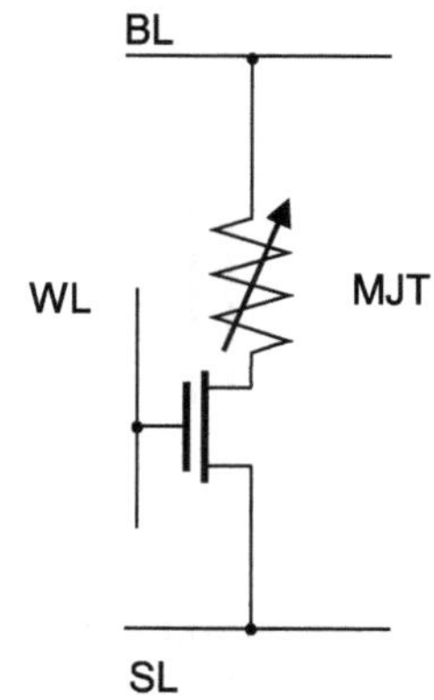

Fig. 4.6 A Spin-Transfer Torque Random Access Memory (STT-RAM) cell, a non-volatile memory that stores data using the spin of electrons. The cell consists of a magnetic tunnel junction (MTJ) between two ferromagnetic layers, where the magnetic alignment of spins represents data

4.2.4 RRAM and Resistive Crossbar

Resistive random-access memory (RRAM or ReRAM) is a type of memory technology where information is stored by altering the resistance of individual cells [22]. In this chapter, we use the term RRAM specifically for memristor-based memory. However, similar principles of resistance change are also found in other technologies we have discussed, such as STT-RAM and phase-change memory (PCM). Unlike SRAM, which requires six transistors for a single cell, RRAM has a compact design, typically consisting of just one transistor and one special resistor called a memristor, as shown in Fig. 4.7a, making it an efficient alternative for high-density storage. A memristor can work similarly to a resistor, but also its resistance can adjusted electronically.

The 1T1R RRAM cell shown in Fig. 4.7a resembles the structure of eDRAM, where data is read and written by applying voltages to specific lines (LL and WL for writing; BL for reading). However, unlike eDRAM, which requires periodic refresh cycles due to charge leakage, RRAM is inherently non-volatile, similar to STT-RAM, allowing it to retain data even when powered off.

The operational principle of RRAM involves setting the cell to either a low-resistance state (LRS) or a high-resistance state (HRS) by applying specific voltages, as illustrated in the I-V characteristics in Fig. 4.7b. Initially, the cell is in HRS, with a current below 1 μA through the memristor. For instance, in an HfO_x-based RRAM cell, applying a bias voltage of approximately 1.3 V across terminals P and N creates additional oxygen vacancies, forming conductive filaments that switch the cell to LRS. This is a notable contrast to the operation of SRAM cells, where data is maintained by stable logic states in transistor arrangements rather than resistance states.

To reset the RRAM cell back to HRS, a voltage lower than −1.3 V is applied, disrupting the conductive filaments and increasing resistance. This resistance-based

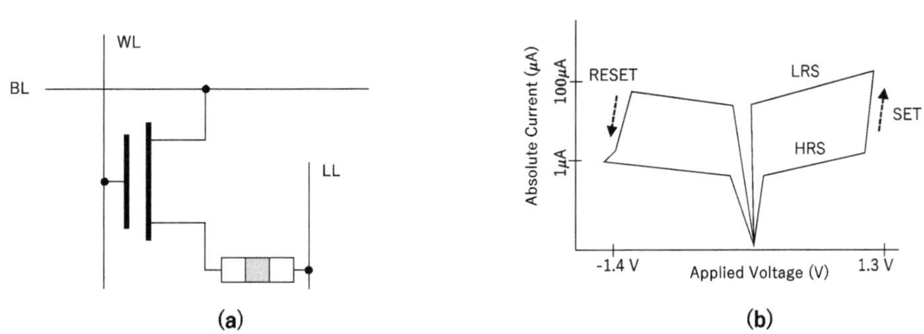

Fig. 4.7 RRAM cell design and characteristics: (**a**) Schematic of a resistive random-access memory (RRAM) cell. (**b**) The I–V characteristics curve of a HfO_x RRAM cell [20], illustrating the current-voltage relationship, where current is shown in absolute values. Readers may find this curve similar to the I-V characteristics of memristors, which also exhibit nonlinear resistance behavior and bistability

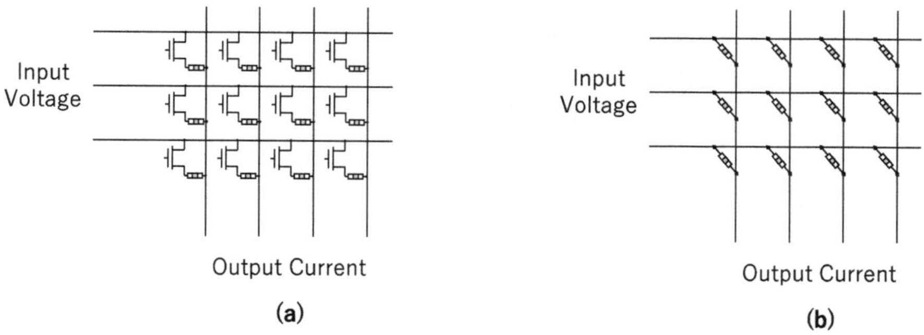

Fig. 4.8 Examples of resistive crossbar designs: (**a**) 1T1R (one-transistor, one-resistor) design, which integrates a single transistor with a resistive element at each crosspoint in the array. (**b**) 0T1R (zero-transistor, one-resistor) design eliminates the need for a transistor at each crosspoint, relying solely on resistive elements

switching is a unique feature of RRAM, setting it apart from SRAM and eDRAM, which rely on transistor states or charge storage in capacitors, respectively. RRAM's low area cost, power efficiency, and CMOS compatibility make it particularly suitable for neuromorphic applications, with essential high-density, low-power, and in-memory computation capabilities.

Figure 4.8 illustrates the resistive crossbar structure, which operates based on RRAM principles. Two configurations are possible: (a) incorporating a transistor, as in the 1T1R design shown in Fig. 4.7a, or (b) utilizing a transistor-free, 0T1R cell setup [22].

In the reading process, a reading voltage is applied to the word line (WL), and the bit line (BL) is monitored. Depending on the memristor's resistance in each cell, the output voltage at BL can be close to 0V or near the WL voltage. It is important to note that, in the 0T1R design, the absence of a transistor introduces a leakage current, potentially impacting accuracy and stability.

The writing process is accomplished by applying a voltage directly across the two terminals of the memristor. However, due to high variability and difficulty in managing leakage currents in high-density RRAM arrays, the 1T1R design, which includes a transistor, is generally preferred. This configuration helps maintain better control over cell operations and reduces leakage, ensuring more reliable performance in neuromorphic applications.

4.2.5 Phase Change Memory

One of the most advanced current memory technologies is Phase Change MMemory (PCM) [5]. PCM relies on materials such as $Ge_2Sb_2Te_5$, which exhibit distinct resistivities depending on whether they are in a crystalline or amorphous phase. In a

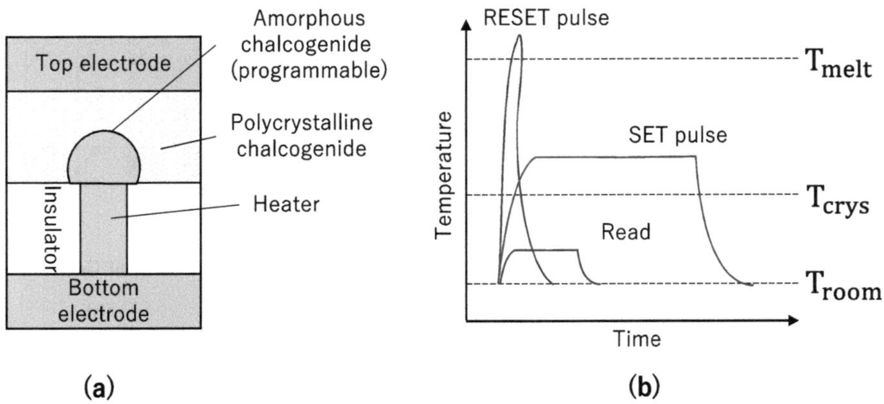

Fig. 4.9 Phase Change Memory (PCM) illustrations: (**a**) A cross-sectional image of a mushroom-type PCM device. The mushroom shape allows for phase transitions between the amorphous and crystalline states. (**b**) The programming pulses and corresponding relative temperature profiles for PCM's RESET, SET, and read operations. During the RESET operation, a high programming pulse melts the material, cooling it rapidly to form an amorphous state. In contrast, the SET operation involves a lower pulse that crystallizes the material. The read operation utilizes a low voltage to sense the resistance of the phase change material without altering its state

typical PCM device, a small amount of this phase-change material is placed between two metal electrodes, as shown in Fig. 4.9a.

Programming the PCM device involves applying SET and RESET pulses, illustrated in Fig. 4.9b. RESET pulses generate heat to form a larger amorphous region, increasing the resistance, while SET pulses encourage crystallization, reducing resistance and enhancing conductivity. This operation is distinct from SRAM, where data is stored through stable transistor states [4], and STT-RAM, which utilizes magnetic states for non-volatile storage [19]. Unlike eDRAM, which requires periodic refreshing due to charge leakage [22], PCM's non-volatile design retains data without a constant power supply.

By leveraging changes in conductance, PCM enables multiple stable states and high-density storage, making it suitable for applications requiring long-term data retention. The phase-change mechanism also offers potential benefits for neuromorphic computing, as the varying resistance levels allow for in-memory computing capabilities similar to those explored with RRAM-based crossbars [22]. PCM is a mature technology extensively investigated for neuromorphic systems [13, 14]. PCM demonstrates advantages in terms of cell size (typically 4–12F^2), write endurance, and power consumption. These attributes make it well-suited for neuromorphic applications where high-density memory and low power are essential. However, PCM is limited by its write latency. A typical SET operation, which utilizes partial pulses at a 50% duty cycle for 100 ns at 90 μA, can require substantial time to transition the material's phase [14] fully. This delay can impact system performance, particularly in applications demanding rapid memory updates.

Furthermore, PCM exhibits conductance drift over time, which can reduce the accuracy of neuromorphic computations due to deviations in resistance levels. Such variations introduce potential errors in analog neuromorphic processing, where precise resistance levels are necessary to emulate synaptic weights reliably. Despite these challenges, PCM remains a competitive candidate for neuromorphic systems, balancing density and endurance, especially when compared to SRAM's faster speeds [4] or STT-RAM's magnetic stability [19].

4.3 Ferroelectric Field-Effect Transistor (FeFET)

Ferroelectric Field-Effect Transistors (FeFETs) [8, 21] are emerging devices that offer non-volatile memory storage properties. Unlike traditional MOSFETs, FeFETs utilize a ferroelectric material as the gate, which can retain its polarization even after the power is switched off. This characteristic makes FeFETs suitable for applications requiring persistent memory, such as synaptic weight storage in neuromorphic systems, where we can classify them into NVM.

In a FeFET, the ferroelectric gate material allows for modulating the channel conductivity by applying an electric field, which changes the material's polarization. Storing and altering this polarization state enables FeFETs to act as non-volatile synapses in artificial neural networks. The state of the ferroelectric gate can represent the strength of the synaptic connection, allowing for long-term potentiation (LTP) and long-term depression (LTD), which are crucial for learning and memory in neuromorphic systems.

FeFETs' ability to perform non-volatile weight storage while simultaneously allowing for logic operations offers a unique advantage in neuromorphic systems. However, the practical implementation of FeFETs faces several challenges, such as precise control of polarization states, integration with other devices, and the endurance of the ferroelectric material under repeated cycling. Despite these challenges, FeFETs remain a promising candidate for future neuromorphic devices.

4.3.1 Other Memory Technologies

Table 4.1 provides an overview of various memory technologies, including advanced options such as Domain Wall Memory (DWM), Flash, and Hard Disk Drives (HDD). Despite its widespread use in data storage, Flash memory suffers from high latency and limited write endurance, rendering it unsuitable for embedded and high-speed neuromorphic applications. DWM, a newer technology, offers low power consumption and high density, but it is still in its infancy and requires further research to realize its full potential. Spintronics, particularly Spin-Transfer Torque RAM (STT-RAM), has shown promise for neuromorphic systems due to its non-volatility and fast switching capabilities.

Of all the memory technologies, SRAM stands out as the most practical choice for neuromorphic system design, particularly in FPGAs and ASICs, due to its low power consumption, reasonable area cost, and well-established design compatibility. While SRAM offers high-speed access with minimal delay, its limitations include relatively high leakage current and lower density than other options like eDRAM and RRAM. However, it remains highly accessible and integrates seamlessly with CMOS, providing a solid foundation for neuromorphic processing.

eDRAM, with a 1T1C or gain cell design, provides a denser alternative to SRAM and reduces area costs. However, it demands periodic refreshing, consuming higher power for retention and complicating circuit design with added refresh circuitry, which impacts its suitability for applications requiring persistent memory states.

STT-RAM, discussed in the context of spintronics, offers a small footprint and non-volatile characteristics, making it a strong candidate for low-power neuromorphic applications. Despite these advantages, STT-RAM suffers from slow write speeds and relatively high write energy, challenging its efficiency in dynamic neural networks where frequent parameter updates are necessary.

PCM, which relies on the phase change between crystallized and amorphous states, exhibits good density (4–12F^2), moderate power consumption, and non-volatility. However, its long latency during phase changes and endurance limitations can degrade neuromorphic system performance, especially in applications demanding real-time responsiveness and high write endurance [14].

RRAM (ReRAM) builds on the principle of resistance change, like PCM and STT-RAM, but benefits from simpler cell architecture and the ability to support in-memory computing. Its crossbar configuration can emulate synaptic connections, as each cell can act as a binary weight, aligning well with neuromorphic network structures. RRAM's low area cost, power requirements, and CMOS compatibility make it attractive for densely integrated neuromorphic designs where efficient data storage and retrieval are essential.

In summary, SRAM is typically the most accessible and compatible solution for neuromorphic applications, particularly for FPGAs and conventional ASIC implementations. However, STT-RAM, PCM, and RRAM are promising alternatives for more experimental and prototype neuromorphic systems where power efficiency, area density, and non-volatility are prioritized.

4.4 Memory Organization

The previous section reviewed different memory cell technologies, including SRAM, eDRAM, STT-RAM, PCM, and RRAM, highlighting their unique advantages and applications in neuromorphic and conventional systems. This section will discuss memory organization within general semiconductor systems, showcasing how these individual memory technologies fit into broader memory arrays and architectures.

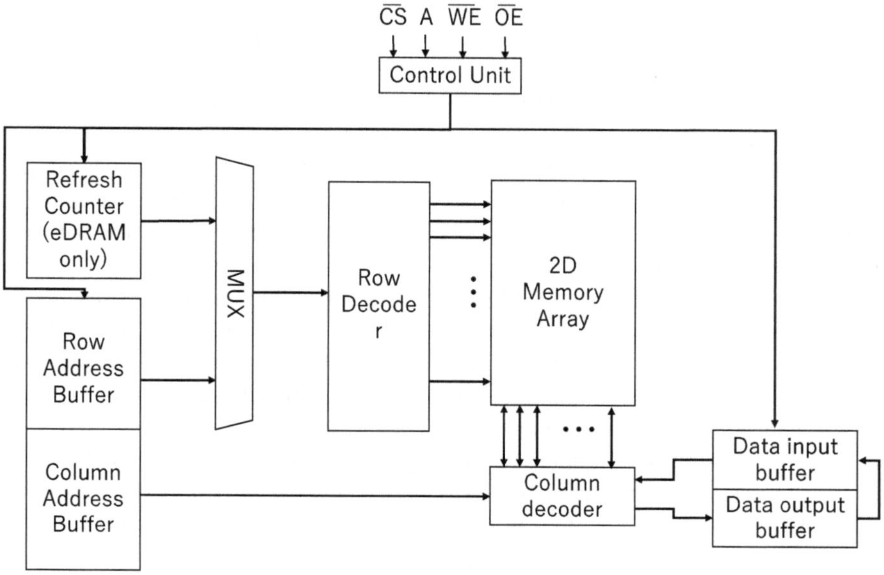

Fig. 4.10 Organization of semiconductor memory consists of several key components: a control unit that manages memory operations, an optional refresh counter for maintaining data integrity in volatile memory types, and row and column address buffers that temporarily hold address signals. The organization also includes a row decoder and a column decoder, which translate address signals into specific locations within the memory array. The structure's core is the 2D memory array, where data is stored in a grid of memory cells. Additionally, data input and output buffers facilitate data transfer to and from the memory array, ensuring efficient read and write operations

Figure 4.10 illustrates a typical organization of semiconductor memory, organized as a 2D array of $M \times N$ cells (with M rows and N columns). Beside the 2D structure, memory can also be organized in stacked 3D structure which exploit the new dimension of integration [15–17]. Regardless of the structure, the arrangement still stay the same. The arrangement of these cells can vary depending on the desired access width or memory type. For instance, eDRAM, which requires refresh circuits, includes an additional refresh counter and circuitry to maintain logic levels within its cells. Similarly, given their resistive nature, technologies like RRAM and PCM may need different peripheral circuits to support current-to-voltage conversion for reading data.

In a typical configuration, if the accessing bit-width matches the number of columns, a column decoder is not required, and data from the memory array can directly go to the output buffer. However, a column decoder must select the appropriate word width from the array for narrower access widths. For instance, a 1-Mbit memory organized in 32-bit words could be configured as a 1024×1024 array, where a 10-bit row address is used to select the row, and a 5-bit column address specifies the word within the row. After accessing the row data, it is cached in an output buffer to ensure timing, etc. Writing to memory also follows a similar logic, with the new word written back after modifying the intended row data.

Each memory type has distinct readout circuitry requirements based on its cell design. For example, eDRAM needs sense amplifiers to detect the stored charge, whereas SRAM directly outputs its stored logic state without needing sense amplification. Resistive memories like RRAM and PCM, on the other hand, are output currents that must be converted to voltage to interpret the cell state accurately. Thus, the organization and supporting circuitry can significantly vary with the memory technology used.

Additionally, Figs. 4.11 and 4.12 provide examples of everyday memory operations. In write operations, the chip select ($\overline{CS}$) and write enable ($\overline{WE}$) signals are set low to allow writing, while the output enable ($\overline{OE}$) is high. During reads, both the chip select ($\overline{CS}$) and output enable ($\overline{OE}$) signals are activated at low, allowing data to appear on the output after a typical one-clock cycle delay.

The input/output (I/O) ports for a memory block include (1) the row and column address lines (A), (2) chip select ($\overline{CS}$), (3) write enable ($\overline{WE}$), and (4) output enable ($\overline{OE}$). Other essential I/O connections, such as power, ground, reset, and clock, are often present but not displayed for simplicity.

This organization strategy demonstrates how each memory cell type fits broader memory architectures, from high-speed, volatile SRAM to non-volatile, resistive memories like STT-RAM, PCM, and RRAM. SRAM remains the practical choice for FPGA-based systems due to its fast access and CMOS compatibility. At the same time, other technologies are leveraged in prototypes and specialized applications where unique attributes like non-volatility or in-memory computation are advantageous.

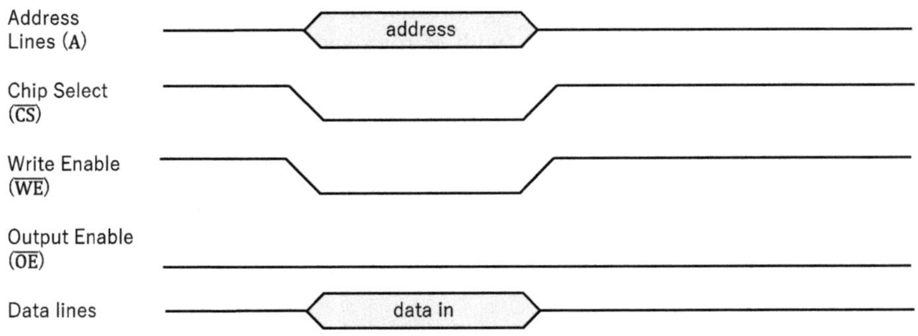

Fig. 4.11 Simplified memory waveform depicting the data writing process. When a write command is issued (enabling Chip Select ($\overline{CS}$) and Write Enable ($\overline{WE}$) while disabling Output Enable ($\overline{OE}$)), the voltages of the data lines are elevated to specific levels, transitioning the memory cells to either a high-voltage state (logical '1') or a low-voltage state (logical '0'). The duration of the high voltage corresponds to the time required for the memory cell to change state. Additionally, an address is provided, which is decoded to ensure the correct location for writing the data. The waveform illustrates the timing relationships between the address signals, data input, and control signals during the read operation

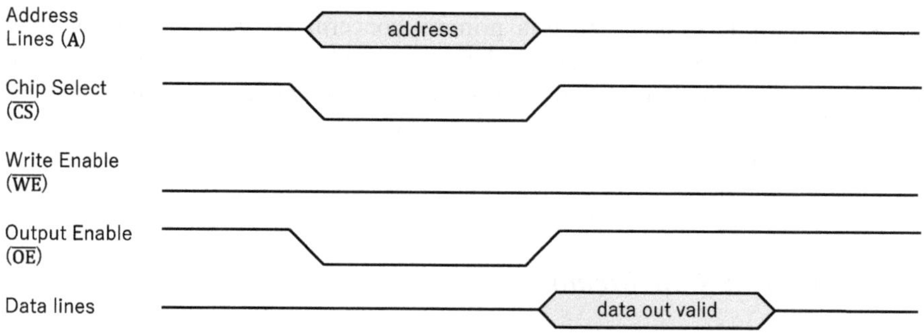

Fig. 4.12 Simplified memory waveform depicting the data reading process. When a read command is issued (enabling Chip Select ($\overline{CS}$) and Output Enable ($\overline{OE}$) while disabling Write Enable ($\overline{WE}$)), the address lines are activated to specify the memory location to be read. The voltage level on the data lines is then driven to reflect the stored value in the selected memory cell, either high (logical '1') or low (logical '0'). This output is stable for a defined period, allowing the data to be captured by the receiving circuit. Additionally, an address is provided, which is decoded to ensure the correct location for reading the data. The waveform illustrates the timing relationships between the address signals, data output, and control signals during the read operation

4.5 Memory for Neuromorphic Systems

Neuromorphic systems typically store three major types of data: action potentials (spikes), neuron states or temporal values, and synaptic information. Based on their role in the system, these data types have different storage and organizational requirements.

Spikes are time-step-based information that requires synchronization across the system. As spikes are discrete events, they are often stored in SRAM or registers for quick access and direct conversion to synapse array addresses. A typical design for spike memory may include a first-in, first-out (FIFO) queue structure or a sorting/scheduling mechanism to manage spike events in an ordered fashion, ensuring correct temporal sequencing.

Neuron states or temporal values represent the ongoing activity or state of individual neurons, and how they are stored depends on whether the neuron model is digital or analog. Digital neurons can store states directly in binary values, while analog models may require more complex storage systems to capture their continuous nature. Additionally, the organization of neuron state memory varies depending on whether neurons are processed serially or in parallel. Serial processing typically requires more superficial memory structures, while parallel neuron operations demand more sophisticated memory systems to handle multiple neuron states simultaneously.

The most significant component of memory organization in neuromorphic systems is the weight of memory. Synaptic weights represent the strength of connections between neurons and are crucial for learning and memory formation. Given the vast number of synapses in any neural network, efficiently storing and accessing synaptic information is a primary concern. Weight memory must be designed for high-density storage and fast retrieval, especially with large-scale networks. In the following sections of this chapter, different neuron models and their operations will be discussed, along with the corresponding memory organization strategies that support them.

4.5.1 Neuron State Memory

As mentioned earlier, there are two types of neurons: (1) *analog* and (2) *digital* (Fig. 4.13). In principle, analog and digital neurons each store two significant types of information: *membrane potential* and *threshold.* The in situ learning system may store additional information for learning purposes. Digital neurons store their information in binary format, typically in registers, and their data management follows standard caching mechanisms. On the other hand, the analog values of a neuron's threshold and membrane potential are more challenging to store, requiring an analog-to-digital converter (ADC) for initial digitization and a digital-to-analog converter (DAC) for reconstruction during computation.

Moreover, neurons can operate in two modes: (1) *serial* and (2) *parallel.* In the parallel model, each neuron has its dedicated physical computing unit, and the neuron's state can remain stored in registers without needing to be reloaded during computation [6]. This eliminates the need for memory loading at the start of the process. Conversely, in the serial model, neurons share a single physical unit, and time-multiplexing is used to compute the states of multiple neurons [1, 9, 10]. In this case, parameters are stored in local memory and loaded sequentially to update

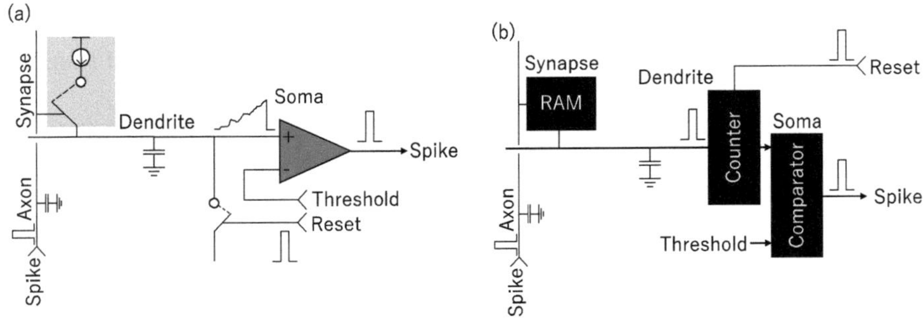

Fig. 4.13 Analog and digital silicon neurons: (**a**) Analog implementation: Incoming spikes on the vertical wire (axon) charge the capacitance (synapse) on the horizontal wire (dendrite), which integrates the charge. The comparator (soma) triggers an outgoing spike when the integrated voltage exceeds a threshold. After the spike, the capacitor is discharged (reset), and the cycle repeats. (**b**) Digital implementation: A counter (dendrite) increments each time a '1' is read from a bit cell (synapse), triggered by incoming spikes (axon). The counter's output is compared (soma) to a digitally stored threshold, and a spike is generated when it exceeds this threshold. The counter is then reset, and the cycle begins anew

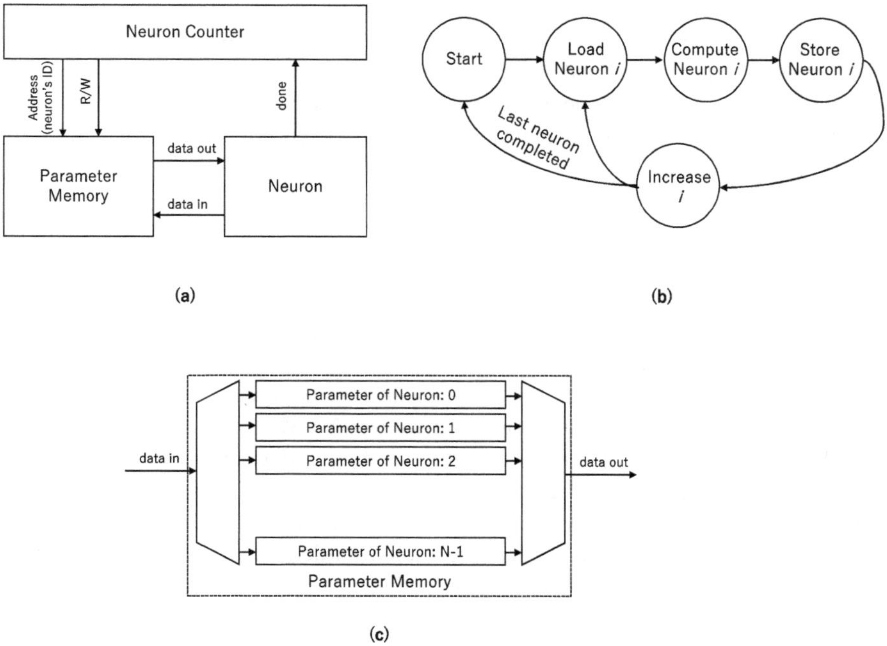

Fig. 4.14 The serial neuron model: (**a**) Model architecture: This diagram illustrates the overall structure of the serial neuron model, comprising key components such as the memory (axon, dendrites) and neuron (soma). The model processes incoming signals sequentially using a neuron counter to switch, integrating them to generate an output spike. (**b**) Finite state machine: This component represents the different states of the neuron, including loading, computing, storing, and starting (idle). (**c**) Parameter structure: This section details the parameters governing the neuron's behavior, such as threshold voltage, refractory period, and time constants

each neuron's state. The serial model is illustrated in Fig. 4.14, with the operation proceeding as follows:

1. Loop over neuron ID i from 0 to N-1 (N: number of neurons).
2. Load the state of neuron ID i (membrane potential, threshold, and other parameters).
3. Perform the neuron operation (integrate, leak, fire).
4. Save the updated state of neuron ID i to memory.
5. Increment the neuron ID i.
6. Repeat the process for all neurons until completion.

The structure of the serial neuron model is shown in Fig. 4.14c, with each row representing the parameters for a single neuron in the cluster.

The primary reason for serializing neuron operation is the limitation on weight access. Most neuromorphic systems use SRAM for weight storage, which typically has a single port for read and write (R/W) operations, making design more straightforward and less complex. However, this single-port access restricts the ability to access multiple weights simultaneously. As a result, to handle this limitation, many systems opt for serializing neuron operations, where each neuron is processed sequentially, and weights are accessed one at a time. This approach reduces the need for simultaneous weight accesses, making it more compatible with the design of memory systems that rely on single-port SRAM.

4.5.2 *Synapse Memory*

In the memory of neuromorphic system, synapse memory plays a central role, typically occupying the most significant portion of the stored memory. State-of-the-art neuromorphic memory systems can be classified into two categories: SRAM-based synapses and non-volatile memory (NVM)-based synapses. SRAM, a well-established and mature technology, is fast and compatible with CMOS fabrication, making it a popular choice for neuromorphic systems [4]. In contrast, NVMs are emerging as a promising alternative, offering significant advantages in low power consumption and smaller size. Non-volatile memory technologies often use resistive crossbars with multiple conductance levels, which mimic the matrix-vector multiplication commonly found in neural networks. While SRAM offers higher speed and is ready for fabrication, NVMs excel in scalability, enabling the design of large-scale neuromorphic systems with reduced power consumption. This section discusses both SRAM-based and NVM-based memory technologies and explores how neuromorphic systems can be designed using these memory types.

4.5.2.1 SRAM Synapse Memory

Like neuron state memories, synapse memory can be organized into *serial* and *parallel* models. In the *parallel* model, each neuron has its dedicated memory for synapses, allowing simultaneous weight reading and updating. This model ensures that each neuron can independently access its synaptic weights. In contrast, the *serial* model shares the physical neuron for multiple emulated neurons, making it inefficient to have numerous weight memories since they are not accessed simultaneously. The overall structure of the parallel model is illustrated in Fig. 4.15, where each neuron is directly connected to its weight memory. Each row in the weight memory corresponds to the value of a synapse. When a spike arrives, the presynaptic neuron ID (i.e., neuron j) is extracted and converted into the memory address to retrieve the corresponding weight. The SRAM weight memory receives the address corresponding to the ID j of the presynaptic neuron. In the next clock cycle, the weight of the synapse between neuron i and neuron j ($w_{i,j}$) is sent to neuron i for integration.

Multiple weights can be merged into a single memory row to optimize the design, especially when the synapse resolution is low. This approach keeps the cell area constant since the number of bits required to represent the synapses remains

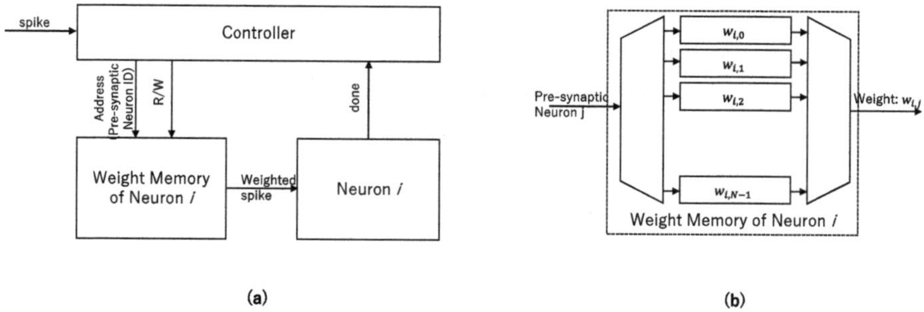

Fig. 4.15 The parallel neuron weight model: (**a**) Model architecture: This diagram illustrates the structure of the parallel neuron weight model, highlighting its capability for parallel processing, where weighted spikes are simultaneously fetched into neurons. (**b**) Weight structure: This section describes the organization of synaptic weights for each connection between neurons, which determines the strength of signal transmission

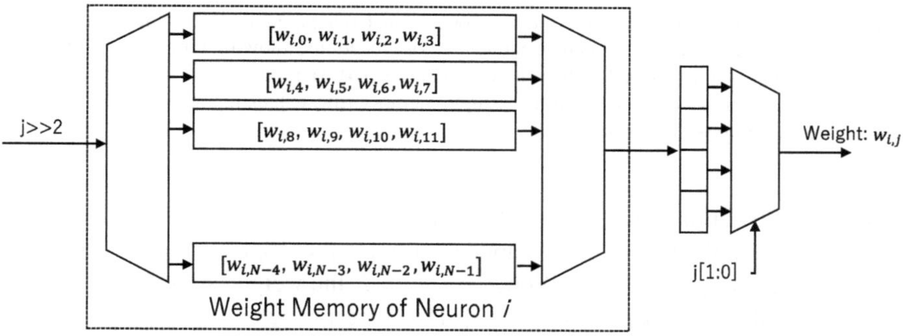

Fig. 4.16 The *parallel* neuron weight memory, featuring four merged weights within a single memory row. This design enhances efficiency by allowing multiple weight values to be stored and accessed simultaneously, facilitating parallel processing in neuron models

the same. However, it reduces the complexity of the SRAM by requiring fewer rows. The structure of this memory model is illustrated in Fig. 4.16, where four consecutive weights are combined into one memory cell. Consequently, the address for the weight between neuron i and neuron j no longer directly corresponds to the address of neuron j. Instead, it is the right-shifted value of the original address. An additional multiplexer then uses the remaining two bits to extract the appropriate weight from the four merged weights.

Examples of regular and merged weights for parallel neurons are illustrated in Fig. 4.17. The pre-synaptic neuron ID is directly fed to the SRAM to access the corresponding memory row in the standard weight model. For instance, Fig. 4.17a shows an array of pre-synaptic spikes: [10, 14, 7, 8, 23]. These values are not sorted in ascending or descending order, which can cause inefficiencies in the merged weight model.

In the merged weight model, the pre-synaptic neuron ID address is split into two parts: (1) the SRAM address ($j >> 2$) used to extract a group of four weights,

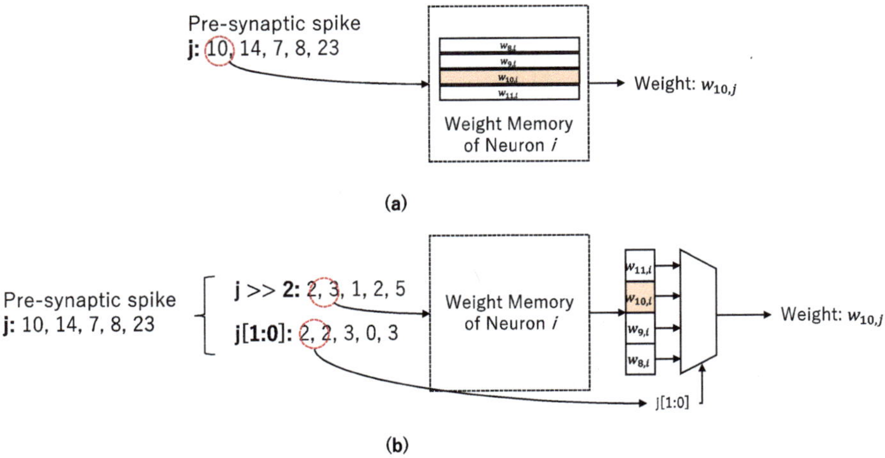

Fig. 4.17 The *parallel* neuron weight memory operation: (**a**) Separated weight: This configuration illustrates individual weights stored in separate memory locations, allowing for precise control and retrieval of each weight value for neuron computations. (**b**) Merged weight: This configuration shows multiple weights combined within a single memory row, enhancing storage efficiency and faster access during parallel processing

and (2) the selection signal ($j[1:0]$) that selects the specific weight within that group. For example, for the pre-synaptic neuron ID $j = 10$, the address is split into $j >> 2 = 2$ and $j[1:0] = 2$. With $j >> 2 = 2$, the weight SRAM outputs a set of four weights: $[w_{8,i}, w_{9,i}, w_{10,i}, w_{11,i}]$. The correct weight, $w_{10,i}$, is then selected using a multiplexer with the selection signal $j[1:0] = 2$.

However, in the merged weight model, the system discards the unused weights ($w_{8,i}$, $w_{9,i}$, and $w_{11,i}$) for the current operation. Additionally, if the spike array is unsorted, repeatedly reading the same memory row for consecutive weights is risky. For instance, if the spikes $j = 10$ and $j = 8$ share the same SRAM address $j >> 2 = 2$, the system will read the same address twice in consecutive cycles. To avoid this inefficiency, sorting the incoming spikes in ascending or descending order is ideal before performing the merge and memory access.

In the *serial* neuron model, multiple dedicated memories are unnecessary because this model does not perform neurons in parallel. The weight structure in this model follows a similar approach to the parallel model, with a slight modification. For separate weights, all weights are stored in a single SRAM. Instead of using the pre-synaptic neuron ID j as the address, the combined address is $i \times N + j$, where N is the number of pre-synaptic neurons. The number of memory banks required for N pre-synaptic and M post-synaptic neurons is $N \times M$. By merging the neurons, the number of banks can be reduced. For example, in systems with limited synapse bandwidth, the weights of an entire neuron can be read at once [1]. All weights for neuron i are read simultaneously, and a multiplexer is used later to separate the individual weights.

The state and weight of the neuron can also be merged in the merged weight mechanism. In the TrueNorth system [1], the SRAM word is 410 bits: 256 bits for the weight (1 bit per synapse), 124 bits for the neuron state (membrane potential and other parameters), and 30 bits for spike representation. Once a serial neuron is loaded, its parameters and weights are retrieved from memory and are ready for computation. Figure 4.18 shows a serial neuron weight memory operation.

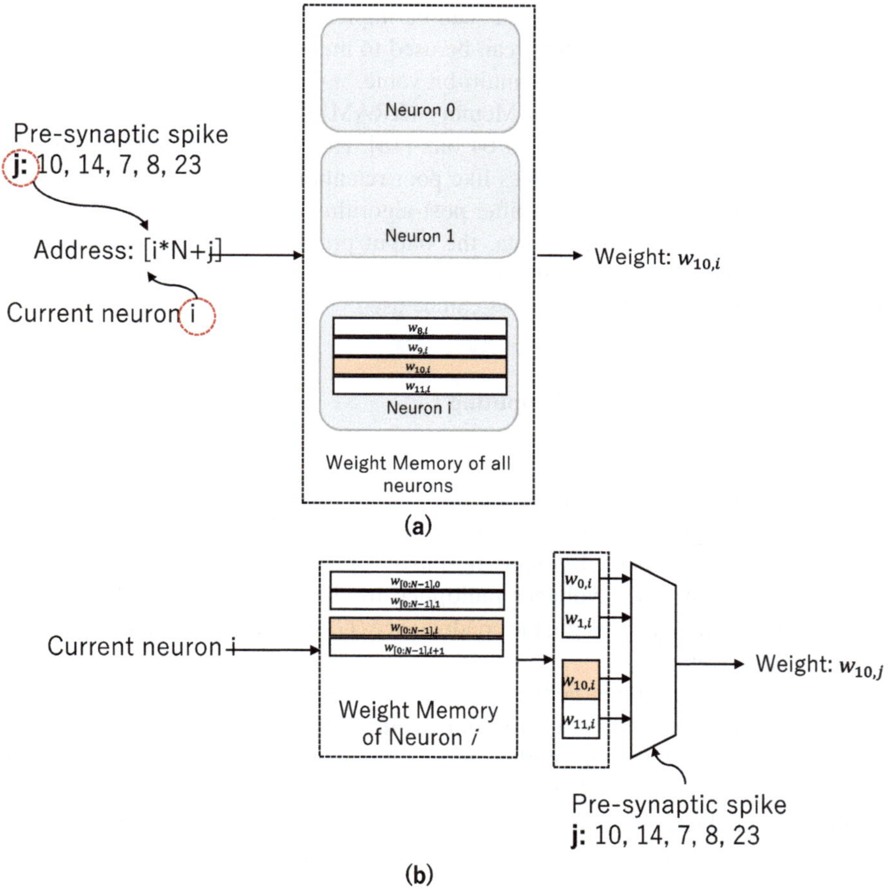

Fig. 4.18 *Serial* neuron weight memory operation: (**a**) Normal weight: This configuration depicts individual weights stored separately in memory, allowing for straightforward access and precise control during the computation process. Each weight can be accessed sequentially, facilitating traditional serial processing methods. (**b**) Merged weight: This configuration illustrates multiple weights combined within a single memory location. This approach reduces memory overhead and enhances access speed, allowing for more efficient processing in serial neuron models where weights are applied in succession

4.5.2.2 Non-volatile Synapse Memory

The first use of Non-Volatile Memory (NVM) in neuromorphic systems is to store data similarly to standard SRAM designs. The NVM cell's resistance (or conductance) can determine the output current from the crossbar, allowing it to function like a DRAM design (1T1C), where the output voltage is compared to a CMOS threshold voltage to obtain the bit value. The NVM can act as standard SRAM in this setup, with each cell storing one bit. Given the wide variability of cell conductance, multi-level cells can be implemented. For example, an ADC (or multiple voltage comparators) can be used to measure the output of the NVM, converting the conductance into a multi-bit value.

For Resistive Random-Access Memory (RRAM) devices, it has been reported that a resistive cell can store up to 64 bits [18]. However, this technology is still in its early stages due to challenges like poor retention time at high temperatures, limited endurance, and instability after post-algorithm operations.

When using NVM to store data, the output process is similar to SRAM, as discussed in Sect. 4.5.2.1. The memory can be organized serially or parallelly, and independent and merged weight rows can be used.

4.5.2.3 NVM In-Memory Computing

The resistive memory design for synapses can emulate neural network connections and matrix multiplications, enabling *in-memory computing*. Figure 4.19a illustrates the crossbar design using resistive memory, precisely a 1T1M configuration, where M represents a memristor. By applying input voltages across all lines, the output current is the sum of the voltages multiplied by the conductance of the resistive devices. In a multi-layer design, the conductance (G_{ij}) is treated as the weight (W_{ij}) between two layers.

To connect layers in the network, an activation unit (e.g., a ReLU for artificial neural networks (ANNs) or a threshold comparator for spiking neural networks (SNNs)) is required to convert the output current into the input voltage for the subsequent layer. The crossbar array of NVMs effectively represents the synapses and plays a vital role in the integration process. The activation unit functions as the neuromorphic system's threshold, mimicking the Leaky Integrate-and-Fire (LIF) neuron operation as shown in Fig. 4.13.

The output current for neuron j (I_j) is calculated as the sum of the currents generated by all presynaptic neurons (I_{ij}), as per Kirchhoff's current law:

$$I_j = \sum I_{ij} \tag{4.1}$$

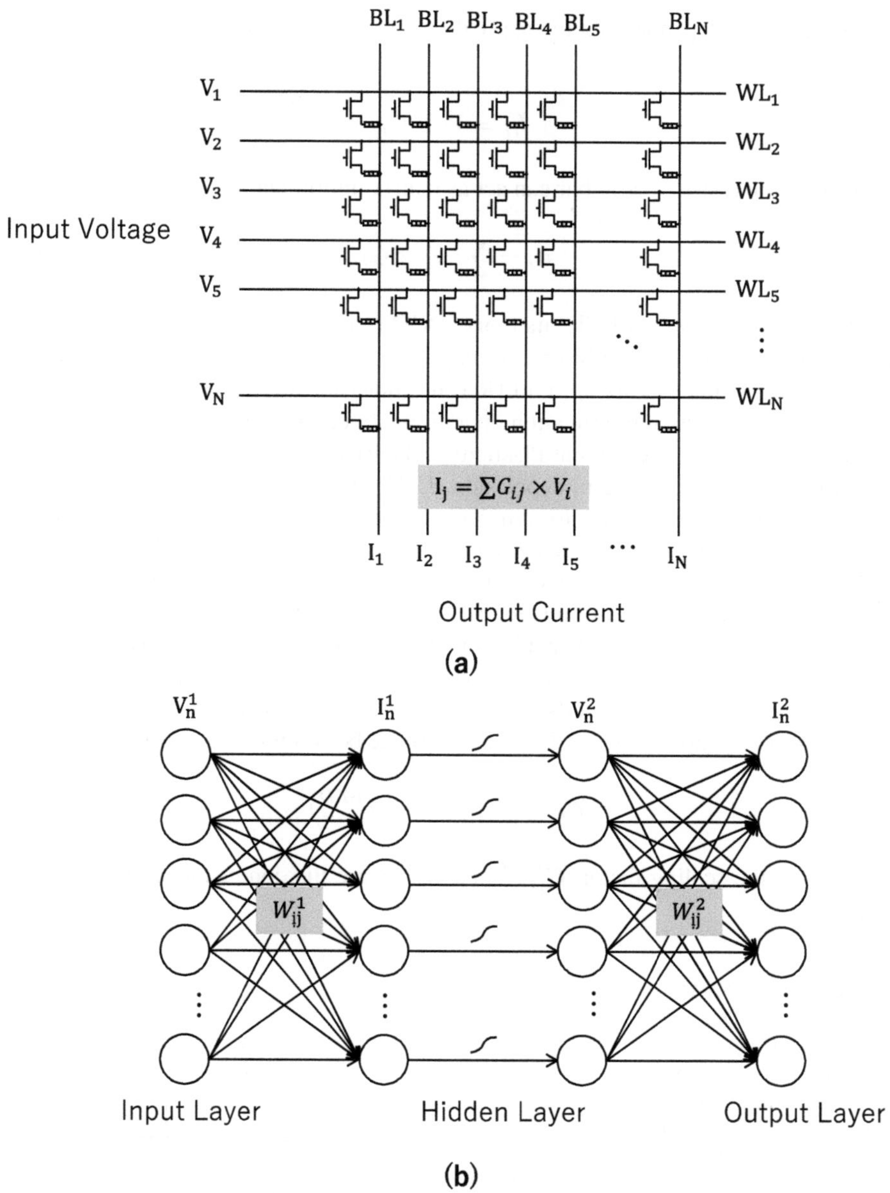

Fig. 4.19 Schematic for a multiple-layer neural network utilizing non-volatile memory (NVM): (**a**) Crossbar configuration for two connected layers: This diagram illustrates the arrangement of memory cells in a crossbar structure, enabling efficient connectivity between the two layers of the neural network. Each intersection of the crossbar represents a synaptic connection, allowing for the storage of weights essential for layer-to-layer communication. (**b**) Three-layer design: This schematic expands on the previous configuration by incorporating an additional layer, demonstrating how multiple layers can be interconnected using NVM

Where I_{ij} is dependent on the applied voltage and the conductance of the NVM cell (as the Ohm's Law):

$$I_{ij} = V_i \times G_{ij} \tag{4.2}$$

Hence, the resistive crossbar can act as matrix multiplication.

$$I_j = \sum V_i \times G_{ij} \tag{4.3}$$

The range of non-volatile memory (NVM) can be classified based on its application in learning and inference-only designs. The inference-only design can be relatively simple, utilizing a 1T1R (one transistor, one resistor) configuration that translates matrix multiplication operations. In contrast, in situ learning, particularly Spike-Timing-Dependent Plasticity (STDP) learning, requires more complex structures to model long-term depression (LTD) and long-term potentiation (LTP). Two resistors are employed to simulate the relationship between the timing of presynaptic and postsynaptic spikes, each corresponding to LTD or LTP behavior. A voltage comparator compares the voltages across the two resistors and determines the synapse output. This design is referred to as the "2-NVM Synapse" [3].

The "2-NVM Synapse" [3] is illustrated in Fig. 4.20. Rather than using a single NVM cell where the conductance is the weight for synaptic connections, the 2-NVM synapse uses two separate cells—one for LTD and the other for LTP. The actual weight of the synapse is defined as the difference between the two resistances:

$$W_{ij} = \beta(G_{ij}^{LTP} - G_{ij}^{LTD}) \tag{4.4}$$

where β is the scaling factor, G_{ij}^{LTP} and G_{ij}^{LTD} are the conductance of two NVM cell.

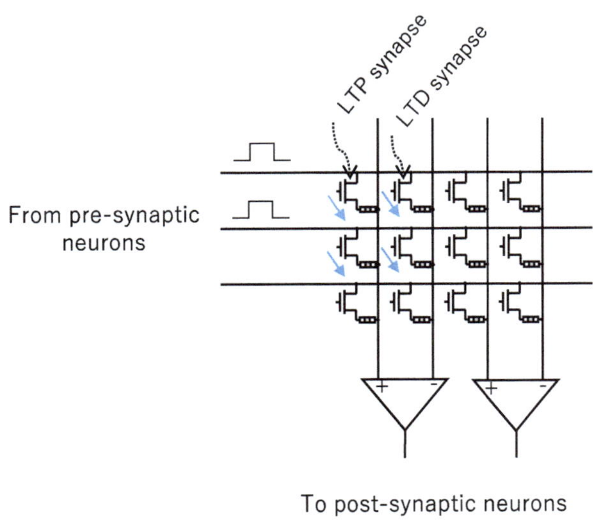

Fig. 4.20 The 2-NVM synapse design: This architecture features two non-volatile memory (NVM) cells integrated to form a synapse. One NVM cell is for LTP and one NVM cell is for LTD. Writing into the cell can help adjust the weight depending on the learning result

The output of the resistive crossbar is analog, and two activation options are available, as shown in Fig. 4.13. A capacitor (virtual ground) wire can capture the output voltage in the analog neuron design. The output voltage is then compared with a threshold voltage to determine if the neuron should fire. A spike is generated once the output voltage exceeds the threshold, and the membrane potential is reset.

For the digital version, the activation unit design depends on how the input voltages are applied. If the input voltages are applied simultaneously, an ADC (Analog-to-Digital Converter) can convert the voltage to a digital value, which is then compared to a threshold. If the input voltages are applied sequentially (one by one), a counter can be used to accumulate the incoming weighted spikes. In either case, converting and comparing values in the digital domain is essential for determining the firing condition.

4.6 Learning with Memory Technologies

In the previous sections, we discussed various technologies used in neuromorphic systems. However, from the programmer's perspective, the key differences between these technologies lie in their speed, density, and retention characteristics. As non-volatile memories (NVMs) become more widely adopted, it is essential to address one of their critical features: the shift in value upon writing and holding.

NVMs offer high density and low power consumption for reading, writing, and holding. However, one challenge is that the conductance values of NVMs are not always stable over time. The nature of NVMs involves drift in their conductance, which can result in values getting stuck at Low Resistance State (LRS), High Resistance State (HRS), ground, or supply voltage. These behaviors lead to gradual changes in the synaptic values, ultimately affecting the system's long-term stability.

Learning in neuromorphic systems can be categorized into two types: online (in situ) and offline (ex-situ). In the ex-situ learning process, weight calculations are performed in a software system, and then the computed weights are loaded into the synapse array. These weights remain fixed during the loading process and are not adjusted afterward. While this is not problematic for SRAM-based synapses, it can be critical for NVM-based systems. For NVMs, maintaining stable conductance during operation is crucial. Even SRAMs can experience transient or permanent errors that change bit values. Thus, ensuring reliability is particularly important in ex-situ learning scenarios.

4.6.1 In-Situ Learning

In in-situ learning, weights are updated directly on-chip during training, allowing for real-time adjustments to the synaptic weights as the system learns. This can either involve training from scratch, where the network's weights are initially set to random values, or fine-tuning, where pre-trained models undergo further refinement to improve performance on specific tasks. In both cases, the primary advantage of in-situ learning lies in its ability to dynamically adjust the weights without the need for transferring large amounts of data between external processing units and memory banks, as is typical in traditional ex-situ learning.

One of the primary goals of in-situ learning is to handle the realistic variations and deviations that arise from the devices used, particularly the non-volatile memories (NVMs) that store synaptic weights. These devices are prone to conductance changes due to the inherent physical properties of NVM materials, such as resistive switching and conductance drift over time. The design weights are adjusted once the variations occur during the learning process to mitigate these issues.

After each training iteration in an in-situ setup, a pre-inference process is needed to calculate the discrepancy between the expected output (based on the current weights) and the actual output (based on the conductance values stored in the NVMs). This discrepancy is used to calculate the error, which informs the subsequent weight update. The weights are adjusted by applying specific voltages to the NVM cells, which either increase (SET) or decrease (RESET) the synaptic connections, mimicking potentiation and depression processes in biological neural systems.

Tuning operations are performed after the error correction process to ensure that the conductance of the NVMs is accurate. These tuning operations aim to adjust the conductance of the NVMs to match the expected values more closely. The tuning process may also include recalibration steps to correct any conductance drift over time, ensuring that the weights reflect the authentic relationships between neurons. Once the weights are tuned, the system must verify the NVM cells' conductance to ensure that the writing process was successful and that the weights are still within acceptable ranges for future computations.

An exciting approach to mitigate the impact of conductance drift is to focus on the sign of the weight during the learning process. This method, which involves updating only the polarity (positive or negative) of the weights, has been shown to reduce the impact of minor deviations in conductance, allowing for more stable learning outcomes even in the presence of conductance drift. This approach was explored in the work of Zhang et al. [23], where the sign-based weight updates helped preserve the overall performance of the neuromorphic system despite the inherent variability in NVM conductance.

The conductance tuning in NVM-based synapses involves applying specific voltages to the NVM cells, as shown in Fig. 4.13. For a single 1-NVM design, increasing the conductance is referred to as "SET", which corresponds to potentiation in neuromorphic systems, while decreasing the conductance is called "RESET", corresponding to depression. These operations are analogous to the biological processes of synaptic strengthening (potentiation) and weakening (depression), which are essential for learning in the brain. In a more advanced 2-NVM design, the relative conductance between two NVM cells determines whether the weight experiences potentiation or depression, offering more nuanced control over synaptic strength.

Conductance drift is an inherent characteristic of NVM devices, and it is crucial to account for this drift when designing neuromorphic learning systems. Retaining the NVM cell's conductance, unlike SRAM cells requiring re-fetching after a reset, is critical. NVM cells can maintain their conductance for extended periods, potentially years, making them ideal candidates for long-term storage of synaptic weights. However, this extended retention can also introduce challenges, as any drift in conductance can lead to inaccuracies in the stored weights, which, if uncorrected, could degrade the performance of the neuromorphic system.

In addition to retention, the endurance of NVM cells is another important factor that needs to be considered, particularly during training. The NVM cells undergo repeated SET and RESET operations, and their ability to withstand these operations without failure is crucial. NVM technologies such as RRAM and PCM typically offer write endurance in the 10^{11} and 10^8 to 10^9 cycles, respectively. As these cells are subjected to numerous write operations, they may eventually fail by becoming stuck at the SET or RESET states or experiencing defects such as open or stuck-at-ground failures. This endurance limitation is a significant challenge for using NVMs in long-term, large-scale neuromorphic systems, as it impacts the longevity and reliability of the devices.

Furthermore, the analog nature of the reading and writing processes in NVMs introduces another layer of complexity. Analog signals are susceptible to noise, which can lead to inaccuracies in the measurement of conductance and, consequently, in the stored weights. While SRAM-based systems can deal with such noise using Error Correction Codes (ECC), this method does not apply to fully analog systems like NVMs. Therefore, additional techniques such as level-based error correction or noise filtering mechanisms may be necessary to ensure reliable performance in NVM-based neuromorphic systems.

Adapting weights in both in-situ and ex-situ learning should consider these factors—conductance drift, retention, endurance, and noise—. Ensuring the accuracy and reliability of weight updates throughout the training process is critical to maintaining the system's overall performance. While SRAM-based systems can overcome some of these challenges with traditional digital error correction techniques, NVM-based systems may require more innovative solutions to address these challenges and fully exploit the potential of non-volatile memory in neuromorphic computing.

4.7 Ex-Situ Learning

The weights and parameters are updated off-chip in ex-situ learning. During this phase, the system undergoes training in a software-based model, typically running on a general-purpose processor or accelerator. The model is trained on a dataset, adjusting the weights and learning parameters to mimic the behavior of the neuromorphic hardware. Once the training process is complete, the optimized weights and parameters are transferred from the software system to the neuromorphic device, where they are loaded into the non-volatile memory (NVM) elements that store the synaptic connections. This enables the device to use the trained weights for inference tasks without further learning or updates.

Unlike in-situ learning, where the weights are updated directly on the device during training, ex-situ learning cannot address the issues related to the variation of values due to device characteristics such as conductance drift and natural process variations. Several factors, including temperature fluctuations, supply voltage fluctuations, and the inherent randomness in the manufacturing process, can cause these variations. As a result, the weights stored in NVM devices may drift over time, potentially causing inaccuracies in the system's behavior.

In-situ learning, by contrast, is designed to dynamically compensate for these variations by adjusting the weights during training to ensure that they remain stable and accurate despite fluctuations. Techniques such as conductance tuning, recalibration, or error correction can help maintain the accuracy of weights over time, even in the face of device drift. In ex-situ learning, however, once the weights are transferred to the NVM device, the system cannot compensate for drift or variations, leaving it vulnerable to the long-term effects of these changes.

Since ex-situ learning cannot predict or correct for the variation of values during writing and holding, it is inherently more sensitive to the instability and drift of NVM-based synapses. This makes ex-situ learning less reliable when working with devices prone to such drift, as it cannot estimate the overall loss of accuracy caused by these variations. In practice, once the weights are transferred into the NVM, they may no longer perform optimally, especially if the devices have undergone significant drift during or after the transfer.

The preferred approach is to perform training in-situ, directly on the device, so that variations can be accounted for during the learning process. This ensures that the weights are continuously adjusted to match the evolving characteristics of the device, which is especially important for non-volatile memory technologies that are susceptible to drift. However, if in-situ training is not possible—such as when the hardware does not support on-device learning or when power constraints prevent continuous learning—it is necessary to accept the accuracy loss caused by drift or try alternative approaches to mitigate it.

One potential solution is to retrain the system periodically. This retraining process can involve reloading the weights back into the system after some time has passed and recalibrating the system based on the actual behavior of the devices. This retraining could mimic an in-situ process, where the system is updated periodically to compensate for the variations in the stored weights. While this can help recover some of the lost accuracies, it still cannot fully replicate the advantages of in-situ learning, where the system continuously adapts in real-time.

The key differences between in-situ and ex-situ learning can be summarized in Table 4.2.

In conclusion, while ex-situ learning provides a more straightforward method by training off-chip and transferring weights into the system, it struggles to handle the variations and instabilities inherent in NVM-based devices. Conversely, in-situ learning presents a more robust approach by adjusting weights during training to accommodate these device variations, thus proving more reliable in dynamic

Table 4.2 Comparison between in-situ and ex-situ learning

Aspect	In-situ learning	Ex-situ learning
Training process	Training occurs on-chip; weights are updated during operation	Training is done off-chip, and weights are updated using a software model
Adaptation to device variations	Continuously adjusts weights to compensate for device variations (e.g., drift)	Cannot account for variations after weights are transferred
Device stability	Maintains stability by dynamically adapting the weights to device characteristics	Vulnerable to drift and unstable once weights are transferred
Error handling	Can use error correction, conductance tuning, or re-calibration during learning	Cannot handle errors caused by device drift after weight transfer
Hardware dependency	Requires devices capable of on-chip learning and updating	Does not require on-chip learning, relying on external computation for updates
Reliability	More robust, as it adapts to changes in device state over time	Less reliable due to lack of adaptation to drift and process variations
Flexibility	More flexible for continuous or real-time learning	Suitable for scenarios where training must be completed offline

environments. When in-situ learning is not feasible, periodic system retraining or tolerating some accuracy loss due to drift are possible alternatives. However, neither approach can fully match the advantages offered by in-situ learning.

4.8 Chapter Summary

In recent years, there has been a significant push towards realizing artificial synapses using post-CMOS devices, such as resistive random access memory (ReRAM), phase change memory (PCM) devices, and magneto-resistive random access memory (MRAM). These innovative memory technologies hold promise for enhancing the performance and efficiency of neuromorphic computing systems, which aim to mimic the architecture and functionality of the human brain. Each of these technologies offers distinct attributes that can be harnessed to replicate the behavior of biological synapses, including the dynamic storage and updating of weights, akin to memristive systems.

This chapter provides an in-depth exploration of these emerging memory technologies and their potential applications in neuromorphic computing. Additionally, it examines the advancements made in developing non-CMOS neurons and discusses the benefits and challenges associated with each type of memory technology. Key issues such as conductance drift, retention, endurance, compatibility with existing architectures, and their effects on in-situ and ex-situ learning processes are thoroughly addressed. The aim is to offer a comprehensive overview of the current landscape of neuromorphic memory systems and their potential to enable more efficient, brain-like computing paradigms.

4.9 Exercises

4.9.1 Exercise 1

Memory is one of the most crucial parts of a neuromorphic system. Understanding the characteristics of different memory locations is very important to have an efficient design; in neuromorphic systems, the following locations, neurons' registers, weight memories, and input/output memories, are the major locations to be considered. Rank them according to the required speed and size for computation.

4.9.2 Exercise 2

Consider a neuromorphic chip where synapses are implemented using Static RAM (SRAM). Each synapse stores a weight value w_i for neuron i, represented by a 10-bit binary number. The synapse array consists of N synapses, and the system operates with a clock frequency of $f = 1\,\text{GHz}$. The read and write operations for each synapse take $t_{\text{read}} = 10\,\text{ns}$ and $t_{\text{write}} = 15\,\text{ns}$, respectively.

The power consumption for read, write, and standby operations are $P_{\text{read}} = 1\,\text{mW}$, $P_{\text{write}} = 1.5\,\text{mW}$, and $P_{\text{standby}} = 0.1\,\text{mW}$, respectively. Assume the system accesses each synapse once per neuron computation cycle, with half of the accesses being reads and the other half being writes. Answer the following questions:

1. Calculate the total number of synapses N in the neuromorphic chip if the chip can store a total of 1 Mbit of weight values.
2. Determine the total energy consumption for one complete neuron computation cycle.
3. If the neuron computation cycle occurs every 1 ms, compute the average power consumption of the SRAM cells over one second.
4. Discuss the impact of reducing the read and write latencies by 50% on the total energy and power consumption.

4.9.3 Exercise 3

Retention time is a critical factor for storing values for a long time. Among the memory types in Ex. 3, which memory has a short retention time, and why? What are the significant benefits of long retention time?

4.9.4 *Exercise 4*

The 6-transistor SRAM cell is one of the most popular memory designs. In this SRAM cell, if WL is '1' and BL is '1', what is the logic value of Q? Please explain how you determine the value of Q.

4.9.5 *Exercise 5*

When designing memory for a neuromorphic system, determining memory size is crucial. Assuming the neuromorphic system is a fully connected model of 784:1200:1200:10, what is the size of the total memories if the weight is 8-bit?

4.9.6 *Exercise 7*

Since the weight's bitwidth could be small and unsuitable for a single word in memory, the merged weight organization is usually applied. With a merged weight organization (8 weights to 1), calculate the address of memory for the following pre-synaptic spikes with ID: 17, 33, 123.

4.9.7 *Exercise 8*

With the network model in Ex. 5 and the merged weight in Ex. 6, calculate the size of the memory word and the bit-width of the address for the memory.

4.9.8 *Exercise 9*

During the designing phase, selecting parallel or serial neurons must be done. Please explain parallel and serial neuron weight memory differences. Explain the scenario when we use parallel neurons and the scenario when we use serial neurons.

4.10 Exercise 10

Consider a neuromorphic system where the synapses are implemented using Static RAM (SRAM). Each synapse stores a weight value, which is used during neuron computations. In this system, the weight values are represented by 8-bit binary numbers. The SRAM cells have the following specifications:

- Read latency: 10 ns
- Write latency: 15 ns
- Power consumption during reading: 2 mW
- Power consumption during writing: 3 mW
- Standby power consumption: 0.5 mW

The system has a total of 1024 synapses. Each synapse is accessed once per neuron computation cycle. Answer the following questions:

1. Calculate the total energy consumption of the SRAM cells for one complete neuron computation cycle, assuming equal numbers of read and write operations.
2. If the neuron computation cycle occurs every 1 ms, what is the average power consumption of the SRAM cells over one second?
3. Considering the standby power consumption, determine the total energy consumption of the SRAM cells over one second.
4. Discuss how the power consumption could be optimized in such a neuromorphic system.

References

1. Akopyan F, Sawada J, Cassidy A, Alvarez-Icaza R, Arthur J, Merolla P, Imam N, Nakamura Y, Datta P, Nam G, Taba B, Beakes M, Brezzo B, Kuang JB, Manohar R, Risk WP, Jackson B, Modha DS (2015) Truenorth: design and tool flow of a 65 mw 1 million neuron programmable neurosynaptic chip. IEEE Trans Comput Aid Des Integr Circuits Syst 34(10):1537–1557
2. Ben Abdallah A, Dang KN (2021) Toward robust cognitive 3D brain-inspired cross-paradigm system. Front Neurosci 15:795
3. Bichler O, Suri M, Querlioz D, Vuillaume D, DeSalvo B, Gamrat C (2012) Visual pattern extraction using energy-efficient "2-PCM synapse" neuromorphic architecture. IEEE Trans Electron Dev 59(8):2206–2214
4. Chang M, Rosenfeld P, Lu S, Jacob B (2013) Technology comparison for large last-level caches (l3Cs): low-leakage SRAM, low write-energy STT-RAM, and refresh-optimized eDRAM. In: 2013 IEEE 19th international symposium on high performance computer architecture (HPCA), pp 143–154
5. Close G, Frey U, Breitwisch M, Lung H, Lam C, Hagleitner C, Eleftheriou E (2010) Device, circuit and system-level analysis of noise in multi-bit phase-change memory. In: 2010 international electron devices meeting. IEEE, Piscataway, pp 29–5
6. Dang, KN, Abdallah AB (2019) An efficient software-hardware design framework for spiking neural network systems. In: The international conference on internet of things, embedded systems and communications (IINTEC 2019)
7. Davies M, Srinivasa N, Lin T, Chinya G, Cao Y, Choday SH, Dimou G, Joshi P, Imam N, Jain S, Liao Y, Lin C, Lines A, Liu R, Mathaikutty D, McCoy S, Paul A, Tse J, Venkataramanan G, Weng Y, Wild A, Yang Y, Wang H (2018) Loihi: a neuromorphic manycore processor with on-chip learning. IEEE Micro 38(1):82–99
8. Dünkel S, Trentzsch M, Richter R, Moll P, Fuchs C, Gehring O, Majer M, Wittek S, Müller B, Melde T, et al (2017) A FeFET based super-low-power ultra-fast embedded NVM technology for 22nm FDSOI and beyond. In: 2017 IEEE international electron devices meeting (IEDM). IEEE, Piscataway, pp 19–7

9. Frenkel C, Lefebvre M, Legat JD, Bol D (2018) A 0.086-mm^2 12.7-pJ/SOP 64k-synapse 256-neuron online-learning digital spiking neuromorphic processor in 28-nm CMOS. IEEE Trans Biomed Circuits Syst 13(1):145–158
10. Frenkel C, Legat J, Bol D (2019) Morphic: a 65-nm 738k-synapse/mm^2 quad-core binary-weight digital neuromorphic processor with stochastic spike-driven online learning. IEEE Trans Biomed Circuits Syst 13:999
11. Furber SB, Lester DR, Plana LA, Garside JD, Painkras E, Temple S, Brown AD (2013) Overview of the spinnaker system architecture. IEEE Trans Comput 62(12):2454–2467
12. Ikechukwu OM, Dang KN, Abdallah AB (2021) On the design of a fault-tolerant scalable three dimensional NoC-based digital neuromorphic system with on-chip learning. IEEE Access 9:64331–64345
13. Joshi V, Le Gallo M, Haefeli S, Boybat I, Nandakumar SR, Piveteau C, Dazzi M, Rajendran B, Sebastian A, Eleftheriou E (2020) Accurate deep neural network inference using computational phase-change memory. Nat Commun 11(1):1–13
14. Nandakumar S, Le Gallo M, Boybat I, Rajendran B, Sebastian A, Eleftheriou E (2018) A phase-change memory model for neuromorphic computing. J Appl Phys 124(15):152135
15. Nguyen ND, Dang KN (2023) A novel yield improvement approach for 3D stacking neuromorphic architecture. In: 2023 IEEE 16th international symposium on embedded multicore/many-core systems-on-chip (MCSoC). IEEE, Piscataway, pp 392–398
16. Nguyen ND, Ahmed AB, Abdallah AB, Dang KN (2023) Power-aware neuromorphic architecture with partial voltage scaling 3-D stacking synaptic memory. IEEE Trans Very Large Scale Integr Syst 31:2016
17. Nguyen ND, Dang KN, Ahmed AB, Abdallah AB, Tran XT (2024) NOMA: a novel reliability improvement methodology for 3-D IC-based neuromorphic systems. IEEE Trans Compon Packag Manufact Technol. https://ieeexplore.ieee.org/document/10738829
18. Pérez E, Cristian Zambelli MKM, Olivo P, Wenger C (2019) Toward reliable multi-level operation in RRAM arrays: improving post-algorithm stability and assessing endurance/data retention. IEEE J Electron Dev Soc 7:740–747
19. Seo J, Brezzo B, Liu Y, Parker BD, Esser SK, Montoye RK, Rajendran B, Tierno JA, Chang L, Modha DS, Friedman DJ (2011) A 45nm CMOS neuromorphic chip with a scalable architecture for learning in networks of spiking neurons. In: 2011 IEEE custom integrated circuits conference (CICC), pp 1–4
20. Tosson AMS, Yu S, Anis MH, Wei L (2018) Proposing a solution for single-event upset in 1t1r RRAM memory arrays. IEEE Trans Nucl Sci 65(6):1239–1247
21. Wu CC, Chiu YC (2024) A physics-based model of charge trapping behavior of Si FeFET with metal/ferroelectric/interlayer/Si structure. IEEE Trans Electron Dev 71(6):738–745
22. Yang JJ, Strukov DB, Stewart DR (2013) Memristive devices for computing. Nat Nanotechnol 8(1):13
23. Zhang Q, Wu H, Yao P, Zhang W, Gao B, Deng N, Qian H (2018) Sign backpropagation: an on-chip learning algorithm for analog RRAM neuromorphic computing systems. Neural Netw 108:217–223

Chapter 5
Communication Networks for Neuromorphic Systems

Abstract Brain connectivity is described at various scales, ranging from synaptic connections between individual neurons at the microscale to networks of neuronal populations at the mesoscale and brain regions linked by fiber pathways at the macroscale. High bandwidth is essential for efficient communication since each neuron is connected to many others, and very low communication latency is crucial as spike timings encode information. This chapter explores network structures used for communication in neuromorphic systems, focusing on Network-on-Chip (NoC) architecture. This network facilitates the reception and transmission of spikes following the Address Event Representation (AER) protocol and aids in memory access. Detailed exploration of the methods of inter-neuron communication highlights their design principles, providing a comprehensive understanding of both on-chip and off-chip communication. The chapter covers neural communication, interconnect design principles, and advanced interconnect technologies for multi-core neuromorphic systems, including 3D-NoC and Si-Photonic NoC. It concludes with exercises designed to reinforce the concepts discussed, providing practical application opportunities for readers.

5.1 Introduction

Early neuromorphic chips were designed by Carver Mead and his students at Caltech [39, 49]. In the initial design, Address Event Representation (AER) was used as the inter-chip communication protocol because many required neurons could not be realized then. AER multiplexes the firing events from neurons and encodes them as a lower-complexity connection. For an N-axon fiber system, with only one active fiber at a time, AER replaces traditional wiring with $(1 + \log(N))$ wires. In more recent neuromorphic designs, AER is a protocol for both on-chip and off-chip communication. Figure 5.1 shows the AER protocol. The neurons in the sender array generate a temporal sequence of digital amplitude events to encode their outputs, a representation conceptually equivalent to a train of action potentials (or spikes). Each neuron has a digital address that is uniquely assigned to it (for instance, 1, 2, 3). Whenever a neuron signals an event, the encoder

A. Ben Abdallah, K. N. Dang, *Neuromorphic Computing Principles and Organization*, https://doi.org/10.1007/978-3-031-83089-1_5

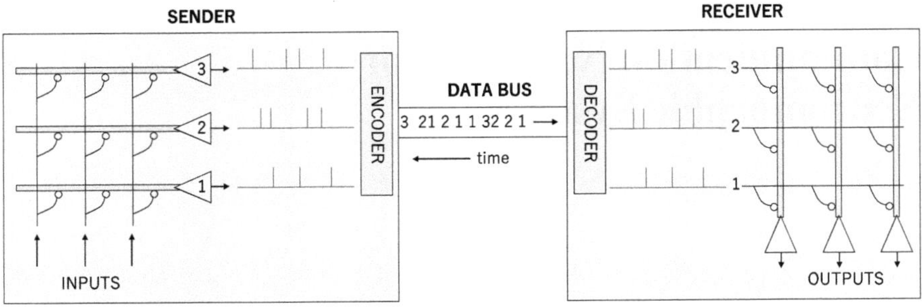

Fig. 5.1 Address-Event Representation (AER) Protocol: In AER, each spike is encoded as a unique address that represents the specific neuron generating the spike. This address is transmitted to downstream neurons or processing units, allowing them to identify the origin of the firing neuron

circuitry broadcasts that neuron's address on the inter-chip data bus. After an action potential, the neuron enters a refractory period, which prohibits its ability to generate new action potentials [45]. Therefore, the inter-spike interval (ISI) at a neuron is longer than the time required to broadcast the neuron's address. This means multiple neurons can use the same bus to transmit their spike events without creating significant bottlenecks, as each neuron's firing event is temporally separated. The receiver then interprets the address as an event corresponding to an action potential from the neuron identified by that address, enabling the correct post-synaptic neurons to receive the spike information.

5.2 Neural Communication

Most biological neurons communicate predominantly via an electrochemical impulse known as an action potential or spike [45]. In neuromorphic systems, this communication model is often mimicked by the 'point neuron model' [25], where the complex dendritic structures are abstracted out, and the assumption is made that all inputs to the neuron effectively arrive at the soma. The size and shape of the spike remain invariant under normal conditions; however, this complexity is not efficient for computing purposes. As a result, a spike can be treated as a unit impulse, conveying information primarily based on its timing rather than its amplitude.

In the context of neuromorphic systems, as shown in Fig. 5.1, there is no need for a global clock, and the signals are transmitted asynchronously. This asynchronous nature of communication means that the timing of the spikes is encapsulated within the events themselves, and there is no reliance on a time step or synchronization typically seen in digital systems. For example, when *neuron 1* fires, its spike is immediately encoded as the value '1' in the data bus between two modules, and no further information is transmitted on the bus until the next spike occurs. Once the spike happens, the neuron's ID is sent to the bus, and the signal is decoded. The post-synaptic neurons receive the spike accordingly. The decoder re-issues the spike to the appropriate destination neurons, mimicking the biological transmission of an action potential across synapses.

Request and acknowledgment protocols are often employed in communication, particularly inter-chip or inter-neuron cluster communication. A request signal is initially sent from the pre-synaptic neuron to indicate that it is ready to transmit a spike. Once the AER signal has been encoded and transmitted, an acknowledgment signal is sent back from the receiver to confirm the arrival of the spike. This ensures reliable communication between the chips or neuron clusters. Figure 5.2a illustrates this process in detail, showing the send/acknowledge handshake between two blocks (clusters of neurons). The arbiter grants permission for a pre-synaptic neuron in the sender block to send the signal to the encoder, which then encodes the spike into the AER format. The encoded spikes are transmitted through the data bus to the decoder at the receiver end. Once the decoder receives the spike, it is unpacked from the AER format and reissued to the post-synaptic neurons.

After the spikes have been delivered to the post-synaptic neurons, an acknowledgment signal is sent back to the sender, signaling the successful reception of the spike. Once this acknowledgment reaches the pre-synaptic neuron, the spike is removed from the communication channel, and the arbiter then allows other neurons in the sender block to fire. This ensures that the spike is not lost during

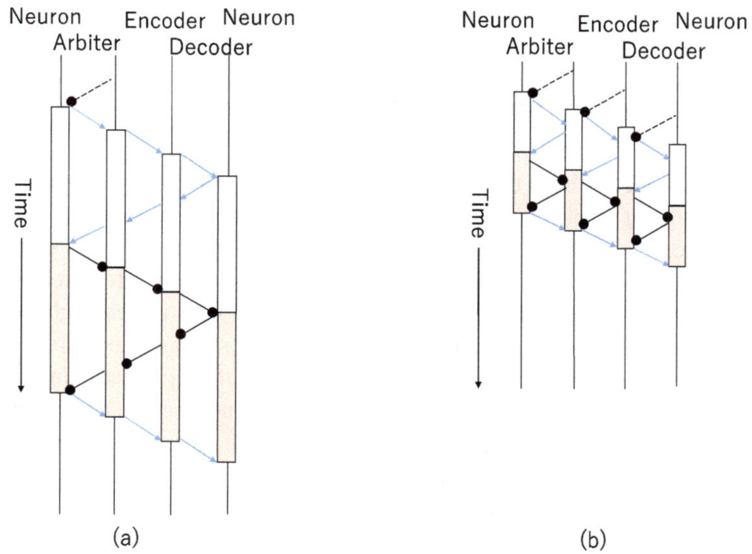

Fig. 5.2 The control signal flow in an AER system begins with a neuron's spike, which travels through the arbiter and encoder on the transmitting side and reaches the decoder and receiving neuron (from left to right). (**a**) illustrates the spike transmission completion from the originating neuron before handshaking concludes in the acknowledgment phase. (**b**) demonstrates how pipelining reduces the overall handshaking duration by enabling signals to continue propagating in the set phase without waiting for acknowledgment, enhancing transmission efficiency

transmission. If no acknowledgment signal is received, the spike is considered lost, and a re-transmission is initiated. To enhance communication efficiency, pipelining can be employed, as depicted in Fig. 5.2b. Pipelining allows a new neuron to fire immediately after the encoder has received the previous signal, reducing idle times between communications and improving the system's overall throughput. The arbiter ensures that the sequencing of neuron firings occurs orderly, preventing race conditions or conflicts in the communication process.

These handshake protocols and asynchronous communication methods provide a robust and efficient way of transmitting spike information between neurons or neuron clusters. They emulate the biological communication mechanisms found in the brain while addressing the challenges of scaling neuromorphic systems. There are two basic types of inter-neural communications: local and global interconnects. While the local interconnect transfers the spikes within a particular area, long-range analog signals help neurons communicate to a different brain area. Therefore, a communication network for a given neuromorphic system should consider local and cluster-to-cluster communication during the design phase.

The communication network in a given neuromorphic system must satisfy the ability to send and receive spikes (action potentials) with low and precise latency. Consequently, unlike early neuromorphic prototypes with hundreds or thousands of neurons, a large-scale system must be explicitly designed to achieve the biological system's real-timeliness. The following section will discuss creating the interconnect for inter-neural communication in neuromorphic systems.

5.3 Inter-Neural Communication

Even though AER has been the de facto protocol for silicon neuron communication, the protocol itself is not exceptionally scalable. While AER can help reduce the traffic between two groups of neurons, it is no longer a straightforward solution for systems with massive numbers of neurons. As more neurons are integrated into clusters with shared encoders and decoders, the design becomes increasingly complex, resulting in longer wire lengths. Therefore, one of the standardized infrastructures for neuromorphic systems is to adopt both on-chip and off-chip interconnects. Many works on neuromorphic systems now support multiple neurocores per system.

The communication between neurons can be done in a synchronous [26] or asynchronous manner [21, 40]. While synchronous systems are easier to manage and control, asynchronous systems offer low power consumption and behavior that more closely resembles biological brains, which perform asynchronously. Table 5.1 shows three significant neuromorphic systems: SpiNNaker by the University of Manchester, TrueNorth by IBM, and Loihi by Intel. While SpiNNaker emulates neurons using ARM cores, TrueNorth and Loihi implement hardware neurons.

The SpiNNaker processor [26] features an array of ARM9 cores that use a custom interconnect fabric for packet-based communication. Each packet has 40 or 72 bits and is supported by hardware. The processor can transmit over 5 billion packets/s.

Table 5.1 Neuromorphic system communication

Architecture	Configuration	Communication
SpiNNaker [26]	Each ARM core performs operations for 1000 neurons. A node consists of 18 ARM cores, with 1024 neurons per ARM core. 16-bit for node, 5-bit for core, 11-bit for axon.	Nodes are connected using six communication links in triangular lattices folded onto the surface of a toroid. Multi-cast based using CAM.
TrueNorth [11]	Each core emulates 256 neurons, with 4096 (64 × 64) cores per chip. 18-bit for core distance, 8-bit for axon.	Formed in 2D-mesh. Uni-cast based with relative X and Y coordinates. X-first routing.
Loihi [21]	The system features 128 neuromorphic cores and 3 × 86 cores per chip, scalable up to 4096 cores. It supports up to 16,384 inter-chip communications. Each core implements 1024 neural units with variable synaptic resolution.	Asynchronous 2D Mesh NoC. NoC only supports uni-cast, and multi-cast is supported by iteration. NoC routing uses the dimension-order routing algorithm (X-first).

The ‘point neuron model’ is also adopted here, where all packets (spikes) must effectively arrive at their desired destinations. Weights alternate the strength of the connections to represent the connections between neurons. These weights can be either positive or negative to represent excitatory and inhibitory connections.

SpiNNaker adopts the AER protocol as the central idea, with modifications to form the connections between neurons. Since the AER format represents a spike by its time and identity (i.e., number), SpiNNaker uses packet-switched communication and broadcast/multicast routing. Once a spike occurs, the AER signal is sent to the packet-switched communication fabric and delivered to the connected neurons.

By enabling communication via electronic fabrics, spikes can instantaneously arrive at their destinations, similar to the biological signals in the brain. This flexibility allows SpiNNaker to map any neuron to any node (cluster of neurons), thus forming the biological topology regardless of the packet-switched communication topology. The problem of efficient mapping has been extensively investigated to reduce transmission time between neurons [13].

In SpiNNaker, 1000 neurons are simulated in each ARM core using fixed time-multiplexing. Figure 5.3 shows the SpiNNaker node architecture. Each node contains 18 ARM processors, meaning 18,000 neurons can be simulated per node. Consequently, SpiNNaker expects a delivery time (spike window) of around 0.2 μs per hop to ensure neurons react to stimuli in order of milliseconds, similar to biological systems. Initially, communication between ARM cores of a SpiNNaker chip is handled by a Network-on-Chip (NoC). This is then converted into off-chip communication using packet-router modules. Six links are merged using a time-division multiplexer to stream spikes from the local NoC. The output stream is then split into six output links. For example, the inter-node communication in SpiNNaker is achieved via packets. These packets are generated by cores and transmitted to the local router, redirecting them to the target cores. The local router sends the packets

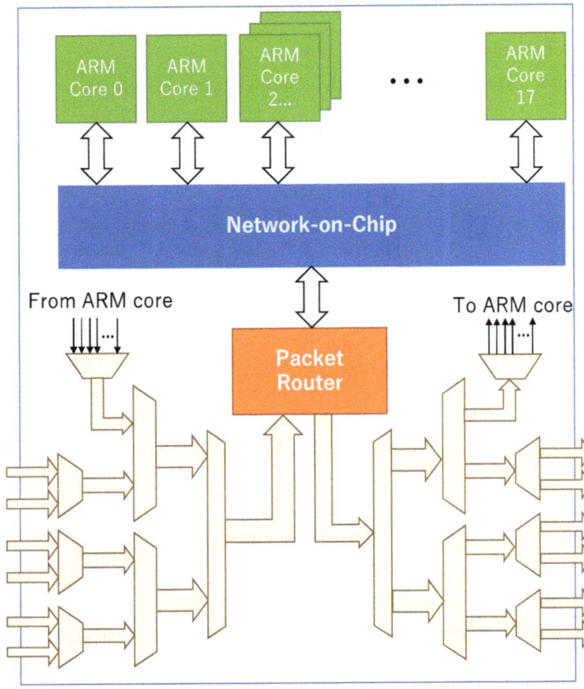

Fig. 5.3 The SpiNNaker node: A core component of the SpiNNaker neuromorphic computing platform, designed to support large-scale, parallel neural simulations. Each node contains 18 ARM processors interconnected by a high-speed, low-latency communication fabric, allowing efficient spike-based communication. The nodes are also connected into a large-scale inter-chip fabric via packet routers and multiplexers/demultiplexers

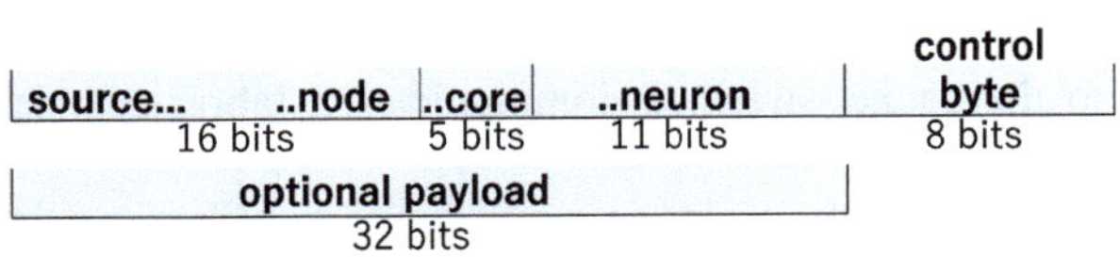

Fig. 5.4 The SpiNNaker Address-Event Representation (AER) system: An event-driven protocol within the SpiNNaker platform that enables efficient spike communication between neurons. SpiNNaker encodes each neural spike as an address, specifying the node, core, and neuron origin

back to the local cores if the destination neurons are located within the same node as the source. However, if the destination is in another node or multiple nodes, the local router forwards the packets to a neighboring node. Since each node can only connect to six other nodes, a routing technique is required to deliver the packets efficiently.

SpiNNaker employs four types of packets, available in either 40-bit or 72-bit formats: (1) Nearest neighbor, (2) Point-to-point, (3) Neural event multicast, and (4) Fixed route. While the nearest neighbor packets initialize the system, flood-fill communication (broadcast) and point-to-point packets enable more detailed communications. Among these, we focus on the *neural event multi-cast* packets, as they represent the interneural communication.

The AER protocol in SpiNNaker can be summarized in Fig. 5.4, where the packet format includes 16 bits for the node ID, 5 bits for the core ID (ARM core), and 11 bits for the neuron ID (neuron within the ARM core). The routing method used for AER follows the Content-Access-Memory (CAM) approach. First, the CAM looks up the address and finds the corresponding output in the output RAM. The word from the output RAM of $6 + 18$ bits encodes the output directly in one-hot format, where the first 6 bits are for the inter-chip link, and the last 18 bits are for the internal core.

Another example is the TrueNorth [11], which is a neuromorphic chip designed by IBM in 2014 [11]. The chip consists of 4096 cores connected via a Network-on-Chip (NoC). Each core simulates 256 neurons using a time-multiplexed method. Each neuron is connected to 256 programmable synapses that emulate the synaptic strength between neurons. Unlike SpiNNaker, which uses ARM cores to simulate neurons, TrueNorth implements the Leaky-Integrate-and-Fire (LIF) model.

The number of connections per neuron is limited to 256; however, TrueNorth achieves much lower power consumption than the large-scale system in SpiNNaker. Unlike SpiNNaker, TrueNorth does not use a global address for node/cluster communication. Instead, it uses the relative distance in the X and Y coordinates, denoted as dx and dy, for communication. These coordinates are represented using 9-bit signed integers, allowing a packet range of $[-256, 255]$ from the source.

TrueNorth employs the X-first routing algorithm. In this algorithm, the relative distance in the X-coordinate (dx) is adjusted first, either increasing or decreasing, until it reaches zero. Once dx becomes zero, the relative distance in the Y-coordinate (dy) is adjusted. In each hop, unless both dx and dy are zero (indicating that the packet has arrived at its destination), it is routed according to the changes in dx and dy. For example, if dx is harmful and is increased in the routing unit, the packet is routed to the east.

The content of the spike data, besides dx and dy, includes the delivery tick (4 bits), the destination axon index (8 bits), and debug bits (2 bits). The delivery tick ensures proper spike timing, while the 8-bit axon index represents the connections between neurons. In TrueNorth, the synapse SRAM has a size of 256×410 for 256 neurons, where the synapse resolution is one bit per connection. Routing in TrueNorth is based on unicast communication with the X-first routing algorithm. Since spikes are sparse, issues like deadlock and live lock are not a concern.

In 2018, Intel released its $60\,\text{mm}^2$ neuromorphic chip, named Loihi, fabricated in a 14 nm process. The Loihi chip consists of 3 $\times$86 cores and 128 neuromorphic cores connected via an asynchronous Network-on-Chip (NoC), and it can be scaled up to 4096 cores. Each core can implement up to 1024 neurons with variable weight lengths (ranging from 1 to 9 bits), affecting the number of synapses per core, ranging from 1 million to 114k. The NoC supports no native multicast, meaning the core must send spikes to a list of destinations iteratively.

Although Loihi's actual packet format is not publicly detailed, it is widely believed that an Address Event Representation (AER) format is used to send spikes. Once a pre-synaptic neuron fires, its spikes are projected to a fan-out core-to-core list, including the cores' IDs with the post-synaptic neurons. These spikes are sent to all connected cores using unicast via the NoC. Upon arrival at the destination cores, the spikes are transmitted to all post-synaptic neurons via a multicast transmission.

5.4 Interconnect Design Principles

When designing interconnects for neuromorphic chips, several crucial aspects must be considered, starting with the system's topology. This design decision significantly impacts the system's performance, as different topologies offer unique advantages and challenges. For instance, SpiNNaker utilizes a folded triangle lattice topology, which is ideal for supercomputer models, whereas other systems prefer a 2D mesh for its simplicity and scalability.

In addition to topology, the system's communications classification is vital. Beyond inter-neural communication, which allows spikes to travel between neurons, other key communications include synchronization, data transactions, and debugging. Synchronization is critical for system operations, often achieved through flooding or gossiping methods, where cores exchange information with their neighbors.

Network support in neuromorphic chips involves various communication types, such as unicast, multicast, and broadcast. SpiNNaker supports multicast, enabling efficient data distribution, whereas TrueNorth and Loihi NoCs rely on unicast, necessitating multiple packets for multi-destination transmissions. Broadcast functions, like flooding and gossiping, are also used to disseminate information system-wide.

Time constraints are another critical factor, especially in ensuring spikes reach their destinations within specific time windows to maintain biological real-time processing. SpiNNaker's infrastructure is designed to deliver packets within milliseconds. This involves managing local and long-range connections crucial for real-time performance. Designers might sometimes tolerate spike dropping to maintain system functionality with minimal accuracy loss. Mapping neural functions within large-scale systems is another complex task. It requires careful clustering of neurons to optimize performance and reduce communication and execution times. Recent studies have explored various mapping techniques to enhance these aspects.

Lastly, fault tolerance is essential for maintaining system reliability. Despite inherent resilience to specific faults, interconnect issues can lead to missing or misrouted spikes, potentially altering the system's behavior. Therefore, ensuring robust fault-tolerance mechanisms is critical to neuromorphic chip design.

5.4.1 OSI Model for Network-on-Chip

The Open Systems Interconnection (OSI) model, traditionally used to standardize telecommunication and computing systems functions, can also be applied to Network-on-Chip (NoC) architectures. By leveraging the OSI model, NoC architectures can achieve scalable, efficient, and trustworthy communication, which is crucial for the performance of multicore and manycore systems. In the context of NoC, the OSI model helps define the layers and protocols necessary for

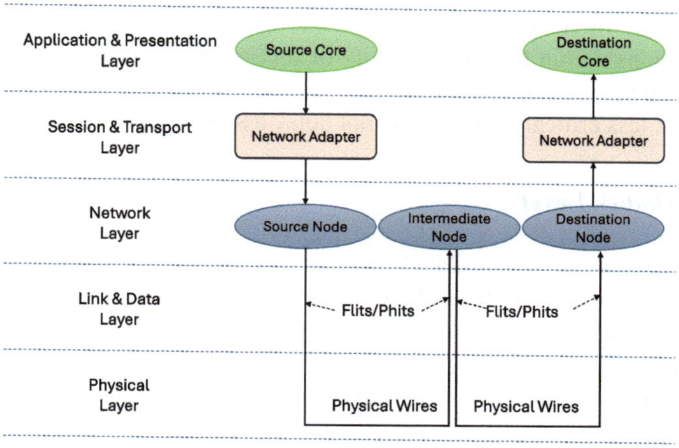

Fig. 5.5 OSI Reference Model for Network-on-Chip (NoC): This model adapts the Open Systems Interconnection (OSI) framework to the context of on-chip networks, providing layered abstractions for data communication within integrated circuits

effective communication between components within a chip. These layers include the physical layer, which handles data transmission over physical interconnects; the data link layer, which is responsible for error detection and correction; the network layer, which manages data routing; and higher layers, which ensure reliable data transfer and application-specific processing.

NoCs are usually packet-switched communication networks derived from the general computer network domain. The OSI reference model for NoC is depicted in Fig. 5.5. This model acts as the framework for building the NoC.

5.4.1.1 Application and Presentation Layers

The data-flow graph is represented at the application and presentation layers. Each task in the graph has a distinct workload, with tasks interconnected through messages or transactions. In neuromorphic systems, these data types may include spikes, data transactions (such as read/write to local memory), or control signals.

5.4.1.2 Session and Transport Layers

In the session and transport layers, messages and transactions are divided into packets or streams and delivered to the network interface for communication. The packet at this layer encapsulates the destination, routing path, and routing instructions. Additionally, quality-of-service (QoS) parameters, such as best-effort or guaranteed services, are handled at this stage. These parameters ensure that the network can meet specific performance criteria, such as latency, bandwidth, and reliability, which are critical for maintaining the efficiency and stability of communications within the NoC. Quality of service mechanisms prioritizes traffic based on importance, allowing time-sensitive data to be transmitted quickly and ensuring that less critical processes do not delay essential tasks.

5.4.1.3 Network Layer

Once the packets are encapsulated, the network interface forwards them to the network layer. The network layer delivers packets from the source network interface (NI) to the destination NI, potentially through intermediate routers. Different switching techniques can be applied in this layer, including circuit switching and packet-switching methods like store-and-forward, virtual cut-through, or wormhole routing.

5.4.1.4 Link and Data Layer

The packet is divided into smaller flow control units (flits) in the link and data layers. Each flit is processed by sub-modules within routers—received, routed, and forwarded. Flow control mechanisms are necessary to ensure synchronization between routers, and error correction codes are used to protect data integrity.

5.4.2 Network Topology

Network topology refers to the structural organization of a network, encompassing the arrangement and connection of nodes or processing elements (PEs), the design of routers, and the interconnecting links between routers and PEs. It is pivotal in determining the performance, efficiency, and scalability of neuromorphic chips. Selecting an appropriate NoC topology involves assessing factors such as communication mechanisms, types of PEs, and router architecture. This choice is typically made through extensive design exploration to optimize for specific performance metrics such as latency, bandwidth, power consumption, and fault tolerance. Effective network topology ensures that data can be efficiently routed across the chip, minimizing delays and energy usage while maximizing throughput. Advanced topologies, such as folded triangle lattice or 2D mesh, offer unique advantages and challenges. This makes the design phase critical for achieving speed, scalability, and reliability in neuromorphic systems.

5.4.2.1 Key Network Topologies

Interconnect designs can feature various topologies, typically regular or irregular. Regular topologies are tailored to specific applications and are well-suited for the system's communication needs, ensuring efficient and predictable data transfer. In contrast, irregular topologies are generally less scalable and may not fully utilize the parallelism offered by Network-on-Chip (NoC) systems. Therefore, our focus here is on regular topologies.

Several regular topologies have been proposed, including mesh, torus, folded torus, concentrated mesh, binary tree, butterfly tree, and clos. Each topology offers unique advantages based on core-to-core distance, the number of cores attached to each router, routing complexity, and layout optimization. The mesh topology is the most common among these due to its simplicity in design, routing, and layout, making it particularly advantageous for neuromorphic applications.

Mesh topology is widely adopted because it provides straightforward routing paths and is easy to implement. It consists of a grid-like structure where each node is connected to its immediate neighbors, facilitating efficient communication with minimal routing complexity. This simplicity helps manage the vast inter-neural communication required in neuromorphic systems, ensuring timely data transfer and reduced latency.

Torus topology, on the other hand, connects the edges of the mesh to form a continuous loop, reducing the maximum distance between any two nodes and enhancing communication efficiency. Folded torus further optimizes this by folding the torus structure, providing even shorter paths for data transfer.

Concentrated mesh reduces the number of routers by grouping multiple cores per router, improving scalability and reducing power consumption. Binary tree and butterfly tree topologies offer hierarchical routing structures that can optimize communication for specific neuromorphic tasks. In contrast, clos topology provides a highly interconnected structure ideal for minimizing latency and maximizing throughput.

The choice of topology in neuromorphic chip design is critical, as it impacts the system's overall performance, scalability, and power efficiency. Among the various topologies, mesh is the most favored for its balance of simplicity and effectiveness, making it a cornerstone in developing neuromorphic systems.

5.4.2.2 2D Mesh Topology

The 2D Mesh topology is illustrated schematically in Fig. 5.6. A 2D Mesh NoC consists of an $M \times N$ array of routers (or switches), each interconnecting a Processing Element (PE) near the router. Each router, except for those at the boundary of the mesh, connects to four neighboring routers and one PE. The total number of routers equals the number of PEs in the system. Communication between routers, or between routers and PEs, is facilitated through two unidirectional links.

In this topology, the assumption is made that all communication links are of similar length, simplifying the physical design. This uniformity typically implies that PEs share a similar architecture. To streamline the design process, a tile—consisting of a router, a Network Interface (NI), and a PE—is first designed as a macro-block, which is then replicated during the physical design phase. This approach accelerates the design time and supports highly scalable systems.

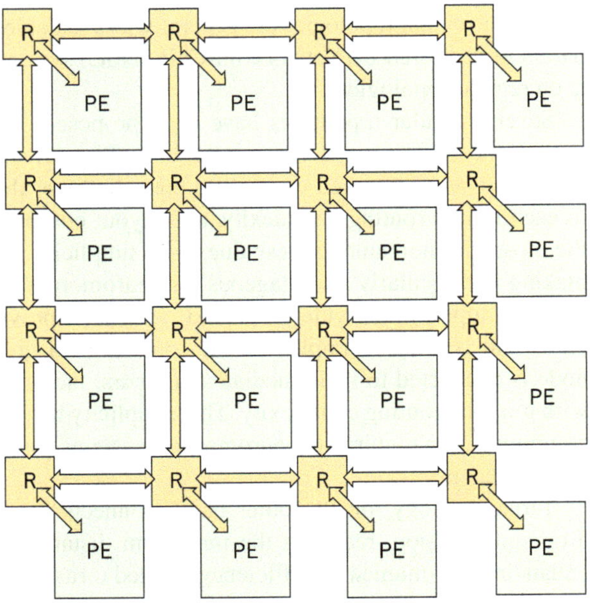

Fig. 5.6 2D Mesh Network-on-Chip (NoC) Topology: This topology organizes processing cores in a two-dimensional grid structure, where each core is connected to its immediate neighbors—north, south, east, and west

Additionally, a multi-chip system can be constructed in neuromorphic applications by extending the NoC across a 2D plane without requiring modifications to the routing scheme.

Communication in a 2D mesh is carried out by transmitting data in flits (flow control units), representing the amount of data a link can send simultaneously. Flits are grouped to form packets, which are transmitted serially. The PE generates the flits via its network interface, travels through the routers using a predefined routing algorithm, and is delivered to the destination PE.

Several routing algorithms have been developed for 2D Mesh topologies, including XY, West-first, North-last, and Negative-first. These are tableless routing algorithms, meaning no routing table is required. Instead, routing is determined by the relationship between the current node, the destination, and the incoming port. Furthermore, adaptive routing algorithms can be employed to manage congestion or faults in the network. Further details on the communication architecture, including switching techniques, packet routing, and quality of service, are discussed in Sect. 5.4.4.

5.4.2.3 3D Mesh Topology

Three-dimensional (3D) stacking technology is an emerging solution that helps sustain the progress of Moore's law, which predicts the doubling of transistors every two years. However, managing cross-layer communication poses a significant

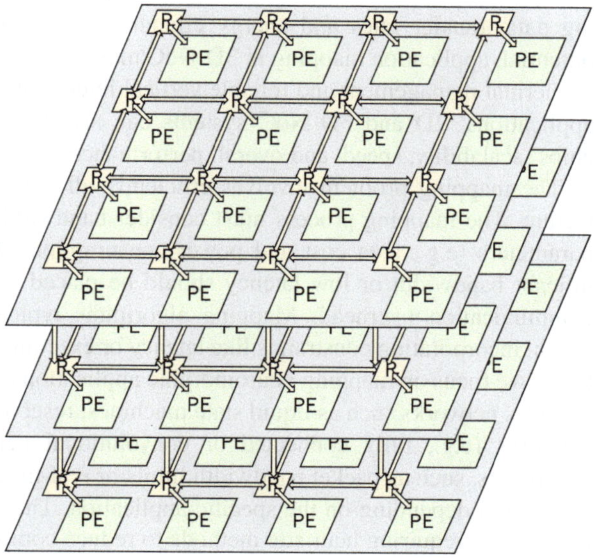

Fig. 5.7 3D Mesh Network-on-Chip (NoC) Topology: This topology organizes processing cores in a three-dimensional grid structure, where each core is connected to its immediate neighbors along three axes—north, south, east, west, as well as up and down

challenge. Expanding the existing 2D Mesh topology into the vertical direction offers a natural and efficient approach to address this issue. Figure 5.7 illustrates the 3D Mesh topology, where each router can connect to up to six neighboring routers and one local processing element (PE). This topology preserves the same ratio of routers to PEs as in the 2D Mesh configuration. The design principles remain similar to those of the 2D Mesh, except for adding a new vertical dimension (Z-direction).

Through-silicon vias (TSVs) are used in stacking 3D integrated circuits (ICs) to enable inter-layer communication. Recent advances in Monolithic 3D ICs now support multiple layers, offering smaller sizes and improved integration. Although the communication architecture in a 3D Mesh can be inherited from a 2D Mesh, routing in this topology must account for the additional Z-direction, which adds complexity to the routing process.

5.4.3 Application Mapping

Application mapping in 2D and 3D Network-on-Chip (NoC) based neuromorphic chips is pivotal for optimizing performance and efficiency. In 2D-NoC architectures, computational and memory elements are arranged on a single plane, necessitating strategies that minimize communication distance and balance workload to avoid hotspots and latency issues. These strategies ensure efficient data transfer, which is crucial for the high-frequency access patterns in neuromorphic systems. On the other hand, 3D-NoC architectures leverage multiple vertical layers, offering enhanced bandwidth and reduced latency through shorter interconnects. This vertical integration facilitates closer proximity between neurons and synapses, improving data transfer rates and energy efficiency. To fully exploit the architecture's potential, application mapping in 3D-NoC must address additional challenges, such as thermal management and reliable vertical interconnects. By effectively mapping applications, 2D and 3D NoC systems can significantly enhance neuromorphic chips' scalability, speed, and overall performance.

The mapping problem involves efficiently allocating tasks to the target architecture. The mapping process must consider bandwidth, latency, and architectural parameters (e.g., area cost and power consumption). Functions that require significant bandwidth or low latency should be placed near each other to minimize communication overhead. Mapping algorithms typically start with a data-flow graph, incorporating constraints like latency or execution time. In the context of this book, we focus on mapping neuromorphic applications to NoC-based systems. This includes networks such as liquid state machines, reservoir computing, or multilayer networks (e.g., fully connected or convolutional neural networks). Additional constraints, such as packet bandwidth limits or real-time requirements, may also be considered depending on the specific application. The mapping problem for NoCs is NP-hard, requiring heuristic methods to reduce complexity, as exhaustive search algorithms are impractical for large systems.

Mapping neuromorphic systems typically consists of two phases: (1) *partitioning* and (2) *placement*. The partitioning phase determines the clusters of nodes within the system. Neuromorphic systems are generally divided into clusters of neurons, each containing a limited number. For example, TrueNorth dedicates 256 neurons per cluster. The partitioning process assigns each neuron to a specific cluster, aiming to group strongly connected or frequently communicated neurons. This strategy minimizes the number of packets that must traverse the NoC. Figure 5.8 illustrates partitioning nine neurons (arranged in a circle) into three clusters. The figure shows

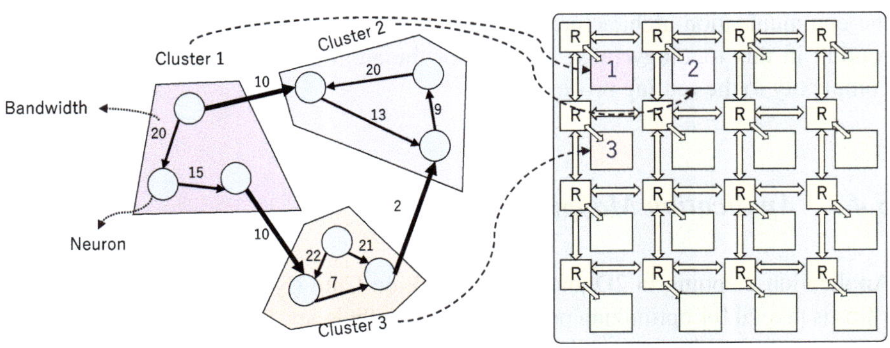

Fig. 5.8 Mapping neuromorphic systems in two phases: *partitioning* and *placing*. The mapping process begins with *partitioning*, where the neural network is divided into manageable subnetworks or clusters to optimize resource use and minimize communication overhead. Following partitioning, *placing* assigns each partitioned sub-network to specific processing cores or hardware units, considering spatial and connectivity constraints to maximize performance and minimize latency

neurons with robust connectivity are placed in the same cluster to reduce network congestion.

Once partitioning is complete, the placement phase maps neuron-to-neuron communication onto node-to-node communication. Each cluster is assigned to a processing element (PE) in the placement process. Figure 5.8 depicts this process, where cluster 1 is placed adjacent to clusters 2 and 3 due to its high communication bandwidth with both. Conversely, clusters 2 and 3 are placed farther apart, as their communication traffic is lower.

The mapping problem can be addressed using Integer Linear Programming (ILP) or other optimization techniques, such as Particle Swarm Optimization [14]. While the method in [14] focuses on optimizing communication costs, the work in [52] optimizes traffic within on-chip network-based neuromorphic systems. In SpiNNaker [25], a linear mapping method is used, where neurons are uniformly distributed across NoC nodes in index order. Although this method is not optimal, it significantly reduces mapping time, making it suitable for large-scale systems. Additionally, [32] presents a technique for mapping deep neural networks onto SpiNNaker.

5.4.4 Neuron Cores Communication Network

The Neuron Cores Communication Network in a neuromorphic chip mimics the brain's neural communication. This network consists of interconnected neuron cores, which handle the computational tasks associated with simulating neuronal activity. Communication between these cores is essential for transmitting information, similar to how neurons in the brain pass signals. Efficient communication protocols ensure that spike timings and synaptic weights are accurately conveyed with minimal latency, maintaining the chip's real-time processing capabilities. Techniques such as Network-on-Chip (NoC) architectures facilitate this communication by providing scalable, high-bandwidth pathways for data transfer. Advanced protocols like Address Event Representation (AER) are often used to encode and transmit neural spikes efficiently. The design and optimization of these communication networks are crucial for enhancing the performance, scalability, and energy efficiency of neuromorphic systems, enabling them to perform complex tasks such as sensory processing, pattern recognition, and decision-making.

This section covers key aspects of the communication architecture, including the switching technique, packet routing, quality of service (QoS), and the design of routers and links.

5.4.4.1 Router Switching Strategies

Router switching strategies for Network-on-Chip (NoC)-based neuromorphic chips are crucial for ensuring efficient communication between neuron cores. These strategies include wormhole switching, which allows partial packets to be forwarded as soon as they arrive, reducing latency and increasing throughput. Virtual channels prevent head-of-line blocking, allowing multiple packets to be in transit simultaneously. Dimension Order Routing (DOR) is a standard algorithm that routes packets based on the destination coordinates, simplifying the routing process. Additionally, multicast routing can handle the one-to-many communication patterns typical in spiking neural networks (SNNs), reducing the communication load and improving performance. These strategies collectively enhance neuromorphic chips' scalability, speed, and energy efficiency, enabling them to perform complex tasks such as sensory processing and pattern recognition more effectively. A comparison of these techniques is presented in Table 5.2. Wormhole switching breaks packets into smaller flits and transmits them in a pipeline, allowing for lower latency and better resource utilization. This is especially beneficial in 3D-NoC architectures with shorter interconnects. Virtual channels enhance wormhole switching by preventing head-of-line blocking through multiple paths, improving throughput, and reducing contention in 2D and 3D layouts. While more straightforward and robust, store-and-forward switching stores the entire packet at each intermediate router. This leads to higher latency and increased buffer requirements, making it less efficient for real-time neuromorphic applications.

On the other hand, circuit switching establishes a dedicated path for the entire communication session, providing guaranteed bandwidth and low latency but at the cost of lower network resource utilization and flexibility. This can be advantageous in scenarios requiring consistent data transfer rates. Wormhole switching with virtual channels is often preferred for neuromorphic chips due to its balanced approach, combining low latency with efficient resource use, especially in more complex 3D-NoC environments.

5.4.4.2 Spiking Packets Routing Methods

An essential aspect of designing a Network-on-Chip (NoC) is determining how to route packets through the network. The network's topology largely influences the

Table 5.2 Comparison of switching techniques

Method	Performance	Buffer size	Design complexity	Flexibility	Transmission latency
Circuit Switching	High for long messages	1 flit	Low	None	Very low
Store-and-Forward	High for short messages	Packet	High	Low	Low
Virtual-Cut-Through	High	Packet	High	Low	Low
Wormhole	High	A few flits	Low	Medium	Low (if not blocked)

routing choice, and in this section, we focus on routing for mesh topologies. Other topologies, such as torus or hypercube, may require different routing strategies.

Packet routing in 2D and 3D electronic and photonic Network-on-Chip (NoC) based neuromorphic chips ensures efficient communication and processing. In 2D electronic NoCs, packet routing involves directing data packets through a mesh or torus topology, balancing the load to minimize latency and energy consumption. As for 3D electronic NoCs, they add a vertical dimension, allowing for more complex and efficient routing strategies that reduce interconnect lengths and enhance bandwidth. Photonic NoCs, both in 2D and 3D, leverage the properties of light to achieve higher data transmission speeds and lower latency compared to their electronic counterparts. In these systems, photonic waveguides replace traditional metal interconnects, enabling ultra-fast communication with minimal heat dissipation. The combination of electronic and photonic routing in 3D NoCs mainly benefits neuromorphic chips by providing scalable, high-bandwidth communication channels that support the high-density interconnectivity and real-time data processing required for simulating neural networks. Overall, advanced packet routing techniques in these architectures significantly enhance neuromorphic systems' performance, energy efficiency, and scalability.

There are three common routing approaches: (1) deterministic routing, (2) adaptive routing, and (3) stochastic routing. Deterministic routing follows predefined paths for packet transmission, ensuring predictability and simplicity in network management. This method is effective for straightforward, low-latency communication but can suffer from congestion and inefficiency in complex, high-load environments. On the other hand, adaptive routing dynamically adjusts paths based on current network conditions, such as congestion and faults. This flexibility allows for better load balancing and resilience, making it suitable for the high-density interconnects in 3D architectures. Stochastic routing introduces randomness in path selection, which can help distribute traffic more evenly and avoid hotspots but may introduce variability in latency. This approach can benefit large-scale neuromorphic networks where uniform traffic distribution is critical. Each routing strategy has its strengths and trade-offs, and the choice of method depends on the specific requirements and constraints of the neuromorphic system in question. These routing techniques enable efficient and reliable communication within 2D and 3D neuromorphic chips, supporting their complex and parallel processing capabilities.

When developing a NoC-based neuromorphic chip, the deadlock problem must be carefully considered during the design phase. The deadlock problem in packet routing for 2D and 3D neuromorphic chips arises when packets get stuck in a cyclic dependency, preventing them from reaching their destination. This issue is more pronounced in 3D-NoC architectures due to the added complexity of vertical interconnects and multiple layers. Deadlocks can severely degrade system performance by causing delays and reducing throughput. Various strategies, such as turn restriction, virtual channels, and deadlock-free routing algorithms, address this. Turn restriction limits packets' directions, reducing the chances of cyclic dependencies. Virtual channels provide multiple paths for packets, preventing them from blocking each other. Deadlock-free routing algorithms, such as the

Prime Perspective Turn Model (PTM-3D), ensure that packets can always find a destination without getting stuck. These techniques are essential for maintaining efficient and reliable communication within neuromorphic chips, enabling them to perform complex tasks effectively.

5.4.4.3 Flow Control

Flow control is a critical component of the communication architecture in neuromorphic chips, responsible for managing the movement of flits (flow control units) between routers and processing elements (PEs). This section shows buffer flow control, explicitly focusing on packet-switching wormhole-based NoCs, which are widely used in neuromorphic systems for their efficiency and performance. These systems employ three primary flow control methods: ACK/NACK, STALL/GO, and CREDIT.

- **ACK/NACK:** This method utilizes a handshaking protocol between two terminals, such as router-router or router-PE. When the sender initiates data transmission, it sends a valid signal to the receiver. If the receiver's buffer is ready to accept and store the data, it responds with an ACK (acknowledgment) signal, allowing the sender to transmit data. If the receiver is unprepared, it sends a NACK (negative acknowledgment) signal, instructing the sender to hold the data until the receiver is ready. This ensures that data is only transmitted when the receiver can handle it, preventing buffer overflow and ensuring reliable communication.
- **STALL/GO:** In this flow control protocol, the receiver notifies the sender of its readiness to receive data. The sender sends a request to the receiver to transmit a flit. Upon receiving this request, the receiver responds with a 'GO' signal when ready to accept the flit, allowing the sender to proceed with the transmission. If the receiver is unprepared, it remains in a 'STALL' state, signaling the sender to wait. This method helps synchronize data transfer and avoid collisions or data loss.
- **CREDIT:** This credit-based flow control method involves the receiver sending information about the status of its input buffer, typically indicating the position of the read pointer. The sender uses this credit information to determine the buffer's availability and adjust the data flow accordingly. This dynamic approach helps efficiently manage buffer resources and prevent overflow, ensuring smooth and continuous data transfer within the network.

5.4.4.4 Quality of Service

Network-on-chip (NoC) architectures must be finely tuned to meet specific application performance requirements. For neuromorphic systems, it is essential to route neural spikes with minimal delay to maintain low execution latency and ensure real-time processing. To achieve this, NoCs can be configured to support various levels of Quality of Service (QoS), such as Best Effort (BE) or Guaranteed Service (GS). Best Effort QoS handles data transmission flexibly without strict delivery guarantees, which is suitable for non-critical spikes. In contrast, Guaranteed Service provides dedicated bandwidth and low-latency routes for critical spike transmissions, ensuring timely delivery and the system's overall performance. By incorporating these QoS levels, neuromorphic chips can effectively balance efficiency and reliability, catering to the dynamic communication needs of neural networks.

- *Best Effort (BE)*: In BE QoS, NoC does not reserve resources for specific packets, meaning transmission time is not guaranteed. While packets are routed with the best effort, they might experience delays, and in some cases, packets may even be dropped if network congestion occurs.
- *Guaranteed Service (GS)*: This approach ensures the timely delivery of packets by pre-allocating resources. Techniques such as packet-switching combined with Time-Division Multiple Access (TDMA) or pure circuit switching can guarantee both the transmission time and successful delivery of packets. This method is beneficial for real-time applications where deadlines must be met.

5.4.4.5 Router Design

The design of a generic router is fundamental to the Network-on-Chip (NoC) architecture. The router's efficiency and performance are closely tied to several NoC parameters, such as the selected topology, flow control methods, and switching techniques. A well-designed router ensures efficient packet routing and seamless communication between processing elements (PEs) within the neuromorphic network. Generally, a router in a NoC architecture for neuromorphic systems is responsible for directing packets between interconnected nodes based on specific routing algorithms. The typical components of such a router include:

- **Input Buffers:** Temporary storage for incoming packets to manage congestion and ensure smooth data flow.
- **Switching Fabric:** The internal mechanism that connects input ports to the appropriate output ports facilitates the transfer of packets.
- **Routing Logic:** The decision-making unit that determines the optimal path for packets based on the routing algorithm.
- **Output Buffers:** Storage for outgoing packets before they are forwarded to the next node, helping to manage timing and synchronization.
- **Flow Control Mechanism**: This ensures that the sender does not overwhelm the receiver with too much data, maintaining an efficient data transfer rate.

By effectively integrating these components, the router ensures that data is efficiently routed across the neuromorphic chip, maintaining the system's overall performance, minimizing latency, and optimizing energy consumption. The design and implementation of these routers are critical for supporting the complex and high-speed communication needs inherent in neuromorphic computing. Several vital parameters for routers are critical in designing neuromorphic chips to ensure efficient communication and performance. Firstly, the network topology and specific location determine the number of ports in a router. For example, a router in a 2D-Mesh topology typically has five ports, whereas a 3D-mesh router features seven ports. In a 2D-Mesh, routers at the borders and corners have fewer ports—four and three, respectively. Another essential parameter is the phit size, which refers to the primary data transmission unit in NoCs. The phit size usually remains consistent across all ports, corresponding to the number of parallel wires in a router link. In a 3D-Mesh topology, inter-layer links might utilize time-division multiplexing (TDM), reducing the number of wires used compared to typical links.

The buffer design is also crucial for effective router operation. This includes the placement, size, and queuing method of the buffers. For instance, a typical setup may involve a FIFO (First In, First Out) 4-flit input buffer but no output buffer, as explored in the case study in the following section. These design choices significantly impact the router's ability to manage data flow and maintain efficient communication within the neuromorphic chip.

Figure 5.9 illustrates the generic architecture of a router with multiple input and output ports. Each input port consists of an input buffer and a routing unit. The

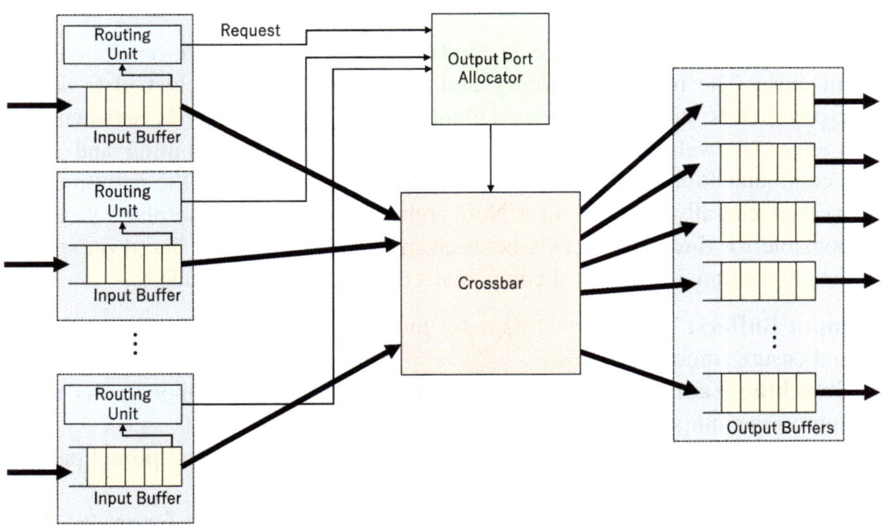

Fig. 5.9 Generic architecture of a Network-on-Chip (NoC) router: This diagram depicts the key components of a NoC router, including input and output ports, a crossbar switch for routing data packets, and a routing unit responsible for determining the output port direction. The operational process involves buffering incoming data, extracting routing information, identifying the destination output port, requesting routing via the crossbar, transmitting the flit to the designated output port, and transferring the data from the output port to the adjacent unit's input port

routing unit uses a routing algorithm to determine the direction of the incoming packet. Afterward, the routing unit sends a request signal to the output port allocator. This module decides which input port is granted access to the crossbar. If access is granted, the packet (or flit) is forwarded through the crossbar to the appropriate output port. Flits are then stored in the output buffer at the output port and transmitted to the next router or the attached processing element (PE).

The *Input Port* typically consists of two main modules: the input buffer and the routing unit (see Fig. 5.10). The input buffer can be implemented using SRAM or standard registers. It may support multiple virtual channels, each capable of storing several flits. The routing unit's responsibility is to select the appropriate channel when various channels are available. Once the channel is selected, the packet routing information is loaded, and the routing unit determines the output port based on the routing algorithm.

The *Output Port Allocator* receives requests from the input ports and decides which input port is granted access to the crossbar. If there are no conflicts (i.e., if each input port requests a different output port), all input ports are granted access. In the case of conflicts, one of the following scheduling policies is applied:

- *Round-robin:* Each input port is assigned a slot in a ring counter token. If no other input port has made a request before, the requesting input port is granted access. If multiple input ports request the same output port, the round-robin policy grants

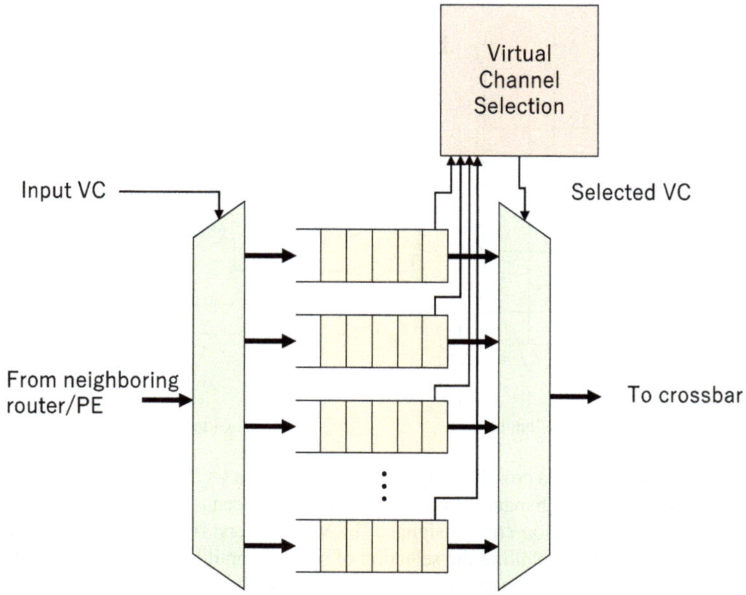

Fig. 5.10 Input buffer architecture with virtual channels: This diagram illustrates the structure of an input buffer designed to support multiple virtual channels within a Network-on-Chip (NoC). The architecture includes separate buffers for each virtual channel and control logic for managing packet arbitration and routing decisions

access to the next input port in the cycle. This policy ensures that each input port periodically receives the highest priority.

- *LRU (Least Recently Used):* This method assigns higher priority to input ports that have not been granted access for the longest time. Once an input port is granted access, its priority drops to the lowest, gradually increasing as time passes without access.
- *Fixed Priority:* Each input port is assigned a fixed priority level. Although easy to implement, this method can lead to unbalanced priority allocation, potentially causing some paths always to be granted access first.

Once an input port has been granted access, it can send the flit to the crossbar or switch fabric, as shown in Fig. 5.11. Two primary crossbar design methods exist (1) pass transistors and (2) multiplexers.

- *Pass Transistors:* In this design, the crossbar is realized through pass transistors, where each transistor shortens the connection from an input to an output port when the connection is granted. The pass transistor acts as a physical switch that establishes the route for the flit.
- *Multiplexers:* In this design, a multiplexer is assigned to each output port, selecting one input signal to drive the corresponding output. The multiplexer allows the output port to choose which input port's flit to forward, providing flexibility in the routing process.

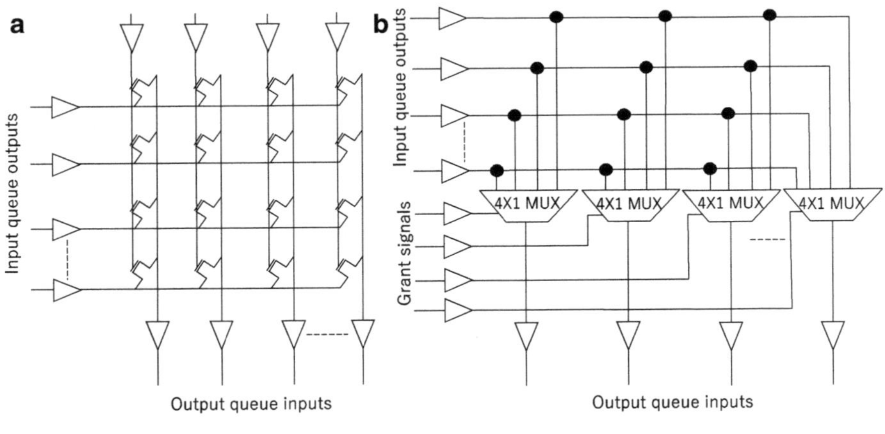

Fig. 5.11 The architecture of a crossbar: (**a**) Pass transistors: this section depicts pass transistors in the crossbar architecture, which manages data transmission between inputs and outputs by allowing signals to pass through based on control signals. (**b**) Multiplexers: this part illustrates the role of multiplexers in the crossbar, enabling the selection of specific input lines for routing to the output lines, thus providing flexible data paths and efficient resource allocation within the network

5.4.4.6 Link Design

In the design of neuromorphic chips, the link between two routers or between a router and a processing element (PE) consists of wires, and several critical design issues must be considered. Wire delay is a primary concern due to the potentially large distances between routers or PEs. Significant wire delay can violate timing constraints, so CAD tools often automatically insert buffers or inverters to maintain signal integrity. If the delay is substantial, inserting registers between the routers can help mitigate the issue, though this may require adjustments in the flow control mechanisms.

Vertical links in 3D-NoCs may be implemented using through-silicon vias (TSVs) or interlayer via Monolithic 3D. Since TSVs are not fully supported by current CAD tools, their placement requires careful planning. Moreover, thermal variations in TSVs can introduce stress on other devices, necessitating the creation of keep-out zones around TSVs to prevent damage to adjacent components. These considerations are crucial for ensuring reliable and efficient communication within the neuromorphic chip.

5.5 Advanced Interconnects for Neuromorphic Systems

Advanced interconnects for neuromorphic systems are crucial for efficiently mimicking the complex communication mechanisms of the human brain. Neuromorphic systems, which aim to replicate the brain's neural architecture, require high-bandwidth and low-latency communication networks to handle the massive data exchange between neurons. Advanced interconnect technologies, such as Network-on-Chip (NoC) and 3D-Integrated Circuits (3D-ICs), play a pivotal role in achieving this. These interconnects enable shorter wire lengths, reduced power consumption, and improved performance, which are essential for the scalability and efficiency of neuromorphic systems. By leveraging these advanced interconnects, neuromorphic systems can better simulate the brain's functionality, leading to more powerful and efficient computing solutions for tasks like machine learning and artificial intelligence.

Studies have shown that 3D-ICs can achieve higher packing density by adding a third dimension to the traditional 2D layout. With reduced average interconnect lengths, 3D-ICs offer improved performance, lower interconnect power consumption, and greater noise immunity [30, 50]. Furthermore, reducing total wiring provides the potential for continued performance improvements using CMOS technology, leading to smaller form factors, higher integration densities, and support for mixed-technology chips [17]. As noted by Topol [50], 3D-ICs can enhance performance even without further scaling.

The 3D NoC architecture is expected to meet the scaling requirements of future multicore and many-core SoCs by utilizing short vertical connections between adjacent layers, significantly boosting system performance.

An efficient router is critical in designing a 3D-NoC, as it forms the backbone of any NoC architecture. Traffic patterns, pipeline design, and network topology influence a router's performance. As Feihui [38] notes, we have less control over traffic patterns than topology and pipeline design. Optimizing the pipeline design is critical to improving router performance, given a fixed topology. By reducing pipeline delay through pipelining optimization, per-hop delay and overall network latency can be minimized.

The pipeline design is closely tied to the routing algorithm used. Routing determines the path a flit takes from source to destination. Minimal routing schemes are more straightforward and require less hardware, while non-minimal routing offers greater path diversity and helps reduce network congestion. Routing algorithms can be adaptive, making decisions based on network congestion and other factors, or deterministic.

Adaptive routing algorithms are sophisticated but require more hardware and complex to implement. Consequently, deterministic routing schemes are often preferred for 3D-NoCs. The Dimension Order Routing (DOR) XYZ algorithm is widely used in 3D-NoCs for its simplicity and freedom from deadlock and live lock. However, it suffers from inefficient pipeline stage usage, leading to additional packet latency and decreased system performance. Improving this algorithm while maintaining simplicity can reduce packet delay and enhance overall system performance.

5.5.1 Three-Dimension Network-on-Chip

Over the past few decades, the number of transistors on a chip has steadily increased, allowing for the reduction in chip size while maintaining high performance. This technology scaling has enabled Systems-on-Chip (SoCs) to grow in component count and complexity, leading to significant challenges such as power dissipation and resource management. Moving to deep submicron technologies, where the features of the transistors are smaller than 100 nm, introduces substantial design and manufacturing challenges. These challenges include increased leakage currents, variability, and difficulties in fabrication. Consequently, 3D integration is an attractive solution for meeting power and performance requirements [34]. By stacking multiple layers of dies or wafers, 3D-ICs can significantly reduce wire lengths, which enhances performance and reduces power consumption. This method mitigates some of the issues in 2D integration and improves overall efficiency.

In neuromorphic systems, which aim to mimic the neural architecture of the human brain, the on-chip interconnection network plays a crucial role in determining the performance and power consumption of the entire chip. Efficiently designed interconnections are essential for achieving the desired power and performance metrics, making 3D integration a critical approach in modern neuromorphic systems design [34].

5.5.1.1 3D-NoC Versus 2D-NoC in Neuromorphic Systems

When comparing 3D Network-on-Chip (3D-NoC) to 2D Network-on-Chip (2D-NoC) in neuromorphic systems, 3D-NoC offers several advantages over its 2D counterpart. By stacking multiple layers of dies, 3D-NoC significantly reduces wire lengths, which leads to improved performance due to faster signal transmission and lower latency. Additionally, 3D-NoC can reduce power consumption as shorter interconnects require less energy. This is crucial for neuromorphic systems that need efficient communication between numerous processing elements to mimic the human brain's neural architecture. However, while 3D-NoC provides better scalability and higher bandwidth, it also presents challenges in heat dissipation, as the stacked layers can lead to thermal management issues. Despite these challenges, the enhanced performance and power efficiency make 3D-NoC a promising approach for advanced neuromorphic systems compared to traditional 2D-NoC designs.

The 3D-NoC has been extensively studied, with numerous works highlighting its advantages over traditional 2D-NoC designs. Feero [23] demonstrated that 3D-NoC can reduce latency and energy per packet by 40%, primarily due to the reduction in the number of hops, a critical factor in evaluating system performance. Pavlidis [43] examined zero-load latency and power consumption, showing that 3D-NoC could achieve a 62% reduction in latency and a 58% decrease in power consumption compared to 2D-NoC for network sizes of $N = 128$ and $N = 256$ nodes. These improvements are primarily attributed to the reduced hop count, which lowers buffer access, switch arbitration, and link traversal, reducing power consumption.

Some previous works have focused on router architecture. Li [37] introduced a hybrid 3D NoC-Bus router by modifying the conventional 7×7 3D router, incorporating a shared bus for inter-layer communication. This design reduces the ports in each router from 7 to 6. However, flits must compete to access the shared bus, which could degrade performance under heavy inter-layer traffic. Yan [56] proposed another 3D router architecture by incorporating all vertical links into a single 3D crossbar, reducing inter-layer distance and enabling single-hop travel between layers. Although this design reduces the number of ports to five and minimizes inter-layer distance, its high implementation complexity and cost may make it unsuitable for more straightforward applications.

Given these considerations, we adopted the conventional 7×7 3D router, which best balances cost, simplicity, and performance. This design provides regularity, concurrent data transmission, and controlled electrical parameters without compromising performance [27, 29].

5.5.1.2 Routing Algorithms

The routing algorithm significantly impacts the design and efficiency of a Network-on-Chip (NoC) based neuromorphic chip by determining how data packets navigate the intricate network of interconnected neurons. An effective routing algorithm minimizes latency and maximizes throughput, ensuring that signals between neurons are transmitted swiftly and reliably. This is critical for the real-time processing needs of neuromorphic systems. Additionally, optimizing the routing path reduces the number of hops and shortens distances, lowering power consumption—a crucial factor given the power constraints of neuromorphic chips. Moreover, scalable routing algorithms are essential for accommodating neural networks' increasing complexity and size, allowing the NoC to manage more nodes without compromising performance. The routing algorithm is a cornerstone of NoC-based neuromorphic chip design, influencing performance, power efficiency, scalability, and thermal regulation.

Routing algorithms for multicore System-on-Chip (MCSoC) systems have primarily focused on 2D network topologies. However, fewer studies have addressed routing algorithms for 3D-NoC. Ramanujam [47] introduced an oblivious routing algorithm called Randomized Partially Minimal (RPM), designed to balance the load and improve worst-case performance. RPM randomly assigns packets to layers, routes them along the X and Y dimensions using XY or YX routing, and sends them along the Z dimension to the destination.

Chao [19] proposed a thermal-aware downward routing scheme to address thermal power issues in 3D-NoC designs. This method routes traffic to lower layers, along the X and Y dimensions, and finally to the destination layer. By avoiding higher layers with critical thermal power, this approach ensures thermal safety with minimal impact on performance.

While both RPM and Chao's algorithms provide load balancing and reduce thermal power, they are non-minimal routing schemes, which increase the number of hops and may delay packets, particularly in large networks. Most 3D-NoC systems employ the minimal Dimension Order Routing (DOR) XYZ algorithm to ensure minimal path traversal, simplicity, and freedom from deadlock and livelock [19, 22, 36]. However, the XYZ algorithm's switch allocation (SA) stage depends on the previous routing calculation (RC) stage, leading to inefficient pipeline stage usage and potential packet delays.

Techniques like look-ahead routing can address these issues. Look-ahead routing reduces pipeline stages by parallelizing them, decreasing router delay, and enhancing overall system performance. Although commonly used in 2D-NoC systems, look-ahead routing has not been widely adopted in 3D-NoC architectures.

Conventional routers using XYZ-based routing schemes also suffer from no-load traffic problems, where flits are unnecessarily stalled in input buffers even when downstream stages are idle. This unnecessary stalling increases packet latency and power consumption, degrading system performance. The no-load bypass technique [54] addresses this by allowing flits to bypass empty buffer stages, reducing router delays.

In [1, 2, 5], the design and performance of the 3D-ONoC were evaluated using a simple application that randomly generated and transmitted flits. However, the absence of specific components prevented the evaluation of real applications. To enable real-world application testing, such as JPEG encoding and matrix multiplication, a network interface was added to the optimized version of 3D-ONoC.

5.5.1.3 3D-NoC Router Architecture Design

The router serves as the central component in the overall 3D-ONoC architecture. Based on the 5 × 5 2D-ONoC router design, each switch in the 3D-ONoC router is configured with a maximum of 7 input ports and seven output ports. Four ports are dedicated to connections with neighboring routers in the north, east, south, and west directions via intra-layer links. An additional port links the router to the local computation tile, enabling packet injection and ejection within the network. The remaining two ports are allocated for inter-layer communication, connecting the router to the upper and lower layers.

As previously mentioned, the number of active ports depends on the router's placement within the design. To reduce power consumption, unused links not connecting to other routers are eliminated.

Figure 5.12 illustrates the architecture of the 3D-ONoC router, highlighting the three primary pipeline stages that define the routing process at each router: Buffer Writing (BW), Routing Calculation and Switch Allocation (RC/SA), and Crossbar Traversal (CT).

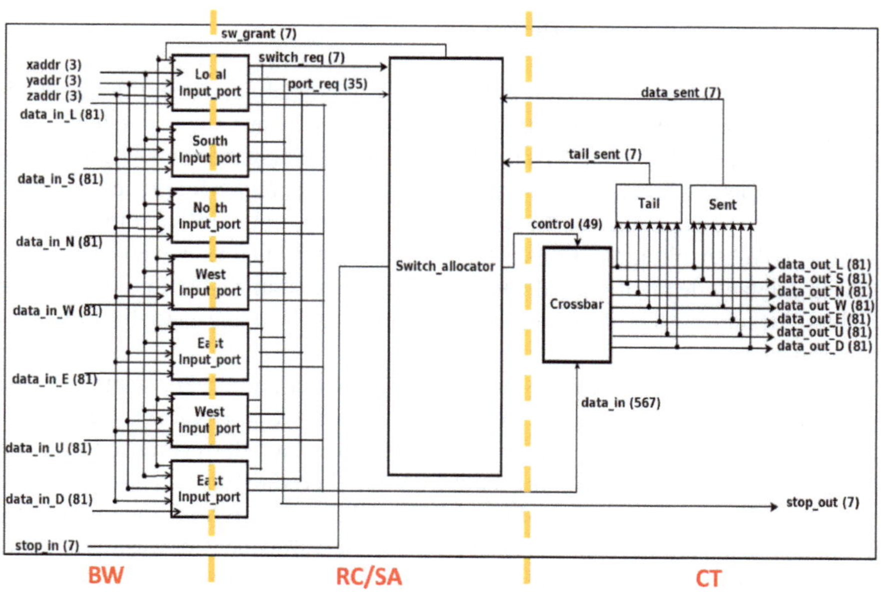

Fig. 5.12 3D-ONoC pipeline stages: This diagram illustrates the key stages in the 3D Network-on-Chip (3D-ONoC) architecture, including (1) Buffer Writing (BW), where incoming data packets are stored in the buffer for processing; (2) Routing Calculation and Switch Allocation (RC/SA): where the optimal routing paths are determined and switch resources are allocated for data transmission; and (3) Crossbar Traversal (CT): the final stage in which packets are routed through the crossbar switch to their designated output ports

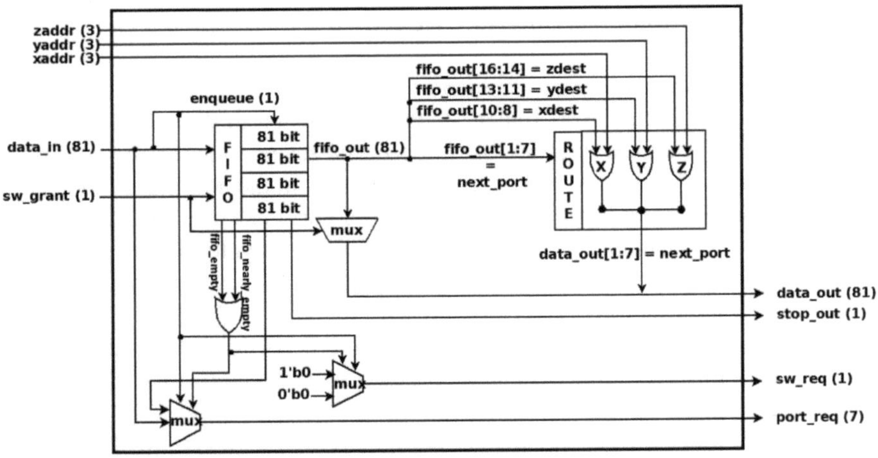

Fig. 5.13 Input port module architecture: The module includes features such as input buffers for temporarily storing incoming data, a route unit for managing data flow and arbitration, and a routing unit that determines the appropriate output port

5.5.1.4 Input Port Module Design

The *Input port* module, depicted in Fig. 5.13, is a crucial component in the router design. The seven input ports have two main components: the *Input buffer* and the *Route* module. Incoming 81-bit flits (*data-in*) from neighboring switches or the connected computation tile is initially stored in the *Input buffer* for processing. This stage marks the beginning of the flit's lifecycle in the router, referred to as Buffer Writing (BW). Arbitration of flits is managed using a FIFO queue, with each buffer having a default depth of four, allowing it to hold up to four 81-bit flits. While input buffers consume a significant router area, they contribute substantially to overall performance.

Once stored, a flit is retrieved from the FIFO buffer and progresses to the next pipeline stage, Routing Calculation and Switch Allocation (RC/SA). Destination addresses (*xdest*, *ydest*, and *zdest*) are decoded to extract destination information along with the pre-calculated *Next-Port* from the preceding upstream node. These values are then forwarded to the *Route* circuit, where the LA-XYZ routing scheme is applied to determine the *New-next-Port* for the subsequent downstream node. Simultaneously, the *Next-Port* identifier triggers a request to the *Switch-Allocator* for a grant to utilize the selected output port via the *sw-req* and *port-req* signals.

As previously mentioned, the 3D-ONoC employs a look-ahead routing scheme (*LA-XYZ*) to expedite routing. This scheme builds upon the dimension-ordered (DOR) X-Y-Z static routing algorithm, ensuring sequential satisfaction of X, Y, and Z coordinates. The simplicity, lack of deadlock, and absence of live lock make X-Y-Z routing ideal for 3D-NoC systems, offering vertically balanced routing and optimal performance. Each flit includes a one-hot encoded *Next-Port* identifier downstream routers use. Because *LA-XYZ* is based on XYZ routing, it operates as a minimal routing algorithm, ensuring that each flit traverses the minimal number of hops between source and destination.

5.5.1.5 Switch Allocator Design

The *sw-req* and *port-req* signals originate from each *Input port* module, transmitting desired output port information to the *Switch-Allocator* for arbitration. When multiple input flits from different ports simultaneously request the same output port, the *Switch-Allocator* decides which input port should be granted access and when. This process runs concurrently with routing computation in the *Input port*, forming the second pipeline stage.

As shown in Fig. 5.14, the *Switch-Allocator* generates two output signals: *sw-cntrl* and *grant-out*. The *sw-cntrl* signal provides the scheduling information the crossbar circuit needs, which is discussed below. The *grant-out* signal returns to the *Input port* to grant access to the selected input port for data transmission through the crossbar toward the next downstream node. The *Switch-Allocator* module is composed of two main components: *Stall-Go flow control* and *Matrix-Arbiter Scheduling*.

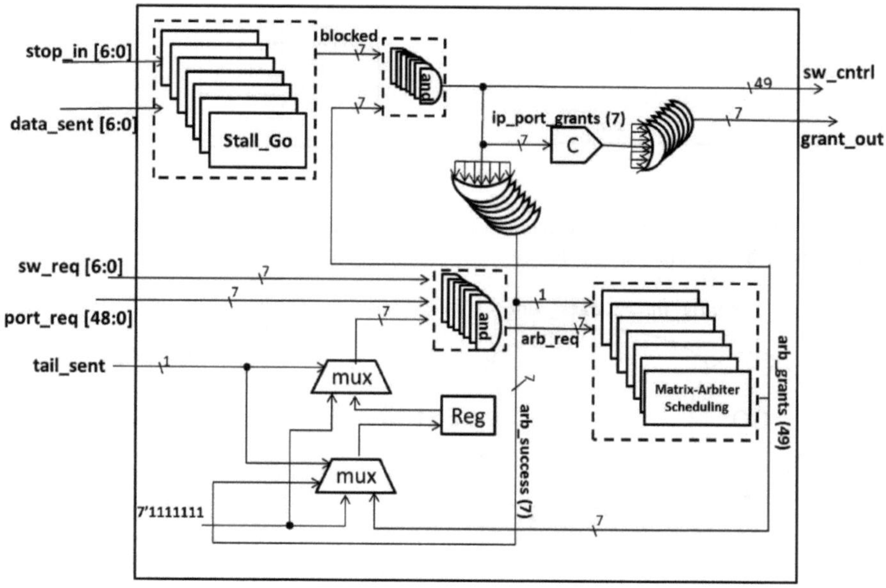

Fig. 5.14 Switch allocator architecture: This diagram illustrates the components and functionality of a switch allocator within a Network-on-Chip (NoC) system. The switch allocator employs stall-go and matrix-arbiter scheduling techniques to manage access to the crossbar switch. Stall-go scheduling dynamically handles input requests by stalling lower-priority requests, while matrix arbitration allocates output ports efficiently, resolving simultaneous requests

5.5.1.6 Stall-Go Flow Control Architecture

Like other flow control mechanisms, the *Stall-Go* module prevents buffer overflow by managing situations where the buffer may exceed its capacity. When the number of flits waiting to be processed surpasses the buffer's capacity, an efficient flow control scheme becomes crucial to avoid overflow and packet loss. The *Stall-Go* flow control was chosen for its efficiency and low overhead, outperforming other schemes such as *ACK-NACK* or *Credit-based* flow control.

The *Stall-Go* module, as shown in Fig. 5.15, operates with two primary control signals: *nearly-full* and *data-sent*. When the input buffer is almost full, the *nearly-full* signal is sent to the upstream node, leaving space for only one additional flit. When receiving this signal, the *FIFO* buffers stop sending flits. The *data-sent* signal indicates that a flit has been successfully transmitted.

Figure 5.16 illustrates the *Stall-Go* flow control state machine, which generates the *nearly-full* and *data-sent* signals. The *GO* state indicates that the buffer can

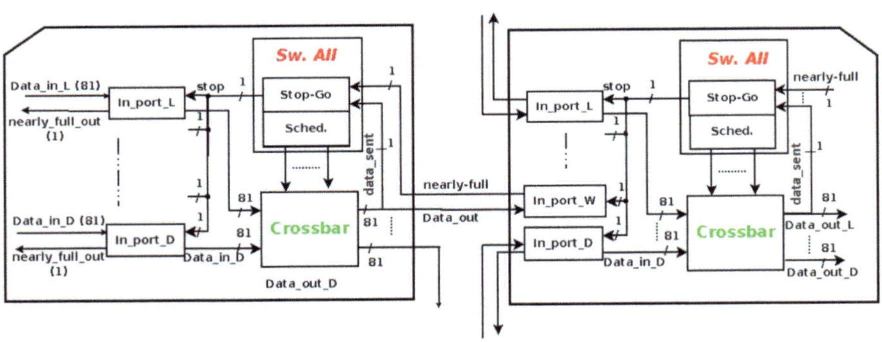

Fig. 5.15 Stall-Go flow control mechanism: Data packets can proceed only when the output port is available; otherwise, they are stalled until resources are free

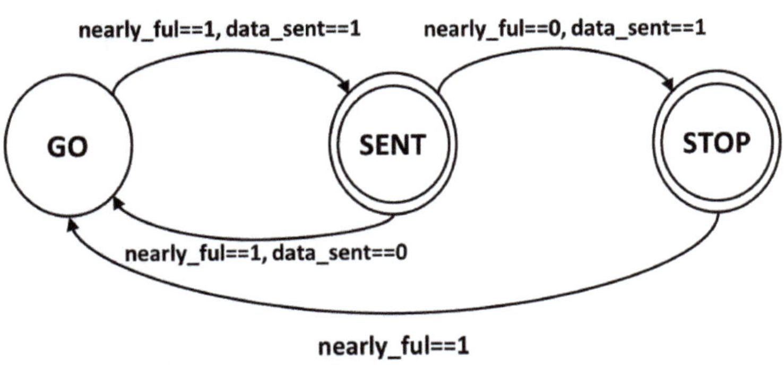

Fig. 5.16 Stall-Go flow control finite state machine: The FSM manages the states of data packets, transitioning between waiting (stop), active (go), and completed (sent) conditions based on the availability of output ports

accommodate two or more flits, while the *SENT* state shows that only one flit can be stored. The *STOP* state signifies that no additional flits can be stored in the buffer.

5.5.1.7 Matrix-Arbiter Scheduling Architecture

The second key component is the scheduling module, depicted in Fig. 5.17. It manages input signals such as *sw-req* and *port-req*, which indicate the input ports requesting access and the output ports they are targeting, respectively. When multiple input ports compete for the same output port, a scheduling scheme is necessary to resolve potential conflicts, as 3D-ONoC allows only one flit transmission per clock cycle.

The switch allocator in this design uses a least recently served (LRS) priority scheme implemented by the matrix arbiter. This ensures that each communication is handled with a partially fixed transmission latency [24, 28].

A 6 × 6 scheduling matrix is used to implement matrix arbiter scheduling in 3D-ONoC. This module collects and prioritizes requests from input ports and their corresponding output ports. Priority assignment determines which input port gains access to the output port. The scheduling module compares priorities in the matrix, ensuring the highest priority request is granted access. When no requests are pending, the priority remains unchanged, guaranteeing fair access to output ports for all input ports.

Figure 5.17 provides an example of the scheduling mechanism. Each row of the matrix represents input port requests and their priorities. The scheduling module evaluates the priority of each request. After serving the highest priority input port, the arbiter shifts the row and column of the granted input port to the lowest priority for the subsequent arbitration round.

In Fig. 5.17a, the *North*, *Up*, and *Down* input ports are requesting grants to transmit their flits to the *Local* port. The *North* request (highlighted in red) has the highest priority, so the arbiter grants it. Afterward, *North* is marked as the lowest priority (green underline), and the priorities of the remaining requests are incremented.

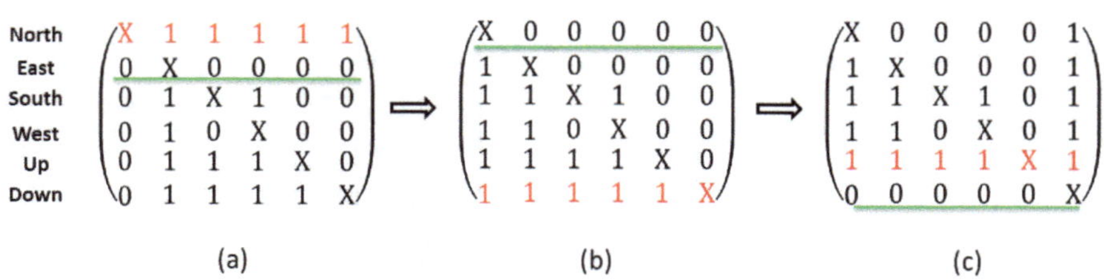

Fig. 5.17 Scheduling-matrix priority assignment: This diagram illustrates the three-phase priority assignment process in a scheduling matrix for data transmission. In phase (**a**), the initial priority is assigned, with North as the highest priority. After North transmits its data, phase (**b**) begins, where North's priority is lowered, and DOWN becomes the highest priority. In phase (**c**), DOWN transmits its flit, and its priority is demoted, allowing North to regain higher priority status. This dynamic priority reassignment ensures fair and efficient data transmission

In the next round (Fig. 5.17b), the *Down* request gains higher priority than the *Up* request. The arbiter grants the *Down* request and demotes its priority. Finally, in Fig. 5.17c, the *Up* request is granted transmission, as it holds the highest priority among the remaining requests.

5.5.1.8 Crossbar Design

The switch allocator sends the generated *control* signal to the crossbar circuit to initiate the third and final Crossbar Traversal pipeline stage (CT). This stage embeds information regarding the selected input port and the *Next-Port*, which is then stored in the *sw-cntrl-reg* register, as shown in Fig. 5.18.

The crossbar retrieves this information, fetches the data from the FIFO buffer of the selected input port, and allocates the appropriate channel for transmission to the decoded *Next-Port*. Finally, the crossbar directs the flit to its destination.

Once all flits are transmitted, the *tail* bit signals the switch allocator via the *tail-sent* signal, indicating the completion of packet transmission and allowing the channel to be released for subsequent packets.

5.5.1.9 Network Interface Architecture

To enable the execution of real applications on the 3D-ONoC system, a Network Interface (NI) was integrated into each router, acting as an intermediary between various Processing Elements (PEs), including cores, memory, and I/O. The system's performance was evaluated using a JPEG encoder application [48].

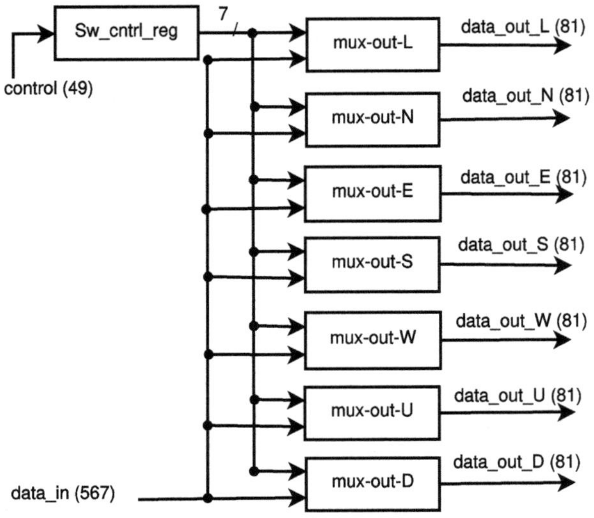

Fig. 5.18 Crossbar circuit: A switch for routing data packets between multiple input and output ports. The control signal arrives at the crossbar controller and is delivered to multiplexers. Based on the control signals, each multiplexer routes the flits from input ports to the correct output ports

The *Transmitter* and *Receiver* NI modules within each switch were explicitly designed to handle this task. The packets were standardized to 99 bits, composed of three 33-bit flits. Each flit includes 17 bits dedicated to routing information (*xdst*, *ydst*, *zdst*, *Next-Port*, and *tail*), with the remaining 16 bits allocated for the payload.

Figure 5.19 illustrates the architecture of the *Transmitter-NI*, while Fig. 5.20 depicts the architecture of the *Receiver-NI*.

The NI module receives 32 bits of data from the JPEG module, which is split into two parts to form the payload for the first two flits of the packet. The third flit's payload carries a 10-bit control signal from the JPEG module, with the remaining six bits left unused.

As shown in Fig. 5.19, the *Control Module* within the *Transmitter-NI* manages the generation of flits. It appends destination addresses and the *Next-Port* direction to each flit and marks the end of the packet by setting the *tail* bit in the third flit. These flits are then injected into the network. On the other hand, the *Receiver-NI* (Fig. 5.20) receives the three incoming flits of each packet, ejected from the network, and stores them in temporary registers. The 16-bit payloads from the first

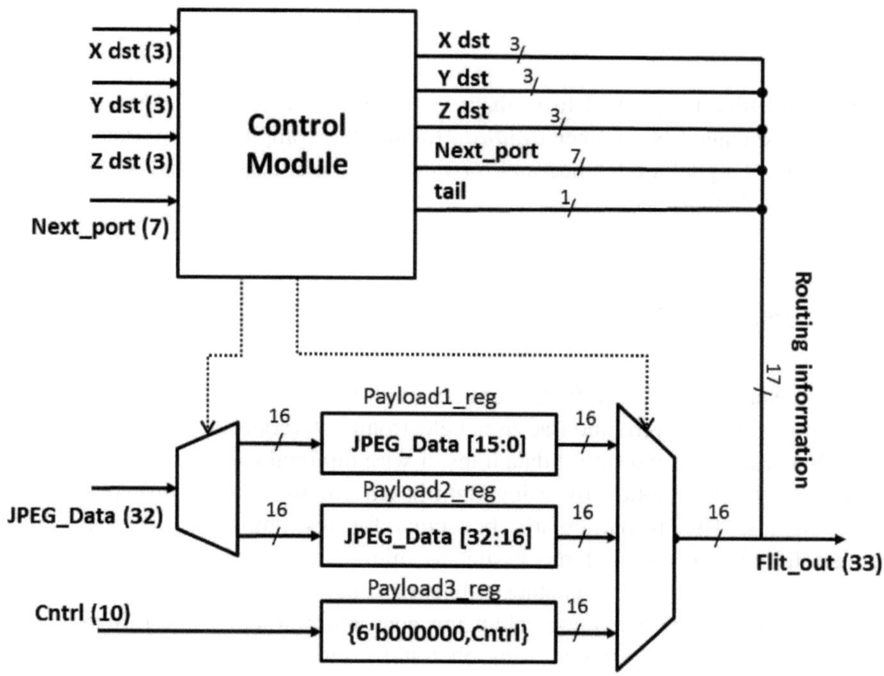

Fig. 5.19 Network Interface Architecture: Transmitter side. This diagram illustrates the transmitter side of a Network Interface for 3D Network-on-Chip (NoC) systems. The architecture includes a control module that utilizes X, Y, and Z coordinates for addressing within the 3D NoC, along with a buffer to store outgoing data. Once the routing information and data are ready, they are merged into a single output flit. This approach optimizes data transmission by consolidating both destination and payload into a single unit, enhancing communication efficiency across the NoC

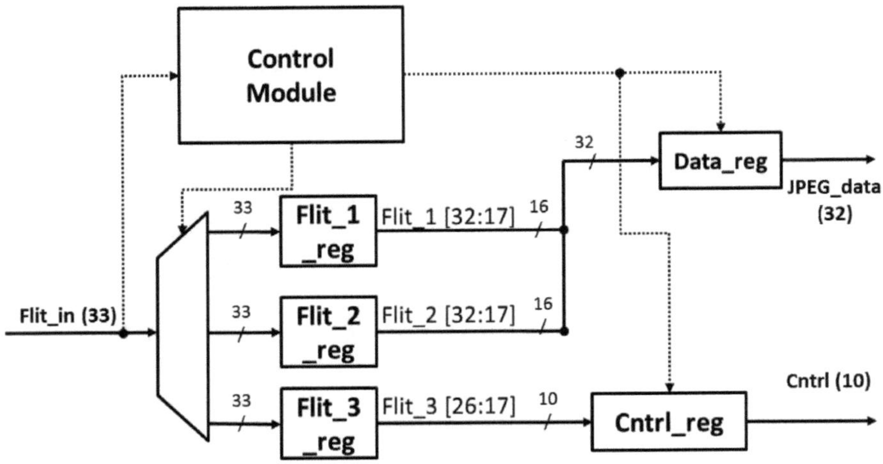

Fig. 5.20 Network Interface Architecture: Receiver side. This diagram illustrates the receiver side of the Network Interface in a Network-on-Chip (NoC) system. It includes a control module that directs incoming data to the appropriate destination buffer based on routing information. By organizing data into the correct buffer, the control module ensures efficient handling of packets

and second flits are fetched from these registers, reassembled, and stored in the *Data-reg*. Managed by another *Control Module*, the complete 32-bit data and the 10-bit control signal are fetched and forwarded to the attached JPEG module once the entire packet has been received.

5.5.2 *Photonic Network-on-Chip*

Photonic Network-on-Chip (NoC) for neuromorphic system design leverages photonics principles to overcome traditional electronic interconnects' limitations. Photonic NoC can achieve ultrafast data transfer with minimal latency and significantly lower power consumption by using light-based communication instead of electrical signals. This is particularly beneficial for neuromorphic systems, which require high-speed, parallel processing to mimic the neural architecture of the human brain. Photonic NoC enables efficient and scalable communication between numerous processing elements, enhancing neuromorphic chips' performance and energy efficiency. Additionally, using photonic components such as lasers, optical interconnects, and frequency microcombs allows for advanced functionalities like adaptive learning and real-time data processing, making Photonic NoC a promising solution for next-generation neuromorphic computing.

Photonic Network-on-Chip (PNoC) [3, 6–9] is a groundbreaking concept that enables ultra-high communication throughput in the terabit-per-second range while maintaining low power consumption and minimal communication latency. Using wavelength division multiplexing (WDM), multiple parallel optical data streams are transmitted simultaneously through a single on-chip waveguide. This contrasts with Electronic Networks-on-Chip (ENoC), which requires a dedicated metal wire for each bitstream.

A distinctive feature of PNoC systems is their ability to transmit optical data end-to-end once a photonic path is established without buffering, repetition, or regeneration. This contrasts ENoCs, where messages are often buffered and regenerated multiple times across inter-router links. Furthermore, photonic routers only switch once per message, regardless of bit rate, leading to energy-efficient transmission and high bandwidth without the power overhead typical of traditional ENoCs.

In a hybrid PNoC configuration, a source node initiates a path configuration packet via a copper-based electrical link containing destination address and control information. This packet is routed through an Electric Control Network (ECN), which reserves photonic switches and channels along the path for the photonic message. After the photonic path is reserved, the source node receives an Acknowledgment (ACK) signal, indicating the start of optical data transmission. Once the transmission is completed, the reserved photonic resources are released.

The circuit-switched nature of hybrid PNoCs significantly influences on-chip communication performance and power efficiency. Research suggests that the energy overhead in hybrid PNoC systems is primarily attributed to the electronic control modules, which consume a significant portion of the overall power budget. Moreover, the latency associated with photonic path configuration is considerably higher than that of photonic data transfer.

While single-layer configurations provide low-loss waveguides and high-performance photonic devices, they are limited by low integration density due to waveguide crossings and space constraints. Multilayered photonic configurations above silicon have been proposed to address these limitations, similar to multilayered electrical interconnects in modern electronic circuits [4, 57].

Fault tolerance is critical for mission-critical applications where system reliability is essential, such as space travel. Repair or replacement is not feasible; failure can result in significant financial losses.

5.5.2.1 Photonic Communication Building Blocks

In neuromorphic system design, the photonic communication building blocks should include photonic integrated circuits (PICs), lasers, optical interconnects, and frequency microcombs. These components enable high-speed, low-latency data transfer, which is essential for mimicking the neural architecture of the human brain. PICs facilitate efficient communication between processing elements, while lasers and optical interconnects provide the means for transmitting data using light. Frequency microcombs offer precise control over optical frequencies, enhancing the system's ability to perform complex computations. These photonic building blocks create a scalable and energy-efficient communication network crucial for advanced neuromorphic computing.

The core components of a photonic NoC (PNoC) include a laser source that generates phase-coherent, equally spaced wavelengths, waveguides that serve as the transmission medium, and modulators and photodetectors that facilitate the conversion between digital electrical and photonic signals [33, 35]. The laser source can emit up to 64 wavelengths per waveguide in a Dense Wavelength Division Multiplexing (DWDM) network.

Laser Source Due to the absence of high-speed, electrically driven on-chip monolithic lasers, PHENIC systems typically incorporate off-chip laser sources such as VCSELs (Vertical Cavity Surface Emitting Lasers). These external sources provide light to the modulators, which convert electrical data into modulated optical signals. Upon entering the chip, optical splitters and waveguides direct the light to various modulators for data transmission.

Modulators Before optical messages can be transmitted, electrical signals from each IP core must be converted into optical signals. PHENIC nodes feature a *Gateway* (Fig. 5.21), which serves as a photonic network interface using silicon optical modulators and SiGe photodetectors. Modulators must be compact (e.g., 10 μm ring-modulators [12]) and fast to minimize conversion time. The performance of these modulators is characterized by the on-to-off light intensity ratio [42],

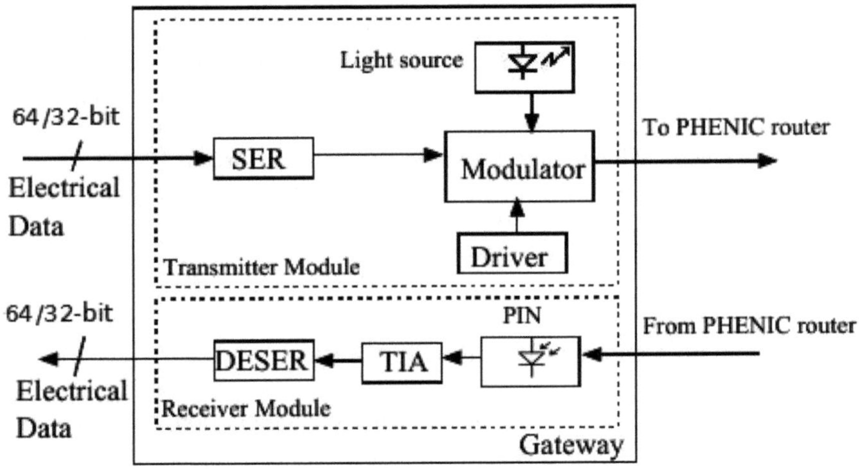

Fig. 5.21 Gateway Organization: This gateway structure comprises two primary modules—the transmitter and the receiver. The transmitter module converts electrical data into photonic signals for transmission across photonic networks. The receiver module, in turn, converts incoming photonic signals back into electrical data for processing within electronic systems. Together, these modules enable seamless data translation between the electronic and photonic domains within the system

which depends on the strength of the electrical input signal. A high extinction ratio (>10 dB) is necessary to ensure accurate signal detection without communication errors.

Waveguides Waveguides form the physical interconnections between all source and destination points, allowing connectivity between various photonic devices within PHENIC systems. These waveguides demultiplex light into appropriate wavelength channels and modulate each channel with a digital data stream generated by electronic components. The photonic signals are then routed to different processing elements (PEs) via routers and waveguides.

The *refractive index* of waveguide materials significantly impacts optical interconnect performance, influencing bandwidth, latency, and area. Typical waveguides have a width of 0.3 μm [16]. At the destination node, where photonic signals are received, they must be converted back into electrical signals. Since PHENIC simultaneously transmits multiple wavelengths per bidirectional waveguide, selective wave filters are necessary to isolate each received wavelength.

Microring Resonator A central component of silicon photonic NoC systems is the microring resonator (MR), which effectively guides optical signals by manipulating their dimensions and positions along the path. Optical signals couple into the ring resonators at specific, evenly spaced wavelengths known as resonant modes [18].

5.5.2.2 Design Challenges

Designing photonic on-chip interconnects for neuromorphic chips presents many complex challenges that span various aspects of technology and engineering. One major challenge is achieving efficient and compact integration of light sources, such as lasers and photodetectors, which are crucial for enabling high-speed data transmission using light. This integration requires precise alignment and packaging to ensure minimal losses and effective communication between photonic components.

Furthermore, the highly dense waveguide circuits necessary for these interconnects must be meticulously engineered to prevent optical crosstalk and signal degradation, which can severely impact performance. Another significant challenge is thermal management; photonic components generate heat, and efficient dissipation is vital to maintain operational stability and avoid thermal crosstalk, which can affect neighboring circuits. Additionally, the variability in material properties at such small scales can lead to inconsistencies in device performance, necessitating robust manufacturing techniques to ensure uniformity and reliability. Overcoming these obstacles requires innovative design strategies and interdisciplinary collaboration to harness the full potential of photonic interconnects, ultimately paving the way for more efficient and powerful neuromorphic systems that better mimic the brain's neural networks.

The photonic domain remains resilient to transient faults caused by radiation [31], yet it is susceptible to process variation (PV), thermal variations (TV), and aging effects. Active components, particularly microring resonators (MRs), are vulnerable to aging and high TV, significantly affecting their reliability [29]. A single MR failure can disrupt message delivery or lead to bandwidth loss, potentially compromising the entire system's operation.

Fabrication-induced PV and TV present substantial concerns for both performance and reliability. TV, for example, can cause microring resonances to shift due to temperature-induced expansions, altering their intended wavelengths [15]. Even small temperature changes, such as 1 °C, can shift resonance wavelengths by up to 0.1 nm [41], highlighting the need for precise temperature control in complex computing systems with thousands of such components. Techniques like trimming dynamically adjust microring frequencies to mitigate thermal drift and fabrication inaccuracies [10, 20, 46].

PV affects critical physical dimensions, such as wafer thickness and waveguide width, directly influencing MR resonance wavelengths. This variability can render some MRs unusable, causing nodes to lose communication bandwidth or wavelengths [53]. Xu et al. [55] proposed flexible wavelength assignment methods to address these challenges, leveraging excess components to compensate for PV-induced variations.

Over time, silicon-based ICs experience aging, which affects both active components like MRs and passive elements like waveguides [51]. This aging necessitates ongoing monitoring and maintenance to ensure continued system reliability.

Recent advancements in Photonic Networks-on-Chip (PNoCs), which focus on network topology, router microarchitecture, performance optimization, and energy efficiency [3, 4, 6–9], have laid the foundation for high-bandwidth, low-energy systems. However, fault tolerance and reliability in photonic interconnects remain underexplored.

This section proposes a fault-tolerant PNoC architecture featuring robust path configuration, routing algorithms, and fault-resilient photonic routers. The system ensures accurate packet transmission even in faulty MRs by integrating minimal redundancy.

5.5.2.3 Design Consideration of Photonic Interconnects in Neuromorphic Chips

While the Photonic Network-on-Chip (NoC) is highly energy-efficient, a significant question remains about its practical application in neuromorphic computing. Photonics is well-established as a communication medium and for its computational capabilities, as demonstrated in [44]. This dual functionality of photonics presents a compelling case for its use in neuromorphic systems. By leveraging photonics for communication, it becomes possible to integrate computational features directly within the communication framework. This approach could lead to significant advancements in the efficiency and performance of neuromorphic chips. Photonic interconnects can facilitate ultra-fast data transfer and reduce latency, addressing the demands of high-speed, parallel processing to mimic the human brain's neural networks. Moreover, photonic systems' inherent low power consumption aligns with the energy constraints of neuromorphic computing. As we continue to explore the integration of photonics in these systems, it is crucial to address the design and implementation challenges, such as thermal management and the precise alignment of photonic components, to fully harness the potential of Photonic NoC in revolutionizing neuromorphic computing. Optoelectronics can perform functions similar to neurons, such as the Izhikevich or Leaky Integrate-and-Fire models. Additionally, optoelectronics can implement matrix multiplication to mimic the operations of neural networks.

Most research on photonic Network-on-Chip (NoC) focuses on wavelength division multiplexing (WDM), where multiple microring resonators generate optical outputs corresponding to different wavelengths. As spikes or action potentials reach the downstream neuron, their connection strengths vary depending on the weights of the upstream and downstream neurons. Each spike can be modulated into various wavelengths, and different microring resonators can be designed to independently control each input wavelength and its weight by fine-tuning the resonance. This approach offers a feasible method for implementing photonic synapses, with demonstrated capabilities to embed 8- or 9-bit weights. Furthermore, summation can also be integrated into the photodetectors to accumulate the weighted action potentials.

Regarding communication, photonic NoCs offer massive parallelism by transferring data using WDM wavelengths. This capability allows spikes from multiple neurons to be moved simultaneously without conflicts in a layer-based neuromorphic system. Photonics also provide significant fan-out (up to 8000, combining WDM and space division multiplexing), enabling much faster multicasting than electronic NoCs. One of the main challenges of photonic NoCs is noise sensitivity; however, neuromorphic systems are known to be resilient to noise. Therefore, when designing photonic NoCs, there can be a relaxation in the stringent bit error rate requirements.

Figure 5.22 illustrates a PNoC-based neuromorphic system. It consists of two silicon layers. The top layer is for photonic communication, and the bottom is for computation and control. Groups of micro rings are connected to dedicated electronic routers to send or receive packets. Spikes are transmitted through waveguides from the source router and delivered to the destination router(s). Upon detection, spikes are forwarded to the neuromorphic core for computation.

5.6 Chapter Summary

In this chapter, the intricacies of building effective communication frameworks for neuromorphic computing are explored in depth. Beginning with Neural Communication, the chapter outlines the foundational principles by which neurons transmit

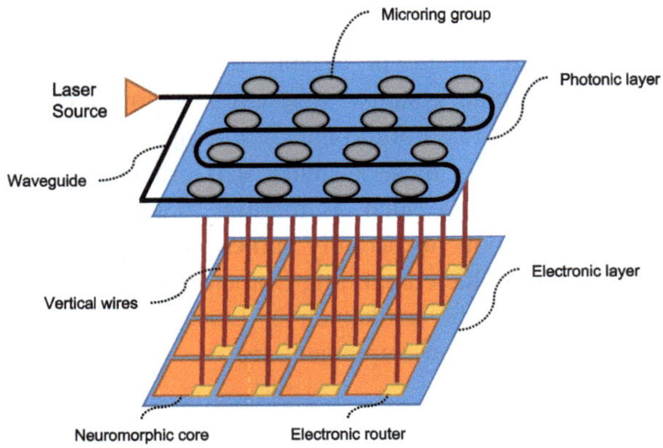

Fig. 5.22 Photonic NoC-based Neuromorphic System: This system architecture consists of two integrated layers. The bottom and electronics layers contain neuromorphic cores and electronic routers facilitating basic data communication. Above it, the photonic layer is designed with microring resonator groups and waveguides, enabling the transmission of photonic signals from an external laser source. The waveguides allow for efficient photonic signal routing, including 90-degree turns, and mirror elements are employed to direct signals for sending or receiving. Vertical interconnects link the electronics and photonic layers, ensuring seamless data transfer

information through electrical and chemical signals, emphasizing the importance of timing and synchronization. Moving to Inter-neural Communication, it shows how neurons interact within networks, covering synaptic plasticity and the role of neurotransmitters in modulating these interactions. Interconnect Design Principles are then discussed, detailing the trade-offs between latency, bandwidth, power consumption, and scalability and examining different interconnect topologies like mesh, torus, and fat tree. The Application Mapping section discusses techniques for efficiently assigning neural network components to hardware resources, considering communication patterns and power constraints, and exploring dynamic reconfiguration strategies. The chapter then addresses Advanced Interconnects for Neuromorphic Systems, highlighting emerging technologies and materials that enhance performance and energy efficiency.

The Three-Dimensional Network-on-Chip (3D-NoC) section focuses on the benefits and challenges of stacking multiple die layers to reduce interconnect lengths, improve performance, and reduce power consumption. The discussion on Photonic Network-on-Chip (PNoC) explores how leveraging photonics for data transmission can achieve ultrafast, low-latency communication, ideal for neuromorphic systems, and address integration challenges. Finally, the chapter concludes with exercises designed to reinforce the concepts discussed and provide hands-on experience with practical applications in neuromorphic system design. This comprehensive overview clearly explains how advanced communication networks can be leveraged to create more efficient and scalable neuromorphic systems.

5.7 Exercises

5.7.1 *Exercise 1*

Address Event Representation (AER) is the most popular protocol for neuromorphic systems. Please explain the Address Event Representation protocol. What are the benefits of this protocol? Given a system of 1024 neurons, how many bits do we need for the AER protocol, and why?

5.7.2 *Exercise 2*

Design a 3D Network-on-Chip (NoC) topology for a neuromorphic chip that consists of 64 processing nodes arranged in an $8 \times 8 \times 1$ grid. Each node has the following parameters:

- The link bandwidth between two adjacent nodes is 20 GB/s.
- The average packet size is 256 bytes.
- The average flit size is 32 bytes.
- The frequency of the processing nodes is 2 GHz.
- The total volume of traffic generated per second by each node is 5 GB/s.

1. Calculate the total number of links in the 3D NoC topology.
2. Determine the average latency for a packet to travel from one node to another, assuming minimal routing and uniform traffic distribution.
3. Compute the required buffer size at each node to handle peak traffic.
4. Assess the power consumption of the NoC, given that each link consumes 2 pJ/bit of data transferred.

5.7.3 *Exercise 3*

In an on-chip network-based neuromorphic system, one of the critical issues is the maximum routing path. This type of routing path is supposed to have the most prolonged latency and could reduce the system's performance. Assuming a system of 64 cores, give examples of a network with the following topologies: 2D Mesh, 3D Mesh, and 2D Torus. What is the maximized routing path in these examples, and what are the distances? Analyze the maximum routing paths of these three topologies.

5.7.4 Exercise 4

When mapping neurons into on-chip networks, the communication must go through an address-based system. Understanding how to address this is important. Given two nodes with index 14 and 35 in the examples in Ex. 3, calculate the addresses for the three topologies.

5.7.5 Exercise 5

In Network-on-Chip, the traveling path of the packets can be different between routing algorithms. From the example of addressing for 3D Mesh in Ex. 4, please list the traveling nodes of a packet from a node indexed 14 to a node indexed 35 with your picked routing algorithm.

5.7.6 Exercise 6

In this chapter, we have discussed the mapping issue, where the mapped neurons' location can significantly impact the overall latency. In this exercise, we perform a mapping for a fully connected model of 14:14:4 into eight nodes with four neurons per node. First, please choose 2D Mesh as the topology of choice. Then, please map the neurons to the cores using the following topology (Fig. 5.23).

5.7.7 Exercise 7

From the mapping solution in Ex. 6, draw the routing path from the neuron indexed 3 of the first layer to the neuron indexed 13 of the second layer.

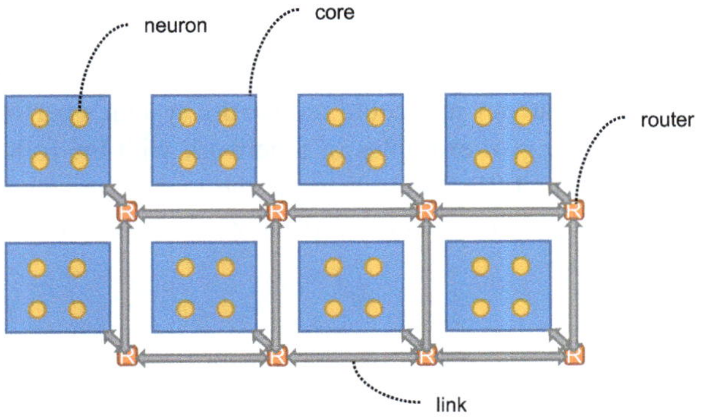

Fig. 5.23 2D Mesh Topology

5.7.8 Exercise 8

In an on-chip network, communication can be done using unicast, multicast, and broadcast. Assuming the on-chip network only supports unicast, please list the routing path and the number of hops for a spike from the neuron indexed 3 of the first layer to all neurons in the second layer.

5.7.9 Exercise 9

Design a multicast routing scheme for a neuromorphic chip that consists of 64 processing nodes arranged in an 8x8 grid. Each node has the following parameters: the link bandwidth between any two adjacent nodes is 25 GB/s; the average packet size is 128 bytes; the average flit size is 16 bytes; the frequency of the processing nodes is 2.5 GHz; the total volume of multicast traffic generated per second by each node is 6 GB/s.

1. Calculate the links required to support multicast communication in the neuromorphic chip.
2. Determine the average latency for a multicast packet to be delivered to all nodes, assuming a tree-based multicast routing scheme and uniform traffic distribution.
3. Compute the required buffer size at each node to handle peak multicast traffic.
4. Assess the power consumption of the multicast routing, given that each link consumes 2.5 pJ/bit of data transferred.

5.7.10 Exercise 10

Design a photonic Network-on-Chip (NoC) topology for a neuromorphic chip that consists of 64 processing nodes arranged in an 8×8 grid. Each node has the following parameters: The optical link bandwidth between any two adjacent nodes is 40 GB/s; the average packet size is 512 bytes; the average flit size is 64 bytes; the frequency of the processing nodes is 3 GHz; the total traffic volume generated per second by each node is 10 GB/s.

1. Calculate the total optical links in the photonic NoC topology.
2. Determine the average latency for a packet to travel from one node to another, assuming minimal routing and uniform traffic distribution.
3. Compute the required buffer size at each node to handle peak traffic.
4. Assess the power consumption of the photonic NoC, given that each optical link consumes 1 pJ/bit of data transferred.

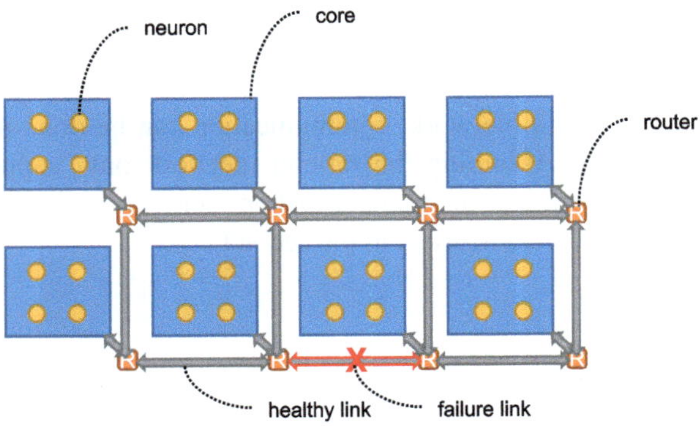

Fig. 5.24 2D Mesh Topology with a link failure

5. Evaluate the advantages and challenges of using a photonic NoC over a traditional electronic NoC regarding power efficiency and data transfer rate (Fig. 5.24).

References

1. Abdallah AB (2013) Multicore systems-on-chip: practical hardware/software design, 2nd edn. Atlantis, Amsterdam
2. Abdallah AB (2017) Advanced multicore systems-on-chip: architecture, on-chip network, design. Springer, Berlin
3. Ahmed AB, Abdallah AB (2013) Phenic: silicon photonic 3D-network-on-chip architecture for high-performance heterogeneous many-core system-on-chip. In: 2013 14th international conference on sciences and techniques of automatic control and computer engineering (STA), pp 1–9
4. Ahmed AB, Abdallah AB (2015) Hybrid silicon-photonic network-on-chip for future generations of high-performance many-core systems. J Supercomput 71:4446–4475
5. Ahmed AB, Abdallah AB, Kuroda K (2010) Architecture and design of efficient 3d network-on-chip (3D NoC) for custom multicore SoC. In: IEEE proceedings of BWCCA-2010, pp 67–73
6. Ahmed AB, Meyer M, Okuyama Y, Abdallah AB (2015) Efficient router architecture, design and performance exploration for many-core hybrid photonic network-on-chip (2d-phenic). In: 2015 2nd international conference on information science and control engineering (ICISCE), pp 202–206
7. Ahmed AB, Meyer M, Okuyama Y, Abdallah AB (2015) Hybrid photonic NoC based on non-blocking photonic switch and light-weight electronic router. In: 2015 IEEE international conference on systems, man and cybernetics (SMC)
8. Ahmed AB, Okuyama Y, Abdallah AB (2015) Contention-free routing for hybrid photonic mesh-based network-on-chip systems. In: The 9th IEEE international symposium on embedded multicore/manycore SoCs (MCSoC), pp 235–242
9. Ahmed AB, Okuyama Y, Abdallah AB (2015) Non-blocking electro-optic network-on-chip router for high-throughput and low-power many-core systems. In: The world congress on information technology and computer applications, June 2015

10. Ahn JH, Fiorentino M, Beausoleil RG, Binkert N, Davis A, Fattal D, Jouppi NP, McLaren M, Santori CM, Schreiber RS, Spillane SM, Vantrease D, Xu Q (2009) Devices and architectures for photonic chip-scale integration. Appl Phys A 95(4):989–997
11. Akopyan F, Sawada J, Cassidy A, Alvarez-Icaza R, Arthur J, Merolla P, Imam N, Nakamura Y, Datta P, Nam G, Taba B, Beakes M, Brezzo B, Kuang JB, Manohar R, Risk WP, Jackson B, Modha DS (2015) Truenorth: design and tool flow of a 65 mw 1 million neuron programmable neurosynaptic chip. IEEE Trans Comput Aid Des Integr Circuits Syst 34(10):1537–1557
12. Almeida VR et al (2004) All-optical switching on a silicon chip. Opt Lett 29(24):2867–2869
13. Balaji A, et al (2019) Mapping spiking neural networks to neuromorphic hardware. IEEE Trans Very Large Scale Integr Syst 28(1):76–86
14. Bhanu PV, et al (2019) Fault-tolerant network-on-chip design with flexible spare core placement. J Emerg Technol Comput Syst 15(1):1–24
15. Bogaerts W, De Heyn P, Van Vaerenbergh T, De Vos K, Kumar Selvaraja S, Claes T, Dumon P, Bienstman P, Van Thourhout D, Baets R (2012) Silicon microring resonators. Laser Photon Rev 6(1):47–73
16. Briere M, et al (2005) Heterogeneous modelling of an optical network-on-chip with systemC. In: 16th IEEE international workshop on rapid system prototyping (RSP'05), pp 10–16
17. Carloni LP, Pande P, Xie Y (2009) Networks-on-chip in emerging interconnect paradigms: advantages and challenges. In: Proceedings of the 3rd ACM/IEEE international symposium on networks-on-chip (NOCS09), pp 93–102
18. Chan J, et al (2010) Phoenixsim: a simulator for physical-layer analysis of chip-scale photonic interconnection networks. In: Design, automation and test in Europe (DATE), pp 691–696
19. Chao CH, Jheng KY, Wang HY, Wu JC, Wu AY (2010) Traffic- and thermal-aware run-time thermal management scheme for 3D NoC systems. In: Proceedings of ACM/IEEE international symposium on networks-on-chip (NoCS), Grenoble, pp 223–230
20. Chu ST, Pan W, Sato S, Kaneko T, Little BE, Kokubun Y (1999) Wavelength trimming of a microring resonator filter by means of a UV sensitive polymer overlay. IEEE Photon Technol Lett 11(6):688–690
21. Davies M, Srinivasa N, Lin TH, Chinya G, Cao Y, Choday SH, Dimou G, Joshi P, Imam N, Jain S, et al (2018) Loihi: a neuromorphic manycore processor with on-chip learning. IEEE Micro 38(1):82–99
22. Dev K (2002) Multi-objective optimization using evolutionary algorithms. Wiley, Hoboken
23. Feero B, Pande PP (2007) Performance evaluation for three-dimensional networks-on-chip. In: Proceedings of IEEE computer society annual symposium on VLSI (ISVLSI), pp 305–310
24. Fu Z, Ling X (2010) The design and implementation of arbiters for network-on-chips. In: 2nd international conference industrial and information systems, pp 292–295
25. Furber S, Temple S (2007) Neural systems engineering. J R Soc Interface 4(13):193–206
26. Furber SB, Lester DR, Plana LA, Garside JD, Painkras E, Temple S, Brown AD (2013) Overview of the spinnaker system architecture. IEEE Trans Comput 62(12):2454–2467
27. Glass CJ, Ni LM (1992) The turn model for adaptive routing. In: Proceedings of 19th annual international symposium computer architecture, pp 278–287
28. Gold BT (2004) Balancing performance, area, and power in an on-chip network. Master's thesis, Department of Electrical and Computer Engineering, Virginia Tech
29. Hu ZS, Hung FY, Chen KJ, Chang SJ, Hsieh WK, Liao TY (2013) Improvement in thermal degradation of ZnO photodetector by embedding silver oxide nanoparticles. Funct Mater Lett 6(1):1793–6047
30. Joyner J, Zarkesh-Ha P, Meindl J (2001) A stochastic global net-length distribution for a three-dimensional system-on-chip(3D-SoC). In: Proceedings of 14th annual IEEE international ASIC/SoC conference
31. Kappeler R (2004) Radiation testing of micro photonic components. Stagiaire Project Report. Technical Report, ESA/ESTEC. September 29 Ref. No.: EWP 2263
32. Kelber F, Wu B, Vogginger B, Partzsch J, Liu C, Stolba M, Mayr C (2020) Mapping deep neural networks on spinnaker2. In: Proceedings of the neuro-inspired computational elements workshop, pp 1–3

33. Koch BR, Fang AW, Cohen O, Bowers JE (2007) Mode-locked silicon evanescent lasers. Opt Exp 15(18):11225–11233
34. Kumar R, Zyuban V, Tullsen DM (2005) Interconnections in multicore architectures: understanding mechanisms, overheads and scaling. In: Proceedings of the 32nd international symposium on computer architecture, Madison, pp 408–419
35. Kumar A, Peh LS, Kundu P, Jha NK (2007) Express virtual channels: towards the ideal interconnection fabric. In: Proceedings of the 34th international symposium on computer architecture, pp 150–161
36. Lahiri K, Raghunathan A, Dey S (2000) Efficient exploration of the SoC communication architecture design space. In: Proceedings of IEEE/ACM ICCAD'00, pp 424–430
37. Li, F, Nicopoulos, C, Richardson, T, Xie, Y, Narayanan, V, Kandemir M (2006) Design and management of 3D chip multiprocessors using network-in-memory. ACM SIGARCH Comput Arch News 34(2):130–141
38. Li F, Nicopoulos C, Richardson TD, Xie Y, Vijaykrishnan N, Kandemir MT (2006) Design and management of 3D chip multiprocessors using network-in-memory. In: The 33rd annual international symposium on computer architecture, pp 130–141
39. Mahowald M (1992) VLSI analogs of neuronal visual processing: a synthesis of form and function. Ph.D. Thesis, California Institute of Technology Pasadena
40. Moradi S, Qiao N, Stefanini F, Indiveri G (2017) A scalable multicore architecture with heterogeneous memory structures for dynamic neuromorphic asynchronous processors (dynaps). IEEE Trans Biomed Circuits Syst 12(1):106–122
41. Nitta CJ, Farrens MK, Akella V (2011) Resilient microring resonator based photonic networks. In: Proceedings of the 44th annual IEEE/ACM international symposium on microarchitecture. ACM, New York, pp 95–104. MICRO-44
42. Parsricha S, Dutt N (2008) Trends in emerging on-chip interconnect technologies. IPSJ Trans Syst LSI Des Methodol 1:2–17
43. Pavlidis VF, Friedman EG (2007) 3-D topologies for networks-on-chip. IEEE Trans VLSI Syst 15:1081–1090
44. Prucnal PR, Shastri BJ (2017) Neuromorphic photonics. CRC Press, Boca Raton
45. Purves D, Augustine G, Fitzpatrick D, Hall W, LaMantia AS, McNamara J: Neuroscience. Sinauer Associates, Sunderland
46. Rafizadeh D, Zhang JP, Hagness SC, Taflove A, Stair KA, Ho ST, Tiberio RC (1997) Temperature tuning of microcavity ring and disk resonators at 1.5-/spl mu/m. In: Conference proceedings. LEOS'97. 10th annual meeting IEEE lasers and electro-optics society 1997 annual meeting, pp 162–163
47. Ramanujam RS, Lin B (2008) Near-optimal oblivious routing on three dimensional mesh networks. In: Proceedings of IEEE international conference on computer design, Lake Tahoe, pp 134–141
48. Rosethal J (2006) JPEG image compression using an FPGA. Master's thesis, Electrical and Computer Engineering, University of California Santa Barbara
49. Sivilotti MA (1991) Wiring considerations in analog VLSI systems, with application to field-programmable networks. Ph.D. Thesis, California Institute of Technology
50. Topol AW, Tulipe JDCL, Shi L, Frank DJ, Bernstein K, Steen SE, Kumar A, Singco GU, Young AM, Guarini KW, Ieong M (2006) Three-dimensional integrated circuits. IBM J Res Develop 50(4–5), 491–506
51. Tu Z, Zhou Z, Wang X (2014) Reliability considerations of high speed germanium waveguide photodetectors. In: Optical components and materials XI, p 89820W
52. Urgese G, Barchi F, Macii E, Acquaviva A (2016) Optimizing network traffic for spiking neural network simulations on densely interconnected many-core neuromorphic platforms. IEEE Trans Emerg Top Comput 6(3):317–329
53. Xiang D, Zhang Y, Shan S, Xu Y (2013) A fault-tolerant routing algorithm design for on-chip optical networks. In: 2013 IEEE 32nd international symposium on reliable distributed systems (SRDS), pp 1–9

54. Xin L, Choy CS (2010) Low-latency NoC router with lookahead bypass. IEEE international symposium on circuits and systems (ISCAS), pp 3981–3984
55. Xu Y, Yang J, Melhem R (2012) Tolerating process variations in nanophotonic on-chip networks. ACM SIGARCH Comput Arch News 40:142–152
56. Yan S, Lin B (2008) Design of application-specific 3D networks-on-chip architectures. In: Proceedings of international conference of computer design, pp 142–149
57. Zhu S, Lo GQ (2015) Vertically-stacked multilayer photonics on bulk silicon toward three-dimensional integration. J Lightw Technol 34(2):386–392

Chapter 6
Fault-Tolerant Neuromorphic System Design

Abstract Neuromorphic computing systems have significantly advanced in various real-world applications, such as object recognition, robotics, and autonomous vehicles. Designers typically leverage large-scale models on dedicated hardware platforms like FPGAs, GPUs, or ASICs to develop these emerging systems. However, collecting datasets, training models, and designing accelerators to maintain privacy and reliability requires substantial time and effort. As neuromorphic systems become increasingly complex, hardware implementations face considerable vulnerabilities. Without knowing these accelerators' internal structures and designs, attackers can still reverse-engineer the neural networks by exploiting various side-channel information. Furthermore, due to the complexity of neuromorphic systems, which integrate numerous neurons and synapses, the accumulation of fault probability presents a growing threat to system reliability. Therefore, ensuring fault tolerance and reliability becomes paramount in the design of these systems. This chapter examines the primary threats to the reliability of neuromorphic systems, highlighting the importance of fault-tolerance mechanisms, and discusses several recovery methods to mitigate these risks, ensuring that neuromorphic systems can operate reliably in the face of various challenges and potential attacks.

6.1 Introduction

Fault tolerance and reliability are paramount in neuromorphic chip design due to these systems' complex and sensitive nature. Neuromorphic chips aim to emulate the human brain's neural networks, involving a dense integration of neurons and synapses that must communicate efficiently and accurately. Any faults or errors in these communication pathways can significantly degrade the system's performance and accuracy. Moreover, neuromorphic systems are increasingly used in critical applications such as autonomous vehicles, medical devices, and defense systems, where reliability is not just a preference but a necessity. Faults in these systems can arise from various sources, including manufacturing defects, environmental stress, and operational wear and tear.

A. Ben Abdallah, K. N. Dang, *Neuromorphic Computing Principles and Organization*, https://doi.org/10.1007/978-3-031-83089-1_6

To mitigate these issues, robust fault tolerance mechanisms must be embedded in the design, such as error detection and correction codes, redundancy, and reconfigurable architectures. These mechanisms help ensure that the system can continue to operate correctly even in the presence of faults, thereby maintaining the integrity and performance of neuromorphic computations. Additionally, reliable neuromorphic systems must be resilient to various attacks, including side-channel and tampering, to protect sensitive data and maintain overall system security. Hence, incorporating fault tolerance and reliability into neuromorphic chip design is crucial for achieving dependable and efficient performance in everyday and mission-critical applications.

When manufacturing Integrated Circuits (ICs), a specific yield rate is critical for ensuring the reliability and functionality of the devices [13]. Inaccuracies during fabrication can introduce variations from the original design, resulting in imperfectly fabricated devices. If such inaccuracies lead to a malfunction in the system, a *fault* is considered to have occurred. For instance, consider a threshold comparison circuit designed to determine a neuron's firing status. If the output line becomes stuck at '1' (high voltage), the neuron will continuously fire regardless of its inputs or the strength of its synapses. This fault can cause errors when the neuron's output drives other neurons, leading to incorrect behavior and potentially altering the system's intended outcome. For example, a different neuron with a wrong label may continuously fire, resulting in a misleading signal or computation.

Other essential factors to consider are the wear-out or aging processes. Assuming the system is initially fabricated correctly and performs as designed wear-out or aging can still occur, leading to erroneous outputs. For example, the wires connecting two clusters of neurons may function properly at first. However, due to the constant current passing through the wires, the *electromigration* effect gradually causes the movement of ions within the conductor, progressively thinning the wires. After several hours of operation, this can result in the wires becoming disconnected, preventing the transmission of spikes between the two clusters.

Hardware faults can be classified according to various aspects. One classification is based on their duration: *permanent*, *intermittent*, and *transient*. A *permanent* fault occurs continuously and never returns to standard functionality. A *transient* fault causes occasional malfunctions, which typically resolve after a short period. An *intermittent* fault oscillates between an active and inactive state. When the fault is active, the component malfunctions; when inactive, the component typically functions as expected.

Another classification of faults is based on their behavior. For example, a fault in a resistive memory cell can be classified as: *stuck-at-ground*, *stuck-at-supply-voltage*, *stuck-at-high-resistance*, and *stuck-at-low-resistance*. When a resistive memory cell is *stuck-at-ground*, the measured voltage at the reading terminal remains fixed at a ground voltage (0 V). This behavior prevents the resistance value from being read or executed correctly.

Since the computation in neuromorphic systems is based on spikes, these systems can be resilient to transient faults, as the impact of faulty spikes can be mitigated. However, *permanent* and *intermittent* faults can lead to malfunctions in neuromorphic system modules, resulting in inaccurate outputs.

6.1.1 Evaluating Fault-Tolerance in Neuromorphic Systems

Fault tolerance is crucial in neuromorphic systems due to their intricate structure and critical applications, such as autonomous vehicles and medical devices. Ensuring that these systems can continue to operate correctly in the presence of faults is essential for maintaining performance and reliability. Evaluating fault tolerance involves several steps, including stress testing under various conditions to identify potential points of failure and implementing error detection and correction mechanisms to monitor and address faults. Techniques such as redundancy, where multiple components perform the same function to provide a backup in case one fails, and reconfigurable architectures that can adapt to changing conditions are commonly used. By rigorously testing these systems and incorporating robust fault-tolerance features, designers can ensure that neuromorphic systems are reliable, resilient, and capable of performing their intended functions even in the presence of faults, enhancing their overall dependability and effectiveness in real-world applications.

Given system reliability's critical nature, an appropriate measurement method is essential. Traditionally, this involves assessing both reliability and availability. Reliability represented as $R(t)$, refers to the probability that the system operates correctly over a specified interval $[0, t]$. A closely related metric is the Mean Time to Failure (MTTF), which denotes the average duration between two consecutive failures. This can be computed using the following formula:

$$MTTF = \int_0^\infty R(t)dt \tag{6.1}$$

Another measurement for repairable systems is the *Mean Time Between Failures* (MTBF), which is the sum of the *Mean Time to Failure* (MTTF) and the *Mean Time to Repair* (MTTR).

Availability, denoted as $A(t)$, is the average fraction of time over the interval $[0, t]$ that the system is operational. The long-term availability (A) can be computed as:

$$A = \lim_{0 \to \infty} A(t) = \frac{MTTF}{MTBF} = \frac{MTTF}{MTTF + MTTR} \tag{6.2}$$

The fault rate $(\lambda(t))$ of a system, which is the inverse of the reliability function $R(t)$, can also be measured as the sum of the fault rates of all modules in the system.

$$\lambda_{system}(t) = \sum_{all\text{-}modules} \lambda_{module_i}(t) \tag{6.3}$$

$$R(t) = \frac{1}{\lambda_{system}(t)} = \frac{1}{\sum_{all\text{-}modules} \frac{1}{Rmodule_i(t)}} \tag{6.4}$$

If redundancies are added, the fault rate computation can be modified. The standard method involves using the *Markov-state* model to calculate the probability of faulty states, with $\lambda(t)$ being the sum of these probabilities [14].

6.1.2 Types of Faults and Their Impact on System Behavior

From a reliability perspective, a typical neuromorphic system is composed of three primary components: (1) the memory or storage unit, (2) the computing unit, and (3) the communication infrastructure. Table 6.1 provides an overview of various faults, categorized by type, behavior, detection methods, and recovery approaches. This section focuses on fault-tolerance methods for hardware faults, highlighting strategies to detect and mitigate defects to ensure the system's robustness and reliability.

In memory systems, specifically SRAM and DRAM, various faults can occur. Common transient faults are caused by alpha particles or cosmic rays, which can flip the bit stored in a memory cell, leading to a single-event upset (SEU). In SRAM, data is stored in two transistors, while in DRAM, it is stored in a capacitor. These errors are unpredictable and unpreventable, so solutions often involve information redundancy techniques such as repetition or error correction codes. Another type of fault is permanent, with a cell value stuck at 0 or 1. Intermittent faults can also occur, often influenced by conditions like thermal elevation. In such cases, some memory damage might happen, and the typical recovery method is to replace faulty cells, banks, or blocks with spare ones. Faults in arbitration modules, responsible for reading and writing operations, can also lead to malfunctions and incorrect data reading or writing results.

Faults in the computing unit often lead to corrupted outputs. For example, a permanent fault, such as a "stuck-at-one" condition on the output wire of a threshold comparator, may cause a neuron to fire continuously. Detecting and recovering from such permanent defects requires redundancy and voting mechanisms. Intermittent faults can also occur under specific conditions. For instance, single-event transients (SETs) can arise in the combinational logic and cause short-term fluctuations in the output. While neuromorphic systems can tolerate noisy inputs and a certain level of transient faults, frequent occurrences of these faults can negatively impact overall accuracy. Implementing redundancies and voting circuits helps to mitigate the impact of these faults, ensuring the reliability and robustness of the system.

In the communication infrastructure, faults behave differently than in the computing unit. Transient faults can lead to data corruption or misrouting of packets. Error detection and correction codes are crucial for identifying and fixing corrupted data. The system must detect and re-route misrouted packets, using flow-control protocols to drop and resend packets to ensure reliable communication. Intermittent and

Table 6.1 Taxonomy of faults: types, causes, behaviors, detection methods, and recovery approaches

Major part	Type	Causes	Behavior	Detection method	Recovery
Memory	Transient	Alpha particles/cosmic rays	Flip bit	Replicating and comparing/Error detection code	Information redundancy
	Permanent/Intermittent	Manufacture imperfection/Aging/Wear-out	Stuck-at, Bridge	Testing algorithm	Spatial redundancy
Computing unit	Transient	Alpha particles/cosmic rays	Inaccurate output	Redundancy-based voting/Multiple executions	Self-resilient/Redundancy-based voting/Multiple executions
	Permanent/Intermittent	Manufacture imperfection/Aging/Wear-out	Stuck-at, Bridge	Voting	Spatial redundancy
Interconnect	Transient	Alpha particles/cosmic rays	Corrupted data, Misrouting	Error detection code/Multiple executions	Error correction code/Network re-routing
	Permanent/Intermittent	Manufacture imperfection/Aging/Wear-out	Corrupted data, Blocking connection	Error detection code	Spatial redundancy, Fault-tolerant routing

permanent faults in the routing unit can corrupt data or block connections entirely. Spatial redundancy, such as extra wires and fault-tolerant routing, can bypass blocked connections to mitigate these issues. While fault-tolerance methods have been well-developed for traditional computer systems over decades, neuromorphic computing is a relatively new paradigm. Thus, adapting existing methods and developing neuromorphic-specific strategies is essential. The following sections will explore fault tolerance in neuromorphic systems in further detail.

6.1.3 Consequences of Faults in Neuromorphic Systems

Faults in neuromorphic systems can have significant and varied consequences, impacting these advanced computing architectures' overall performance, reliability, and functionality. Neuromorphic systems, designed to mimic the human brain's neural networks, rely on the precise and efficient communication between numerous interconnected neurons and synapses. Faults, such as transient, intermittent, or permanent errors, can disrupt this delicate balance, leading to data corruption, loss of information, and incorrect processing of neural signals. Transient faults may cause occasional data errors, which neuromorphic systems can tolerate to some extent, but frequent occurrences can degrade system accuracy. Intermittent faults, influenced by environmental conditions or operational stress, can introduce sporadic errors that are challenging to diagnose and fix. Permanent faults, such as stuck-at faults in memory or computing units, can result in persistent errors and malfunctioning components, requiring redundancy and fault-tolerant mechanisms to maintain system operation. Moreover, communication infrastructure faults can lead to data packet misrouting or blocking critical connections, further compromising system performance. These faults impact the immediate computational tasks and pose long-term threats to the system's robustness and resilience, emphasizing the need for rigorous fault-tolerance strategies and reliable design principles to ensure the dependability of neuromorphic systems in real-world applications.

To analyze the effects of random faults on Spiking Neural Networks (SNNs), random faults were introduced and tested with 10,000 cases from the MNIST dataset. The SNN model, structured as 784:100 with lateral inhibitory connections described by Diehl et al., was simulated using BindsNet. The network operates on the winner-take-all principle, where firing neurons inhibit others. Weights were pre-trained using the Spike-Timing Dependent Plasticity (STDP) algorithm. Figure 6.1 illustrates the accuracy drop upon introducing faults into the weight SRAM.

Introducing stuck-at-0 faults into the weight memory (Fig. 6.1) resulted in only a minimal decrease in accuracy with a small number of faulty weights, underscoring the natural fault resilience of Spiking Neural Networks (SNNs). However, as the number of faulty weights increased, accuracy significantly declined. In contrast, faults in the computational units proved more critical. For example, a single stuck-at-0 fault affecting 1% of the neurons in a threshold register could cause a neuron to fire constantly, reducing accuracy to approximately 10%, equivalent to assigning

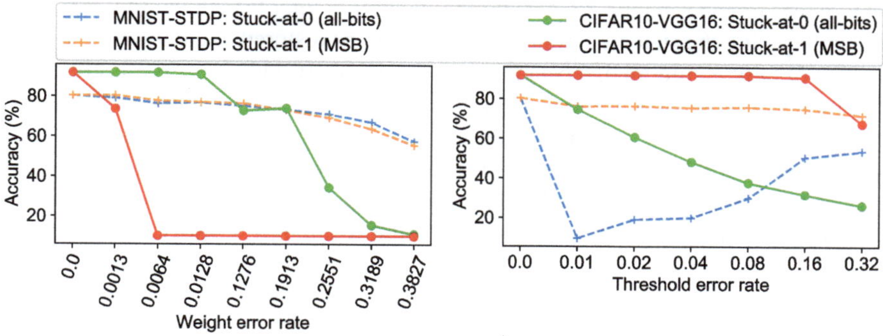

Fig. 6.1 Impact of faults in neuromorphic systems: (**a**): Weight error, (**b**) Threshold error. The errors, classified as "stuck-at-0" or "stuck-at-1", were evaluated using two benchmarks: Spike-Timing Dependent Plasticity (STDP) for the MNIST dataset and the VGG16 model for the CIFAR10 dataset. The analysis highlights the system's resilience and accuracy under different fault conditions, providing valuable insights into the robustness of neuromorphic architectures

a single label to all MNIST test images. When two or more neurons experienced stuck-at-0 faults in their threshold registers, their competition intensified, but accuracy remained substantially lower than in fault-free scenarios. Similarly, in deep neural networks like the VGG-16 model on the CIFAR-10 dataset, the introduction of faults led to a notable decline in accuracy.

6.2 Fault Tolerance in Traditional Computing Systems

Traditional fault-tolerance techniques can be adapted and applied to neuromorphic chips to enhance their reliability and resilience. Methods such as redundancy, error detection and correction, and checkpointing, which have been effectively used in conventional computing systems, can be tailored to address the specific challenges of neuromorphic systems. By incorporating these techniques, designers can ensure that neuromorphic chips can continue to function correctly even in the presence of faults, thereby maintaining their performance and reliability in critical applications. This approach leverages the well-established fault tolerance principles while considering the unique requirements and characteristics of neuromorphic architectures.

Conventional systems utilize various methods to achieve fault tolerance, including redundancy, error detection and correction, and checkpointing. Redundancy involves duplicating critical components so that another can take over without disrupting system functionality if one fails. This can be implemented at various levels, such as hardware (using redundant processors, memory, or disks) or software (employing backup algorithms or parallel processing). Error detection and correction techniques, such as parity checks, checksums, and more sophisticated methods like Reed-Solomon codes, help identify and correct data errors, ensuring data integrity and reliability. Checkpointing, another vital technique, involves periodically saving the state of a system so that it can be restored to a known good state in case of failure, minimizing data loss and downtime. In addition to these strategies, traditional systems may use fault-tolerant architectures, such as Tandem computers, designed with built-in fault detection and recovery mechanisms to handle faults seamlessly. Overall, fault tolerance in traditional computing systems is fundamental for maintaining high availability, reliability, and performance, particularly in mission-critical applications where system failures can have severe consequences.

6.2.1 Hardware Approach

The hardware approach remains the most well-established fault-tolerance technique in computing systems. Before evaluating the reliability of a hardware structure, it is crucial to consider how the modules are interconnected, as the connectivity can significantly impact overall reliability. Generally, there are three types of module interconnect structures: *parallel*, *serial*, and *mixed*, as illustrated in Fig. 6.2.

In the *serial* system, the modules are connected so that if one of the modules fails, the whole system will malfunction. Assuming the modules fail independently, the reliability of the system is the product of the reliability of all modules:

$$R_{\text{serial}}(t) = R_1(t) \cdot R_2(t) \cdot \ldots \cdot R_n(t) \tag{6.5}$$

In the *parallel* system, the system only fails when all modules have failed. Consequently, the reliability of the parallel system is:

$$R_{\text{parallel}}(t) = 1 - (1 - R_1(t)) \cdot (1 - R_2(t)) \cdot \ldots \cdot (1 - R_n(t)) \tag{6.6}$$

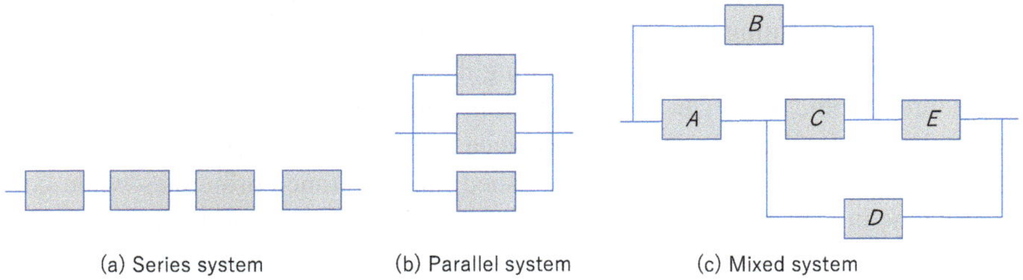

Fig. 6.2 Types of hardware systems: This illustration compares three types of hardware system architectures—serial (**a**), parallel (**b**), and mixed (**c**). In the serial system, modules are connected sequentially, each processing data in turn. The parallel system allows modules to operate simultaneously. The mixed system combines elements of both serial and parallel configurations

For the *mixed* system, we can divide it into sub-systems for analysis. However, this might become overwhelmingly complicated. Here, the efficient approach is to build the Markov-state model. The model consists of all possible states of the system that might occur. There are links between states with a certain probability. The reliability of a system can be obtained by finding the likelihood of the faulty condition.

In summary, the *parallel* system is usually used for tolerating faults. Spare modules are added to allow the system to work under one or more faulty modules. The generalized model of this fault-tolerance method is called *M-of-N* systems. The system consists of N modules, requiring at least M to work correctly. For example, one of the most popular fault-tolerant systems is TMR (Triple Modular Redundancy), where a module is tripled and can tolerate at least one failed module. Figure 6.3 depicts the overall structure of a TMR. TMR can be considered as a 2-of-3 system. The reliability function of the M-of-N system is:

$$R_{\text{M-of-N}}(t) = \sum_{i=M}^{N} \binom{N}{i} \cdot R(t)^i \cdot (1 - R(t))^{N-i} \tag{6.7}$$

Since the voter is connected in series to the three parallel modules, the overall system reliability is given by

$$R_{\text{system}}(t) = R_{\text{TMR}}(t) \times R_{\text{voter}}(t),$$

where $R_{\text{TMR}}(t)$ is the reliability of the TMR system (a 2-of-3 configuration) and $R_{\text{voter}}(t)$ is the reliability of the voter. The reliability of the TMR system can be computed using the M-of-N formula, and the overall system reliability depends on the reliability of both the TMR modules and the voter.

The voter becomes the system's most critical component, as its failure is undetectable and cannot be corrected.

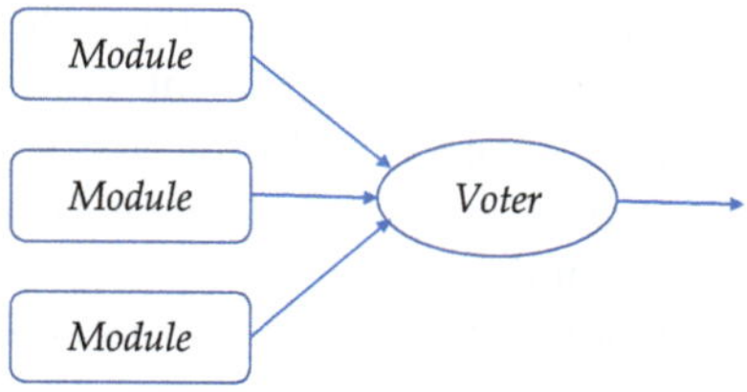

Fig. 6.3 Triple Modular Redundancy (TMR) architecture. This configuration features three modules operating in parallel, with outputs fed into a voting mechanism. The voter compares the outputs and identifies discrepancies, allowing it to determine and discard an incorrect value. This TMR approach enables the system to tolerate faults in one module, ensuring reliability through redundancy

There are also variations of M-of-N with voters, which include:

- *Sub-system TMR:* Instead of applying TMR to the entire system, each module is replicated three times, with three separate voters to conduct the voting system. The outputs of these voters are then passed to the next module, preventing faulty voters from propagating through the system by enabling correction.
- *Dynamic redundancy:* Redundant modules remain inactive during regular operation. If the voter or fault detection module identifies a faulty output, the system reconfigures by replacing the failed module with a spare one.

In addition to using spare modules for correction, these spares can also be used for replication, enabling comparisons that help identify faults. In processor-based computing, similar approaches are used to predict failure situations. For example, the *watchdog* processor is employed with assertions during operation to ensure the processor continues functioning without crashing. This technique is also applied in other computing paradigms, such as *runtime detection*, which can indicate failures. In multi-core systems, *executing parallel threads* of the same program can help detect potential errors.

The hardware fault-tolerance approach relies on redundancy to detect and correct failed modules. This approach can also be applied to neuromorphic systems. For instance, instead of relying on 256 working neurons in a cluster, the system can include 16 spare neurons, resulting in a 256-of-272 cluster. If a neuron fails, a spare neuron can take its place. Additionally, the TMR method can be applied to the computing units in the neuron. For example, a fault in the threshold comparator could lead to incorrect outputs. The system can detect and correct such faults in neuron firing behavior using three comparators and a voter.

6.2.2 Information Redundancy

While adding redundancies and monitors is common in hardware fault tolerance, implementing them in data storage can be inefficient. For instance, applying TMR (Triple Modular Redundancy) to data would triple the system's storage requirements. An appropriate *information redundancy* strategy is necessary to address this issue. The most common form of this strategy is *coding*, where the data is encoded into a codeword. The codeword is then stored and decoded to detect and correct possible errors.

When *encoding*, a d-bit data word is transformed into a c-bit codeword ($c > d$). This introduces redundancy ($c - d$ bits) into the information. Note that the possible codewords do not cover all 2^c binary combinations, which results in some combinations being invalid. The system may encounter a valid or invalid codeword during decoding. A valid codeword can be decoded to retrieve the original d-bit data word, while an invalid codeword needs to be processed to infer the possible original data.

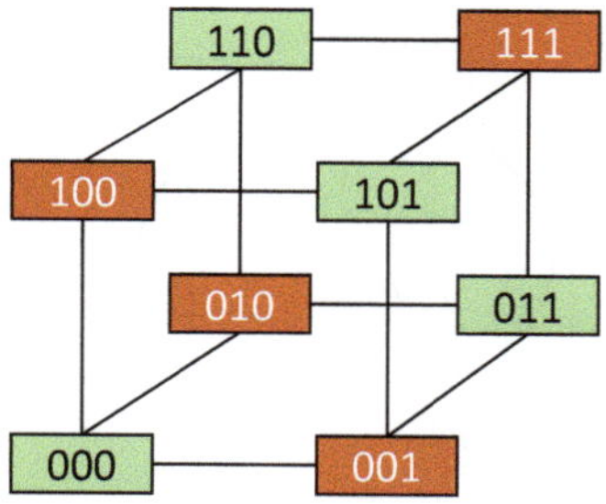

Fig. 6.4 3-Bit codeword space: This diagram illustrates the concept of Hamming distance within a 3-bit codeword space. Each codeword is represented in the space, with green boxes indicating valid codewords and red boxes indicating invalid codewords. The Hamming distance between codewords helps to identify and correct errors by measuring the number of differing bits between them

An important metric of the codeword space is the *Hamming distance*, defined as the number of different bits between two codewords. For example, the Hamming distance between the codewords "110" and "011" is shown in Fig. 6.4. This *Hamming distance* helps determine the ability to detect and correct errors. To detect k error bits, the *minimum* Hamming distance must be at least $k + 1$. In the previous example, the minimum distance is two, which means this codeword space can detect up to 1 error bit. For example, if we receive the codeword "010", we can observe that it has a Hamming distance of 1 from "110" and two from "011". Therefore, upon receiving "010", the decoder can detect the error but cannot identify the original codeword. To identify the original codeword, the minimum Hamming distance must be higher.

To correct k error bits, the minimum distance must be $2k + 1$. Once the system receives an invalid codeword, it can determine which valid codeword is closest, choosing it as the original codeword. For example, using TMR for a single bit results in a similar codeword space as shown in Fig. 6.4, where only two valid codewords exist: "000" and "111". The minimum Hamming distance between these codewords is three, meaning the system can correct one error bit. If the decoder receives the codeword "010", it can determine the original codeword as "000" because the Hamming distance between "010" and "000" is 1, while the distance to "111" is 2.

6.2.2.1 Parity Code

One of the most basic coding techniques is *parity* code. The parity codeword consists of the d-bit data and one parity bit ($c = d + 1$). The parity bit is the output of the parity check on the d-bit data word. The parity check can be performed using the XOR function, which can be implemented using several XOR gates in hardware, as shown in Fig. 6.5. Thus, this *coding* technique is simple and fast.

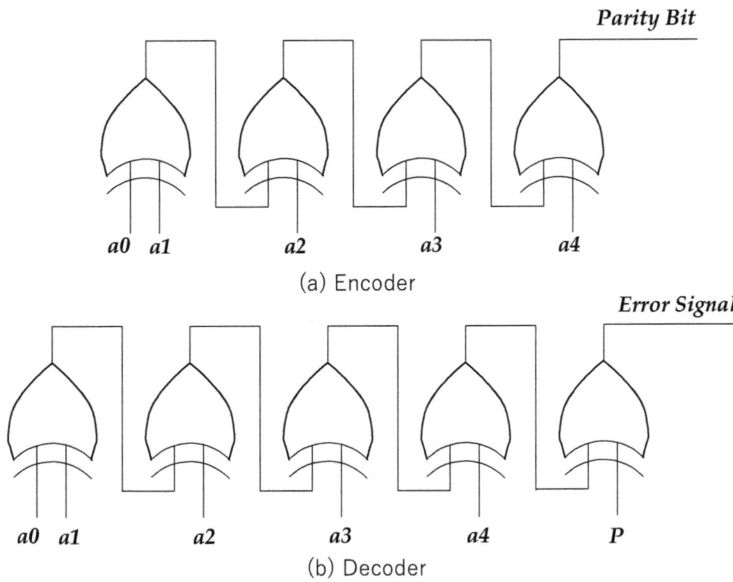

Fig. 6.5 Even parity code: (**a**) Encoder; (**b**) Decoder. The encoder (**a**) uses XOR gates to compute the parity of an input array of bits, ensuring an even number of 1s for error detection. The decoder (**b**) checks the parity of received bits to verify data integrity. If a bit has flipped during transmission, the decoder detects the error by identifying an unexpected parity value

Parity codes come in two types: *odd* and *even*. The *even* parity bit ensures the codeword has an output parity of '0', while the *odd* parity bit ensures the output parity is '1'. For example, consider the 8-bit data word "01010110" as shown in Eq. (6.8). The *odd* parity bit would be '1', and the *even* parity bit would be '0'.

The minimal Hamming distance of the parity code is two, meaning the *parity* code can detect a single error bit.

$$\begin{aligned} \text{Data} &: 0\,1\,0\,1\,0\,1\,1\,0 \\ \text{Even parity codeword} &: 0\,1\,0\,1\,0\,1\,1\,0\,\mathbf{0} \\ \text{Odd parity codeword} &: 0\,1\,0\,1\,0\,1\,1\,0\,\mathbf{1} \end{aligned} \tag{6.8}$$

6.2.2.2 Hamming Code

Another fundamental coding technique is *Hamming* code, which can correct single-bit errors. A variation of this, known as *SECDED* (Single Error Correction, Double Error Detection), can detect two-bit errors, as suggested by its name.

The Hamming code consists of a data word of $2^r - r - 1$ bits and a corresponding codeword length of $2^r - 1$ bits, where $r \geq 2$. On the other hand, the SECDED

Table 6.2 Parity bit combination for hamming code: This table maps the positions of data bits that contribute to each parity bit in the Hamming or Single Error Correction Double Error Detection (SEC-DED) code. A mark (x) indicates that the corresponding bit is included in the calculation of the respective parity bit, helping to ensure error detection and correction in data transmission

Data bit position		1	2	3	4	5	6	7	8	9	10	11
Parity bit (Hamming)	1	x	x		x	x		x		x		x
	2	x		x	x		x	x			x	x
	3		x	x	x				x	x	x	x
	4					x	x	x	x	x	x	x
Extended parity bit (SECDED)		x	x	x	x	x	x	x	x	x	x	x

code adds an extra parity bit, resulting in a codeword length of 2^r bits. Table 6.2 illustrates an example of the Hamming code parity combinations. The Hamming code works by applying parity checks to different parts of the data word. The minimum Hamming distance for Hamming code is 3, allowing it to detect and correct single-bit errors but not distinguish between two-bit errors. An additional parity bit is introduced to detect two-bit errors, which extends the Hamming distance to 4 in the SECDED code, providing the ability to detect two-bit errors while still correcting single-bit errors.

Since SECDED can correct one error bit and detect two, it is widely used in computing systems, such as ECC-DRAM. Several variations of SECDED have been proposed that can fix and detect adjacent error bits. These enhanced codes achieve this capability by explicitly designing the parity bit patterns and decoding algorithms. Other coding methods, such as Cyclic Redundancy Check (CRC) and Reed-Solomon codes, are often used for error detection in systems where correction is not required.

In summary, information redundancy is critical in detecting and correcting error bits within a system. This approach is essential for maintaining data integrity in memory, caches, or on-chip communication.

6.2.3 *Software Approach*

Software approaches to fault tolerance are critical in ensuring system reliability and continuity despite faults or errors. These approaches include techniques like error detection and correction, redundancy, and checkpointing. Error detection and correction mechanisms, such as checksums, cyclic redundancy checks (CRCs), and more advanced methods like Hamming codes, help identify and correct data errors at the software level, maintaining data integrity. Redundancy involves running multiple instances of critical software components, so if one instance fails, another can seamlessly take over, ensuring continuous operation. This can be implemented through techniques like load balancing and replicated databases. Checkpointing, another vital strategy, involves periodically saving the system's state, allowing it to roll back to a known good state in the event of a failure, thereby minimizing data loss and recovery time. Additionally, software-based fault-tolerance can leverage self-healing algorithms that detect faults and automatically attempt to rectify them or switch to backup components. Together, these approaches significantly bolster the resilience of traditional computing systems, allowing them to manage faults smoothly and uphold high levels of availability and reliability.

6.3 Enhancing Fault-Tolerance in Neuromorphic Systems

This section comprehensively reviews major work on safeguarding neuromorphic systems, emphasizing three critical aspects: communication, computation, and memory. In communication, it discusses methods to ensure data integrity and efficient signal transmission across neuromorphic networks, addressing challenges such as latency, bandwidth, and fault resilience. For computation, the section explores various fault-tolerance techniques designed to maintain accurate processing within neuromorphic cores, including redundancy, error detection, and correction mechanisms. Memory protection strategies are also examined, highlighting methods to prevent data corruption and enhance the reliability of storage units, such as error correction codes and redundant memory architectures. Furthermore, this section shows the mapping techniques for Spiking Neural Networks (SNNs) specifically designed to recover from faults. These techniques involve allocating neural network components to hardware resources to maximize fault tolerance and system resilience. By leveraging dynamic reconfiguration and fault-aware mapping algorithms, neuromorphic systems can effectively adapt to and mitigate the impact of hardware faults, ensuring robust and reliable operation.

6.3.1 Memory Protection

Memory vulnerabilities to both permanent and temporary faults necessitate robust protection methods. One effective approach is using Error Correction Codes (ECC), such as Hamming or its extensions [7], which can correct single-bit errors in data. For correcting multiple errors, methods like Orthogonal Latin Square Code [8] or Triple Adjacent Error Correction [18] are commonly used. Another method involves adding spare rows or columns to replace faulty ones [11].

In neural network applications, memory errors can often be tolerated by accepting a loss in accuracy. For example, a CNN application experienced a 5.7 accuracy loss with an error rate of 0.0065, as studied in [5]. The analysis shown in Fig. 6.1 demonstrates a similar acceptable loss with comparable error rates. In summary, memory protection can be achieved either through error correction codes or by accepting some loss in accuracy under specific noise conditions.

For Spiking Neural Network (SNN) applications, the works in [19, 20] proposed a splitting architecture for weights, dividing them into subsets to handle manufacturing defects. In this approach, faults are allowed in the least significant subsets, while faults in the most considerable subsets are not tolerated. Additionally, swapping techniques are proposed to redirect faulty subsets to different positions, enabling the system to tolerate faults. Although initially intended for yield improvement, these techniques can also be applied to handle run-time defects without requiring modifications.

6.3.2 Communication Protection

In neuromorphic systems, spikes, neuron parameters, or weights transmitted within the system or to external memories are vulnerable to corruption, potentially leading to inaccurate results. Safeguarding their integrity is, therefore, crucial. One effective method is Error Correction Codes (ECC), which ensures data integrity despite bit errors. Like those used in memory protection, these codes can detect and correct errors to maintain system reliability.

Another standard communication error is misrouting or arbitration failures. In such scenarios, recovery strategies such as alternative routing paths or redundancy can help mitigate these issues. Fault-tolerant routing algorithms are essential in circumventing failure points and establishing reliable routes. Additionally, integrating redundant modules enables the system to replace faulty components with functional ones, thereby facilitating recovery and maintaining overall system performance.

6.3.3 Computation Protection

Faults in computation modules can severely impact Spiking Neural Networks (SNNs), making protecting these units crucial. Zhang et al. [23] proposed safeguarding systolic arrays through bypassing and retraining, allowing the system to tolerate faults by pruning and retraining the affected computations. Johnson et al. [10] also adjusted spiking models by modifying thresholds and frequencies to enhance fault tolerance. Alternatively, traditional methods, such as N-modular redundancies with majority voting [16], ensure correctness but incur significant area and power costs.

In large-scale Spiking Neural Network (SNN) systems utilizing Network-on-Chip (NoC), spare cores and remapping algorithms are employed to protect computations. Fault-tolerant NoC systems with homogeneous cores often use Integer Linear Programming (ILP) to optimize communication costs [3]. However, ILP's NP-completeness limits its scalability. Works by Sahu et al. [21] and Bhanu et al. [3] have applied Particle Swarm Optimization (PSO) to reduce mapping complexity, although these approaches do not guarantee optimality.

While PSO offers runtime reduction, its space complexity remains significant. For reliability-aware mapping, Namazi et al. [17] proposed a Mixed Non-Linear Programming model for task allocation in homogeneous NoC architectures, showing promise. However, it is primarily focused on conventional multi-core systems. In large-scale SNN setups, internal node recovery is feasible, reducing the need for external spare cores, though migration times between cores are not accounted for.

6.3.4 Error-Resilient Mapping Strategies for SNNs

Remapping neurons to avoid faulty ones is an effective method to correct faults in a neuromorphic system. In Network-on-Chip (NoC)-based multi-core systems, both Spiking Neural Network (SNN) mapping methods [1, 2, 9, 12, 15] and traditional multi-core NoC mapping [3] are employed for neuron placement. The method in [3] optimizes communication costs, while [22] focuses on on-chip network traffic in neuromorphic systems. However, mapping for neural networks (NN) remains complex due to the many neurons.

Conventional SNN mapping typically involves two phases [2]: (1) *Partitioning*, which clusters neurons into groups, and (2) *Mapping*, which assigns these groups to hardware. Challenges arise from NP-hard graph partitioning and mapping, often resulting in suboptimal solutions. For layered SNN applications, nodes are treated as distinct layers, yet traditional methods overlook communication multicast. Lagrange multipliers [12] help reduce runtime complexity but may increase execution times. For practical applications, partitioning approaches like those in [15] offer promising results despite the NP-hard nature of the problem. In [2], the Kernighan-Lin (KL) method is used to manage complexity, although it yields less-than-optimal results.

6.3.5 Fault-Tolerant Mapping Techniques for Neuromorphic Systems

Fault-tolerant mapping techniques for neuromorphic systems are essential for ensuring the reliable operation of these advanced computing architectures in the presence of faults. These techniques involve strategically assigning neural network components, such as neurons and synapses, to the hardware resources to maximize fault tolerance and system resilience. One approach is redundancy, where multiple instances of critical components are mapped to different hardware resources, allowing the system to switch to a backup component if a fault occurs. Dynamic reconfiguration is another crucial technique, which involves continuously monitoring the system for faults and dynamically remapping the neural network components to avoid faulty areas. This can be achieved through algorithms that detect real-time faults and reallocate resources to maintain optimal performance.

Additionally, error detection and correction codes can be employed to identify and correct data errors during communication between neurons and synapses, ensuring data integrity. Particle Swarm Optimization (PSO) and other heuristic algorithms are often used to reduce the complexity of the mapping process, providing efficient solutions for large-scale neuromorphic systems. These techniques enhance the system's fault tolerance and contribute to its overall robustness and reliability, allowing neuromorphic systems to maintain high-performance levels even in the face of hardware faults. By leveraging these fault-tolerant mapping strategies, designers can ensure that neuromorphic systems can operate effectively in real-world applications where reliability is paramount [4].

6.3.6 Problem Formulation

Here, we consider a working system S comprising N nodes (or neuron clusters), with each node containing E_i neurons ($i = 0, 1, \ldots, N - 1$). In serial systems [1, 6], the number of neurons corresponds to the available memory slots per node.

The value of E_i varies based on design and can differ across clusters in heterogeneous systems.

In summary, the total number of neurons in system S is $X = \sum_{i=0}^{N-1} E_i$. We assume the SNN application requires W neurons, where $W \leq X$ for the application to be feasible.

Fault Tolerance

Since the system architecture supports fault tolerance, we allocate R spare neurons, where $R = X - W$, for repairs. When up to $k \leq R$ neurons become faulty and need removal from the system, our problem involves remapping these k neurons to the R spare neurons. If $k > R$, the system S cannot rectify the faults, necessitating off-chip migration (e.g., replacing the chip and migrating to it). Achieving k-fault tolerance entails remapping the function, parameters, and weights of k neurons. Repairability is categorized into two levels:

- *Node-level recovery*: Nodes with sufficient spare neurons internally remap failed ones. Otherwise, *system-level recovery* is initiated, where weights and parameters are read from external storage and written to spare neurons.
- *System-level recovery*: When a node lacks sufficient spare neurons, neurons migrate across nodes. Migrating neurons carry their weights, mapping LUT elements and status to new locations. Excess neurons beyond E_i design limits are migrated.

For *system-level recovery*, reliable communication guarantees support up to R fault tolerance ($k = R$). Figure 6.6 illustrates the system model S with $N = 9$ nodes, each containing $E_i = 256$ neurons ($X = 2304$), and a proposed solution. The application requires $W = 2000$ neurons and employs uniform neuron mapping,

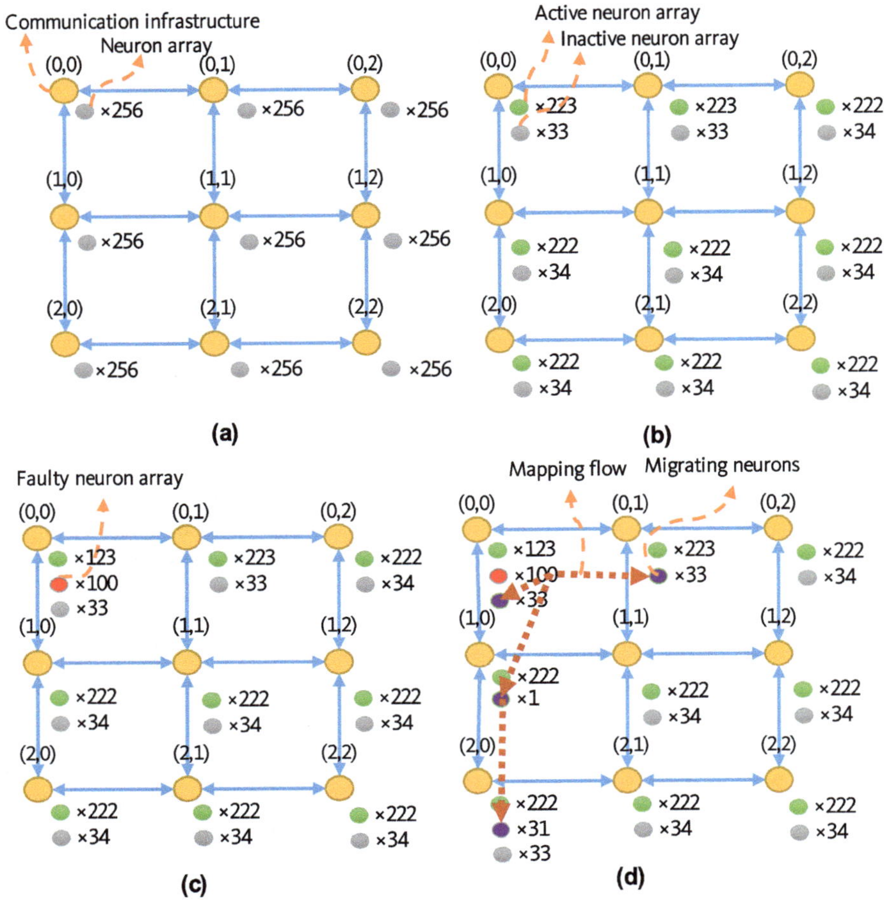

Fig. 6.6 System model for fault-tolerant SNN: (**a**) Designed SNN system with initial node mapping; (**b**) *Node-level recovery*; (**c**) Failure of *node-level recovery* to correct; (**d**) *System-level recovery*: flow of 100 faulty neurons mapped to neighboring nodes. Numbers near circles indicate neuron counts (green: healthy and utilized; gray: healthy and spared; red: faulty; purple: migrating)

as depicted in Fig. 6.6a. Each node in this example has 33 or 34 spare neurons, allowing correction of up to 33 or 34 faulty neurons per node.

Figure 6.6b demonstrates *node-level recovery*, where node (0,0) rectifies ten defective neurons internally. Conversely, Fig. 6.6c shows *node-level recovery* failing when 100 neurons are defective in the node (0,0). In response, Fig. 6.6d outlines a mapping strategy where 100 faulty neurons are redistributed among nodes (0,0), (0,1), and (1,0), leveraging *system-level recovery*.

One of the primary challenges is how to remap the SNN to recover from faulty neurons. Traditionally, a key optimization goal for remapping is minimizing the communication cost, as defined by [3]:

$$F_{cost} = \sum_{i=0,j=0}^{W} d_{ij} \times c_{ij} \tag{6.9}$$

where d_{ij} and c_{ij} represent the distance and connection status between node i and j. When c_{ij} is binary (0/1), F_{cost} becomes the sum of distances traveled by neurons. This optimization strategy involves rerunning the mapping algorithm with information about faulty neurons. However, migrating neurons in large-scale systems entails significant memory access. Hence, this study focuses on optimizing the migration cost, defined by:

$$M_{cost} = \sum_{i=0,j=0}^{W} d_{ij} \times m_{ij} \tag{6.10}$$

where m_{ij} denotes the number of migrating neurons between node i and j.

Since data within faulty neurons (weight memory, threshold, etc.) can be corrupted, the system must write back from its host CPU. The migration distance is calculated from the node (0), typically where the I/O module is attached. This optimization aims to ensure high system availability with minimal repair time.

6.3.6.1 Max-Flow Min-Cut Based Algorithm

In this section, we introduce an algorithm to enhance the reliability of the SNN system by optimizing M_{cost} in Eq. (6.10).

Max-Flow Min-Cut Theorem Graph models widely use The max-flow min-cut theorem to find optimal flows between sources and sinks. Here, we apply a similar approach: faulty neurons act as sources, and spare neurons as sinks. Dealing with multi-source and multi-sink scenarios is complex but can be simplified using a virtual sink and source.

The choice of max-flow min-cut for remapping stems from its efficiency in balancing execution time and memory footprint compared to greedy search approaches. Unlike greedy methods that directly move from faulty to spare neurons, max-flow min-cut creates optimal migration paths, limiting migration distances (evaluated later). It also offers lower complexity than meta-heuristic methods like Genetic Algorithms or Particle Swarm Optimization (PSO), which require substantial memory and may not be suitable for low-cost host CPUs. While reusing the mapping method for system-wide remapping is feasible, high migration costs due to extensive memory transactions are a concern.

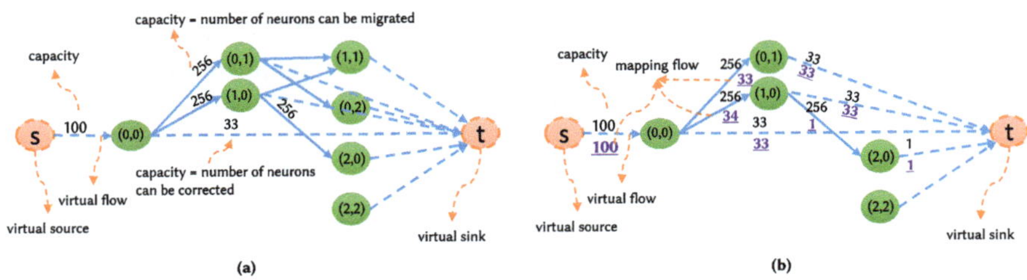

Fig. 6.7 Flow graph for the max-flow min-cut problem: (**a**) Derived Flow from the NoC-Based Spiking Neural Network (SNN); (**b**) Solution to the Max-Flow Min-Cut Problem. Figure (**a**) illustrates the flow of defects requiring correction in a NoC-based SNN, with the capacities representing the number of defects or available spare resources. Figure (**b**) presents the solution, where the channels are filled with migrating neurons, effectively addressing the identified defects

Figure 6.7 illustrates a flow graph for fault tolerance, derived from Fig. 6.6c. By establishing virtual sources and sinks, we support neuron migration. For instance, the connection from the virtual source to a faulty node has a capacity equivalent to the number of faulty neurons (e.g., 100 in Fig. 6.7a). Nodes connected to this source can accept flows up to their healthy neuron count. Figure 6.7a shows a flow capacity of 256 from (0,0) to (0,1), as node (0,1) hosts 256 neurons available for migration. Each node also connects to a virtual sink with flow capacity corresponding to available spare neurons (e.g., 33 spare neurons at (0,0) in Fig. 6.7a). Restricting migration distances to one hop ($d_{ij} \leq one$) reduces migration costs, as per Eq. (6.10). Solving this with a max-flow min-cut approach yields the flow map in Fig. 6.7b, facilitating the transition to NoC-based SNN for new mappings.

The Edmonds-Karp Algorithm implements the Ford-Fulkerson method with a complexity of $O(|V||E|^2)$, translating to $O(N^3)$ for 2D and 3D networks (where N is the number of nodes). This guarantees P-complexity versus NP-completeness for Integer Linear Programming (ILP) or $O(N!)$ for heuristic searches. PSO approaches, like [21], operate at $O(GKN^2 \log N)$ (where G and K are generations and particles, respectively). Scaling particles with nodes, PSO complexity reaches $O(N^4 \log N)$, higher than our $O(N^3)$. Moreover, PSO requires more memory due to particle counts, contrasting our approach's lower footprint.

Graph-Based Algorithm Algorithm 6.1 details our proposed method for tolerating defective neurons. First, it constructs a flow graph (lines 2–7) linking sources and sinks. Each node n_i connects to a source with a capacity matching its faulty neurons and to a sink with spare neuron capacity. Nodes with surplus redundancy can recover locally (line 10). The algorithm then establishes inter-node flows within a maximum distance d_{max} (line 14), capped by the destination's healthy neuron count. Using Edmonds-Karp for system-level repair augments paths to maximize flows (lines 17–19). Successful flow matching k faulty neurons completes the algorithm; otherwise, it indicates failure, necessitating retraining or maintenance.

Algorithm 6.1 The proposed max-flow min-cut neuron cluster replacement algorithm

```
// Build flow graph
add source s and sink t for (node n_i in the system) do
    add vertex for the node n_i
    add edge from the source s to the vertex n_i
    add capacity n_i → s = number of defective neuron in the vertex n_i
    add edge from the vertex n_i to the sink t
    add capacity n_i → t = number of available redundant neurons attached to vertex n_i

for (node n_i in the system) do
    // Node-level repair
    if node n_i has more redundancies than defects then
        node-level recovery vertex n_i;
for (node n_i in the system) do
    for (node n_j in the system) do
        if (d_ij ≤ d_max) then
            add edge from the vertex n_i to the vertex n_j
            add capacity n_i → n_j = number of healthy neurons in n_j
// System-level repair with Edmonds-Karp
while no augmenting path do
    Breadth first search to find minimum path
    Augmenting the found minimum path with capacity
    Save the flow
// Finish the algorithm and require re-training or maintenance if it
    failed
if (max-flow == k ) then
    // done
    return 0;
else
    // The approach fails to correct.
    return 1;
```

Figure 6.8 illustrates the algorithm's operation in a 3D-NoC-based neuromorphic system with $N = 36$ nodes and $X = 9216$ neurons. Mapping 9060 neurons leaves 156 spares, repairing eight faulty nodes with 138 defective neurons. Node (2,2,0) recovers with local nodes, while system-level recovery migrates others to nearby nodes. Successful remapping yields 18 spares post-repair, highlighting minimal migration distances within one hop.

Augmenting Migrating Distance

Although the max-flow min-cut method can optimize neuron migration cost, it is not always optimal. To increase the minimum cut, we can relax the value of d_{max}; however, this increases the complexity of the Edmonds-Karp Algorithm (increasing the number of edges).

According to the max-flow min-cut theorem, the maximum number of neurons that can be corrected is limited by the minimum cut of the flow network. Therefore, the system might be unable to fix as many neurons as there are redundancies.

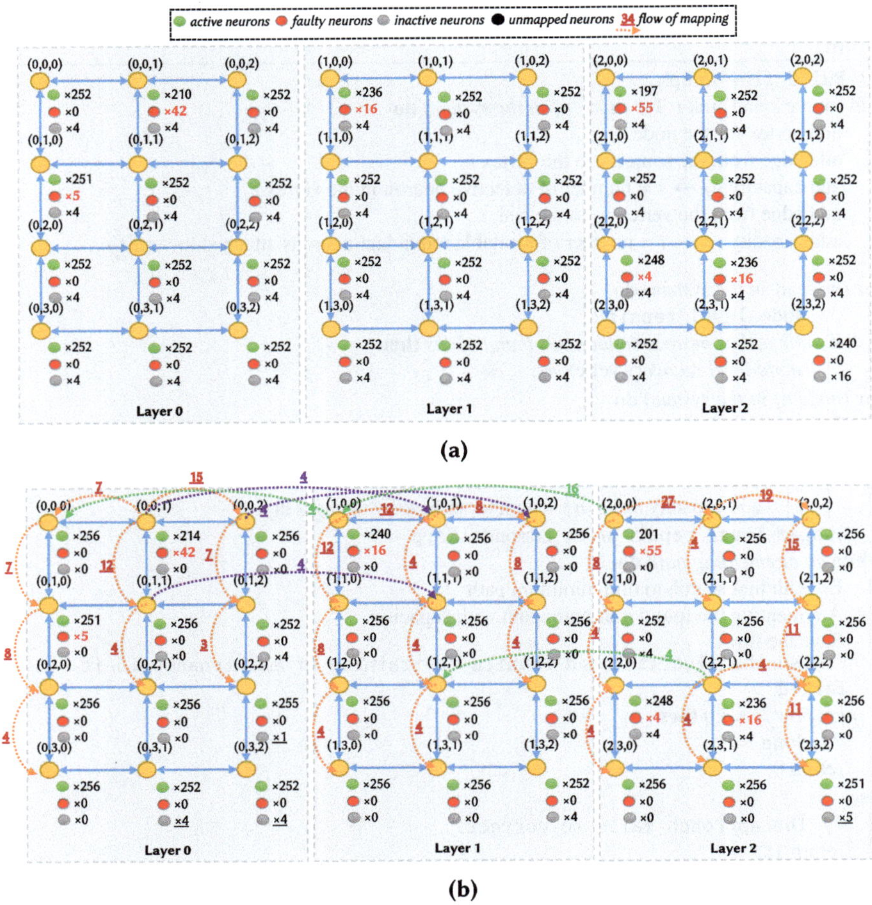

Fig. 6.8 Illustration of the proposed algorithm: (**a**) Faulty Scenario; (**b**) Post-Mapping Using the Proposed Algorithm. Figure (**a**) depicts the distribution of active, faulty, inactive, and unmapped neurons, with unmapped neurons resulting from excess active neurons compared to the available healthy ones. Figure (**b**) shows the proposed remapping solution, where arrows indicate the direction of migration and the associated numbers specify the number of neurons to be migrated

Consider node (0,0) or (0,0,0) in Fig. 6.9. These nodes have 200 faulty neurons and are surrounded by nodes with 210 faulty neurons. After *node-level* recovery, there are 177 unmapped neurons.

However, the maximum flow from these nodes to their neighbors is 112 for a 2D mesh topology and 168 for a 3D mesh topology. In this situation, the system fails to recover despite having redundancies in other nodes.

To address this, we need to consider a communication cost of two, allowing neurons to move by two hops. The flow graph must be reconstructed for this different d_{max}.

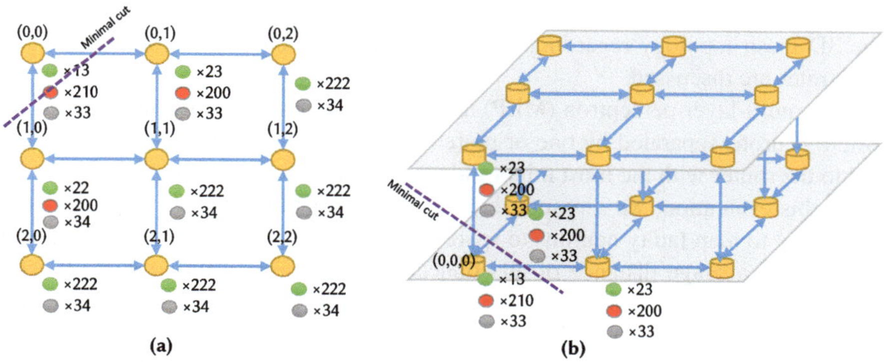

Fig. 6.9 Examples of the minimal cut drawback: (**a**) 2D Mesh; (**b**) 3D Mesh. These figures illustrate that the corners of the mesh topology represent the minimal cut points, where the least number of neurons can be migrated theoretically

---

Algorithm 6.2 Augmenting migrating distance algorithm (MFMC-AMD)

$d_{max} = 1$
while *(mapping success* **or** $d_{max} >$ *(number of layers +number of rows + number of columns))* **do**
  run Algorithm 6.1
  $d_{max} ++$;

Algorithm 6.2 presents our algorithm for increasing the maximum migrating distance to address the issue of a small minimal cut. If the number of faults exceeds the number of spares, the mapping is unsuccessful.

We run Algorithm 6.1 based on whether the SNN has single or multiple layers. Afterward, we perform retraining or maintenance to fit the SNN into the neuromorphic system.

We gradually increase the migrating distance to find the smallest value needed to recover from system failure. This allows us to balance the trade-off between the maximum migrating distance (d_{max}) and recovery. By increasing the d_{max} value to the maximum distance within the NoC, we can ensure mapping for $k \leq R$ cases.

6.3.6.2 Evaluation

In this section, the proposed algorithms (MFMC: *max-flow min-cut* adaptation and GA: *Genetic Algorithm*), 1-hop and N-hop, and *Greedy Search* (GS) are evaluated to understand their efficiency.

The *Greedy Search* runs each node once and looks for a spare node within a 1-hop range or the entire system (N-hop) with the shortest distance. The algorithms are implemented in Java. We insert faults into the system to test the algorithms' efficiency.

The focus is on the communication cost function F_{cost} in Eq. (6.9) and evaluating the 3D mesh topology regarding migration efficiency. Different system sizes and fault rates are discussed.

The multi-layer perceptron (MLP) network is evaluated and organized in layers where neurons separated by one or more layers are disconnected. Input spikes are fed to the router with the most minor indexes (i.e., (0,0) or (0,0,0)).

In this evaluation, we measure three significant parameters: *(1) mapping rate:* the ability to map faulty neurons to spare ones; *(2) average spike transmission cost* (F_{cost})*:* the average distance of all connections; and *(3) Migration cost* (M_{cost})*:* the amount of read/write neurons needed to adapt the system. The evaluation configuration is shown in Table 6.3.

Figure 6.10 shows the results for the proposed system for 3D-NoC configurations (see Table 6.3). Our methods can map all faulty neurons to the spare ones regardless of the size or topology.

We note that the MFMC algorithm is not optimal for communication costs, and the 1-hop *Greedy Search* can only map about 60% (around 80% in the worst cases) of the faulty neurons. This is because the 1-hop *Greedy Search* only runs once and looks for one mapping solution of its neighbor, failing to map easily. Meanwhile, the N-hop *Greedy Search* and the Genetic Algorithm can map all neurons.

The average F_{cost} (communication cost) varies between different approaches. The average communication distance per neuron remains unchanged since the 1-hop GS mostly fails to map the neurons. The average F_{cost} for other methods fluctuates between different sizes. However, as shown in Fig. 6.10, they are reduced when we increase the size of the NoC. This is because, as we increase the size of the NoC, the impact of moving neurons is reduced. The effects are also minor, with lower fault rates (k values). We can see that the communication cost is maintained with remapping, but we observe a slight reduction with the migration-based algorithm. Also, GA seems to have a better average F_{cost} since it reduces that value as the second factor.

Table 6.3 Configuration for the evaluation[a]

Parameter	Value
# neurons per node (E)	256
# nodes (N)	2D-NoC: 4×4 to 16×16
	3D-NoC: $4 \times 4 \times 4$ to $16 \times 16 \times 16$
# spare neurons (R)	$0.2 \times X$
# spare node	1
# faults (k)	$0.05 \times X$, $0.10 \times X$, $0.15 \times X$, and $0.20 \times X$
SNN # layers	4
SNN configuration[a]	784:0.5*(W-10): 0.5*(W-10): 10

[a] MLP model for MNIST. For example, the SNN configuration for E=256 and 4×4 is 784:1633:1633:10

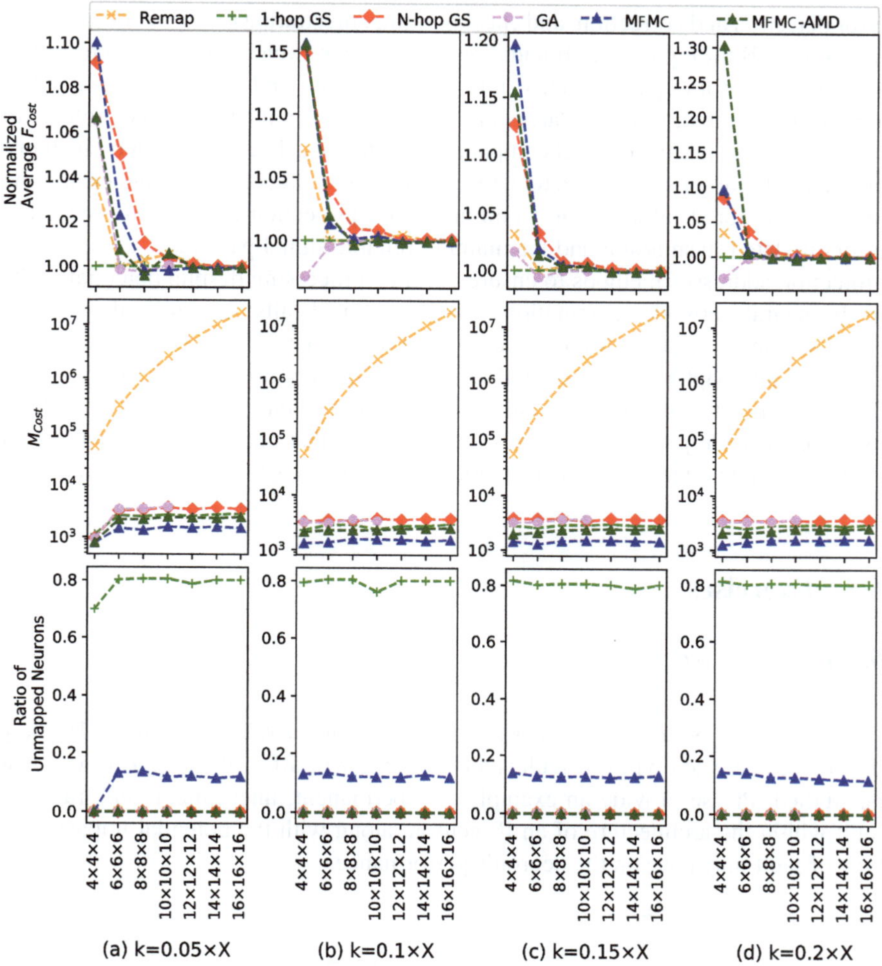

Fig. 6.10 Output mapping for migrated neurons with the minimal-cut cases in 3D NoC: (**a**) 5% error rate; (**b**) 10% error rate; (**c**) 15% error rate; and (**d**) 20% error rate. The system has 256 neurons per node; 20% of neurons are spare with one redundant node without any allocated neuron at 0% fault rate. MFMC-AMD: the augmenting migrating distance d_{max} method

6.4 Chapter Summary

This chapter shows the intricate mechanisms and strategies employed to enhance the reliability and robustness of neuromorphic systems. The introduction sets the stage by discussing the fundamental importance of fault tolerance in neuromorphic computing, drawing comparisons to traditional computing systems where fault-tolerance techniques have long been developed and implemented. The following section provides a comprehensive overview of established methods such as redundancy, error detection and correction, and checkpointing, illustrating their effectiveness and limitations. Building on this foundation, the chapter explores tailored approaches specific to neuromorphic systems' unique architecture and operational principles. Within this context, three key areas are thoroughly examined: memory protection, communication protection, and computation protection. The discussion on memory protection highlights strategies to safeguard against data corruption and ensure the integrity of stored information. Communication protection focuses on preventing errors in data transmission and maintaining reliable signal pathways. Computation protection addresses methods to ensure accurate processing despite potential faults in the neural network computations. Each section details current methodologies and discusses innovative solutions and future directions. To reinforce the concepts covered, the chapter concludes with exercises designed to challenge readers and deepen their understanding of fault-tolerant neuromorphic system design. These exercises provide practical scenarios and problems that encourage the application of theoretical knowledge, ensuring readers gain a robust grasp of the material.

6.5 Exercises

6.5.1 Exercise 1

Fault tolerance is an important aspect of designing a reliable system. The key differences between types of faults and how they will affect the performance must be studied. Please provide an example of a permanent, intermittent, and transient fault within the architecture of an IF neuron, along with the potential impact each type of fault may have on the neuron's performance.

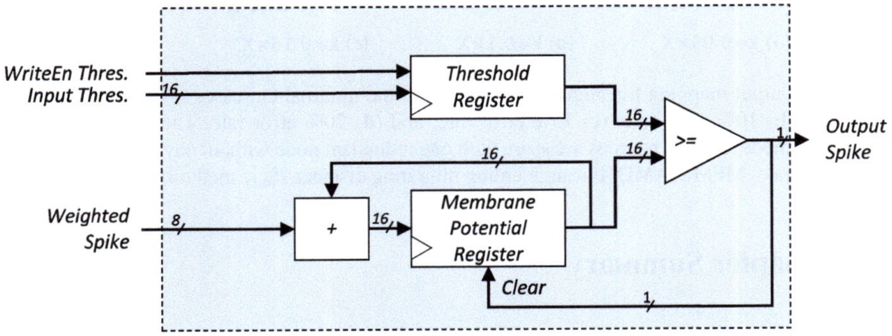

In this exercise, permanent faults will be analyzed. In terms of fault location, the following modules must be analyzed: (1) Threshold register, (2) 16-bit adder, (3) Membrane Potential Register, and (4) Comparator.

6.5.2 Exercise 2

What is the main difference between transient and permanent faults? By applying the previous exercise, please provide the analyses for all modules and compare them to the transient fault.

6.5.3 Exercise 3

There are several well-known techniques for tolerant faults. One of them is triple modular redundancy (TMR). With the architecture of the LIF neuron as in Exercise 1, employ TMR (Triple Modular Redundancy) to protect each circuit module. Illustrate the updated circuit for each alternative protective design and explain how it can correct the potential fault.

In terms of protected location, the following modules must be analyzed: (1) Threshold register, (2) 16-bit adder, (3) Membrane Potential Register, and (4) Comparator.

Once the TMR is applied, please analyze which part of the modified LIF neuron is protected and which is not. Moreover, please analyze the significant drawback of TMR in this scenario.

6.5.4 Exercise 4

Since TMR is very cost-efficient, what can we do to reduce the area cost while keeping the protection of the threshold register?

6.5.5 Exercise 5

To protect against memory errors, using an Error Correction Code (ECC) is a popular approach. Among all ECCs, the Hamming Code is one of the most popular methods. Given the Hamming Code (7, 4) is as in the following table.

Bit position		1	2	3	4	5	6	7
Encoded data bits		p1	p2	d1	p3	d2	d3	d4
Parity bit coverage	p1	#		#		#		#
	p2		#	#			#	#
	p3				#	#	#	#

where the data word is $d1, d2, d3, d4$ and the codeword is $p1$, $p2, d1$, $p3, d2, d3$, $d4$. The values of $p1$, $p2$, and $p2$ are based on the above table. Here, # stands for where the parity bit takes in.

In this exercise, please first illustrate this Hamming Code's encoding circuit (input: 4-bit, output: 7-bit). Then, given the $d1$ bit is flipped after reading the codeword, illustrate how to correct it using Hamming (7,4). Finally, given the $d1$ and $p3$ bits are flipped after reading the codeword, please illustrate how you can correct them.

6.5.6 Exercise 6

If the register is 8-bit, how can we use Hamming Code?

6.5.7 Exercise 7

The Hamming Code (7,4) in Exercise 3 protects the registers (4 separate sets of Hamming (7,4)). Then, compare TMR and Hamming Code approaches regarding area cost and overall reliability.

6.5.8 Exercise 8

Assuming the neuromorphic system consists of a 2D Mesh NoC of 4×4 (in total 16 cores). Each core consists of 4 neurons (64 physical neurons). Please do a mapping for an SNN model of 28:28:4 (in total, 60 neurons; 4 spare physical neurons). Initial mapping is linearly from the core (0,0) (X first: (0,0) then (0,1), then Y: (0,3) then (1,0)). All four spare neurons are in the highest index node (3,3).

6.5.9 Exercise 9

In this exercise, we use the initial mapping from the previous one. Under a fault scenario of all four physical neurons in the core (1,1) are faulty, please suggest (1) a remapping approach for the fastest repairing time or (2) a remapping approach for better communication.

6.5.10 *Exercise 10*

One of the main drawbacks of fault-tolerant mapping is that we need enough neurons to correct the faults. If we do not have enough neurons, please suggest a solution.

References

1. Akopyan F, et al (2015) Truenorth: design and tool flow of a 65 mw 1 million neuron programmable neurosynaptic chip. IEEE Trans Comput Aid Des Integr Circuits Syst 34(10):1537–1557
2. Balaji A, et al (2019) Mapping spiking neural networks to neuromorphic hardware. IEEE Trans Very Large Scale Integr Syst 28(1):76–86
3. Bhanu PV, Kulkarni PV, Soumya J (2019) Fault-tolerant network-on-chip design with flexible spare core placement. J Emerg Technol Comput Syst 15(1):1–23
4. Dang KN, Doan NAV, Abdallah AB (2022) Migspike: a migration based algorithms and architecture for scalable robust neuromorphic systems. IEEE Trans Emerg Top Comput 10(2):602–617
5. Denkinger BW, Ponzina, F, Basu SS, Bonetti A, Balási S, Ruggiero M, Peón-Quirós M, Rossi D, Burg A, Atienza D (2019) Impact of memory voltage scaling on accuracy and resilience of deep learning based edge devices. IEEE Des Test 37:84–92
6. Frenkel C, et al (2018) A 0.086-mm^2 12.7-PJ/SOP 64k-synapse 256-neuron online-learning digital spiking neuromorphic processor in 28-nm CMOS. IEEE Trans Biomed Circuits Syst 13(1):145–158
7. Hsiao MY (1970) A class of optimal minimum odd-weight-column SEC-DED codes. IBM J Res Dev 14(4):395–401
8. Hsiao M, Bossen D, Chien R (1970) Orthogonal latin square codes. IBM J Res Develop 14(4):390–394
9. Jin X (2010) Parallel simulation of neural networks on spinnaker universal neuromorphic hardware. Ph.D. Thesis, The University of Manchester
10. Johnson AP, Liu J, Millard AG, Karim S, Tyrrell AM, Harkin J, Timmis J, McDaid LJ, Halliday DM (2017) Homeostatic fault tolerance in spiking neural networks: a dynamic hardware perspective. IEEE Trans Circuits Syst I Regul Pap 65(2):687–699
11. Kim I, Zorian Y, Komoriya G, Pham H, Higgins FP, Lewandowski JL (1998) Built in self repair for embedded high density SRAM. In: Proceedings international test conference 1998 (IEEE Cat. No. 98CH36270), pp 1112–1119
12. Kim G, Kornijcuk V, Kim J, Hwang CS, Jeong DS (2020) Optimal distribution of spiking neurons over multicore neuromorphic processors. IEEE Access 8:69426–69437
13. Koren I, Breuer MA (1984) On area and yield considerations for fault-tolerant VLSI processor arrays. IEEE Trans Comput 100(1):21–27
14. Koren I, Krishna CM (2020) Fault-tolerant systems. Morgan Kaufmann, Burlington
15. Li S, Guo S, Zhang L, Kang Z, Wang S, Shi W, Wang L, Xu W (2020) Sneap: a fast and efficient toolchain for mapping large-scale spiking neural network onto NoC-based neuromorphic platform. arXiv:2004.01639
16. Lyons RE, Vanderkulk W (1962) The use of triple-modular redundancy to improve computer reliability. IBM J Res Develop 6(2):200–209
17. Namazi A, Abdollahi M, Safari S, Mohammadi S (2017) A majority-based reliability-aware task mapping in high-performance homogenous noc architectures. ACM Trans Embed Comput Syst 17(1):1–31

18. Neale A, Jonkman M, Sachdev M (2014) Adjacent-MBU-tolerant SEC-DED-TAEC-yAED codes for embedded SRAMS. IEEE Trans Circuits Syst II Express Briefs 62(4):387–391
19. Nguyen ND, Dang KN (2023) A novel yield improvement approach for 3D stacking neuromorphic architecture. In: 2023 IEEE 16th international symposium on embedded multicore/many-core systems-on-chip (MCSoC). IEEE, Piscataway, pp 392–398
20. Nguyen ND, Ahmed AB, Abdallah AB, Dang KN (2023) Power-aware neuromorphic architecture with partial voltage scaling 3-D stacking synaptic memory. IEEE Trans Very Large Scale Integr Syst 31:2016
21. Sahu PK, Shah T, Manna K, Chattopadhyay S (2013) Application mapping onto mesh-based network-on-chip using discrete particle swarm optimization. IEEE Trans Very Large Scale Integr Syst 22(2):300–312
22. Urgese G, Barchi F, Macii E, Acquaviva A (2016) Optimizing network traffic for spiking neural network simulations on densely interconnected many-core neuromorphic platforms. IEEE Trans Emerg Top Comput 6(3):317–329
23. Zhang JJ, Basu K, Garg S (2019) Fault-tolerant systolic array based accelerators for deep neural network execution. IEEE Des Test 36(5):44–53

Chapter 7
Reconfigurable Neuromorphic Computing Systems

Abstract The human brain is renowned for its vast parallel reconfigurable synapses that connect billions of neurons, playing a crucial role in learning and adaptability. The synaptic weight represents the strength of the connection between two neurons. Spiking Neural Networks (SNNs) leverage this biological inspiration for applications ranging from vision systems to brain-computer interfaces. Traditionally, the design of these systems has focused on fixed functionality using off-the-shelf components, which lack the flexibility to adapt to various computing environments. In contrast, the reconfigurable design approach supports multiple target applications through dynamic reconfigurability, network topology independence, and expandability. This chapter explores the architecture and hardware design of a reconfigurable neuromorphic processor. The architecture features an SNN that can be reconfigured to recover from faults using suitable methods that employ Field-Programmable Gate Arrays (FPGAs) without relying on proprietary intellectual property. This reconfigurable approach facilitates the implementation of neuromorphic processors in Application-Specific Integrated Circuits (ASICs), enhancing their versatility and robustness.

7.1 Introduction

Reconfigurable neuromorphic computing systems represent a groundbreaking approach to neural network design, drawing inspiration from the adaptability and learning capabilities of the human brain. These systems leverage reconfigurable hardware, such as Field-Programmable Gate Arrays (FPGAs), to dynamically adjust their architecture and functionality based on the requirements of specific tasks or applications. This capability allows for the efficient implementation of Spiking Neural Networks (SNNs) that can recover from faults and reconfigure themselves to maintain performance and reliability. Unlike traditional fixed-function systems, reconfigurable neuromorphic computing systems offer the flexibility to modify network topologies, adjust synaptic weights, and integrate new computational units. This versatility is essential for various applications, from vision systems and brain-computer interfaces to autonomous systems and robotics, where the ability to adapt

A. Ben Abdallah, K. N. Dang, *Neuromorphic Computing Principles and Organization*, https://doi.org/10.1007/978-3-031-83089-1_7

and reconfigure on the fly can significantly enhance performance and resilience. By leveraging the principles of dynamic reconfigurability, these systems aim to bridge the gap between biological neural networks and artificial computing architectures, paving the way for more robust, scalable, and efficient neuromorphic processors.

Reconfigurable neuromorphic systems offer numerous compelling advantages, making them a pivotal innovation in neural network computation. These systems are inherently adaptable and capable of dynamically adjusting their architecture to meet the specific needs of various applications. This adaptability ensures they can efficiently manage diverse tasks, from vision systems and brain-computer interfaces to autonomous robotics and complex data analysis. One of the most critical merits of reconfigurable neuromorphic systems is their enhanced fault tolerance. By incorporating redundancy, error correction, and dynamic reconfiguration techniques, these systems can quickly recover from faults, maintaining their performance and reliability even in challenging conditions.

Additionally, reconfigurable neuromorphic systems can be implemented on flexible platforms like Field-Programmable Gate Arrays (FPGAs), offering unparalleled scalability and customization. This flexibility allows for continuous improvements and updates without requiring entirely new hardware. Overall, reconfigurable neuromorphic systems combine the adaptability, resilience, and efficiency necessary to mimic the human brain's extraordinary capabilities, making them an essential component of future advancements in artificial intelligence and computing. A typical Deep Neural Network (DNN) accelerator organization is a sophisticated setup designed to handle the intensive computational requirements of neural network processing. As shown in Fig. 7.1, a typical DNN accelerator features numerous processing elements (PEs) arranged in parallel, enabling the simultaneous execution of arithmetic operations like multiplication and addition, which are essential for neural network computations. To support these operations efficiently, the accelerator includes a hierarchical memory subsystem. This memory hierarchy consists of on-

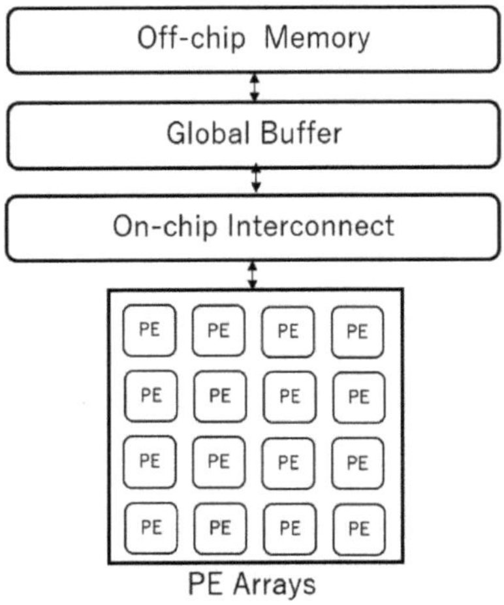

Fig. 7.1 Typical DNN accelerator organization: This figure illustrates the organizational structure of a Deep Neural Network (DNN) accelerator, highlighting its key components and their interconnections. The accelerator comprises multiple processing elements (PEs) arranged in a grid to enable parallel computation of neural network operations

chip memory, such as registers and scratchpads, for fast access to critical data and off-chip memory, like DRAM, for storing larger datasets. The interconnect network is pivotal in this organization, connecting PEs with memory modules and facilitating data movement. The network can take various forms, such as a bus, mesh, or Network-on-Chip (NoC), and its design greatly influences the performance and scalability of the accelerator.

A well-structured control unit orchestrates the operations of these components, managing the execution of neural network layers, data flow, and synchronization. It may include specialized controllers for specific tasks, such as convolution, pooling, and activation functions. DNN accelerators often adopt specific dataflow architectures, like weight-stationary, output-stationary, and row-stationary dataflows, to optimize the processing of neural network layers. Energy efficiency is another critical consideration, with accelerators incorporating techniques like data reuse, compression, quantization, and dynamic voltage and frequency scaling (DVFS) to reduce power consumption. Programmability and flexibility are key features that enable the accelerator to support a wide range of neural network models and applications. This flexibility is achieved through programmable PEs, configurable memory hierarchies, and adaptable dataflow architectures, allowing the accelerator to be tailored to specific tasks and accommodate advancements in neural network algorithms. Lastly, integration with host systems, such as CPUs or GPUs, ensures that the accelerator can offload computationally intensive tasks, leaving the host system to handle preprocessing, data transfer, and system management. This comprehensive organization enables DNN accelerators to deliver high-performance neural network processing capabilities, essential for deploying complex neural networks across various applications, from edge devices to data centers.

Each layer in a Deep Neural Network (DNN) is typically represented as a two-dimensional (2D) structure, resulting in the overall network being a three-dimensional (3D) arrangement of interconnected layers. This 3D structure poses significant challenges when mapping onto a two-dimensional circuit. One of the primary difficulties is the need for long wires to connect neurons from different layers, which can lead to increased signal latency and potential communication bottlenecks. These long interconnects affect data transmission speed and contribute to higher power consumption and increased susceptibility to signal degradation. Additionally, the physical layout can lead to congestion points where multiple connections converge, causing further delays and complicating the routing process. This congestion can exacerbate heat dissipation issues, as densely packed areas generate more heat, potentially affecting the reliability and longevity of the hardware. Efficiently mapping a 3D neural network onto a 2D substrate thus requires sophisticated design strategies to minimize wire lengths, balance load distribution, and optimize the placement of components to mitigate congestion. Advanced routing algorithms, innovative architectural designs, and the use of three-dimensional integrated circuits (3D ICs) are some approaches being explored to address these challenges and enhance the performance and efficiency of DNN accelerators.

The primary challenges include achieving efficient on-chip communication and network routing, developing lightweight spiking neuro-processing cores, implementing on-chip learning, and creating an efficient neuro-coding scheme. Additionally, it's essential to recognize that the number of neurons to be connected is several orders of magnitude (at least 10^3) more significant than the number of cores that need to be interconnected on recent multicore system-on-chip platforms [15]. These obstacles make constructing such a neuromorphic integrated circuit a formidable task regarding on-chip interconnect [7].

7.1.1 Design Consideration

Designing a reconfigurable neuromorphic chip involves several critical considerations to ensure its functionality, adaptability, and efficiency. One of the primary aspects is the architecture's flexibility, which must allow for dynamic reconfiguration of neural network components such as neurons and synapses. This flexibility enables the chip to adapt to different tasks and recover from hardware faults, enhancing its reliability. Another critical factor is the integration of efficient communication and data routing mechanisms. Given the complex and data-intensive nature of neuromorphic systems, ensuring low-latency and high-bandwidth communication paths between processing elements is vital. Lightweight and efficient spiking neuro-processing cores are also essential, as they directly impact the chip's computational performance and power consumption.

Additionally, the chip must support on-chip learning capabilities, allowing it to adapt and improve its performance over time without relying on external systems. Implementing robust error detection and correction methods is crucial to maintaining data integrity and system reliability. Furthermore, an efficient neuro-coding scheme is necessary to encode and decode neural signals accurately and efficiently. Lastly, scalability is a significant consideration, as the design should accommodate the integration of more neurons and synapses as required by advanced applications, making the chip suitable for a wide range of neural network models and use cases. Balancing these considerations ensures that the reconfigurable neuromorphic chip can deliver high performance, adaptability, and resilience in various computational environments.

Brain connectivity is generally described at three levels of scale: first, the single synaptic connections that link individual neurons at the micro-scale; second, the networks connecting neuronal populations at the mesoscale; and third, brain regions linked by fiber pathways at the macro-scale [23]. A crossbar is one of the approaches employed in representing these connections in neuromorphic systems. However, it has been recorded that the size of a crossbar directly affects the power consumption of a neuromorphic system, and this limitation in neuromorphic systems that employed single large crossbars [40, 42] has been demonstrated [1]. Therefore, partitioning and mapping its synapses into smaller local crossbars linked using shared interconnect is a better approach for a scalable neuromorphic system supporting large SNN with many synapses to maintain low power. Sadly, with shared interconnect, the challenge of latency, which affects the timing of spikes, is introduced.

7.2 Fault-Tolerant Neural Networks

Fault-tolerant neural networks are designed to maintain performance and functionality even in hardware faults, errors, or adverse conditions. These networks incorporate various techniques to detect, isolate, and mitigate the effects of faults, ensuring reliable and accurate operation. In Spiking Neural Networks (SNNs), fault tolerance is often achieved through dynamic reconfiguration, where the network can adapt its structure to bypass faulty neurons or synapses. This adaptability is supported by redundancy, allowing multiple components to perform the same function and take over if one fails. Error detection and correction codes ensure data integrity during spike communication. At the same time, fault-aware mapping techniques allocate neural network components to hardware in a way that minimizes the impact of faults.

Non-spiking neural networks also leverage error correction methods, often inspired by biological systems, to protect neural states against noise and errors. Techniques like redundancy and dropout during training enhance the robustness of these networks, allowing them to handle faults effectively. Both types of neural networks benefit from adaptive learning algorithms that adjust to new errors and maintain high performance, making them suitable for critical applications where reliability is essential. Several methods are used to solve the fault occurrence problem in hardware implementations of neural networks. They are generally classified into learning, architecture, and hybrid-based approaches.

Figure 7.2 shows a self-detect and self-repair mechanism mimicking capability in the human brain [26]. This mechanism involves the network's ability to detect faults or errors autonomously and initiate repairs without external intervention. For instance, in a spiking neural network (SNN), if a synaptic connection fails, the network can identify the fault and adjust the weights of other synapses to compensate for the loss, ensuring continued performance. This self-repair capability enhances the network's robustness and fault tolerance, making it more reliable for critical applications such as autonomous systems and medical diagnostics.

7.2.1 Learning-Based Approach

The learning-based methods utilize modified conventional learning rules to address faults occurring in neural network systems. In [35], the authors introduced a fault-tolerant technique that temporarily injects faults into hidden neurons during training, randomly affecting one to three neurons for each input example. Another approach,

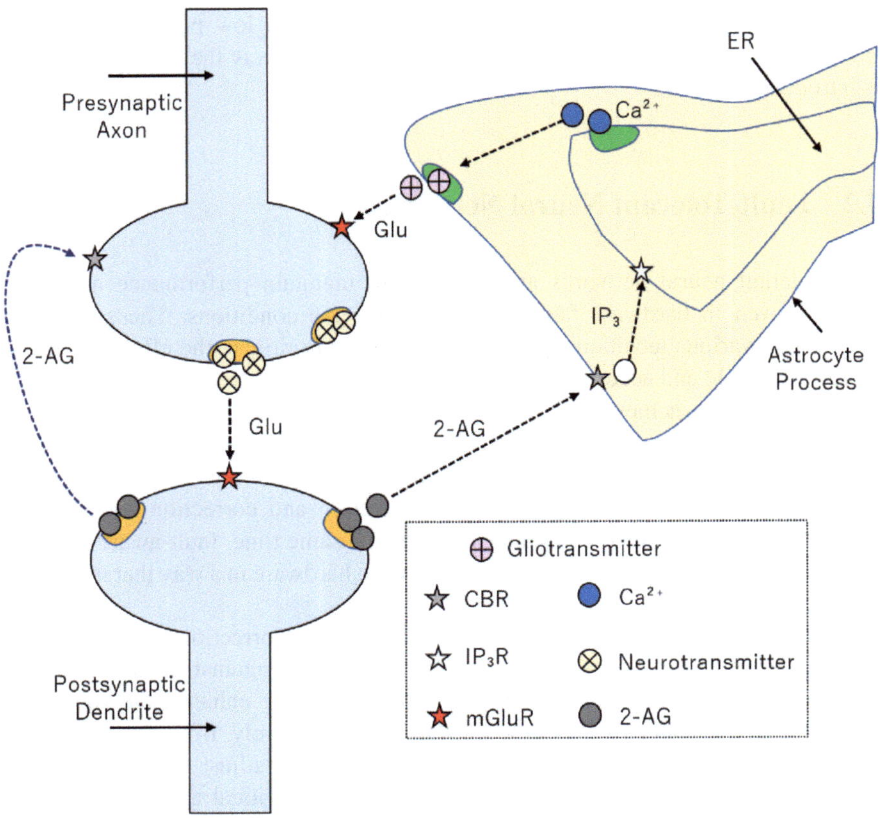

Fig. 7.2 A self-detect and self-repair mechanism mimicking capability in the human brain [26]. This mechanism is based on indirect feedback from the astrocyte cell (i.e., the most abundant type of glial cell in the brain), regulating the synaptic transmission probability of release when faults occur

described in [33], involves adding a regularization term to the cost function as a modified training rule. In [39], a backpropagation-based method was proposed for handling faults in classification tasks by constraining weights within a limited range. Although these modified learning methods do not require external interactions post-training, they significantly increase computation costs and lengthen the training process.

Besides the methods above, retraining techniques are also widely employed. In [18], the authors suggested a periodic retraining technique to enhance fault tolerance in GPGPU systems, which does not necessitate reprogramming or recompilation. The work in [11] introduced a retraining method to mitigate the effects of timing errors in hardware-based neural networks, activating the retraining process when timing errors impact output results. In [29], the authors presented a novel learning rule that emulates the brain's self-repair capability, enabling the learning rule to reestablish the firing rate of neurons when synaptic faults occur.

7.2.2 *Architecture-Based Approach*

In architecture-based methods, fault tolerance primarily relies on the redundancy of the architecture, which is implemented in pre-trained networks, including hidden neurons and their connections. In [9], a fault-tolerant architecture was proposed that emphasizes the monotony of specific critical neurons to reduce hardware costs. This method involves storing multiple sets of weights in a processor and recomputing neural computations with various processors, allowing the system to detect and correct processor faults, thus enhancing fault tolerance. Similarly, [14] introduced redundancy for critical hidden neurons combined with augmentation, where the weights of connections between augmented neurons and output layer neurons are halved from their original values.

Faults in the connections between neurons are also a significant concern. To address faults in both connections and neurons, [21] proposed a weight shipping method. This method shifts the weights of defective connections to other fault-free connections of the same neuron while also considering the output connections of a faulty neuron as defective. Liu et al. [26] presented a self-repairing hardware architecture featuring self-detection and self-repair of synaptic faults, maintaining system performance with a fault rate of up to 40%. However, this architecture, tested with only two neurons, may face scalability issues due to its area overhead.

In the SpiNNaker system [41], an emergency routing mechanism was introduced to manage congested or broken links in a 2D-NoC torus topology. This algorithm uses redundancy in the NoC architecture to automatically reroute blocked packets through adjacent links to their destination, thereby preventing timing violations in Spiking Neural Networks (SNNs) during congestion or faults.

7.2.3 *Hybrid-Based Approach*

Hybrid approaches, which combine learning-based and architecture-based methods, have shown significant promise in enhancing fault tolerance in neural networks. In [32], a two-phase method was proposed to improve the fault tolerance of a system. The first phase involves removing less important hidden neurons by feeding input and measuring their sensitivity. Following this, redundant neurons are added, and the network undergoes retraining. Evaluation results demonstrated that this method improved the system's fault tolerance in two multiclass classification problems. This work was further extended in [8], where the authors introduced three innovative methods: (1) During backpropagation training, weights are restricted to low magnitudes to prevent degradation in fault tolerance caused by high-magnitude weights. Hidden nodes are automatically added to the network to maintain the desired performance. (2) Artificial faults are injected into some neurons and connections during training to simulate potential failures and improve the network's robustness. (3) Unimportant neurons are removed, and new neurons are added to share the role of critical neurons in the network, ensuring that the network can continue to function effectively even if some neurons fail.

These hybrid methods effectively blend the strengths of both learning-based and architecture-based approaches, providing a more comprehensive solution to fault tolerance. Integrating redundancy and retraining ensures the network can adapt to and recover from faults, maintaining performance and reliability. Additionally, injecting artificial faults during training helps the network learn to cope with real-world imperfections, further enhancing its robustness. The evaluation results from these studies have shown that hybrid approaches can achieve better fault tolerance than other methods, making them a valuable strategy for designing resilient neural networks.

7.3 Interconnect Architectures for Neuromorphic Systems

Inter-neuron communication in neural networks is a complex and essential process miming how neurons interact in the human brain. This communication occurs through synapses, which are the connections between neurons. When activated, a neuron generates an electrical signal called an action potential. This action potential travels down the neuron's axon to the synapse, triggering neurotransmitter release. These neurotransmitters cross the synaptic cleft—a small gap between the neurons—and bind to receptors on the dendrites of the neighboring neuron.

This process involves electrical and chemical signals in biological neural networks, making it highly dynamic and intricate. The strength and efficacy of these synaptic connections are critical for learning and memory formation, as they determine how signals are transmitted and processed within the network. The synaptic weights, which represent the strength of these connections, can be adjusted through various learning mechanisms, allowing the network to adapt and improve over time.

In artificial neural networks, inter-neuron communication is represented by mathematical functions and weight adjustments. Each neuron receives inputs from multiple other neurons, processes these inputs through an activation function, and then passes the output to subsequent neurons. The weights of these connections are modified during the training process using algorithms like backpropagation, which help the network learn by minimizing the error in its predictions.

In Spiking Neural Networks (SNNs), which more closely emulate the timing-based nature of biological neural networks, neurons communicate through discrete spikes or pulses. The timing and frequency of these spikes convey information, making the communication more biologically plausible. SNNs use mechanisms like spike-timing-dependent plasticity (STDP) to adjust synaptic weights based on the precise timing of spikes, enabling more efficient and adaptive learning.

Hardware implementations were proposed as alternative solutions to overcome the problems of the software simulation mentioned above. Such systems require

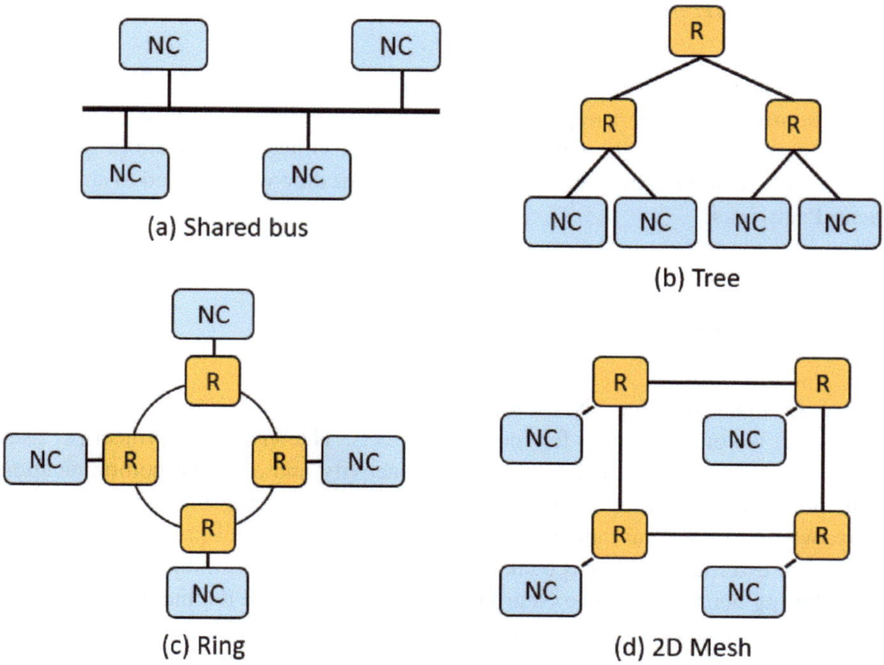

Fig. 7.3 Interconnect architectures for neuromorphic systems

high parallelism and scalable interconnect architecture to convey many spikes generated from SNPCs.

As illustrated in Fig. 7.3, neuromorphic chip design incorporates various topologies to optimize communication and computation efficiency. The Ring topology connects each neuron core to its two immediate neighbors, forming a circular data path that reduces latency and resource usage, ideal for low-power applications. With its hierarchical structure of nodes, tree topology excels in multicast routing, efficiently managing communication in large-scale systems. Meanwhile, the Shared-bus topology simplifies design by allowing all neuron cores to share a common communication bus. However, it may experience bottlenecks under heavy loads, making it suitable for smaller-scale systems. The 2D-Mesh topology features a grid of neuron cores connected to their four nearest neighbors, providing high connectivity and parallelism, essential for robust and scalable large-scale neuromorphic systems. Each topology offers distinct advantages, catering to specific system requirements and performance goals.

7.3.1 Hierarchical Bus-Based

Low-cost shared-bus-based SNN architectures are proposed in [22, 28]. Although these approaches support multicast and broadcast routing, they suffer from scalability limitations when the network size increases. Other works were proposed in [5, 25]. These architectures boosted throughput, but they were limited to small-size neural networks.

7.3.2 2D Packet-Switched-Based

There are many ongoing SNN research projects based on 2D-NoC interconnects. Hereafter, we only review a few notable projects. The *Neurogrid* project [4] uses analog computation to emulate ion-channel activity and a digital communication scheme to support synaptic connections. The main building block is the neuro-core, which can accommodate 65,536 quadratic integrate-and-fire neuron models. It uses an external FPGA and bank of SRAMs for digital communication between neighboring neuro-cores. The Neurogrid has a limitation on the maximum number of neurons per layer (up to 2175 neurons) that makes it unable to offer biological real-time behavior [4].

H-NoC [6] uses a hierarchical star-mesh topology to connect neurons. The *H-NoC* is organized into three layers: module, tile, and cluster. At the bottom, each module router can connect up to ten neural cells, each as a main neural computation element that can host one or multiple neurons. Similarly, ten module routers are connected to a tile router. An attractive work in [27] proposed combining hierarchical architecture and mesh routing strategies. The architecture consists of multiple levels of routers.

In SpiNNaker [16], the interconnection between each node is handled by a NoC using six links, which is wrapped into a triangular lattice; this lattice is then folded onto the surface of a toroid. A node comprises a processor core and two NoC routers, in which one handles the communication between the microprocessors and the peripherals, and the second controls the communications between processors and neighbor nodes.

7.3.3 3D Packet-Switched-Based

The work in [2] investigated the architecture and design of a 3D stacked neuromorphic accelerator. The architecture targeted processing applications on a CMOS vision sensor next to the first neural network layer. The authors claimed that only modest adaptations would be required to use the system for other applications. The 3D stacking architecture used face-to-face bonding of two 20 cm wafers using micro-bumps. Recent work was presented in [44] about a real-time digital neuromorphic system for simulating large-scale conductance-based SNNs. The architecture was implemented in six Altera Stratix III FPGA boards to simulate one million neurons [44]. An *AER* multicast routing mechanism was used for inter-neuron communications. Although the NoC architecture meets the system's requirements, it is hardly deployed in embedded neuromorphic systems [13].

Apart from the mentioned works, routing methods for NoC-based SNNs must be considered. This is because the spike routing method affects the network's load balance and the spike latency. In general, these works can be classified as unicast-based [43], path-based [12], and tree-based [34]. A comparison between these methods is presented in [12]. The basic ideas of these algorithms are shown in Fig. 7.4. Compared to the others, unicast-based [43] is an easy way of implementing multicast with no hardware overhead. A multicast package will be replicated at the source node and sent sequentially to destinations. However, this method leads to much traffic by injecting multiple copies. In the path-based [12] approach, a routing path is established from the source to each destination. Before sending, every packet header must contain a list of all destinations. Whenever the packet reaches a target, the information of that destination will be removed from the header. This helps the packet to be sequentially delivered to all destinations. A disadvantage of this method is that it requires a long time to prepare the packet at the source node. Besides, when increasing the size of destination sets (large size of SNNs), it is not efficient to implement because of the large header size of packets.

The drawbacks of path-based can be overcome by tree-based [34]. This approach constructs a "virtual" tree with the source node as the root and destinations as leaves. The packets are sent from the source, going along branches and reaching given destinations. Apart from advantages, a shortcoming of this method is high congestion in wormhole networks [24].

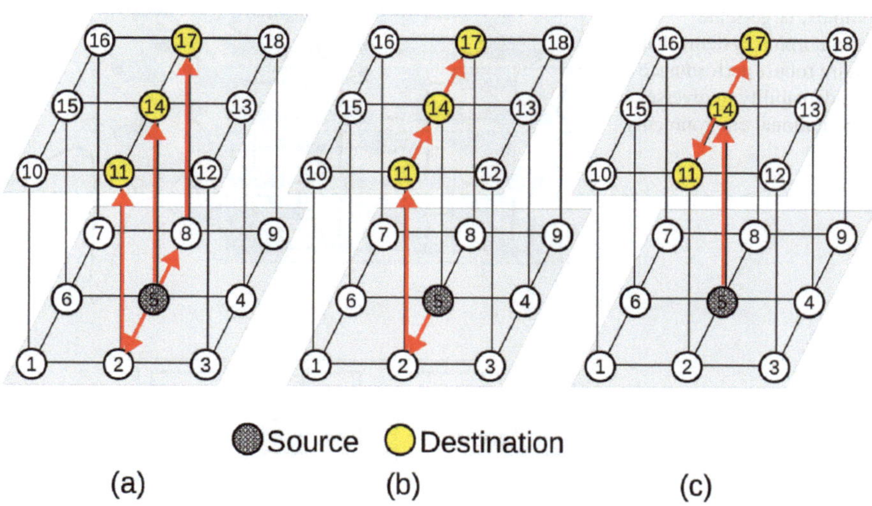

Fig. 7.4 Multicast routing mechanisms: (**a**) Unicast-based (**b**) Path-based (**c**) Tree-based

7.4 Core Components of Reconfigurable Neuromorphic Systems

Reconfigurable 3D-NoC-based neuromorphic architecture enables dynamic and adaptive neural network configurations to enhance performance and fault tolerance. This architecture leverages a three-dimensional Network-on-Chip (3D-NoC) structure to interconnect multiple neuromorphic cores efficiently, providing high bandwidth and low-latency communication. By utilizing reconfigurable elements, the system can adapt to various neural network models and applications, facilitating scalability and flexibility. This approach also integrates fault-tolerant mechanisms, such as redundancy and dynamic re-routing, to ensure reliable operation despite hardware faults.

Figure 7.5 illustrates the architecture of a 3D NoC-based neuromorphic system named NASH, consisting of several nodes. Each node comprises a Spiking Neuron Processing Core (SNPC), a network interface (NI), and a fault-tolerant multicast 3D router (FTMC-3DR), all connected in a 2D mesh topology and stacked to form a 3D architecture. A 4 $\times$ 4 2D tile configuration stacked and interconnected with Through-Silicon Vias (TSV) to create a 3D structure is shown for design illustration. Each SNPC contains 256 Leaky Integrate-and-Fire (LIF) neurons with a crossbar-based synapse array. The LIF model is used in NASH due to its proven effectiveness in learning applications and its suitability for digital implementation with modest

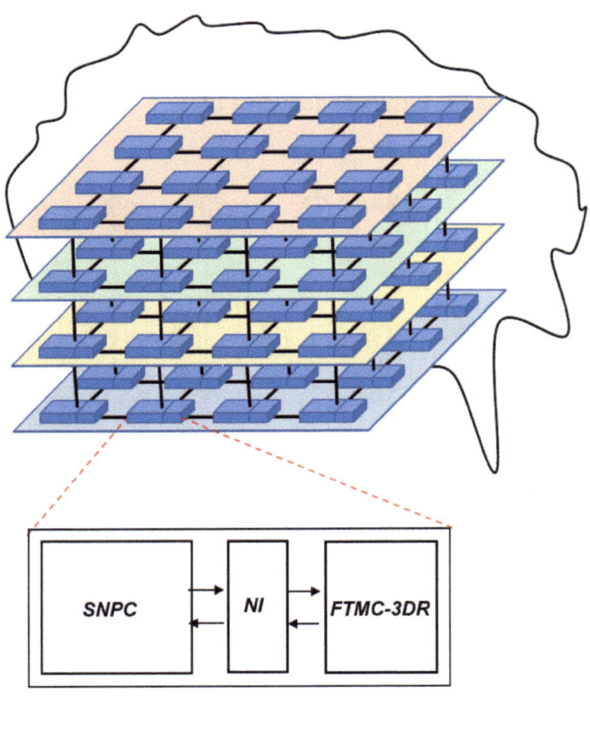

Fig. 7.5 Reconfigurable 3D-NoC based neuromorphic architecture. The reconfigurable 3D-NoC-based architecture is particularly suitable for complex, large-scale neuromorphic systems that require robust performance and adaptability in diverse computational environments

hardware costs [20]. When a LIF neuron generates an output spike, it is sent to the postsynaptic neurons within the same SNPC or another node in the 3D network. The synaptic weights are retrieved via the crossbar if the postsynaptic neuron is in the same SNPC. However, if the destination SNPC is different, the spike is encoded into a packet at the network interface, transmitted to the local FTMC-3DR, and routed to the target SNPC where the postsynaptic neuron is located. At the destination SNPC, the packet is decoded into a spike, the postsynaptic neuron is identified, and the synaptic weight is obtained through the crossbar for processing.

7.4.1 Spiking Neuron Processing Core

The Spiking Neuron Processing Core (SNPC) architecture features a compact, efficient design for neuromorphic computing. Each SNPC integrates 256 Leaky Integrate-and-Fire (LIF) neurons, utilizing a crossbar-based synapse array for connectivity. The architecture supports intra-core and inter-core communication, facilitating the transfer of spikes between neurons within the same core or across the network. Including a network interface (NI) and fault-tolerant multicast 3D router (FTMC-3DR) enhances robustness and scalability, making the SNPC architecture well-suited for large-scale, reconfigurable neuromorphic systems. The spiking neuron processing core (SNPC) described in Fig. 7.6 is the processing element (PE) in the NASH system.

The SNPC also has a crossbar-based synapse, a control unit, a synapse memory, an STDP learning block, and an encoder/decoder. The SNPC uses a spike array for spike events, and this was chosen in place of AER (Address Event Representation) to avoid memory overflow and extended pipeline time, which occurs when a large

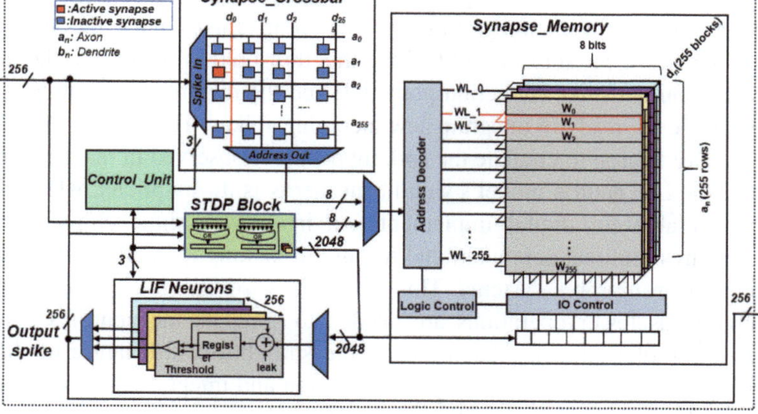

Fig. 7.6 Spiking Neuron Processing Core Architecture (SNPC): The SNPC architecture is designed to handle spiking neural network operations [19] efficiently

number of spikes are fired in the same time step. The SNPC design enables the state of neurons to be multiplexed onto a single shared bus of 256 bits, each bit taking the value of one or zero to signify the presence or absence of a spike event.

The operation of the SNPC is controlled by the SNPC control unit Using seven states: *Idle*, *Download_spike*, *Generate_spike_&_Comp*, *Leak*, *Fire*, *Upload_spike*, and *Learn*. At the *Idle* state, the default state, the SNPC does nothing while waiting for input spikes. The arrival of an input spike train triggers the control unit to change its state to the *Download_spike* state to receive the input spike train. After receiving the spike train, the next state, the *Generate_spike_&_Comp* state, is enabled. This state activates the crossbar to identify and update the destination neurons by activating their synapses using the addresses generated from the input spike train. After the last address has been updated, a signal is sent to the control unit to move to the *Leak* state, enabling a leak signal that causes a decay in the membrane potential value to be sent to the neurons. This state is followed by the *Fire* state, which activates the neurons to check for an output spike by comparing the membrane potential value with the set threshold. At the *Upload_spike* state, the spikes generated by the neurons are sent to the destination neurons.

7.4.1.1 LIF Neuron

The Leaky Integrate-and-Fire (LIF) neuron is a fundamental model used in neuromorphic computing to mimic the behavior of biological neurons. The LIF neuron operates based on the principles of integration and leakage of electrical signals. The neuron's membrane potential increases when receiving an input spike (or stimulus). This membrane potential is a variable that represents the difference in electric charge inside and outside the neuron. The "integrate" part of the model refers to the accumulation of incoming spikes, which causes the membrane potential to rise. Concurrently, the "leaky" aspect means that this potential gradually decays over time, simulating the natural leakage of ions in biological neurons.

The neuron continues integrating the incoming spikes until the membrane potential reaches a certain threshold. Once this threshold is surpassed, the neuron generates an output spike (or action potential) and the membrane potential is reset to a baseline level, ready to integrate new incoming spikes. This simple mechanism allows the LIF neuron to emulate the spiking behavior observed in real neurons.

One of the LIF neuron model's significant merits is its simplicity, which makes it highly suitable for digital implementation in neuromorphic chips. The LIF neuron requires minimal computational resources, making it an efficient choice for large-scale neuromorphic systems. This simplicity also translates to lower power consumption, as fewer operations are needed to simulate the neuron's behavior than more complex models. Additionally, the straightforward nature of the LIF neuron facilitates more accessible hardware design and integration, contributing to the overall efficiency and scalability of neuromorphic processors.

These characteristics make LIF neurons particularly advantageous for applications where power efficiency and simplicity are critical, such as edge devices

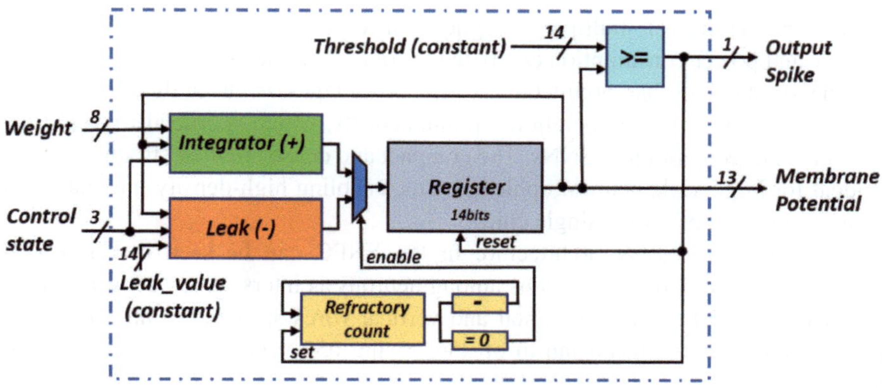

Fig. 7.7 LIF neuron architecture: The Leaky Integrate-and-Fire (LIF) neuron architecture is designed to emulate the behavior of biological neurons with computational efficiency

and large-scale neural network implementations. LIF neurons play a crucial role in advancing the development of neuromorphic computing systems by providing a balance between biological realism and computational efficiency. The block diagram of the implemented LIF neuron model is depicted in Fig. 7.7. The neuron's membrane potential is accumulated by summing the input weighted spikes in the integrator, which includes an additional 5 bits to manage overflow. The resulting value is stored in a 14-bit register, with 13 bits used for the membrane potential value and 1 bit for overflow. To simulate the leak current observed in the neural membrane, the neuron is assigned a specific leak value that causes the membrane potential to decay at the end of each accumulation time step when the leak is activated. When the accumulated membrane potential surpasses the threshold constant, an output spike, represented by 1 bit, is fired. A signal is then sent to the register to reset the membrane potential to zero and initiate the refractory period, which counts down from the set refractory period to zero at each step. After the refractory period, the neuron can accumulate incoming spikes again.

7.4.1.2 Crossbar Architecture

The crossbar architecture in a spiking neural network (SNN) chip is a highly efficient and scalable design to implement synaptic connections between neurons. This architecture typically employs a grid of perpendicular nanowires, forming a crossbar structure, where the junctions between the wires act as memristive devices or resistive RAM (RRAM) cells. These memristive devices store the synaptic weights, determining the strength of the connections between neurons.

When a neuron fires, the corresponding voltage is applied across the crossbar junctions, causing a change in the conductance of the memristive devices. This change in conductance represents the synaptic weight update, mimicking the plasticity observed in biological synapses. The crossbar architecture allows for parallel processing of multiple synaptic connections, significantly reducing the latency and power consumption compared to traditional methods.

One of the crossbar architecture's key advantages is its ability to perform both reading and writing operations simultaneously, which is crucial for real-time learning and recognition in SNNs. The compact and dense crossbar structure makes it ideal for large-scale neuromorphic systems, enabling high-density integration of neurons and synapses on a single chip.

The synapse crossbar architecture in the SNPC can be seen in Fig. 7.6. It represents the synaptic connections among neurons as intersections between axons and dendrites, defined as horizontal and vertical wires arranged in an orthogonal manner. Each neuron has a fan-in of 256, giving 65k synapses for all embedded neurons.

7.4.1.3 Learning Algorithm

NASH implements on-chip learning based on the trace-based Spike-Timing-Dependent Plasticity (STDP) learning rule. Trace-based STDP is an extension of the traditional STDP learning rule, incorporating the concept of synaptic traces to capture the temporal dynamics of spike interactions. Each neuron traces its recent spike activity in this method, which decays over time. When a presynaptic spike occurs, it updates the trace of the postsynaptic neuron and vice versa. The synaptic weight adjustments are then based on the overlap between these traces, allowing the network to learn complex temporal patterns more effectively. This approach enhances the biological plausibility and computational efficiency of neuromorphic systems by considering the cumulative effect of spikes over time rather than relying solely on the precise timing of individual spike pairs.

The implemented trace-based STDP update logic is presented in Fig. 7.8. A single learning operation requires 16 presynaptic spike trace vectors, each from a simulation time step. To begin learning, a postsynaptic spike trace vector is verified. Then, the presynaptic spike trace vectors are grouped into 8 $Before$ and 8 $After$ based on their arrival time relative to the postsynaptic trace vector. An OR operation is performed on the $Before$ spike vectors and the $After$ spike vectors to obtain two vectors. These two vectors are converted into synapse memory addresses, and Using the postsynaptic spike trace vector, the neurons whose synapses are to be updated are identified. The weights of these synapses are then fetched from synapse memory (SM), increased for the $Before$ and decreased for the $After$, and then written back to synapse memory. The implemented trace-based STDP enables the parallel update of synapses.

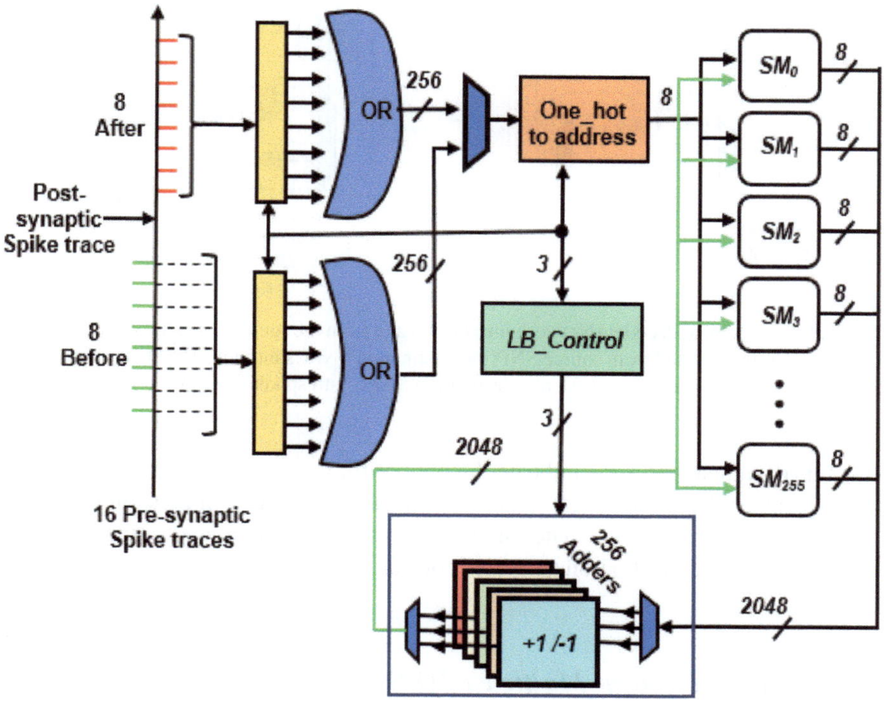

Fig. 7.8 STDP learning module architecture: This architecture encapsulates the dynamic and adaptive processes involved in Spike-Timing-Dependent Plasticity (STDP) learning. The module integrates several core components, including synaptic trace accumulators, synaptic memory, weight update logic, and timing control units [19]

7.4.2 Network Interface

The Network Interface (NI) in a neuromorphic Network-on-Chip (NoC)-based chip is crucial in managing communication between system components. It acts as a bridge, facilitating the transfer of spike events and other data between neurons, synapses, and other processing elements within the chip. The NI ensures efficient and reliable data exchange, enabling parallel processing and real-time learning capabilities. The NI contributes to the neuromorphic system's overall performance, scalability, and energy efficiency by optimizing communication pathways and reducing latency. This efficient communication is essential for implementing complex neural network models and achieving high computational power with low power consumption.

The NI consists of two modules: encoder and decoder. The encoder is the output interface between an SNPC and its local FTMC-3DR. As presented in Fig. 7.9, the encoder encodes spikes into packets for transmission while the decoder decodes received packets to spikes. The 81-bit flit format is also shown in Fig. 7.9. The first

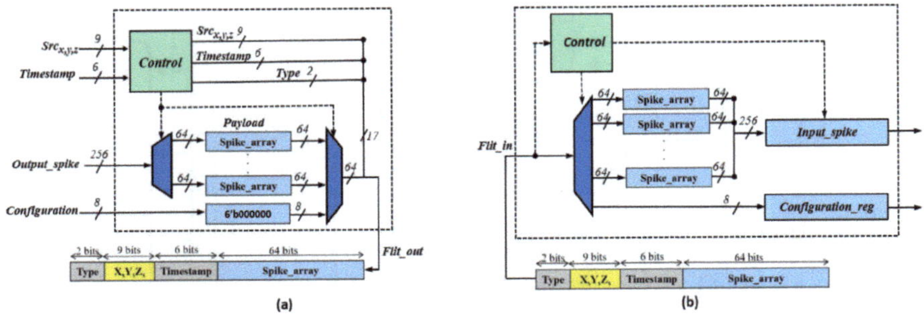

Fig. 7.9 Encoder and decoder (Network interface to and from the router). (**a**) The encoder encodes output spikes transmitted from source SNPC to destination SNPCs into flits. (**b**) On the other hand, the Decoder decodes flits that arrive at a destination SNPC into spikes [19]

two bits designated as Type indicate the type of flit it is; "00" for configuration and "11" for spike. The following 9 bits (3 bits for each X, Y, and Z dimension) represent the source neuron's address. The following 6 bits record the time the source neuron fired the spike. The last 64 bits are used for the spike array.

7.4.3 *Fault-Tolerant Multicast 3D Router*

The Fault-Tolerant Multicast 3D Router Architecture (FTMC-3DR) ensures robust and reliable communication within a 3D Network-on-Chip (NoC) environment, specifically for neuromorphic computing systems. It incorporates fault-tolerant mechanisms to handle potential faults and errors, ensuring seamless data transmission even in adverse conditions. The router supports multicast routing, which allows a single packet to be sent to multiple destinations simultaneously, improving communication efficiency and reducing latency. The 3D aspect of the architecture leverages vertical and horizontal links, connected through Through-Silicon Vias (TSVs), to enable efficient data routing across multiple layers of the chip. This setup enhances bandwidth and reduces the average hop count for data packets, improving overall system performance. The architecture includes error detection and correction modules to identify and mitigate the impact of faults, ensuring data integrity. It also features dynamic re-routing capabilities, allowing the system to bypass faulty links or nodes and maintain reliable communication paths. This combination of fault tolerance, multicast capability, and 3D integration makes the architecture well-suited for high-performance, scalable neuromorphic systems, ensuring consistent and efficient data flow despite hardware imperfections.

Figure 7.10 describes the architecture of the FTMC-3DR, which is based on [3, 10]. It has seven input(output) ports: one port for connecting to the local SNPC with which packets (spikes) can be injected into or received from the network, four for connecting to neighboring routers in the north, east, south, west, direction using

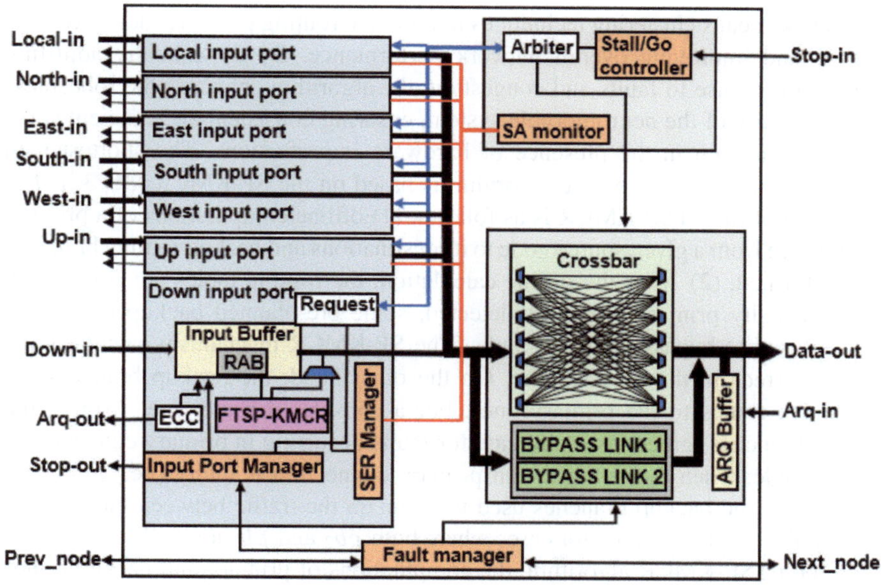

Fig. 7.10 Fault-tolerant multicast 3D router architecture: This advanced router architecture ensures efficient and reliable communication within a 3D Network-on-Chip (NoC) environment, especially for neuromorphic computing systems [19]

the intralayer links, and the remaining up and down ports for those in the closest layers through TSVs. The switch allocator (SA) and the crossbar control packets (spikes) transfer to the appropriate port. Each FTMC-3DR routes packets in four pipeline stages. In the first stage, buffer writing (BW), the received packets (spike) are stored in the port's input buffer. The second pipeline stage routing calculation (RC) obtains the source address of the stored packet from it and uses it to derive the next address, either in the X, Y, or Z dimension. After this address is derived, the switch-allocator, which handles the flow control (stall/go) and matrix arbitration (matrix-arbiter scheduler), is triggered in the third stage to allocate/make available the right port to the next router or local SNPC. After the right output port has been made available, the fourth stage, crossbar traversal(CT), begins, and the packet traverses the crossbar to the allocated output port.

7.5 Fault-Tolerant Spike Routing Algorithm

The Fault-Tolerant Spike Routing Algorithm is designed to ensure reliable and efficient communication within a 3D Network-on-Chip (NoC) for neuromorphic systems. This algorithm incorporates fault-tolerant mechanisms to detect and bypass faulty links or nodes, maintaining uninterrupted data flow. It combines shortest-path and k-means clustering techniques to optimize routing paths, reducing average latency and improving overall network performance. By dynamically adjusting routes in response to faults and congestion, the algorithm enhances the robustness and scalability of the neuromorphic system, ensuring consistent and efficient spike transmission even in the presence of hardware imperfections. The shortest path fault-tolerant multicast routing algorithm is based on the SP-KMCR [36, 37]. The basic idea of the FTSP-KMCR is as follows: (1) offline computations of a primary routing tree from a given source node to its destinations and backup routing branches are performed. (2) After the offline calculation, the routing tables are configured. When a faulty primary branch is detected, some pre-planned backup branch(es) is (are) used to bypass the faulty links. The SP-KMCR mechanism calculates the branches (red) in the primary tree. On the other hand, the backup branches are alternative routes to the primary ones. For a considered router (i.e., "son"), the backup branches (green) are computed for faults occurring in primary connections. For example, when the father-to-son primary connection is faulty (i.e., pb_1), bb_1 and bb_2 are the backup branches used to maintain the traffic between the "father" and "son". This is the same for cases where both pb_2 and pb_1 are faulty.

In the FTSP-KMCR algorithm, the computations of primary and backup routes are critical computational tasks. These calculations are performed offline. This reduces the proposed routing algorithm's runtime overhead. Hence, we avoid any possible timing violations in SNNs. Figure 7.11 show an example of SP-KMCR for a 6×3×2 3D-NoC-SNN system, where nodes in *L1* send spike packets to all nodes in *L2*.

7.6 Neuron Mapping in a 3D-NoC-Based Neuromorphic Chip

In a 3D Network-on-Chip (NoC)-based neuromorphic chip, neurons are mapped across multiple layers of the chip to leverage the vertical and horizontal communication pathways. This mapping strategy utilizes Through-Silicon Vias (TSVs) to connect different layers, enabling efficient data transfer and reducing latency. The neurons are typically organized in clusters or patterns that optimize the use of available resources and minimize communication overhead. Advanced algorithms, such as genetic algorithms or heuristic-based partitioning, are employed to determine the optimal placement of neurons, considering factors like firing patterns, connectivity, and thermal management. This approach ensures that the neuromorphic system can handle complex neural network models with high efficiency and scalability while maintaining low power consumption and high performance.

An efficient mapping approach and method is crucial to achieving good performance and energy efficiency and providing a guide for efficiently scaling neuromorphic models. Figure 7.12 illustrates the mapping of a spiking neural network (SNN) configured with 784 input neurons, 225 hidden neurons, and 10

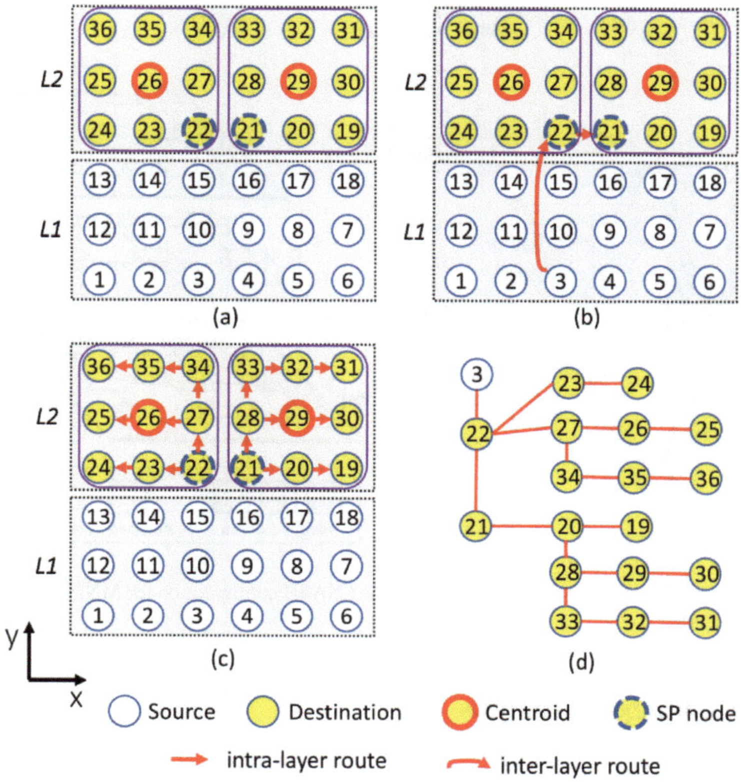

Fig. 7.11 Example of SP-KMCR for a 6×3×2 3D-NoC-SNN system, where nodes in *L1* send spike packets to all nodes in *L2*: (**a**) destinations are partitioned by adopting K-means clustering with centroids *26* and *29*, (**b**) the formation of the first part of the tree from a given source (node *3*) to shortest path node of each subgroup (SP node), (**c**) the second part of the tree from SP nodes to its destinations, (**d**) the routing tree from the given source to destinations [38]

output neurons onto a 3 × 3 × 3 NASH configuration. The NASH configuration employs a three-dimensional Network-on-Chip (3D NoC) design, facilitating efficient communication and parallel processing across multiple chip layers. In this setup, the 784 input neurons are responsible for processing the pixel values of the MNIST images, the 225 hidden neurons perform intermediate computations, and the 10 output neurons correspond to the digit classes (0–9). The 3D NoC architecture enhances the scalability and performance of the neuromorphic system, ensuring rapid and reliable spike transmission between neurons. By leveraging the vertical and horizontal connections provided by the 3D NoC, this mapping efficiently utilizes the available resources, enabling high-accuracy classification of handwritten digits with low power consumption and minimal latency.

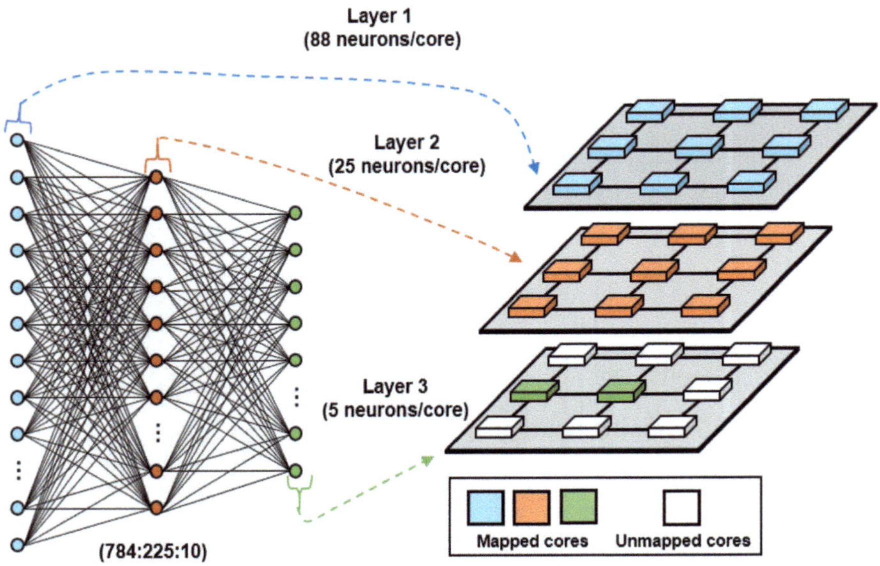

Fig. 7.12 784:225:10 SNN mapping on a $3 \times 3 \times 3$ NASH configuration for MNIST classification application [19]

7.7 Complexity Analysis

In analyzing the complexity of NASH described in Sect. 7.4, the hardware design of the system was described in Verilog-HDL, and its synthesis and layout were made with Cadence tools. For ASIC implementation, the NANGATE 45 nm open-cell library [30] was used as the standard cells. OpenRAM [17] was used for generating the system memory, and TSV from FreePDK3D45 [31] was used for interlayer connection. Using the MNIST application SNN and mapping approach described in Sect. 7.6, the accuracy of classifying 10K MNIST images on NASH using various synapse precision can be seen in Fig. 7.13. With 8-bit synapse precision, NASH reached an accuracy of 97.6%. However, it can be seen that as the synapse precision decreases, so does the accuracy. The effect of varying synapse precision on design complexity can be seen in Fig. 7.13. With increased precision, the area and power complexity increases and reduces otherwise (Table 7.1).

7.8 Chapter Summary

This chapter presents the intricacies of reconfigurable neuromorphic computing systems, beginning with an introduction and critical design considerations that lay the groundwork for understanding this field's unique challenges and opportunities. The discussion then transitions to fault-tolerant neural networks,

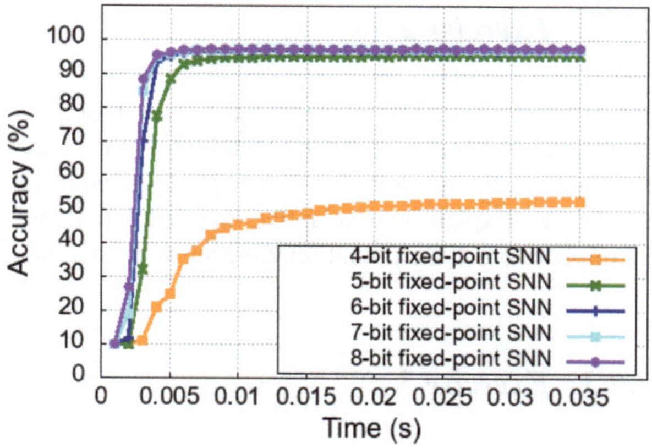

Fig. 7.13 Accuracy evaluation over various synapse precision: This figure illustrates the impact of different synapse precision levels on the accuracy of the neural network. The evaluation assesses how varying the bit-width of synaptic weights affects the network's performance, showcasing the trade-offs between precision and accuracy [19]

Table 7.1 Design complexity comparison of NASH and the baseline nodes

System	XY-UB	XYZ-UB	SP-KMCR		FTSP-KMCR	
Architecture	Baseline	NASH	Baseline	NASH	Baseline	NASH
Area (mm^2)	1.194	1.197	1.197	1.202	1.200	1.205
Power (mW)	49.29	50.02	49.58	50.10	50.86	51.76

highlighting methods to enhance the resilience of these systems against hardware faults. The various interconnect architectures for neuromorphic systems, including ring, tree, shared-bus, and 2D-mesh topologies, are examined for their benefits and trade-offs. Core components such as adaptive memory, reconfigurable processing units, and programmable interconnects are explored, emphasizing their roles in enabling reconfigurability. The chapter also introduces a fault-tolerant spike routing algorithm designed to ensure reliable communication within the network despite potential faults. Finally, exercises are provided to reinforce the concepts discussed, encouraging readers to engage practically with the material and deepen their understanding of reconfigurable neuromorphic computing systems.

7.9 Exercises

7.9.1 Exercise 1

What are the key considerations and techniques for reconfiguring a neuromorphic computing system? How can one adapt the system to different tasks or optimize its performance by adjusting its configuration? Please provide an explanation of the process of reconfiguration and any challenges associated with it.

7.9.2 Exercise 2

Adaptive learning and plasticity are crucial in our ability to learn, adapt, and make decisions in response to changing circumstances. These mechanisms enable artificial neural networks to learn, process information, and adjust to changing conditions. Explain how adaptive learning functions in a neuromorphic chip and its implications for artificial intelligence and machine learning applications.

7.9.3 Exercise 3

How does adaptive learning function in a neuromorphic chip, and what are its implications for artificial intelligence and machine learning applications? How is learning implemented in reconfigurable neuromorphic systems, and what mechanisms or algorithms are typically used to facilitate this process?

7.9.4 Exercise 4

Spike-timing-dependent plasticity (STDP) is a biological process that adjusts the strength of connections between neurons in the brain. This process operates based on the relative timing of a particular neuron's output and input action potentials. How is STDP learning implemented in reconfigurable neuromorphic systems, and what are the main components and processes involved in this implementation?

7.9.5 Exercise 5

Neuromorphic chips hold great promise for robotics and autonomous systems. Researchers have developed adaptable devices using innovative materials, which can transform into various key electronic components needed for artificial intelligence hardware. How can reconfigurable neuromorphic chips enhance the performance and adaptability of robotic systems?

7.9.6 Exercise 6

Supervised learning is crucial in training spiking neural networks (SNNs) to perform specific tasks. Suppose you're designing an SNN-based controller for a mobile robot. The robot needs to learn to avoid obstacles and reach a target area. You decide to use reward-modulated Spike-Timing-Dependent Plasticity (R-STDP) for training. Explain how you would set up the supervised learning process using R-STDP to achieve this behavior.

7.9.7 Exercise 7

Fault tolerance is needed when designing a large-scale Spiking Neural Network (SNN) for several reasons, including vulnerability to soft errors, maintaining accuracy, and energy efficiency. Suppose you create a safety-critical system that utilizes convolutional neural networks (CNNs) for real-time image classification. The system must be fault-tolerant to handle soft errors caused by high-energy particles, abnormal voltage, or temperature fluctuations. Discuss how you would enhance the fault tolerance of the CNN inference process while minimizing runtime overhead. Consider algorithm-based fault tolerance (ABFT) techniques and the trade-off between generalization and classification accuracy.

7.9.8 Exercise 8

3D-IC (Three-Dimensional Integrated Circuits) technology allows stacking multiple layers of integrated circuits, improving performance and reducing power consumption. Suppose your task is to design a mapping strategy for implementing an SNN on a 3D-IC hardware platform. Explain the different steps needed for this task. In addition, propose metrics to evaluate the effectiveness of your mapping strategy (e.g., energy efficiency, spike latency) and discuss trade-offs between accuracy and hardware efficiency.

7.9.9 Exercise 9

Reconfigurable Spiking Neural Networks (RSNNs) allow dynamic adaptation of network architecture, connectivity, and parameters during runtime. RSNNs are helpful for applications where network requirements change over time, or energy efficiency is crucial. Your task is to design an RSNN that can adapt to different functions while minimizing energy consumption. Suggest metrics to evaluate the effectiveness of the RSNN (e.g., accuracy, energy consumption, adaptability) and discuss how reconfiguration affects these metrics.

7.9.10 Exercise 10

In spiking neural networks, reconfigurable computation involves adjusting specific parameters, such as coupling strength, neuron model parameters, and threshold voltage, to achieve robustness and adaptability. For coupling strength reconfiguration, networks of spiking neurons can be reconfigured by changing the coupling strength. For example, after the loss of a neuron, the system can adapt this global parameter to achieve different required numbers of winners (k) and handle disruptions effectively. How can spiking neural networks achieve reconfigurable computation by choosing the value of k via a global system parameter? What role do inhibitory pulse-couplings play in this process?

References

1. Balaji A, Das A, Wu Y, Huynh K, Dell'Anna F, Indiveri G, Krichmar JL, Dutt N, Schaafsma S, Catthoor F (2019) Mapping spiking neural networks to neuromorphic hardware. IEEE Trans Very Large Scale Integr Syst 28:76–86
2. Belhadj B, Valentian A, Vivet P, Duranton M, He L, Temam O (2014) The improbable but highly appropriate marriage of 3D stacking and neuromorphic accelerators. In: 2014 international conference on compilers, architecture and synthesis for embedded systems (CASES), pp 1–9
3. Ben Ahmed A, Ben Abdallah A (2016) Adaptive fault-tolerant architecture and routing algorithm for reliable many-core 3D-NoC systems. J Parallel Distrib Comput 93–94:30–43
4. Benjamin BV, Gao P, McQuinn E, Choudhary S, Chandrasekaran AR, Bussat JM, Alvarez-Icaza R, Arthur JV, Merolla PA, Boahen K (2014) Neurogrid: a mixed-analog-digital multichip system for large-scale neural simulations. Proc IEEE 102(5):699–716
5. Boahen KA (1998) Communicating neuronal ensembles between neuromorphic chips. In: Neuromorphic systems engineering. Springer, Berlin, pp 229–259
6. Carrillo S (2013) Scalable hierarchical networks-on-chip architecture for brain-inspired computing. Ph.D. Thesis, University of Ulster
7. Carrillo S, Harkin J, McDaid LJ, Morgan F, Pande S, Cawley S, McGinley B (2013) Scalable hierarchical network-on-chip architecture for spiking neural network hardware implementations. IEEE Trans Parallel Distrib Syst 24(12):2451–2461
8. Chin CT, Mehrotra K, Mohan CK, Rankat S (1994) Training techniques to obtain fault-tolerant neural networks. In: Proceedings of IEEE 24th international symposium on fault-tolerant computing, pp 360–369
9. Chu L, Wah BW (1990) Fault tolerant neural networks with hybrid redundancy. In: 1990 IJCNN international joint conference on neural networks, vol 2, pp 639–649
10. Dang KN, Ahmed AB, Okuyama Y, Abderazek BA (2017) Scalable design methodology and online algorithm for TSV-cluster defects recovery in highly reliable 3D-NoC systems. IEEE Trans Emerg Top Comput 8:577–590
11. Deng J, Rang Y, Du Z, Wang Y, Li H, Temam O, Ienne P, Novo D, Li X, Chen Y, Wu C (2015) Retraining-based timing error mitigation for hardware neural networks. In: 2015 design, automation test in Europe conference exhibition (DATE), pp 593–596
12. Ebrahimi M (2014) Reliable and adaptive routing algorithms for 2D and 3D networks-on-chip. In: Routing algorithms in networks-on-chip. Springer, Berlin, pp 211–237

13. Ehsan MA, Zhou Z, Yi Y (2017) Modeling and analysis of neuronal membrane electrical activities in 3D neuromorphic computing system. In: 2017 IEEE international symposium on electromagnetic compatibility signal/power integrity (EMCSI), pp 745–750
14. Emmerson MD, Damper RI (1993) Determining and improving the fault tolerance of multilayer perceptrons in a pattern-recognition application. IEEE Trans Neural Netw 4(5):788–793
15. Furber S, Temple S (2006) Neural systems engineering. J R Soc Interface 4(13):193–206
16. Furber SB, Galluppi F, Temple S, Plana LA (2014) The spinnaker project. Proc IEEE 102(5):652–665
17. Guthaus MR, Stine JE, Ataei S, Chen B, Wu B, Sarwar M (2016) Openram: an open-source memory compiler. In: 2016 IEEE/ACM international conference on computer-aided design (ICCAD), pp 1–6
18. Hashmi A, Berry H, Temam O, Lipasti M (2011) Automatic abstraction and fault tolerance in cortical microachitectures. In: 2011 38th annual international symposium on computer architecture (ISCA), pp 1–10
19. Ikechukwu OM (2022) On the design of adaptive digital neuromorphic system. Ph.D. Thesis
20. Indiveri G, Linares-Barranco B, Hamilton TJ, van Schaik A, Etienne-Cummings R, Delbruck T, Liu SC, Dudek P, Häfliger P, Renaud S, Schemmel J, Cauwenberghs G, Arthur J, Hynna K, Folowosele F, Saighi S, Serrano-Gotarredona T, Wijekoon J, Wang Y, Boahen K (2011) Neuromorphic silicon neuron circuits. Front Neurosci 5:73
21. Khunasaraphan C, Vanapipat K, Lursinsap C (1994) Weight shifting techniques for self-recovery neural networks. IEEE Trans Neural Netw 5(4):651–658
22. Lazzaro J, Wawrzynek J, Mahowald M, Sivilotti M, Gillespie D (1993) Silicon auditory processors as computer peripherals. IEEE Trans Neural Netw 4(3):523–528
23. Leergaard T, Hilgetag C, Sporns O (2012) Mapping the connectome: multi-level analysis of brain connectivity. Front Neuroinf 6:14
24. Lin X, Ni LM (1993) Multicast communication in multicomputer networks. IEEE Trans Parallel Distrib Syst 4(10):1105–1117
25. Liu SC, Kramer J, Indiveri G, Delbrück T, Burg T, Douglas R (2001) Orientation-selective aVLSI spiking neurons. Neural Netw 14(6–7):629–643
26. Liu J, Harkin J, Maguire LP, McDaid LJ, Wade JJ (2018) Spanner: a self-repairing spiking neural network hardware architecture. IEEE Trans Neural Netw Learn Syst 29(4):1287–1300
27. Moradi S, Manohar R (2018) The impact of on-chip communication on memory technologies for neuromorphic systems. J Phys D Appl Phys 52(1):014003
28. Mortara A, Vittoz EA, Venier P (1995) A communication scheme for analog VLSI perceptive systems. IEEE J Solid-State Circuits 30(6):660–669
29. Naeem M, McDaid LJ, Harkin J, Wade JJ, Marsland J (2015) On the role of astroglial syncytia in self-repairing spiking neural networks. IEEE Trans Neural Netw Learn Syst 26(10):2370–2380
30. NanGate Inc, Nangate open cell library 45 nm. http://www.nangate.com/. Accessed 16 June 2016
31. NCSU Electronic Design Automation, FreePDK3D45 3D-IC process design kit. http://www.eda.ncsu.edu/wiki/FreePDK3D45:Contents. Accessed 16 June 2016
32. Piche S (1992) Robustness of feedforward neural networks. In: [Proceedings 1992] IJCNN international joint conference on neural networks, vol 2, pp 346–351
33. Poggio T, Girosi F (1990) Networks for approximation and learning. Proc IEEE 78(9):1481–1497
34. Samman F, Hollstein T, Glesner M (2010) New theory for deadlock-free multicast routing in wormhole-switched virtual-channelless networks-on-chip. IEEE Trans Parallel Distrib Syst 22(4):544–557
35. Sequin CH, Clay RD (1990) Fault tolerance in artificial neural networks. In: 1990 IJCNN international joint conference on neural networks, vol 1, pp 703–708
36. Vu TH, Ikechukwu OM, Abdallah AB (2019) Fault-tolerant spike routing algorithm and architecture for three dimensional NoC-based neuromorphic systems. IEEE Access 7:90436–90452

37. Vu TH, Murakami Y, Abdallah AB (2019) Graceful fault-tolerant on-chip spike routing algorithm for mesh-based spiking neural networks. In: 2019 2nd international conference on intelligent autonomous systems (ICoIAS)
38. Vu TH, Okuyama Y, Abdallah AB (2019) Comprehensive analytic performance assessment and k-means based multicast routing algorithm and architecture for 3D-NoC of spiking neurons. ACM J Emerg Technol Comput Syst 15(4):1–28
39. Wei N, Yang S, Tong S (1996) A modified learning algorithm for improving the fault tolerance of BP networks. In: Proceedings of international conference on neural networks (ICNN'96), vol 1, pp 247–252
40. Wijesinghe P, Ankit A, Sengupta A, Roy K (2018) An all-memristor deep spiking neural computing system: a step towards realizing the low power, stochastic brain. IEEE Trans Emerg Top Comput Intell 2(5):345–358. https://doi.org/10.1109/TETCI.2018.2829924
41. Wu J, Furber S (2009) A multicast routing scheme for a universal spiking neural network architecture. Comput J 53(3):280–288
42. Xia Q, Yang JJ (2019) Memristive crossbar arrays for brain-inspired computing. Nat Mater 18(4):309–323
43. Xiang D, Shen K (2016) A new unicast-based multicast scheme for network-on-chip router and interconnect testing. ACM Trans Des Autom Electron Syst 21(2):1–23
44. Yang S, Wang J, Deng B, Liu C, Li H, Fietkiewicz C, Loparo KA (2018) Real-time neuromorphic system for large-scale conductance-based spiking neural networks. IEEE Trans Cybern 49:2490–2503

Chapter 8
Practical Design of a Reconfigurable 3D-NoC-Based Neuromorphic System

Abstract This chapter presents the design and evaluation of the reliable three-dimensional digital neuromorphic processor (R-NASH), which is built to mimic the 3D structure of biological brains using 3D-integrated circuits (3D-ICs). The platform achieves high integration density and minimizes spike transmission delays in spiking neural networks, offering scalability for diverse applications. R-NASH leverages Through-Silicon-Via (TSV) technology to implement spiking neural networks across neuron clusters via a Network-on-Chip (NoC) architecture. In addition to the core processing capabilities, R-NASH features an advanced memory interface that connects seamlessly to a host CPU. This integration enables real-time training and inference of neural networks, significantly enhancing the system's operational efficiency and flexibility. The processor's design ensures high-speed communication between the neuron clusters and the central processing unit, facilitating rapid and accurate data processing essential for complex neural computations. Furthermore, R-NASH incorporates sophisticated fault detection and recovery mechanisms. These mechanisms are crucial for maintaining system reliability, allowing the processor to detect and address errors dynamically. The system ensures continuous operation despite faults by implementing strategies for gradual performance degradation rather than abrupt failures. This robustness is essential for applications in critical environments where downtime or performance lapses can have significant consequences. Overall, this chapter provides a comprehensive overview of the practical design and implementation of the R-NASH system, highlighting its innovative use of 3D-IC technology and fault-tolerant features. The detailed analysis demonstrates how R-NASH balances high performance, reliability, and scalability, making it a versatile solution for modern neuromorphic computing applications. To reinforce the concepts discussed, the chapter concludes with exercises facilitating deeper understanding and practical application of the material.

A. Ben Abdallah, K. N. Dang, *Neuromorphic Computing Principles and Organization*, https://doi.org/10.1007/978-3-031-83089-1_8

8.1 Introduction

In spiking neural networks (SNNs), information is encoded using different methods, including coincidence, rate, and temporal coding [18]. SNNs commonly employ integrate-and-fire neuron models, in which neurons generate voltage spikes, typically lasting around 1 ms each. These spikes propagate along nerve fibers when neurons receive adequate stimuli from other neurons or external inputs. While spikes can vary in amplitude, shape, and duration, they are generally considered similar in their role in signal transmission. To more accurately simulate the nonlinear and random behavior of ion channels in biological neurons, the Hodgkin-Huxley conductance-based neuron model is often used [13]. However, this model is too complex for large-scale simulations or hardware implementations.

Software simulation of spiking neural networks (SNNs) [14, 24] offers flexibility for studying neuronal systems. On the other hand, dedicated multi-core hardware architectures can provide high processing speeds and low power consumption by exploiting the parallelism inherent in neural networks. This makes SNNs ideal for low-power applications, such as embedded neuromorphic devices, motor control systems, or medical devices [25]. SNN hardware systems typically consist of multiple nodes (groups of neurons) connected via a Network-on-Chip (NoC) infrastructure [2, 20] (refer to Chap. 5 for on-chip communication). Scaling neuromorphic systems is achieved by extending both on-chip and off-chip connections, enabling the integration of multiple neuromorphic chips [2, 3, 7, 12, 22].

Designing an efficient neuromorphic system requires addressing several challenges. These include creating lightweight neuron and synapse architectures with low energy consumption, developing efficient coding methods for action potentials, and enabling in-situ learning and tuning capabilities. Another significant challenge is connectivity, as the number of neurons to be connected is expected to be at least 10^3 times greater than the number of cores in conventional System-on-Chip (SoC) platforms [11].

While most modern deep neural network (DNN) designs are based on 2D structures (chips, systems, and connections), biologically plausible neuromorphic systems typically feature a 3D structure similar to the human brain. Mapping a 3D structure onto 2D circuits results in more extended wiring and potential bottlenecks [5]. These constraints implement brain-like integrated circuits (ICs), a challenging problem in on-chip interconnect design [25]. Figure 8.1 illustrates a possible mapping of a 3D silicon brain. Instead of flattening and placing modules in a single plane, this approach mimics the brain's natural structure. 3D structures offer an extra dimension, improving scalability even without actual connectivity. As discussed in Chap. 6, reliability issues present significant challenges in large-scale neuromorphic systems. While 3D-IC technology offers enhanced scalability, it also introduces more complex reliability concerns. This chapter presents a case study of RNASH, a hardware-software design for a 3D-NoC-based neuromorphic system.

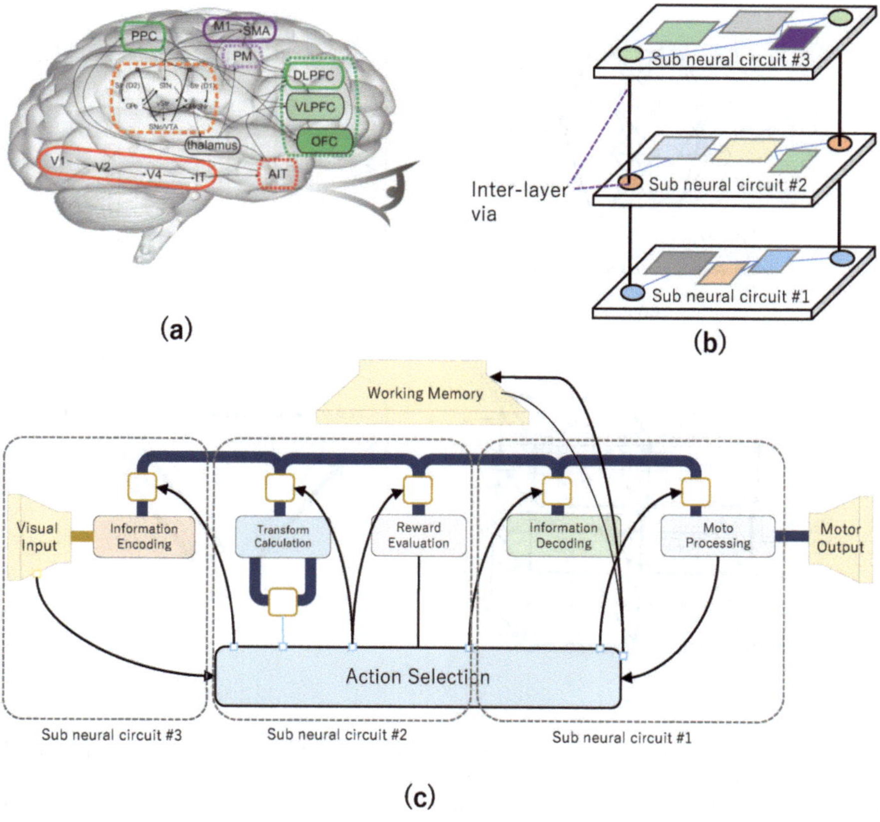

Fig. 8.1 Neuro-inspired 3D silicon brain: (**a**) The anatomical structure of Spaun, showing the main brain regions and their connections [10, 25]; (**b**) A potential mapping of the Spaun system onto 3D-IC technology; (**c**) Spaun's architecture, thick dark-yellow lines representing communication between cortical elements and thin lines indicating connectivity between the Basal Ganglia and the cortex. This figure is adapted from "Toward Robust Cognitive 3D Brain-Inspired Cross-Paradigm System" by Ben Abdallah and Dang, used under CC BY-SA 4.0

8.2 Reconfigurable 3D-NoC-Based Neuromorphic System (R-NASH) Architecture

As illustrated in Fig. 8.2, the R-NASH platform design is organized into four main phases. First, the software spiking neural network *model* is created using Python/Matlab, with customizable parameters such as neurons, synapses, thresholds, learning methods, and connections. The next phase involves neuron mapping, which consists of several key steps: (1) *transformation*, converting specified values into a binary format suitable for neuromorphic hardware, (2) *clusterization*, determining optimal neuron groupings, (3) *scheduling*, and (4) *configuration*. (a) Genetic algorithm is employed to streamline these processes and enhance efficiency.

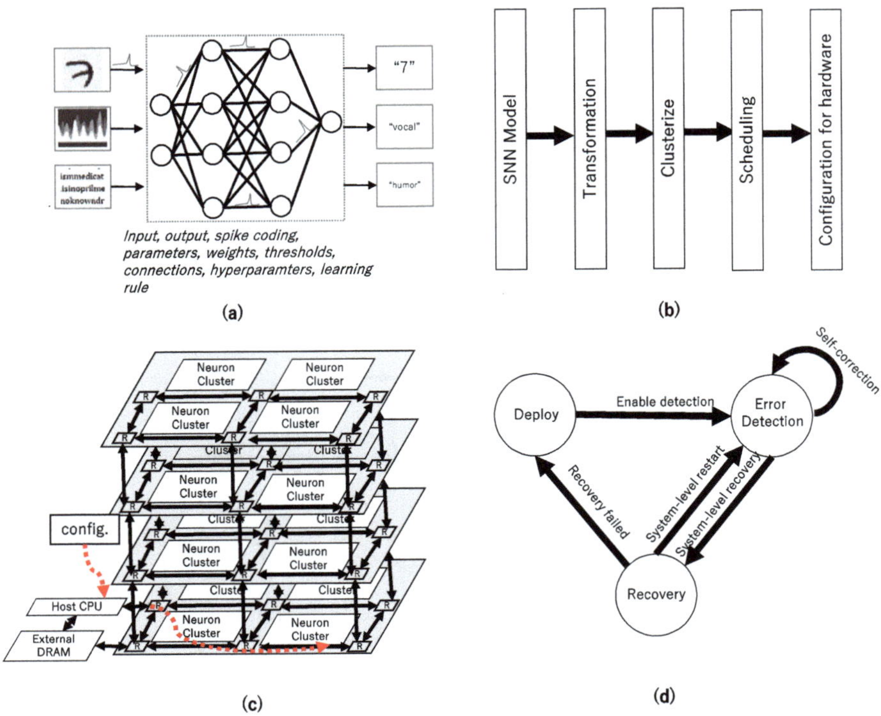

Fig. 8.2 R-NASH system platform: (**a**) SNN model; (**b**) Mapping into the neuromorphic hardware; (**c**) Our neuromorphic hardware in 3D-ICs; (**d**) Runtime maintenance for R-NASH. This figure is adapted from "Toward Robust Cognitive 3D Brain-Inspired Cross-Paradigm System" by Ben Abdallah and Dang, used under CC BY-SA 4.0 (https://creativecommons.org/licenses/by-sa/4.0/)

Given the complexity of neuromorphic hardware, it is susceptible to both temporary and permanent faults, which can degrade performance. Therefore, the *runtime maintenance* phase is dedicated to detecting and addressing these faults in real-time.

8.3 R-NASH Hardware Components

The architecture of the neuromorphic system, as shown in Fig. 8.3, employs a 3D-IC approach to replicate the brain's three-dimensional structure. This design organizes neurons and synapses into clusters or nodes, moving away from traditional point-to-point connections in favor of a packet-switched, mesh-based 3D Network-on-Chip (NoC) architecture.

Within this framework, a 3D-Mesh NoC manages communication, while computation occurs within neuron clusters (nodes), as depicted in Fig. 8.3. The Address-

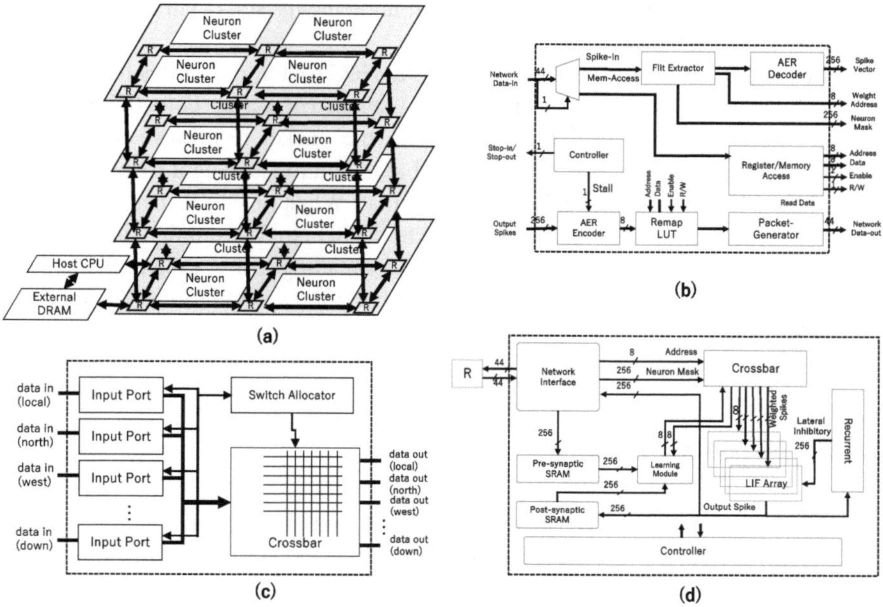

Fig. 8.3 R-NASH architecture: (**a**) Neuromorphic System, (**b**) Network-Interface. (**c**) 3D-Router, (**d**) SNPC Core. This figure is adapted from "Toward Robust Cognitive 3D Brain-Inspired Cross-Paradigm System" by Ben Abdallah and Dang, used under CC BY-SA 4.0

Event-Representation (AER) protocol stores incoming spikes in memory, decodes them to retrieve addresses and generates enabling signals for accessing weight memory. The system simulates weighted spikes for input to Leaky Integrate-and-Fire (LIF) neurons by fetching synapse data from memory.

Once the correct synapse address and enable signal are received, the weighted inputs are directed to the appropriate LIF neuron. The neuron accumulates these values, applies leak subtraction, and checks the firing conditions. The output spike is then stored in a postsynaptic SRAM and transmitted through the Network-on-Chip.

For further details on neuron clusters and 3D NoC router architectures, please refer to Sects. 8.3.1 and 8.3.5, respectively.

8.3.1 Spiking Neural Processing Core (SNPC)

Figure 8.3 shows the architecture of the SNPC, the backbone of the R-NASH neuromorphic system. The SNPC consists of four main modules: (1) the Network Interface (NI), which handles communication via the 3D NoC; (2) the Crossbar, which decodes spikes and retrieves the corresponding weights; (3) the LIF array, which contains multiple Leaky Integrate-and-Fire (LIF) neurons that operate in parallel; and (4) the Learning module, which implements Spike-Timing-Dependent Plasticity (STDP) learning.

When the NI receives a packet from the 3D-NoC router, it decodes it to identify its type. There are two types of packets: (1) spikes (or action potentials) and (2) memory access (read/write). The NI decodes the packet to retrieve the relevant memory address and forwards it to the crossbar to obtain the weight for spike flits in the Address-Event-Representation (AER) format. When an SNPC neuron fires, its index or address is encoded and transmitted to the 3D NoC to simulate inter-neuron communication. The NI provides an interface for reading and writing each neuron's weight memory and parameters in single and burst transaction modes for memory access.

8.3.2 Network Interface

The Network Interface (NI) facilitates neuron communication via the on-chip network infrastructure in the R-NASH system, supporting two types of flits: spike flits in AER format and memory flits. Spike flits in AER format are used to identify the address in the weight SRAM.

Each flit carries instructions and the necessary addresses for reading from or writing to memory cells and registers within the neuron cluster. Memory access flits are generated by the system's master processor or an external host processor.

The NI handles two types of read/write commands: single and burst. Single commands access one element per request, while burst commands specify a length argument for multiple accesses. The NI translates the requested addresses into local addresses for each weight memory or LIF array. Figure 8.4 illustrates the two types of flits in R-NASH. The first bit distinguishes between spike (0) and

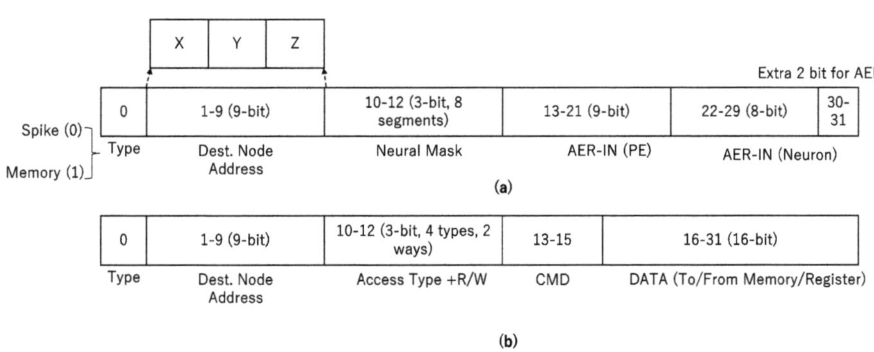

Fig. 8.4 R-NASH Flit Formats: (**a**) Spike flit, (**b**) Memory access flit. These formats are optimized for low latency and minimal power consumption, crucial for maintaining the high performance and efficiency of neuromorphic systems. This figure is adapted from "Toward Robust Cognitive 3D Brain-Inspired Cross-Paradigm System" by Ben Abdallah and Dang, used under CC BY-SA 4.0

memory access (1) flits. Spike flits consist of four fields: destination node address (9-bit), neuron mask for sparse connections (3-bit, supporting 8 types), AER of the source node (9-bit), and AER of the neuron within the source node. Firing neuron AERs are represented by node and neuron addresses, allowing scalability up to $8 \times 8 \times 8$ 3D-NoC nodes (512 nodes) with 256 neurons per node. Expansion to 10 bits accommodates 1024 neurons per node, enabling R-NASH to support 0.5 million neurons and 0.5 billion synapses. All fields are extendable to meet larger-scale requirements. Memory access flits have four types: (1) single read, (2) burst read, (3) single write, and (4) burst write. The two-bit command field indicates the transaction status: completed, ongoing, corrupted (requiring a rewrite or reread), or canceled. Since R-NASH is byte-addressable, the command field is followed by the memory/register address of the R-NASH node (16-bit). The NI sends the data corresponding to the host node's address for single reads. For burst reads and writes, the next flit contains the length of the transaction.

Figure 8.3 shows the Network Interface (NI) block diagram. Input flits are classified as either spikes or memory accesses. For memory accesses, the NI provides an interface for reading and writing data in all registers and memory blocks of the node. A read instruction prompts the NI to return the value from the requested address to the master processor. When processing input spikes from the network, the NI decodes the weight SRAM address and forwards it to the weight memory. For multi-layer SNNs or sparse connections, the Flit Extractor generates the read enable (RE) signal for different layers or links in the weight memory. This allows a node to handle multiple AERs at the same address for other neurons. The output spike from the LIF array is passed to the AER decoder, which extracts the address of the firing neuron. This address is then serially sent to the remap Look-Up Table (LUT) to retrieve the AER value of the receiving nodes.

8.3.3 Crossbar Architecture

The design of a crossbar with SRAM for a neuromorphic chip involves integrating a crossbar array with Static Random-Access Memory (SRAM) to implement synaptic connections between neurons efficiently. In this architecture, the crossbar array consists of perpendicular nanowires, with memristive devices or resistive RAM (RRAM) cells at the junctions, storing synaptic weights. The SRAM stores additional information, such as neuron states and configuration parameters, providing fast access and low latency.

The crossbar array enables parallel processing of multiple synaptic connections, significantly reducing latency and power consumption. The SRAM component complements the crossbar by offering high-speed data storage and retrieval, ensuring efficient communication between neurons and synapses. This combination allows for real-time learning and adaptation in spiking neural networks, mimicking the plasticity observed in biological brains.

As described in the previous subsection, the input spikes—events characterized by timestamps and polarities—are decoded into the weight address and neuron mask (read-enable signal) before being transmitted to the crossbar. The crossbar comprises several SRAMs, each storing the synapses associated with a particular neuron. The neuron mask signal filters out any unused weighted spikes. Once the address and enable signal are received, the crossbar reads the corresponding synapses from memory and forwards them to the LIF array.

8.3.3.1 Leaky Integrate and Fire Neuron Design

Due to its simplicity, the Leaky-Integrate-and-Fire (LIF) neuron model is chosen for the R-NASH hardware architecture. Figure 8.5 illustrates the architecture of a LIF neuron. Weighted spike inputs (*i_wspike*) are fed into an adder and register structure for accumulation. The inverted leak value is added to the accumulator at each step, decrementing the membrane potential. The neuron then checks if the membrane potential exceeds the firing threshold to determine whether it should fire. When the neuron fires, a refractory countdown begins, and the neuron remains inactive until the countdown completes. This period is known as the refractory period. The following equation theoretically represents the computational framework for a LIF or IF neuron:

$$V_j(t) = V_j(t-1) + \sum_i w_{i,j} \times x_i(t-1) - \lambda \tag{8.1}$$

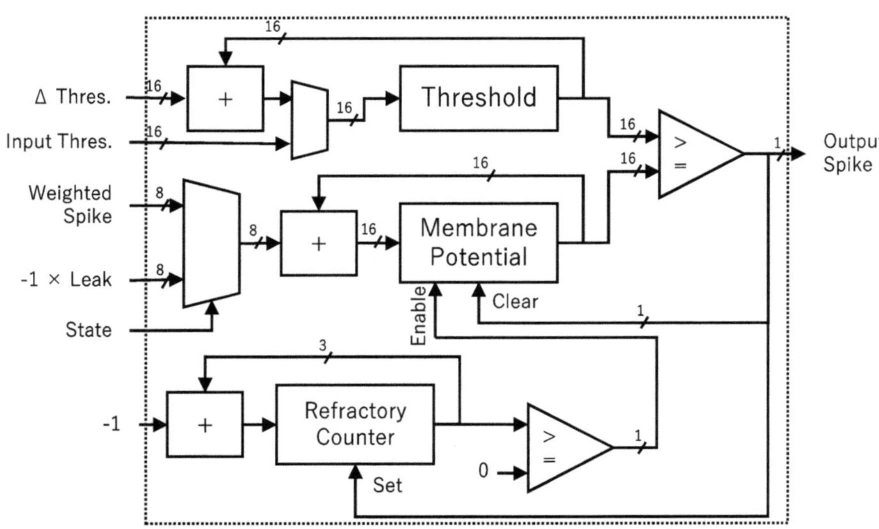

Fig. 8.5 LIF neuron architecture. This figure is adapted from "Toward Robust Cognitive 3D Brain-Inspired Cross-Paradigm System" by Ben Abdallah and Dang, used under CC BY-SA 4.0

Where $V_j(t)$ represents the membrane potential of neuron j at time step t, $w_{i,j}$ denotes the synapse weight from presynaptic neuron i to postsynaptic neuron j, $x_i(t-1)$ indicates the output spike of presynaptic neuron i, and λ represents the leak constant ($\lambda = 0$ for IF). The output of neuron j is described by the equation below:

$$x_j(t) = \begin{cases} 1, & \text{if } V_j(t) \geq Vt \\ 0, & \text{otherwise} \end{cases} \tag{8.2}$$

At the crossbar, input spikes are weighted by multiplying them with synapse weights to produce weighted inputs. These inputs are accumulated to form the membrane potential, and when this accumulated value surpasses the threshold, a spike is generated. The memory module manages the multiplication of input spikes and synapse weights. Due to the binary nature of input spikes, actual multiplication hardware is unnecessary. Instead, a straightforward approach using registers and adders handles the accumulation process.

8.3.4 R-NASH Control

The system enters a learning phase after each time step when the training mode is activated. If a postsynaptic spike occurs during the emulated training time step, weights are adjusted; otherwise, the system proceeds to the next step. During inference, R-NASH begins by synchronizing time steps. Each node's registers are accessible via interfaces, allowing the system to indicate, confirm, and adjust each node's time step. This flexibility in defining time steps facilitates transitions within the LIF array from integration to the leaky phase, enabling neurons to operate at different time steps as needed.

The operation of the SNPC involves four phases: (1) loading spikes, (2) integration, (3) leak and firing, and optionally (4) learning. In the loading spikes phase, spikes are fetched from presynaptic neurons via the interconnect. Due to the limited size of the input cache, spikes are decoded and directly sent to the crossbar. Alternatively, spikes are packed into a spike vector for learning purposes, optimizing memory usage.

8.3.5 Inter-Neural Communication Method

R-NASH utilizes a 3D-NoC that incorporates fault-tolerance mechanisms in its input buffers, crossbar, routing hardware, and pipeline [6]. The inter-neural interconnect comprises multiple routers (R) responsible for facilitating communication between neuron clusters [4].

The system supports two types of flits. The first type facilitates spikes between neurons in AER format, with the AER format flit translated into the address of the weight SRAM. The second type supports memory access, providing instructions and necessary arguments (addresses) for reading and writing to memory cells and registers within the neuron cluster. Memory access flits are generated by the master processor or an external host processor within the system. We support two types of read/write commands: single and burst. Single read/write commands access one element per request, while burst commands require a subsequent argument specifying the length. The Network Interface (NI) translates requested addresses into local addresses for each weight memory or LIF array.

Figure 8.3b depicts the Network Interface (NI) block diagram. Input spikes are classified into two categories: input spikes or memory accesses. For memory accesses, the NI provides an interface to manage data read and write operations across all registers and memory blocks of the node. When a read instruction is executed, the NI retrieves the value from the requested address and returns it to the master processor.

When handling input spikes from the network, the NI's decoding phase identifies the address in the weight SRAM and forwards it to the weight memory. In scenarios involving multi-layer SNNs or sparse connections, the *Flit Extractor* generates the read enable (RE) signal tailored for different layers or links within the weight memory. This capability allows multiple Address-Event Representations (AERs) to coexist at the same address, corresponding to other neurons.

The output spike from the LIF array is processed by the AER decoder, which identifies the address of the firing neuron. Subsequently, this address is transmitted sequentially to the remap Look-Up-Table (LUT) to retrieve the appropriate AER value for the receiving nodes.

8.4 R-NASH Learning Methods

As previously discussed, neuromorphic systems operate with asynchronous and independent execution of neurons within neural networks, providing greater flexibility and the capability to learn timing information. The R-NASH platform accommodates two learning methods: (1) off-chip learning, which involves straightforward parameter mapping from a pre-trained Artificial Neural Network (ANN) to an equivalent and accurate Spiking Neural Network (SNN), and (2) online learning, employing the Spike-Timing-Dependent Plasticity (STDP) approach.

8.4.1 Off-Chip Learning

We implement the approach outlined in [9] for off-chip learning. The feed-forward neural network functions as a fully connected model employing ReLU (rectified linear units) as its activation function.

During training, standard back-propagation is used without bias. Once training concludes, we transition the network's RELU weights to the IF (Integrate and Fire) model. Subsequently, these weights undergo normalization and conversion into an SNN format. Finally, the converted weights are integrated into our R-NASH model for inference. Notably, no refractory or leaky materials are employed in this conversion process. After normalization, the weights are quantized into a fixed-bit format and transferred to the R-NASH system via a host CPU. Our system defaults to an 8-bit format, but reducing the bit-width can potentially decrease overall area costs, given that memories constitute a significant portion of the system's footprint. Offline learning can be approached through various methods, such as converting from ANN/CNN [21, 23], direct learning with SNN [26, 27], or bio-inspired learning mechanisms like STDP or SDSP [14]. These different approaches offer flexibility when adapting to our R-NASH system.

8.4.2 Adaptive Learning Through STDP

While the R-NASH system supports loading pre-trained weights and parameters solely for inference, it also facilitates online learning. Specifically, we employ the online unsupervised Spike-Timing-Dependent Plasticity (STDP) mechanism with a winner-take-all approach [8]. Upon firing, a neuron enters a refractory state, and an inhibitory spike is broadcasted to other neurons to reduce their membrane potential. Figure 8.6 illustrates our system utilizing STDP learning.

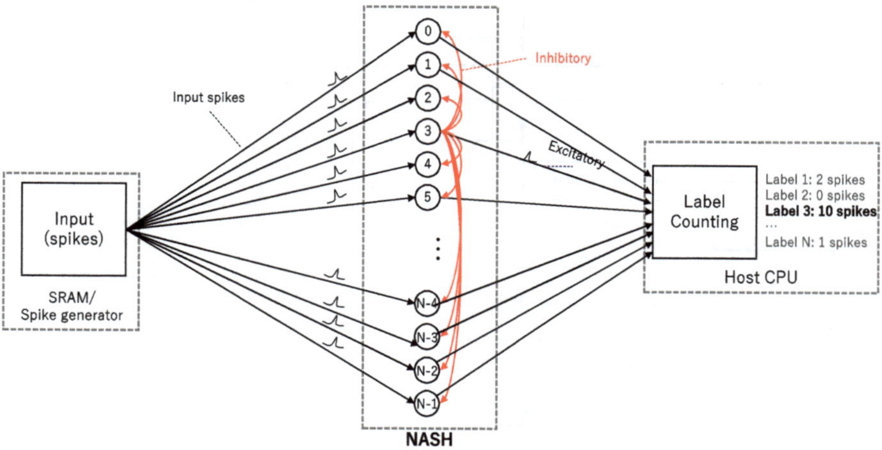

Fig. 8.6 R-NASH System using on-chip Spike-Timing-Dependent Plasticity (STDP) learning. STDP learning models in neuromorphic chips enable synaptic weights to adjust dynamically based on the precise timing of spikes, mimicking biological learning processes. This figure is adapted from "Toward Robust Cognitive 3D Brain-Inspired Cross-Paradigm System" by Ben Abdallah and Dang, used under CC BY-SA 4.0

The input spikes can be stored in SRAM, loaded into the system, or generated by the host CPU. Our 3D-NoC manages the transmission of these spikes interconnect. When a neuron fires, it transmits the spike to the host CPU for counting purposes. Ultimately, the label associated with the maximum spikes determines the selected label. Conversely, upon firing, neurons emit inhibitory spikes to reduce the membrane potential of other neurons. Given that STDP is an unsupervised learning method, label assignment by the host CPU is based on input spike labels.

Figure 8.7 illustrates the online STDP learning block. To streamline complexity, we employ a simplified STDP mode where synapse weights adjust to a fixed value based on the relative arrival time of presynaptic spikes. If neuron i's presynaptic spike arrives before neuron j's postsynaptic spike event, the synapse weight w_{ij} increases by a fixed amount Δw. Conversely, if neuron i's presynaptic spike arrives after neuron j's postsynaptic spike event, the weight decreases by Δw.

The R-NASH system incorporates various reconfiguration techniques using two methods:

- *Adaptive threshold:* Upon firing, a neuron's threshold is incrementally adjusted within a specific range; however, it decays if the neuron remains inactive.
- *Weight normalization:* The STDP learning module aims to maintain the average weights of neurons unchanged throughout the learning phase.

However, R-NASH faces limitations in achieving high resolution due to hardware constraints such as the floating-point computation unit of the CPU or GPU. For adaptive thresholding, an additional adder in the LIF neuron adjusts the threshold

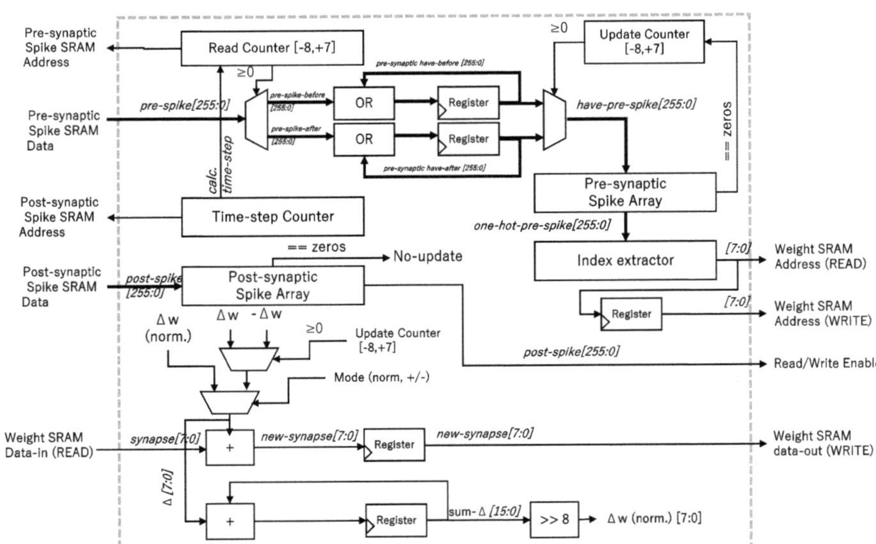

Fig. 8.7 On-chip STDP learning architecture. This figure is adapted from "Toward Robust Cognitive 3D Brain-Inspired Cross-Paradigm System" by Ben Abdallah and Dang, used under CC BY-SA 4.0

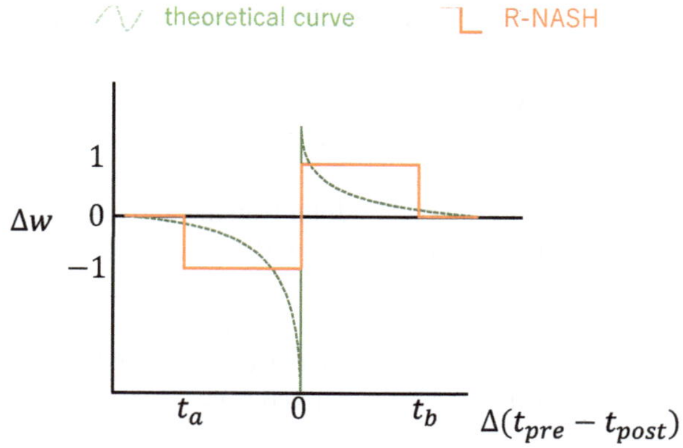

Fig. 8.8 On-chip STDP learning mechanism. This figure is adapted from "Toward Robust Cognitive 3D Brain-Inspired Cross-Paradigm System" by Ben Abdallah and Dang, used under CC BY-SA 4.0

(ΔThres.), as depicted in Fig. 8.5. The adjustment varies depending on whether the neuron fires: the threshold increases until reaching its maximum value when firing and decays to its minimum value when not firing. This adaptive mechanism helps balance the neuron's firing pattern with incoming rates. Nevertheless, unbalanced weights may cause neurons with higher values to fire maximally, potentially inhibiting others from firing and hindering learning in a winner-take-all mechanism. The STDP learning update mechanism is depicted in Fig. 8.8. It categorizes presynaptic and postsynaptic spikes based on their respective timestamps: (1) increasing the weight if the presynaptic neuron's spike precedes the postsynaptic neuron's spike, and (2) decreasing the weight if the presynaptic spike follows the postsynaptic one. This illustration uses 16 timesteps and fixed weight adjustments to simplify the process. Additionally, these values can be reconfigured through the memory interface facilitated by NI.

8.5 R-NASH Hardware Mapping

This section discusses the R-NASH system's hardware mapping approach. Breaking down the neuromorphic system into groups of neurons interconnected via a Network-on-Chip raises significant concerns about division and placement, as these factors can profoundly impact performance. For example, positioning two interconnected neurons far apart can create critical delay paths within the system. Consequently, the system must wait for spikes to traverse longer distances before progressing to the next time step. This leads to increased power consumption and heightened thermal dissipation in the packet-switching network.

R-NASH employs a genetic algorithm (GA) to determine the positioning and configuration of neurons. We outline the GA methodology and illustrate its application within R-NASH.

8.5.1 Genetic Algorithm for Spiking Neurons Mapping

A Genetic Algorithm (GA) addresses both constrained and unconstrained optimization problems. As demonstrated later, the initial mapping GA operates under unconstrained conditions. GA mimics biological evolution through natural selection, initially developed by John Holland and his colleagues [15], which is rooted in Charles Darwin's theory of natural selection.

GA employs random search and rank-based selection to operate on evolving string structures. Each generation defines survival rules that selectively retain certain members while removing others from the population. GA involves a crossover process where offspring are generated from parents to maintain a consistent or specified number of members. Typically, offspring inherit parts of their string structures from their parents. Furthermore, the mutation process introduces stochastic changes to the string structure. The Genetic Algorithm typically progresses through several stages: (1) Initialization, (2) Selection, (3) Crossover, and (4) Mutation. These stages of selection, crossover, and mutation occur iteratively across generations.

8.5.1.1 Population Initialization

GA initializes the population by randomizing it to establish a starting point. The string structure of each GA population member is randomized within optional constraints. The initial population size is typically larger to ensure an effective starting pool. Figure 8.9a shows an example string structure, where each structure comprises six binary bits (0 or 1). During initialization, GA randomizes M members, as illustrated in Fig. 8.9b. The structure size and string format depend on specific applications and configurations.

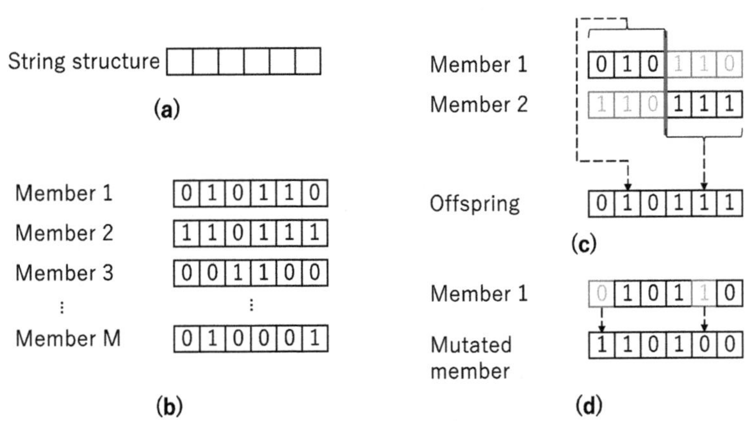

Fig. 8.9 Genetic algorithm (GA): (**a**) Example string structure; (**b**) Initialization process; (**c**) Crossover; (**d**) Mutation

8.5.2 *Selection*

The selection process in GA is governed by survival rules. Typically, a cost function or fitness function determines which members of the population survive. The fitness function, which is the inverse of the cost function, ranks members from lowest to highest cost to decide their survival.

There are various methods for selecting survivors. A straightforward approach involves ranking the entire generation for selection. Alternatively, tournament selection can be used, where multiple tournaments are conducted among population subsets to identify survivors.

8.5.3 *Crossover for Combining Two Parents*

Crossover in GA involves combining two parents to create offspring. Offspring inherit their string structure from their parents. For instance, one parent's first half might combine with the second half of another parent to produce an offspring. Figure 8.9c illustrates an example crossover between *Member 1* and *Member 2*, where each offspring is generated by combining 50% of each parent's structure.

8.5.4 *Mutation for Modifying Member's String Structure*

The mutation process introduces random changes to a member's string structure. This variability allows GA to explore new local solutions. The mutation must adhere to constraints set during initialization. Figure 8.9d illustrates a mutation example, where the first and fifth indices of a string structure are modified (e.g., 0 changes to 1 and vice versa).

After the Genetic Algorithm (i.e., after G generations), the selection process identifies a single surviving member from the entire population.

8.5.5 *Genetic Algorithm for Neurons Mapping on R-NASH Hardware*

When addressing mapping issues, several design factors require careful consideration: computation, communication, and memory. Given the architecture's node-based computation on-chip, it becomes evident that communication poses the most significant challenge. A bottleneck in communication arises when data does not flow swiftly enough to the parallelized computation units.Since mapping in multicore systems is NP-hard, R-NASH employs a simplified Genetic Algorithm

(GA) for optimization. This choice is made because ILP is NP-complete, and heuristic searches involve factorial complexity. Initially, the algorithm randomizes K mapping solutions. Subsequently, across G generations of refinement, the GA executes the steps outlined in Algorithm 8.3.

Algorithm 8.3 Genetic Algorithm for neurons mapping

`// Initialization phase`
S1: Load the system configuration.
S2: Randomize K mapping solutions.
`// Evolving phase`
for *(generation g_i in 1 to G)* **do**
  S3: Remove the wrong mapping solutions
  S4: Calculate cost function (communication cost) for each solution of the population
  S5: Select the B best out of K solutions based on the cost function
  S6: Crossover the new K solutions to have new population
  S7: Mutate the B best solutions to have new K solutions
  S8: Check if it satisfies the communication cost or does not improve over several generations
`// Finalization phase`
S9: Calculate cost function for each solution of the population
S10: Select the $B = 1$ best out of K solutions based on the cost function

Throughout these generations, the algorithm first eliminates incorrect mappings that either exceed the designed node's computational capacity or fail to map all computations. Then, the GA computes the cost function, which evaluates communication costs.

$$F_{cost} = \sum_{i=0,j=0}^{W} d_{ij} \times c_{ij} \tag{8.3}$$

Where d_{ij} and c_{ij} denote the distance and connection status between neurons i and j respectively. Since data transfer is multicast at each node, c_{ij} represents the connection between two processing elements (PEs). F_{cost} denotes the communication cost evaluated by our GA. The best communication costs among the K mapping solutions are then selected. Here, the communication cost is inversely related to the fitness function.

After having B's best solutions, they are crossed over to obtain K solutions. We keep the original B solutions and create a K-B solution using the crossover. The crossover method is shown in Fig. 8.10a. Assuming the crossover probability is 0.4 (randomly picked), the offspring take 0.4 of a parent and 0.6 of another parent to generate its mapping. Figure 8.10a shows two parents' mappings with configured neurons for [L1, L2, L3] (layer of neural net) as [100, 100, 50] and [40, 30, 80]. After the crossover process, an offspring is generated as 40% of [100, 100, 50] plus 60% of [40, 30, 80], which is [76, 72, 62].

After generating K solutions through crossover, the GA mutates these solutions to produce mutated configurations based on a specified probability. Figure 8.10b

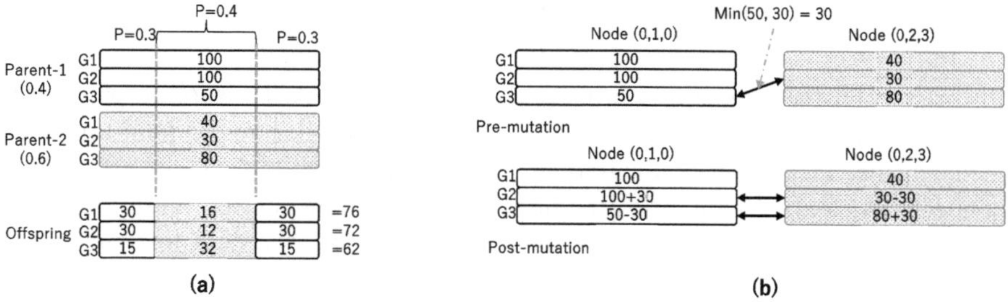

Fig. 8.10 Crossover and mutation method for GA mapping: (**a**) Crossover, (**b**) Mutation. This figure is adapted from "Toward Robust Cognitive 3D Brain-Inspired Cross-Paradigm System" by Ben Abdallah and Dang, used under CC BY-SA 4.0

illustrates the mutation process. Since the number of neurons mapped in each layer and processing element (PE) remains constant, strict adherence to this constraint is necessary. In Fig. 8.10b, we present a scenario where Layer 3 of node (0,1,0) undergoes random mutation. To maintain the total number of mapped neurons, we adjust Layer 2 of node (0,2,3) accordingly. The minimum configuration for both layers is 30, allowing us to decrease one configuration by 30 units while increasing the other by the same amount.

Following the mutation, we adjust the configurations to ensure the proper utilization of unused neurons. Subsequently, we evaluate whether the resulting communication cost meets the specified criteria. If the communication cost is satisfactory, the mapping process can be terminated. The GA concludes its operation after G generations.

After obtaining the best solutions from set B, they undergo crossover to generate K solutions. We retain the original B solutions and create K-B solutions through crossover operations. The crossover process is illustrated in Fig. 8.10a assumes a crossover probability of 0.4. The offspring inherit 40% of one parent's configuration and 60% from another parent's configuration to form their mapping. Figure 8.10a depicts two parents' mappings for layers [L1, L2, L3] as [100, 100, 50] and [40, 30, 80]. Following the crossover, an offspring's configuration results in [76, 72, 62].

Once crossover generates K solutions, the GA mutates these solutions to introduce variations under a specified probability. Figure 8.10b demonstrates a mutation scenario where a neuron configuration is randomly altered while maintaining the constant number of neurons mapped per layer and processing element (PE). In this example, Fig. 8.10b shows a mutation affecting L3 of node (0,1,0), where it is decreased by 30 units, compensated by an increase of L2 in node (0,2,3) by 30 units. The adjustment values are randomized but constrained to ensure minimal disruption.

After mutation, configurations are updated to accommodate unused neurons and ensure they conform to communication cost specifications. If the communication cost criteria are met satisfactorily, the mapping process may conclude. The GA completes its operations after G generations.

8.6 R-NASH Run-Time Maintenance

Ensuring robustness remains a primary objective for R-NASH neuromorphic hardware, which is why the system integrates a comprehensive set of fault-tolerance mechanisms. Protection is focused on three critical areas: data integrity, interconnectivity, and computational engines. Initially, strategies for preserving data integrity against corruption are discussed. Following this, the fault-tolerance measures to enhance communication reliability within R-NASH are detailed. Finally, methods for detecting and recovering from irreparable faults within the system are addressed.

8.6.1 Data Integrity Protection

Fundamental to the reliability of any robust system is its ability to withstand data corruption. In this context, data is categorized into two distinct types: (1) one-time load data and (2) data being transferred. One-time load data, such as weights and thresholds, is crucial and can be safeguarded by storing them in on-chip SRAM or registers. An error correction code may be employed to protect these data types. However, our investigation revealed that soft errors minimally impact overall accuracy. Hence, periodic verification and writing can suffice to ensure their correctness.

The other data category involves transfers within the system, particularly spikes and synchronizations, which are significant types of signals. System initialization is also crucial. Synchronization signals are vital as they ensure system operability. To safeguard this data type, our 3D-NoC incorporates two sets of (22,16) SECDED codes [16]. Consequently, for transferring 32-bit data, the 3D-NoC must handle 44 bits. This setup enables R-NASH to tolerate one fault per set and detect up to two. Our 3D-NoC provides up to 2-bit correction and 4-bit detection capability for optimal reliability.

8.6.2 Neurons Communication Protection

As discussed earlier, data integrity in our R-NASH system is ensured by implementing two sets of SECDED (22,16) codes [16]. Additionally, R-NASH safeguards its communication infrastructure with specific measures. Firstly, the Random Access Buffer technique [1] isolates faulty buffers from read and write processes, ensuring data reliability. Moreover, in case of crossbar faults, backup links within the crossbar facilitate uninterrupted communication [1]. Furthermore, a fault-tolerant routing algorithm is employed to recover from faults in input ports, output ports, or the entire router [1].

8.6.3 Fault-Tolerant Neurons Mapping Scheme

Another challenge in large-scale SNN architectures is the occurrence of uncorrectable faults in modules during runtime. This indicates that a module becomes corrupted and cannot gracefully maintain functional accuracy. Therefore, we propose a method to remap the neuromorphic system under such faulty conditions.

We employ two strategies to mitigate faults in neural computing units: (1) each neuron node includes spare neurons along with their weight SRAM, and (2) the system includes spare nodes. When a neuron or node fails, R-NASH remaps it to a spare neuron or node to maintain operation. Figure 8.11a illustrates a layer configuration with varying numbers of spare neurons per node, facilitating remapping in case of failures. Figure 8.11b depicts an example where 25 faulty neurons from node (0,0,0) are remapped to node (0,3,2), reducing the spare neuron count in the node (0,3,2) from 34 to 9.

While traditional SNN mapping methods can be applied for neuron replacement, remapping offers an alternative approach, especially in the context of faults. For instance, minimizing downtime and reducing memory transfers within the system are critical considerations. However, mapping can be challenging in disconnected regions caused by faulty network segments. To address these challenges, we explore two conventional methods: (1) Greedy Search, which scans faulty nodes once to find replacements, and (2) Genetic Algorithm adaptation for mapping, which aims to optimize the remapping solution. In addition to the communication cost discussed in Eq. (8.3), we introduce the concept of migration cost to minimize system repair time, as follows:

$$M_{cost} = \sum_{i=0,j=0}^{W} d_{ij} \times m_{ij} \tag{8.4}$$

where m_{ij} represents the number of migrating neurons between node i and j. The primary motivation for introducing the migration cost is to minimize repair time, as reloading neuron weights is costly and can impact the real-time operation of R-NASH.

Algorithm 8.4 presents the Remapping Genetic Algorithm, structured into three phases: initialization, evolution, and finalization. The initialization phase commences with the first step (**S1**), where the count of unmapped and available neurons is gathered and transmitted from each node in the system. Figure 8.11a illustrates a layer after this initial phase. Based on these metrics, the second step (**S2**) proceeds to randomly generate K mapping solutions (as depicted in Fig. 8.11b). This step selects a node with available neurons and an unmapped one based on the data from **S1**. By the end of step **S2**, the algorithm produces K valid mapping solutions, which, although not optimal, serve as starting points for further optimization. In the *evolve* phase, the GA method iterates through G generations, with each generation consisting of four sequential steps. Initially, step **S3** computes the cost function

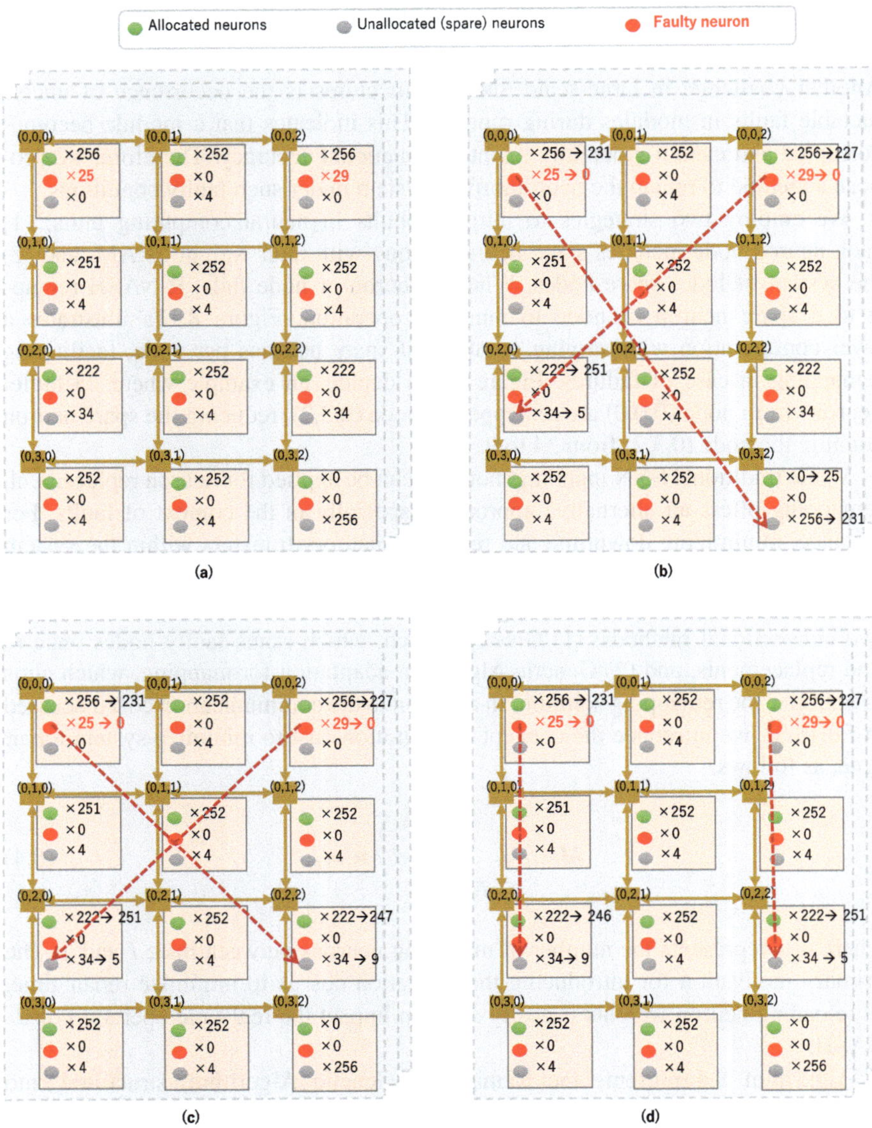

Fig. 8.11 Illustration of fault-tolerance remapping of the Genetic Algorithm: (**a**) Unmapped and free neurons per node; (**b**) A randomized mapping solution; (**c**) Mutating by finding a shorter distance for a flow; (**d**) Mutating by swapping the flow's destination. This figure is adapted from "Toward Robust Cognitive 3D Brain-Inspired Cross-Paradigm System" by Ben Abdallah and Dang, used under CC BY-SA 4.0

Algorithm 8.4 Genetic Algorithm for remapping SNN

`// initialize phase`
S1: build the unmapped and free neurons per node
S2: randomize the K mapping solutions
`// evolve phase`
for *(generation g_i in 1 to G)* **do**
    S3: calculate cost function for each solution of the population
    S4: select the B best out of K solutions based on the cost function
    S5: crossover the new K solutions to have new population
    S6: mutate the B best solutions to have new K solutions
`// finalize phase`
S7: calculate cost function for each solution of the population
S8: select the $B = 1$ best out of K solutions based on the cost function

for each solution, focusing solely on M_{cost} from Eq. (8.4). Simultaneously, the communication cost F_{cost} is evaluated in step **S4** during the selection process of the top B solutions from K. In cases where multiple solutions exhibit similar M_{cost} values, their F_{cost} is considered to maintain a straightforward single-objective optimization approach while integrating migration and communication costs.

Following selecting the best B solutions, the process advances to two subsequent steps: **S5**—crossover and **S6**—mutation. Step **S5** involves mixing two randomly selected mapping solutions, wherein each parent contributes 50% to generate offspring inheriting characteristics from both parents.

The mutation step **S6** introduces two types of mutations. The first type identifies an immediate node between two nodes in a mapping flow, ensuring that the immediate node with available neurons is closer to the source node than the original flow destination. For example, Fig. 8.11b illustrates a scenario where 25 unmapped neurons from the source node (0,0,0) are mapped initially to the destination node (0,3,2). Subsequently, node (0,2,2) is identified as the immediate node meeting the criteria: it possesses free neurons and is closer to (0,0,0) than (0,3,2). The neurons are then remapped to node (0,2,2) instead of the original destination, as depicted in Fig. 8.11c.

The second mutation type involves swapping mappings to achieve a shorter migration distance (M_{cost}). This mutation is executed when exchanging destinations between two flows can reduce their migration distance. For instance, in Fig. 8.11c, neurons initially mapped from the node (0,0,0) to (0,2,2) and from the node (0,2,0) to (0,0,2) each have a migration distance of four. Both flows achieve a migration distance of two by swapping destinations, as demonstrated in Fig. 8.11d. Upon completing G generations, the algorithm finalizes by selecting the best solution in steps **S7** and **S8**. This optimal solution is then employed for the mapping process. Early termination criteria can be applied based on the best-found solution to expedite the mapping process. This GA methodology extends the optimization framework for remapping faulty neurons beyond traditional mapping algorithms focused solely on communication costs. It leverages the migration cost function to enhance optimization outcomes for neuromorphic systems.

8.7 R-NASH Evaluation Results

This section evaluates the performance of our R-NASH platform across various dimensions. Initially, we address the efficiency of the GA (Genetic Algorithm) model in tackling the initial mapping challenge. We map multi-layer feed-forward networks onto 3D NoCs of different sizes, ranging from $4 \times 4 \times 4$ to $10 \times 10 \times 10$. We assess how these factors influence system performance by varying the node sizes (256, 128, 64, and 32 neurons per node) and exploring different topologies. Additionally, we compare the benefits of 3D topology over 2D to highlight the structural advantages. To enhance the robustness of our neuromorphic hardware, we introduce fault-tolerant mapping, contrasting it with conventional methods such as greedy search. This approach effectively mitigates system failures. Next, we show the hardware complexity of our system, utilizing NANGATE 45 nm and FreePDK45 TSV library for evaluation. Furthermore, we explore the performance of our R-NASH platform through offline and online training using the MNIST dataset. Offline learning involves using pre-trained weights from a multi-layer feed-forward neural network for classification on R-NASH. Meanwhile, online learning leverages on-chip STDP with a winner-take-all mechanism facilitated by inhibitory connections.

Finally, we discuss our approach's strengths and limitations, encapsulating the findings and implications of our evaluations.

8.7.1 Initial Mapping Evaluation

8.7.1.1 Mapping over Different 3D-NoC Sizes

To evaluate the efficiency of the GA method for initial mapping, we compare it against three linear mapping approaches. These approaches include Linear X, Linear XY, and Linear XYZ, derived from SpiNNaker's linear mapping method [17], adapted to the 3D topology. Each variant prioritizes mapping directions based on specified configurations detailed in Table 8.1. Notably, each node reserves 20% of neurons as spare capacity, and an additional node (the highest indexed node) remains unused for mapping purposes, serving as a fault-tolerance measure discussed further in Sect. 8.7.2. Here, we employed GA with a population size of $K = 100$, selecting the best $B = 5$ solutions and using a mutation rate of 0.5. In Fig. 8.12, we compare the results of GA against linear mapping methods. For a smaller network size of $4 \times 4 \times 4$, after approximately 60 generations, GA reaches a saturation point where the lowest communication cost remains unchanged throughout subsequent generations. The final communication cost is lower than that of manual mapping solutions, with an overall cost of approximately 0.4 times that of manual mapping.

Table 8.1 Configuration for the mapping evaluation[a]

Parameter	Value
# neurons per node (E)	256
# nodes (N)	4 × 4 × 4 to 10 × 10 × 10
# spare neurons (R)	0.2×X
# spare node	1
# faults (k)	0.05×X , 0.10×X, 0.15×X, and 0.20×X
SNN # layers	4
SNN configuration[a]	784:0.5*(W-10): 0.5*(W-10): 10

X: number of neurons in R-NASH.
[a] MLP model. For example, the SNN configuration for E=64 and 4 × 4 × 4 is 784:1633:1633:10.

Larger NoCs require more generations to achieve lower costs compared to linear mapping. Specifically, while a 4×4×4 network stabilizes in around 60 generations, larger configurations such as 6 × 6 × 6, 8 × 8 × 8, and 10 × 10 × 10 require approximately 120, 180, and 320 generations, respectively, to stabilize. Across all tested cases, linear mapping methods consistently exhibit significantly higher communication costs compared to genetic algorithms.

8.7.1.2 Mapping over Different Node Sizes

Figure 8.13 illustrates the impact of varying node sizes (from 32 to 256 neurons) while mapping the same system across different 3D NoC configurations, ranging from 4 × 4 × 4 to 8 × 8 × 8. As depicted in Fig. 8.13, smaller NoCs benefit from reduced inter-node distances, resulting in lower communication costs. The smallest network size achieves the lowest communication cost (4039).

However, increasing the network size and reducing the number of neurons per node leads to higher communication costs. Specifically, with 128, 64, and 32 neurons per node, the communication costs rise to 21,768, 107,838, and 529,440, respectively. Consolidating neurons from the same layer into a single node reduces the need for multiple unicast flits for spikes, thereby significantly decreasing traffic. It's important to note that scaling the number of neurons per node is constrained by crossbar limitations and on-chip communication bottlenecks.

Additionally, larger node sizes present challenges such as lower operating frequencies due to longer critical paths, difficulties in placement and routing due to complex structures and macro SRAM, and reduced NoC performance due to longer inter-node distances. Typically, neuromorphic clusters range between 256 and 1024 neurons per node, balancing these considerations.

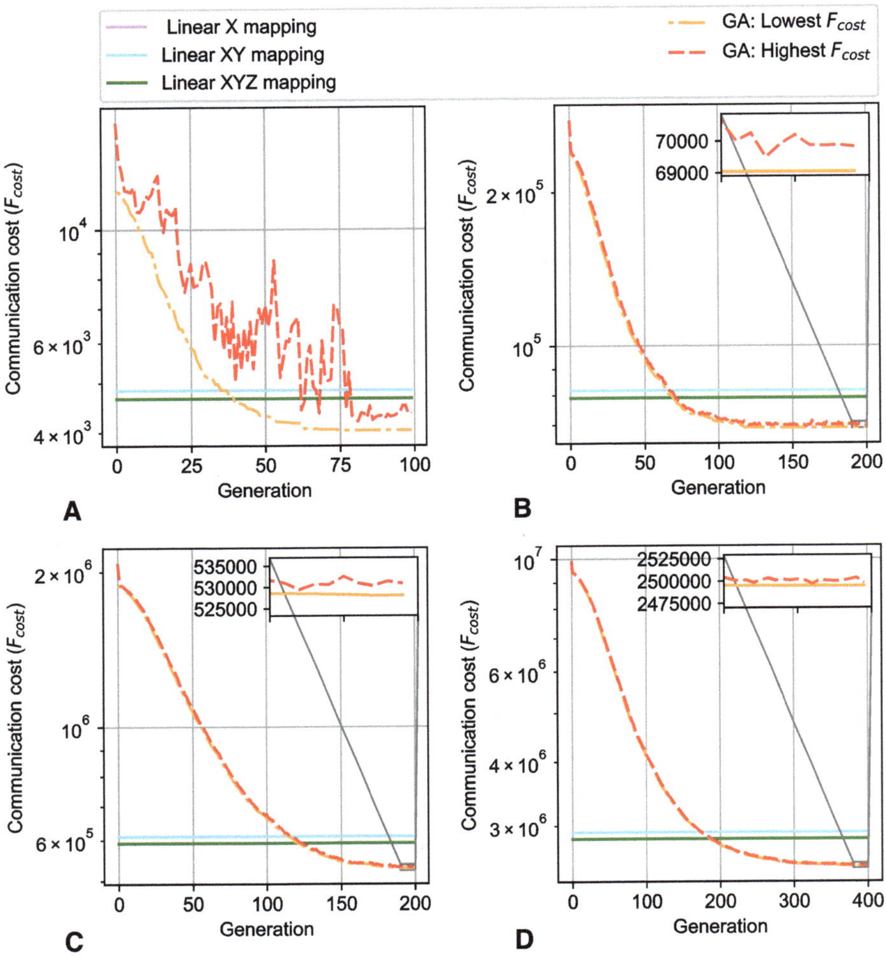

Fig. 8.12 Genetic Algorithm Result for initial mapping: (**a**) 4 × 4 × 4 NoC-based, 256 neurons/node, (**b**) 6 × 6 × 6 NoC-based, 256 neurons/node, (**c**) 8 × 8 × 8 NoC-based, 256 neurons/node, (**d**) 10 × 10 × 10 NoC-based, 256 neurons/node (CC BY-SA 4.0 "Toward Robust Cognitive 3D Brain-Inspired Cross-Paradigm System" by Ben Abdallah and Dang)

8.7.1.3 Comparison Between 3D and 2D in Initial Mapping

As previously mentioned, the advantages of a 3D structure are evident. To demonstrate these benefits, we compare the communication costs between 3D and 2D configurations using linear mapping and GA, as shown in Fig. 8.14. To ensure a fair comparison, we maintain a consistent node size of 256 neurons per node and vary the sizes of the NoCs (64, 128, 256, and 512 nodes) between the 3D and 2D configurations.

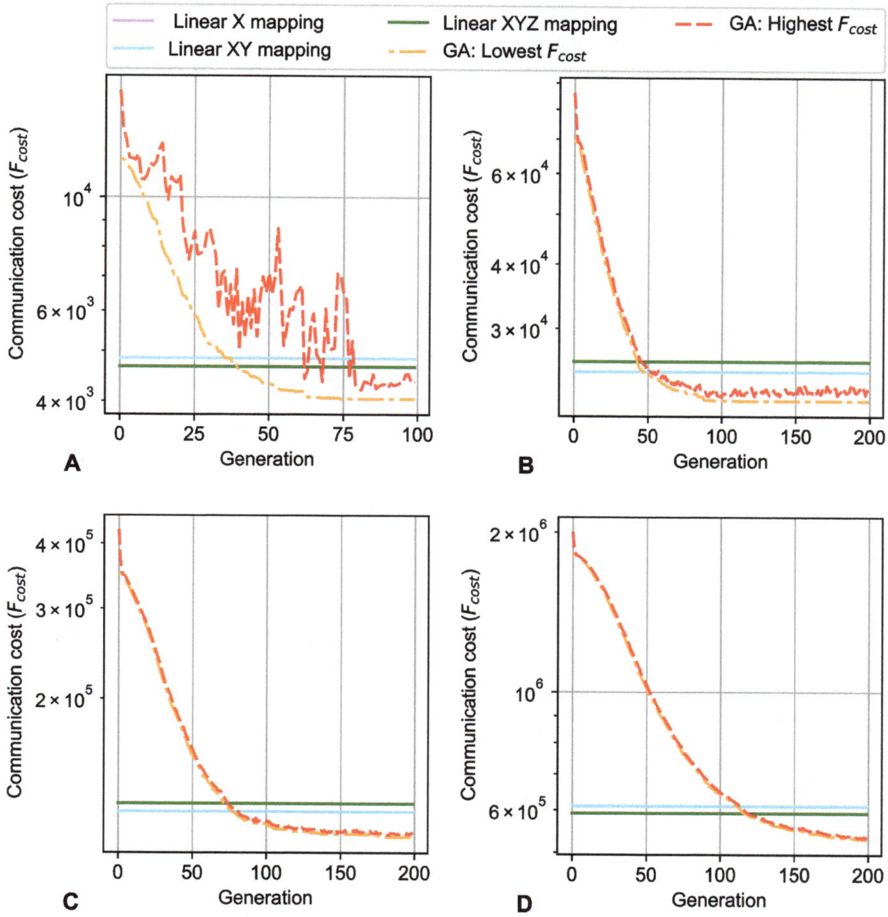

Fig. 8.13 Genetic Algorithm Result of the initial mapping of 3D NoC-based:: (**a**) 4 × 4 × 4, 256 neurons/node; (**b**) 4 × 4 × 8, 128 neurons/node; (**c**) 4 × 8 × 8, 64 neurons/node; (**d**) 4 × 8 × 8, 32 neurons/node

Figure 8.14 demonstrates that mapping on a 3D structure significantly lowers communication costs. Across all tested configurations (64, 128, 256, and 512 nodes), GA's performance on 3D structures is 1.4–2.0 times lower compared to 2D configurations. Even with linear mappings (X, XY, or XYZ), 3D consistently outperforms 2D. This advantage stems from the inherent characteristics of 3D structures, which enable shorter traversal paths between different chip regions. Consequently, spikes can propagate more quickly on 3D architectures, potentially enhancing overall performance and reducing power consumption.

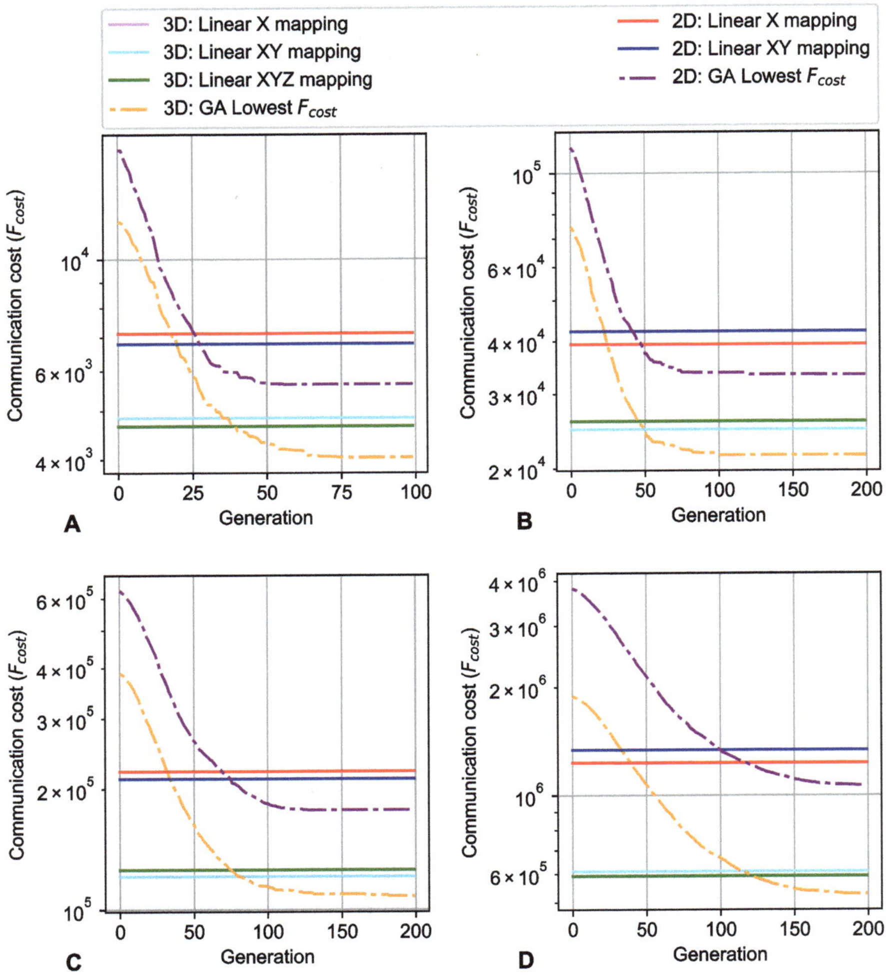

Fig. 8.14 Comparison between 3D and 2D mapping: (**a**) 64 nodes (4 × 4 × 4 and 8 × 8) NoC-based, 256 neurons/node; (**b**) 128 nodes (4 × 4 × 8 and 8 × 16) NoC-based, 256 neurons/node; (**c**) 256 nodes (4 × 8 × 8 and 16 × 16) NoC-based, 256 neurons/node; (**d**) 512 nodes (8 × 8 × 8 and 16 × 32) NoC-based, 256 neurons/node. This figure is adapted from "Toward Robust Cognitive 3D Brain-Inspired Cross-Paradigm System" by Ben Abdallah and Dang, used under CC BY-SA 4.0

8.7.2 Fault-Tolerant Mapping

In this section, we evaluate the Genetic Algorithm (GA) for remapping and compare it with 1-hop and N-hop Greedy Search (GS) to assess its efficiency. Greedy Search examines each node once and identifies a spare node within a 1-hop range or across the entire system (N-hop) with the shortest distance. The evaluation configuration is detailed in Table 8.1. This evaluation focuses on three key parameters:

- *Mapping Rate*: The effectiveness of mapping faulty neurons to spare nodes.
- *Average Spike Transmission Cost* (F_{cost}): The average distance of all connections.
- *Migration Cost* (M_{cost}): The amount of read/write operations required to adapt the system.

Figure 8.15 illustrates the results of the system using various 3D-NoC configurations (see Table 8.1).

As shown in Fig. 8.15, our GA method successfully remaps all faulty neurons to spare ones, irrespective of the size or topology. Notably, 1-hop Greedy Search can only map approximately 60% (or up to 80% in worst-case scenarios) of the faulty neurons. This limitation arises because 1-hop Greedy Search attempts a single mapping solution from its immediate neighbors, making it prone to failures in mapping. In contrast, both N-hop Greedy Search and the Genetic Algorithm demonstrate the ability to map all neurons.

The average communication cost (F_{cost}) varies across different approaches. Specifically, the 1-hop Greedy Search shows a consistently high F_{cost} due to its frequent inability to map neurons effectively. Other methods exhibit fluctuating

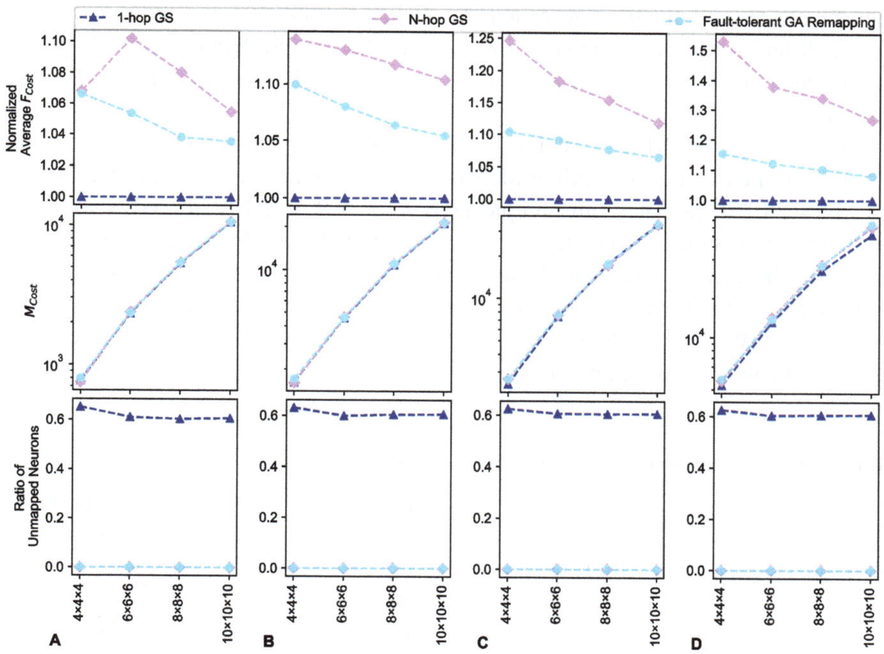

Fig. 8.15 Output mapping for the migrated neurons with random fault patterns in 3D-NoCs. The system has 256 neurons per node; 20% of the neurons are spares with 1 redundant node without any allocated neuron at 0% fault rate. (**a**) 5% defect rate. (**b**) 10% defect rate. (**c**) 15% defect rate. (**d**) 20% defect rate (CC BY-SA 4.0 "Toward Robust Cognitive 3D Brain-Inspired Cross-Paradigm System" by Ben Abdallah and Dang)

F_{cost} values across different NoC sizes, with reductions observed as the NoC size increases. This reduction can be attributed to decreased impact on neuron movements with larger NoCs, particularly with lower fault rates (k values). Additionally, remapping tends to maintain communication costs, albeit slight reductions are noticed with migration-based algorithms. Notably, the Genetic Algorithm tends to achieve a lower average F_{cost}, reflecting its effectiveness in optimizing communication costs as a secondary factor.

In conclusion, we have demonstrated the efficiency of adapting the Genetic Algorithm to address the remapping problem. While the Genetic Algorithm may exhibit higher F_{cost} in some instances than other methods, it excels in managing migration and overall communication costs. Despite high defect rates, it proves effective, consistently achieving lower communication costs than alternative methods.

8.7.3 Hardware Complexity

Table 8.2 presents the hardware complexity of the architecture. The Network Interface (NI), crucial for supporting the mapping method, is integrated with the neuron cluster and the 3D-NoC router. According to Table 8.2, the additional LUTs for AER and Address collectively account for 23.35% and 28.83% of the Network Interface area, respectively. The overhead imposed by these two LUTs is relatively minimal.

In contrast, the NI designed to support migration techniques occupies only 25.95% of the tile area, excluding SRAM (neuron cluster + network interface).

Figure 8.16 illustrates our sample layout for a 2 × 2 NoC-based SNN layer with migration support. The cluster configuration includes 256 spike inputs in AER format, 8-bit synapse weights, 32 physical neurons, and 32 synapse crossbars per cluster. Each crossbar is implemented using OpenRAM with a 256-bank, 8-bit dual-port SRAM. We limit each node to 32 neurons to facilitate reasonable Place&Route times and enhance visual layout clarity.

Table 8.2 Hardware complexity of the R-NASH node

Module		Area (μm^2)	Power (mW)	Max Freq. (MHz)
Network Interface	AER LUT	16,747	–	–
	Address LUT	20,768	–	–
	Total	72,032	30.4043	699.30
Neuron Cluster		205,608	81.682	751.87
		64KB SRAM	–	–
3D-NoC router [6]		41,739	14.6128	537.63
Vertical TSVs (up and down)		2901.1136	–	–

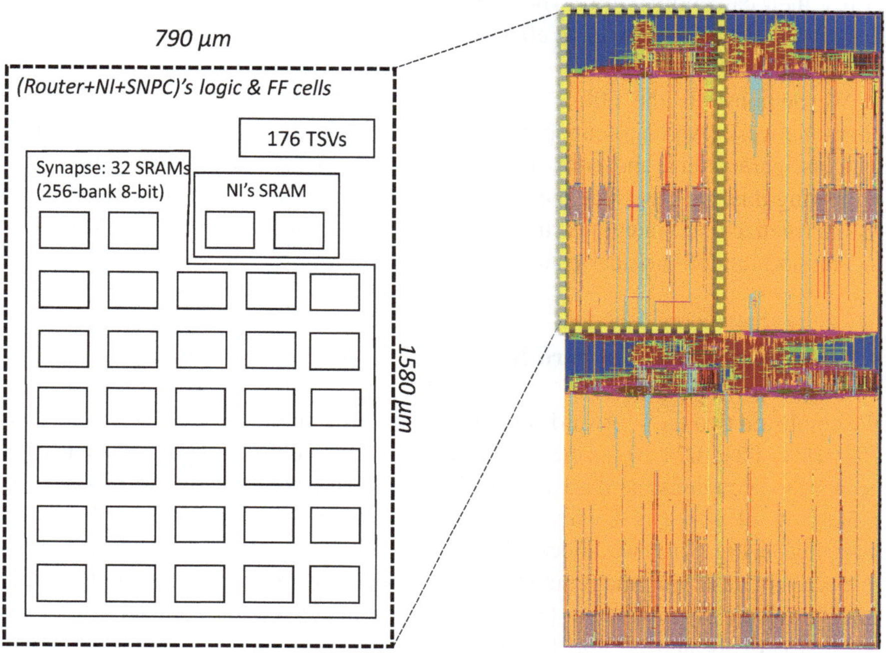

Fig. 8.16 Layout of a 2 × 2 3D-NoC-based R-NASH die. A tile's size is 790 μm × 1580 μm (CC BY-SA 4.0 "Toward Robust Cognitive 3D Brain-Inspired Cross-Paradigm System" by Ben Abdallah and Dang)

To support inter-layer interconnects in the 3D-NoC, we utilize TSVs from FreePDK3D45, each with dimensions of 4.06 μm^2 × 4.06 μm^2, and a Keep-out-Zone of 15 μm^2 × 15 μm^2 for each TSV. As depicted in the layout, approximately 80% of the area is allocated for macro SRAM placement. Given the lightweight design of the LIF neurons, the most complex component remains the crossbar.

The Network Interface (NI) necessitates two dedicated SRAMs: one for converting AER from local to global values and another for a destination lookup table. Further optimization of the design footprint could involve reducing synapse bit-width or exploring alternative memory technologies such as eDRAM, STT-RAM, or memristors. Additionally, additional stacking layers dedicated to memory could help minimize the overall footprint.

8.7.4 System Validation

This section presents the results of online and offline training conducted on our R-NASH system. Given the complexity of the 3D-NoC in modeling neuromorphic systems, conventional MNIST classification neural networks are often too small to utilize their capabilities fully. Therefore, we have scaled up the hidden layer of the feed-forward neural network to effectively map it onto our R-NASH platform in the validation phase.

We demonstrate the offline conversion process from a feed-forward artificial neural network (ANN) to our spiking neural network (SNN). This involves loading weights, parameters, and configurations into the system via a memory interface. Following this, we introduce the online STDP method. Initial weights, randomized and normalized, are integrated into our R-NASH system, given that R-NASH does not support random number generation.

8.7.4.1 Offline Feed-Forward Network

We employed two feed-forward networks for offline training: 784:1024:1024:10 and 784:1024:1024:1024:10 for the MNIST dataset. The hidden layer was fixed at 1024 neurons to accommodate the 10-bit SRAM model in our hardware design. Utilizing a 3D-NoC of $4 \times 4 \times 4$ with 64 neurons per node, as determined by the initial mapping in Fig. 8.13, we allocated 2058 and 3082 neurons for the two networks respectively, reserving the remainder as spare neurons to tolerate potential defects. Additionally, an extra node at (3,3,3) and sparse neurons (approximately 31/32 for the first network and 2/3 for the second network) were allocated across all active nodes. Scaling the 3D-NoC and increasing the neurons per node could support more extensive networks, so we opted for the feed-forward above sizes to avoid extensive SRAM models. Although sparse synapses could reduce SRAM size, we focused solely on validating R-NASH's operation.

Figure 8.17 presents the accuracy results of the 784:1024:1024:10 network on the R-NASH system compared to its software counterpart. The R-NASH system employed an 8-bit signed weight representation, yielding results comparable to the Matlab-converted version. The simulation utilized 350 time steps (1 millisecond per time step). We also evaluated the fixed-point SNN in software, where we truncated the least significant bit in the representation. Similarly, in R-NASH, 8-bit signed fixed-point values were converted to integer values for hardware implementation. Initially, a drop in accuracy was observed when comparing the floating-point SNN to the fixed-point version, particularly significant when using fewer than five representation bits. This discrepancy arises because larger and deeper networks accumulate value differences, resulting in more significant inaccuracies. Nevertheless, the 8-bit signed fixed-point approach proved optimal for implementation, offering nearly identical accuracy with slightly slower response times.

Our results demonstrate that R-NASH can effectively infer pre-trained and converted networks without issue, yielding performance identical to the software version. Notably, R-NASH reaches saturation around the 55th time step in both cases. Implementing clock gating as described in Mahmoodi et al. [19] could save up to 85%

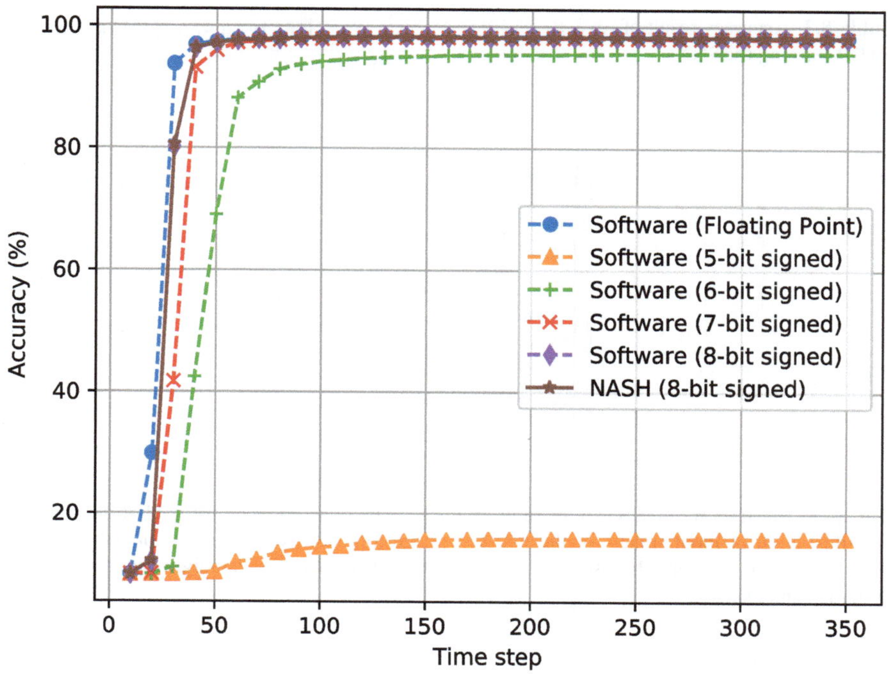

Fig. 8.17 Accuracy result of offline training for MNIST dataset with the network model 784:1024:10 (CC BY-SA 4.0 "Toward Robust Cognitive 3D Brain-Inspired Cross-Paradigm System" by Ben Abdallah and Dang)

8.7.5 Unsupervised STDP

This section evaluates the online STDP method using the MNIST benchmark. We adopt the network architecture from [8]. Precisely, the recurrent version detailed in [14]. To align with our hardware implementation, we simplify the architecture to match our specifications. The original network size in [8] is 784:N:N, while our adapted network is 784:N. Given the manageable number of neurons, we utilize a small 3D-NoC configuration of $1 \times 4 \times 4$ with 64 neurons per node. Versions of the network with N = 100 and N = 400 are mapped onto 2 and 4 nodes, respectively. Since there are no sparse connections, the communication cost remains unchanged regardless of neuron placement.

For testing purposes, we employ the BindsNet platform [14] to develop an RTL-like version of the LIF neuron for training and testing on our PC. After completing the testing and debugging phase, we perform Verilog model training and compare it against the golden reference software.

In the SNN software model [8], the authors used adaptive weight changes ($\Delta w = w \times$ learning_rate). However, this approach is unsuitable for our hardware STDP implementation due to two primary reasons: (1) the limited resolution of

Table 8.3 Accuracy result of STDP learning for SNNs

N	Floating Point Software	R-NASH
100	79.44%	71.32%
400	88.87%	84.05%

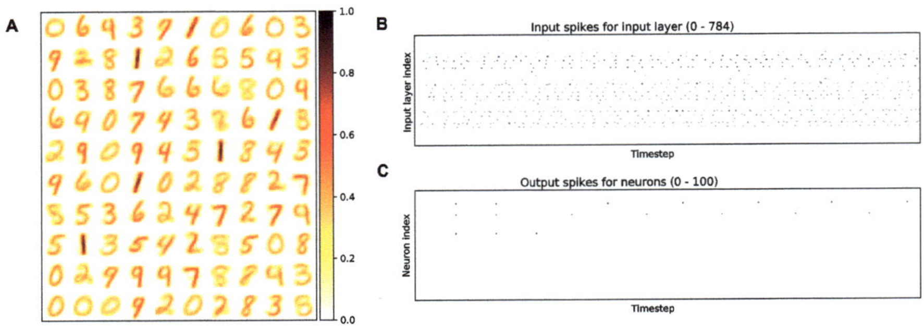

Fig. 8.18 Illustration of the STDP learning result: (**a**) The final 2D receptive field of the weights. (**b**) Illustration of input spikes for the first test image (digit 8). (**c**) Illustration of output spikes (CC BY-SA 4.0 "Toward Robust Cognitive 3D Brain-Inspired Cross-Paradigm System" by Ben Abdallah and Dang)

weights (8-bit) makes this principle impractical, and (2) the architectural complexity of multiplication. Therefore, we employ fixed weight changes and conduct further evaluations for deeper insights. Table 8.3 presents the accuracy comparison between the software version of STDP learning and our hardware-based STDP SNN. A noticeable decrease in accuracy is observed with our RTL model compared to the software implementation by Diehl et al. [8]. This discrepancy arises from the simplified hardware model and lower resolution (fixed 8-bit weights, 16-bit membrane potential, and 16-bit normalization).

Figure 8.18 illustrates the weights for N = 100 and the input/output spikes extracted from our R-NASH software model, adapted for MNIST. However, limitations of the hardware model result in some weights having similar distributions. Consequently, these neurons fire simultaneously and persist across subsequent time steps, as depicted in Fig. 8.18. Furthermore, weights continue to evolve during training due to pure STDP without intervention, sometimes exhibiting mixed values (e.g., 8 and 5, 1 and 7).

8.8 Chapter Summary

This chapter introduces R-NASH, a resilient three-dimensional neuromorphic system that leverages 3D Network-on-Chip (NoC) technology to maximize parallelism while maintaining a compact form factor. By utilizing 3D-integrated circuits (3D-ICs), R-NASH saves space and enhances system performance through sophisticated data protection and fault recovery mechanisms at the system level. The chapter demonstrates the efficacy of R-NASH by applying it to classify the MNIST dataset, showcasing the system's capability in handling real-world data.

Additionally, the chapter presents the platform's innovative mapping method, which significantly outperforms manual mapping techniques by minimizing the number of hops required for communication between Spiking Neural Networks (SNNs). This efficiency is bolstered by introducing a genetic algorithm designed to enhance fault recovery in SNNs, ensuring robust and reliable system operations even in the presence of hardware faults.

Future work will focus on optimizing bit widths to reduce power consumption further and improve computational efficiency. The exploration of low-power strategies will aim to enhance the system's overall energy efficiency, making R-NASH a more sustainable and scalable solution for neuromorphic computing applications. The chapter concludes with exercises designed to reinforce the concepts discussed and provide practical experience in applying the techniques covered.

8.9 Exercises

8.9.1 Exercise 1

It is essential to understand the phases and why we need them when implementing a platform. In R-NASH, we have several stages of implementation. Please name the main phases of the R-NASH system platform and briefly explain what they are.

8.9.2 Exercise 2

The NoC fabric is implemented to communicate between cores. However, the core must understand how to communicate using a Network Interface. Please explain the central role of the Network Interface. To deploy a new system, what data must be sent or received at each NI? What information should we store at the Network Interface to allow it to operate as intended?

8.9.3 Exercise 3

In R-NASH, we have two types of data. During a regular operation (inference), what does an NI need to be transferred? What data needs to be moved if we need to perform some fault tolerance?

8.9.4 Exercise 4

Please illustrate again the two types of flits in RNASH. What is the limitation of this flit format, and how can we improve it?

8.9.5 Exercise 5

In Spiking Neural Network, all computation must be done using a neuron circuit. As in R-NASH, a Leaky-Integrate-and-Fire (LIF) neuron is adopted. In the LIF neuron architecture, one part is called the refractory counter. Please explain what it is and why we need to do so.

8.9.6 Exercise 6

There are two types of connections (or synapses): inhibitory and excitatory. Please explain the differences between them. What kind of connection do we need for STDP learning? Why do we need them, and what are their roles?

8.9.7 Exercise 7

There are several types of STDP equations and curves. Understanding them and finding a suitable solution is necessary. In R-NASH, what is the significant difference between the theoretical curve of STDP and R-NASH's implementation? Please explain the reason behind it. What should we do if we want to match the theoretical curve precisely?

8.9.8 Exercise 8

A Genetic Algorithm (GA) is an optimization technique inspired by natural selection. In this technique, solutions evolve over generations to find the best ones. GA consists of the following processes: selection, crossover, and mutation. Please briefly explain these above processes. In this work of R-NASH, what are the main modifications from a general Genetic Algorithm?

8.9.9 *Exercise 9*

Understanding the evolution process is critical for designing GA. Please explain why the Genetic Algorithm has good results and started to improve after several generations.

References

1. Ahmed AB, Abdallah AB (2014) Graceful deadlock-free fault-tolerant routing algorithm for 3d network-on-chip architectures. J Parallel Distrib Comput 74(4):2229–2240
2. Akopyan F, et al (2015) TrueNorth: design and tool flow of a 65 mW 1 million neuron programmable neurosynaptic chip. IEEE Trans Comput Aid Des Integr Circuits Syst 34(10):1537–1557
3. Benjamin BV et al (2014) Neurogrid: a mixed-analog-digital multichip system for large-scale neural simulations. Proc IEEE 102(5):699–716
4. Dang KN, Ben Abdallah A (2019) An efficient software-hardware design framework for spiking neural network systems. In: 2019 international conference on internet of things, embedded systems and communications (IINTEC), pp 155–162
5. Dang KN, Ahmed AB, Okuyama Y, Abderazek BA (2017) Scalable design methodology and online algorithm for TSV-cluster defects recovery in highly reliable 3D-NoC systems. IEEE Trans Emerg Top Comput 8:577–590
6. Dang KN, Ahmed AB, Okuyama Y, Abdallah AB (2020) Scalable design methodology and online algorithm for TSV-cluster defects recovery in highly reliable 3D-NoC systems. IEEE Trans Emerg Top Comput 8(3):577–590
7. Davies M, et al (2018) Loihi: a neuromorphic manycore processor with on-chip learning. IEEE Micro 38(1):82–99
8. Diehl PU, Cook M (2015) Unsupervised learning of digit recognition using spike-timing-dependent plasticity. Front Comput Neurosci 9:99
9. Diehl PU, et al (2015) Fast-classifying, high-accuracy spiking deep networks through weight and threshold balancing. In: 2015 international joint conference on neural networks (IJCNN), pp 1–8
10. Eliasmith C, Stewart TC, Choo X, Bekolay T, DeWolf T, Tang Y, Rasmussen D (2012) A large-scale model of the functioning brain. Science 338(6111):1202–1205
11. Furber S (2016) Large-scale neuromorphic computing systems. J Neural Eng 13(5):051001
12. Furber SB, et al (2014) The SpiNNaker project. Proc IEEE 102(5):652–665
13. Goldwyn JH, Imennov NS, Famulare M, Shea-Brown E (2011) Stochastic differential equation models for ion channel noise in Hodgkin-Huxley neurons. Phys Rev E—Stat Nonlinear Soft Matter Phys 83(4):041908
14. Hazan H, et al (2018) BindsNET: a machine learning-oriented spiking neural networks library in Python. Front Neuroinf 12:89
15. Holland JH, et al (1992) Adaptation in natural and artificial systems: an introductory analysis with applications to biology, control, and artificial intelligence. MIT Press, Cambridge
16. Hsiao MY (1970) A class of optimal minimum odd-weight-column sec-ded codes. IBM J Res Develop 14(4):395–401
17. Jin X (2010) Parallel simulation of neural networks on spinnaker universal neuromorphic hardware. The University of Manchester
18. Levin JA, Rangan V, Malone EC (2014) Efficient hardware implementation of spiking networks, 2014. Patent No. US 2014/0351190 A1, Filed May 1, 2014, Pub. Date Nov. 27, 2014

19. Mahmoodi H, et al (2008) Ultra low-power clocking scheme using energy recovery and clock gating. IEEE Trans Very Large Scale Integr Syst 17(1):33–44
20. Ogbodo M, Vu T, Dang K, Ben Abdallah A (2020) Light-weight spiking neuron processing core for large-scale 3D-NoC based spiking neural network processing systems. In: 2020 IEEE international conference on big data and smart computing (BigComp), pp 133–139
21. Rueckauer B, et al (2017) Conversion of continuous-valued deep networks to efficient event-driven networks for image classification. Front Neurosci 11:682
22. Schemmel J, et al (2010) A wafer-scale neuromorphic hardware system for large-scale neural modeling. In: Proceedings of 2010 IEEE international symposium on circuits and systems, pp 1947–1950
23. Sengupta A, Ye Y, Wang R, Liu C, Roy K (2019) Going deeper in spiking neural networks: VGG and residual architectures. Front Neurosci 13:95
24. Stimberg M, Brette R, Goodman DF (2019) Brian 2, an intuitive and efficient neural simulator. eLife 8:e47314
25. Vu TH, Okuyama Y, Ben Abdallah A (2019) Comprehensive analytic performance assessment and K-means based multicast routing algorithm and architecture for 3D-NoC of spiking neurons. J Emerg Technol Comput Syst 15(4):34:1–34:28
26. Wu Y, Deng L, Li G, Zhu J, Shi L (2018) Spatio-temporal backpropagation for training high-performance spiking neural networks. Front Neurosci 12:331
27. Yin S, Venkataramanaiah SK, Chen GK, Krishnamurthy R, Cao Y, Chakrabarti C, Seo JS (2017) Algorithm and hardware design of discrete-time spiking neural networks based on back propagation with binary activations. In: 2017 IEEE biomedical circuits and systems conference (BioCAS). IEEE, Piscataway, pp 1–5

Chapter 9
Case Study: Advanced Neuromorphic Prosthetic Design

Abstract This chapter explores the cutting-edge advancements in prosthetic technology embodied by the AIzuHand. The discussion begins with 3D printing technology to create a lightweight and durable chassis, providing exceptional comfort and long-term use for individuals with upper limb amputations. It then presents the sophisticated control systems powered by Artificial Neural Networks (ANN) and Spiking Neural Networks (SNN), which allow for highly adaptive and precise movements, closely mimicking natural hand functions. Furthermore, the chapter highlights the development of a user-friendly smartphone application, offering real-time control and extensive customization options to enhance user experience. In addition, the revolutionary implementation of Virtual Reality (VR) for rehabilitation is examined, showcasing how immersive, interactive environments can significantly improve motor skill recovery and user confidence. By integrating these advanced technologies, the AIzuHand prosthetic stands as a testament to the potential of modern engineering to transform the lives of those with limb loss, setting a new standard in prosthetic design and functionality.

9.1 Introduction

Prosthetic hands have become essential tools for individuals with upper limb loss, providing functional utility and enhancing the quality of life by restoring capabilities that many take for granted, such as grasping objects, typing, or engaging in everyday activities [3, 6]. 3D printing technology in prosthetic hands has revolutionized the field, allowing for greater customization, rapid prototyping, and cost reduction compared to traditional manufacturing methods. With 3D printing, prosthetic devices can be tailored to fit each user's unique anatomy and functional requirements, making them more comfortable and practical. Moreover, this technology facilitates the incorporation of innovative designs that enhance functionality without significantly increasing weight.

Control methods for prosthetic hands have also seen notable advancements [2, 4], particularly in integrating artificial neural networks (ANNs) and spiking neural networks (SNNs). ANNs mimic how humans learn from experience, enabling

A. Ben Abdallah, K. N. Dang, *Neuromorphic Computing Principles and Organization*, https://doi.org/10.1007/978-3-031-83089-1_9

prosthetic hands to recognize and classify signals related to the user's motor intentions, such as those from surface electromyography (sEMG). This allows for more intuitive control, as the prosthetic can adapt to the user's specific movements and patterns over time, providing a seamless interface between the user and the device. On the other hand, SNNs, which closely resemble how biological neurons communicate through spikes, offer real-time processing capabilities and improved responsiveness. This advantage is crucial in quick-reaction scenarios, such as catching a falling object or adjusting grip strength when handling fragile items. The combination of 3D printing technology and advanced control methodologies like ANN and SNN not only enhances the functionality and usability of prosthetic hands but also represents a significant leap forward in making these devices more accessible, intuitive, and sensitive to the needs of users, ultimately fostering greater independence and improving overall quality of life.

The AIzuhand system harnesses the latest advancements in neural network technologies to create a prosthetic hand that is both cost-effective and highly functional. By incorporating deep learning techniques and exploring the potential of spiking neural networks, AIzuhand aims to develop a system that intuitively and accurately interprets the user's intentions from surface electromyographic (sEMG) signals, enabling a fluid and natural user experience. This project aspires to address the shortcomings of current prosthetic hands by providing a device that is not only accessible but also proficient in performing intricate, real-world tasks with remarkable accuracy. By prioritizing user-centric design and advanced neural processing, AIzuhand seeks to redefine prosthetics' capabilities, ultimately enhancing users' quality of life.

In this chapter, we explore the design process for the AIzuHand prosthetic based on 3D printing technology. We also present a detailed overview of the control methodologies employed, explicitly focusing on implementing artificial neural networks (ANN) and spiking neural networks (SNN). These advanced control techniques enhance the prosthetic's functionality and responsiveness, ensuring a seamless interaction between the user and the device.

9.2 Prosthetic Design

The prosthetic design has undergone remarkable transformations from ancient times to the present, reflecting advances in materials, technology, and our understanding of human anatomy and biomechanics. Early prosthetics were rudimentary, often crafted from wood or metal, and primarily used to replace a missing limb's essential functions. Although primitive, these designs provided their users a semblance of normalcy and mobility.

In the nineteenth and early twentieth centuries, prosthetics began incorporating more sophisticated mechanical joints and harness systems, allowing for a more fantastic range of motion and functionality. The introduction of lighter materials like aluminum and later plastics marked significant milestones, improving the comfort and usability of prosthetic limbs. The latter half of the twentieth century saw the advent of myoelectric prosthetics, which utilized electrical signals from the user's muscles to control movements. This innovation allowed for a more natural and intuitive use of prosthetic limbs. In recent decades, the field has advanced even further with the integration of microprocessors, advanced materials, and neurotechnology. Modern bionic prosthetics can now mimic natural limbs' complex movements and functions with high precision.

Additionally, 3D printing has revolutionized the customization and affordability of prosthetics, allowing for personalized designs tailored to each user's unique needs and anatomy. This technology has significantly reduced production times and costs, making advanced prosthetic solutions more accessible. As we look to the future, the continued convergence of biotechnology, artificial intelligence, and advanced materials promises even more groundbreaking developments, paving the way for prosthetics that are more functional, comfortable, and seamlessly integrated with the human body and mind.

9.2.1 3D Printed-Based Prosthetic

3D printing technology, widely recognized as additive manufacturing, has significantly impacted various industries through its ability to produce intricate and customized objects with remarkable accuracy and efficiency. This transformative process involves creating three-dimensional items by successively layering materials based on digital models, allowing for unprecedented design flexibility. One of the most compelling applications of 3D printing is in prosthetic design, which has revolutionized how prosthetic limbs are created and tailored for individual users.

Traditionally, prosthetic devices required extensive time and resources for custom fitting and manufacturing, often leading to high costs and limited accessibility for many users. However, with 3D printing, prosthetics can be designed using advanced software that takes precise measurements and considers the user's lifestyle and preferences. The ability to rapidly prototype and modify designs ensures that the resulting prosthetic is not only a perfect fit but also tailored to the specific functional requirements of the individual. This customization translates to enhanced comfort and usability for the wearer, leading to better outcomes and increased adoption of prosthetic devices. Furthermore, 3D printing allows for lightweight yet durable materials, which can significantly improve the performance of prosthetics while reducing fatigue during use. The technology also supports the creation of intricate internal structures that can mimic the biomechanics of a natural limb, resulting in prosthetics that offer more excellent dexterity and movement capabilities. Additionally, 3D printing can lower production costs and lead times, making advanced prosthetic designs more accessible to individuals who may have previously faced barriers to obtaining high-quality devices.

As technology evolves, ongoing research and development are expanding the boundaries of what can be achieved, including the potential for integrating electronics and sensors into 3D-printed prosthetics for improved functionality. Ultimately, the intersection of 3D printing and prosthetic design exemplifies how this innovative technology can enhance the quality of life for users, providing them with more personalized, effective, and affordable solutions that foster independence and empowerment. By breaking down traditional barriers in prosthetic design and manufacturing, 3D printing is paving the way for a new era of assistive technology that prioritizes user needs and adaptability, ensuring individuals can lead more fulfilling lives.

9.3 AIzuHand Prosthetic Design Overview

The AIzuHand prosthetic [10] exemplifies the extraordinary advancements in prosthetic technology, combining cutting-edge 3D printing techniques with sophisticated control systems. 3D printing technology has created a lightweight and durable prosthetic chassis, ensuring long-lasting comfort and usability. Integrating Artificial Neural Networks (ANN) and Spiking Neural Networks (SNN) into its control system showcases the power of modern AI in replicating the nuanced movements of a natural hand. This dual AI approach enhances the prosthetic's responsiveness and efficiency, providing users with a highly adaptive and intuitive device that seamlessly fits into their daily lives.

Developing a smartphone-based application to control the AIzuHand adds another layer of accessibility and customization. This app offers users a familiar and user-friendly interface, allowing them to fine-tune the prosthetic's functions to match their individual preferences and needs. By harnessing smartphones' widespread availability and advanced features, the app enables real-time adjustments and greater control over the prosthetic's movements, thus enhancing the overall user experience.

Furthermore, integrating Virtual Reality (VR) into the rehabilitation process marks a revolutionary step in how individuals with limb loss regain functionality and confidence. The VR training system provides an immersive and interactive environment where users can practice and perfect their motor skills safely and engagingly. By simulating realistic scenarios, the VR tool bridges the gap between virtual exercises and real-world applications, making the transition smoother and more effective. This innovative approach accelerates the rehabilitation process and makes it more enjoyable and motivating for users, addressing the physical and psychological aspects of recovery.

The AIzuHand, with its advanced design and intelligent control systems, represents a significant leap in prosthetic technology. The addition of a smartphone-based control app and the revolutionary use of VR for rehabilitation highlights this innovation's comprehensive and user-centric nature. These developments collectively enhance the functionality, accessibility, and overall quality of life for individuals with upper limb amputations, setting a new benchmark in prosthetics.

9.3.1 Design Considerations

The AIzuhand design considers functionality and affordability, ensuring the prosthetic hand is lightweight, durable, and capable of performing various gestures and grasps. To achieve these goals, different materials and design configurations are explored. The material selection is critical, with choices made based on strength, flexibility, and cost-effectiveness. Commonly used materials in 3D printing the AIzuhand include PLA (Polylactic Acid) and ABS (Acrylonitrile Butadiene Styrene), which provide an excellent balance of durability and ease of printing. TPU (Thermoplastic Polyurethane) is also considered for flexible parts, such as joints and fingertips. The AIzuhand features a modular design, allowing for easy customization and replacement of individual parts, making it essential to adapt the prosthetic to different users' needs and facilitate quick maintenance. Furthermore, the design emphasizes ergonomics, ensuring comfort during use and considering aesthetics to create a natural-looking hand. This attention to visual appeal is crucial for user acceptance and confidence in their prosthetic device.

9.3.2 Printing Process

The 3D printing process involves several essential steps to transform a digital design into a physical prototype of the prosthetic hand. The initial step is modeling, where a 3D model is created using CAD (Computer-Aided Design) software. This model encompasses all components, including the palm, fingers, joints, and connectors, and undergoes multiple iterations based on feedback from test prints and user trials. Once the model is finalized, it is sliced into layers using slicing software, which converts the 3D design into a set of instructions that the 3D printer can understand. This slicing process determines the printer's path to lay down each material layer. The slice is then sent to the 3D printer, where printing occurs. This process can take several hours, depending on the complexity and size of the components, as the printer builds the hand layer by layer, fusing the material to create the final structure. After printing, the parts typically require post-processing steps, including removing support structures, sanding, or applying a finish.

These post-processing steps ensure that the parts fit together smoothly and that the hand operates correctly, completing the transformation from digital design to functional prototype.

9.3.3 Assembly and Testing

Once all the parts are printed and undergo the necessary post-processing, the assembly of the AIzuhand begins. This process involves carefully fitting together the fingers, joints, and other components, typically using screws or adhesive to ensure secure connections. During assembly, the Myo armband and additional sensors are integrated into the design to guarantee they are securely attached and correctly aligned with the user's arm, optimizing functionality and responsiveness.

After the assembly is complete, the prosthetic hand undergoes rigorous testing to assess its ability to perform a variety of gestures, such as gripping and pinching. Each gesture is evaluated to ensure accurate and intuitive movement. Additionally, the hand is subjected to stress tests that analyze its durability under real-world conditions. These tests focus on joint strength, material fatigue, and the device's resilience to environmental factors like moisture and temperature fluctuations.

The AIzuhand project represents a significant advancement in making cutting-edge prosthetic technology accessible to users. By harnessing 3D printing's capabilities, we can produce customizable and affordable prosthetic hands that empower users and enhance their overall functionality and quality of life. This innovative approach aims to bridge the gap between advanced technology and individuals' needs, facilitating greater independence and improving their daily experiences.

9.4 AIzuHand Control

As illustrated in Fig. 9.1, the AIzu Hand operates through a sophisticated integration of surface electromyography (sEMG) signals and deep learning models. An array

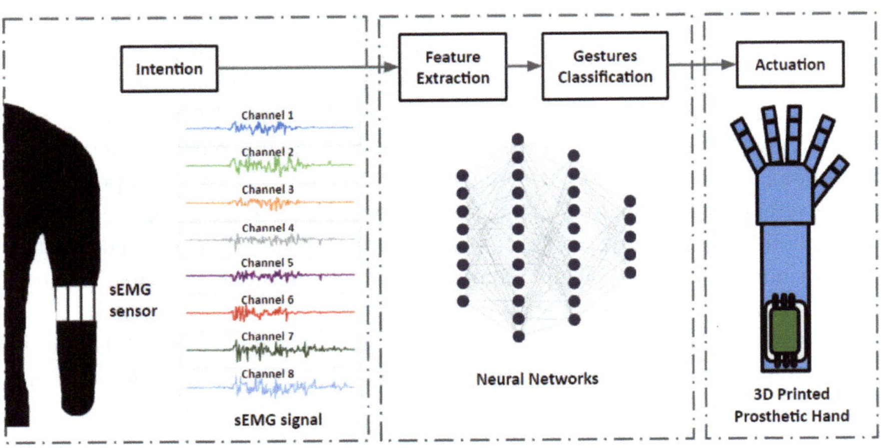

Fig. 9.1 Overview of AIzuHand prosthetic design method. The prosthetic design begins with Intention, identifying the user's movement goals to tailor the device accordingly. Feature Extraction follows, where sensors capture and analyze muscle signals or other biofeedback, enabling Gesture Classification to interpret these movements accurately through advanced algorithms. Finally, Actuation translates these classified gestures into precise, natural movements, ensuring the prosthetic responds seamlessly to the user's intent

of sensors captures the sEMG signals by detecting muscle activity in the user's arm. These signals are then processed and classified to discern the user's intended gestures accurately. Once processed, the signals are translated into corresponding actions by the prosthetic hand, enabling intuitive and responsive control that closely mimics natural movement. This innovative approach enhances the overall usability of the AIzu Hand, demonstrating how advanced technology can improve the functionality and effectiveness of prosthetic devices.

As shown in Fig. 9.1, the sEMG sensors are strategically positioned on the user's forearm to capture muscle activation signals across multiple channels. In this particular setup, we employ eight channels, each corresponding to different muscle groups, enabling comprehensive monitoring of muscle activity. The raw sEMG signals undergo several preprocessing steps, including noise filtering, normalization, and feature extraction, ensuring the neural network's data input is reliable and accurate.

Feature extraction plays a vital role in effectively distinguishing between various hand gestures. We extract various characteristics from the sEMG signals, including time-domain, frequency-domain, and time-frequency-domain features. This diversity in feature selection is essential for capturing the variability in muscle activation patterns, thereby enhancing the model's capacity to classify gestures with precision. The AIzu Hand can achieve more accurate and responsive control by utilizing these comprehensive features, ultimately improving user experience and functionality.

9.4.1 *Optimizing Neural Networks for Gesture Recognition*

Optimizing neural networks for gesture recognition in prosthetic hands involves integrating advanced machine learning algorithms to accurately interpret user intentions and translate them into precise movements. By fine-tuning both Artificial Neural Networks (ANN) and Spiking Neural Networks (SNN), we can enhance the prosthetic's ability to recognize and classify various hand gestures with high accuracy and minimal latency. ANNs are particularly effective for continuous gesture recognition due to their robust pattern recognition capabilities, while SNNs offer efficiency and low power consumption by mimicking the biological neurons' spiking activity.

Combining these networks allows for a dynamic system that adapts to the user's unique neural signals, providing a seamless and intuitive control experience. The training phase is critical to this optimization process, where the neural networks are exposed to extensive datasets of gesture patterns, ensuring that the system can generalize from the training data to real-world scenarios. Additionally, incorporating real-time feedback mechanisms helps fine-tune the network's performance, reducing errors and improving responsiveness. This sophisticated approach not only enhances the functionality of prosthetic hands but also significantly improves the quality of life for users, enabling them to perform everyday tasks with greater ease and confidence.

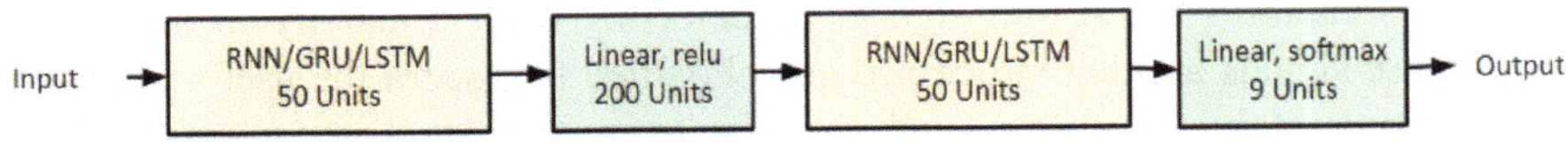

Fig. 9.2 Artificial neural networks architecture of the AIzuHand prosthetic. ANNs are pivotal in enhancing prosthetic control through their ability to learn and generalize from complex, non-linear data

Table 9.1 Accuracy performance based on window sizes (32-bit model)

	Raw sEMG data		
Window sizes	SimpleRNN	LSTM	GRU
60	54.09%	86.85%	85.31%
100	59.54%	87.87%	87.20%
120	53.58%	88.22%	85.86%
150	46.53%	87.63%	88.94%
200	47.78%	85.26%	88.59%

The neural network architecture developed for classifying gestures of the AIzu Hand [11] is a sophisticated hybrid model that combines Recurrent Neural Networks (RNNs) with Long Short-Term Memory (LSTM) networks [7], as illustrated in Fig. 9.2. This model features two layers of RNNs/GRUs/LSTMs, each containing 50 units, followed by a fully connected layer with ReLU activation and 200 units. To conclude the architecture, a softmax layer with nine units outputs the probability distribution across the nine possible gestures: close, open, one, two, three, four, pinch, thumb up, and rest.

The architecture diagram effectively visualizes the flow of input sEMG signals through various network layers, culminating in the output that determines the intended gesture of the prosthetic hand [1]. By leveraging the sequential characteristics of sEMG data, this design takes advantage of RNN-based models' capacity to capture the temporal dependencies inherent in muscle activation patterns. This approach enhances the model's ability to classify gestures accurately, resulting in more intuitive and responsive control of the AIzuHand. Table 9.1 presents the average accuracy performance for offline evaluations using raw sEMG data input. Within the RNN group, the standard RNN demonstrates the lowest accuracy, while both LSTM and GRU models exhibit comparable performance. As the window sizes increase, the GRU model shows a slight advantage over LSTM [12].

While there is a general trend of improved accuracy with larger window sizes, the differences in performance are minimal. Interestingly, the largest window size of 200 ms tends to yield slightly lower accuracy compared to the 120 and 150 ms window sizes. This suggests that a larger window size does not inherently lead to better performance. Instead, there appears to be an optimal window size that balances accuracy with response time, highlighting the need for careful consideration in selecting the appropriate window size for effective gesture classification.

The models utilizing a window size of 150 ms were employed for online evaluation, enabling test experiments to be conducted on a Raspberry Pi [13].

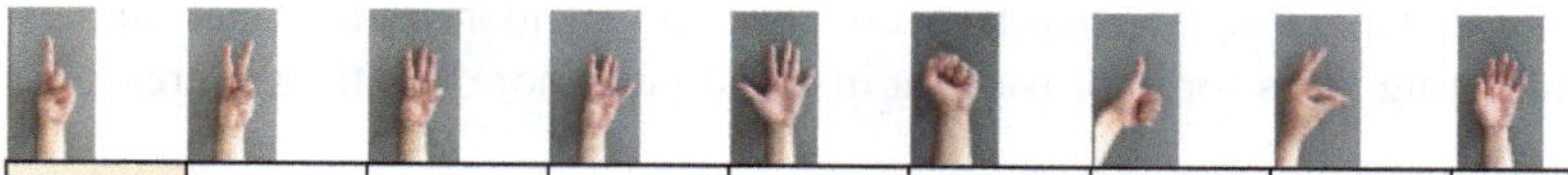

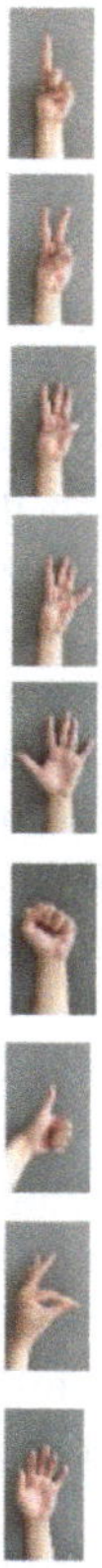

47 94%	0 0%	0 0%	0 0%	0 0%	2 4%	1 2%	0 0%	0 0%
0 0%	32 64%	16 32%	2 4%	0 0%	0 0%	0 0%	0 0%	0 0%
0 0%	0 0%	39 78%	10 20%	1 2%	0 0%	0 0%	0 0%	0 0%
0 0%	0 0%	0 0%	50 100%	0 0%	0 0%	0 0%	0 0%	0 0%
0 0%	4 8%	9 18%	0 0%	37 74%	0 0%	0 0%	0 0%	0 0%
0 0%	0 0%	0 0%	0 0%	0 0%	50 100%	0 0%	0 0%	0 0%
0 0%	0 0%	0 0%	0 0%	0 0%	1 2%	49 98%	0 0%	0 0%
0 0%	0 0%	0 0%	1 2%	0 0%	0 0%	0 0%	49 98%	0 0%
0 0%	0 0%	0 0%	0 0%	0 0%	0 0%	0 0%	0 0%	50 100%

Fig. 9.3 GRU-based raw sEMG classification online testing accuracy (150 window size, 8-bit model). The model leverages Gated Recurrent Units (GRUs) to process sequential electromyography (sEMG) data, providing robust feature extraction and classification performance. The classification accuracy is evaluated through online testing, where real-time data is fed into the model with a window size of 150 and an 8-bit resolution. This setup ensures efficient data processing and accurate classification, highlighting the model's ability to handle complex, real-world sEMG signals effectively

Results from the online tests, specifically for the GRU model, are presented in Fig. 9.3, demonstrating an overall accuracy of approximately 89.55%. Notably, the online accuracy performance of the GRU is consistent with its offline performance. However, the classification of the "two fingers" gesture exhibited the lowest accuracy, followed by the "open" and "three fingers" gestures. A significant portion of the misclassifications for "two fingers" was mistakenly identified as "three fingers," accounting for 32% of errors. This confusion may stem from the similarities in the sEMG signals associated with these two gestures. Conversely, gestures with distinctly different activation patterns achieved accuracy rates of 100% or near

100%, underscoring the model's effectiveness in identifying clear signals while highlighting areas for improvement in classifying more similar gestures.

9.5 SNN-Based Control

Spiking Neural Networks (SNNs) are a type of artificial neural network designed to closely emulate the biological neural networks found in the human brain. These networks are increasingly utilized in computation and machine learning, offering robust capabilities for classification and recognition tasks [5, 9]. One of the critical advantages of SNNs over traditional artificial neural networks (ANNs) is their ability to achieve higher computational speed while consuming significantly less energy. This efficiency results from the unique manner in which SNNs process information; rather than performing arithmetic operations on every individual data point, SNNs operate similarly to biological neural networks by activating only in response to spikes or patterns of spikes. This event-driven computation allows SNNs to efficiently manage resources, making them highly advantageous for applications requiring real-time processing and low power consumption.

Figure 9.4 illustrates the Spiking Neural Network (SNN) architecture designed for processing raw sEMG spike inputs. The network consists of three layers: the first layer features 300 Leaky Integrate-and-Fire (LIF) units, which initially capture and process the incoming signal spikes. The intermediate layer contains 50 LIF units that refine the signal processing before it moves to the final output layer. This output layer comprises 9 LIF units, each classifying one of the nine identified gestures. This structured layering enhances the network's ability to accurately interpret the incoming sEMG data and perform gesture classification effectively.

Figure 9.5 illustrates the Spiking Neural Network (SNN) architecture for processing raw sEMG spike inputs. This architecture consists of three layers: the first layer features 100 Leaky Integrate-and-Fire (LIF) units, which are responsible for the initial processing of input signals. The middle layer comprises 50 LIF units that refine the signal representation, while the final output layer contains 9 LIF units, each designated to classify one of the nine target gestures. This structured layering

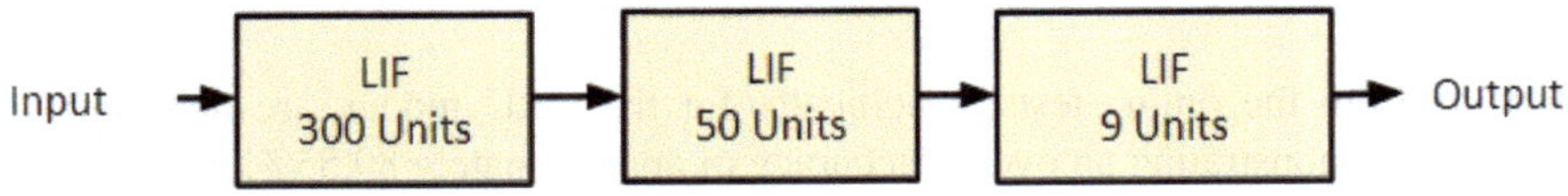

Fig. 9.4 SNN model architecture used for raw sEMG spike input. The Spiking Neural Network (SNN) architecture is designed to process raw sEMG spike inputs. The network consists of three layers: the first layer contains 300 Leaky Integrate-and-Fire (LIF) units for initial signal processing, the second layer includes 50 LIF units for further refinement, and the final output layer features 9 LIF units dedicated to classifying the nine target gestures. This structure enhances the network's ability to accurately interpret and classify muscle activation patterns

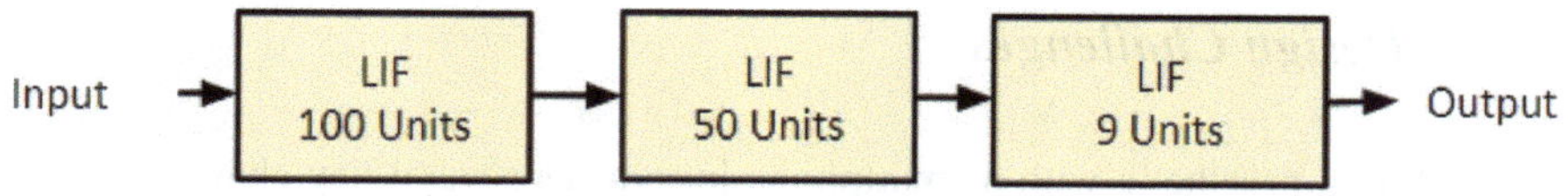

Fig. 9.5 SNN model architecture used for Standard Deviation And Root Mean Square features spike input. The architecture consists of multiple layers, including the input layer receiving spike trains, hidden layers processing spikes, and an output layer generating the final predictions. Each layer is designed to extract and process specific features from the spike input, allowing for efficient computation and accurate analysis

enables the network to interpret muscle activation patterns through spike-based computations effectively. The highest accuracy in Spiking Neural Network (SNN) for raw sEMG spike inputs is achieved is 65.39% with the smallest sEMG window size of 60 ms, after which the accuracy declines as the window size increases. This decrease in performance may be attributed to the limited number of layers and neurons in the model, which restricts its ability to capture the complexities in the data. In contrast, when using standard deviation (SD) and root mean square (RMS) features derived from sEMG signals, the accuracy plummets to approximately 10%, which is deemed inadequate. Since SD and RMS are already processed features of sEMG data, they contain significantly less information than the raw input signals. Therefore, relying on these features for classification may not be appropriate, as they fail to provide the rich detail necessary for effective gesture recognition.

9.6 Smart Phone Controlled 3D Printed AIzuHand Prosthetic

Controlling a prosthetic with a smartphone brings users a world of convenience and customization. The ubiquity of smartphones means that users can easily access and manage their prosthetic devices from a familiar interface, eliminating the need for specialized control hardware. This setup allows for real-time adjustments and fine-tuning of movements, enhancing the prosthetic's responsiveness and functionality. The mobile app can also offer features like gesture control, pre-set movement patterns, and data tracking to monitor usage and progress. By leveraging the power of smartphone technology, users gain greater autonomy and a more seamless, integrated experience with their prosthetic devices. Through a dedicated mobile application, users can directly access a range of features and functionalities to manage the movements and gestures of the prosthetic hand, as illustrated in Fig. 9.7.

9.6.1 Design Challenges

Controlling a prosthetic with a smartphone introduces several key challenges that must be addressed to ensure a seamless user experience. Connectivity issues, such as unreliable Bluetooth or Wi-Fi connections can disrupt the prosthetic's performance, causing users frustration. Battery life is another concern, as both the smartphone and the prosthetic need sufficient power to operate over extended periods. The user interface must be intuitive and user-friendly yet complex enough to offer complete control, which can be challenging to balance, especially for those who are not tech-savvy. Latency is critical; any delay between issuing a command on the smartphone and the prosthetic's response can undermine the user's confidence and functionality. Security is paramount, as personal data and control signals must be protected from unauthorized access. Furthermore, ensuring the app's compatibility with various smartphone models and operating systems adds another layer of complexity. Lastly, the system must be robust and durable enough to function reliably in diverse environments and conditions. Addressing these challenges is essential to make smartphone-controlled prosthetics a viable and efficient solution.

9.6.2 AIzuHand Smartphone-Based Control

The AIzuHand prosthetic hand is a state-of-the-art device that seamlessly integrates smartphone control with advanced artificial intelligence for unparalleled functionality and precision. At its heart is a powerful microcontroller unit (MCU) that processes real-time inputs from the smartphone, enabling the hand to execute complex movements and gestures. This MPU is paired with various sensors, including vibration and pressure sensors, which provide crucial data on the hand's orientation and the forces it encounters. These sensors ensure precise and responsive control, crucial for tasks ranging from delicate manipulations to firm grips. The prosthetic's motor units, driven by these real-time commands, translate electrical signals into smooth, reliable mechanical actions.

The smartphone and the AIzuHand communication is facilitated through robust Bluetooth technology, allowing for a wireless and user-friendly interface. The dedicated mobile application enhances this experience, offering an intuitive platform where users can customize and control the hand's movements. Users can choose from hand gestures and pre-set functions within this app, tailoring the prosthetic's responses to their needs and preferences. Moreover, the AIzuHand is powered by an efficient battery system that ensures long-lasting performance, reducing the need for frequent recharges. The prosthetic chassis is designed with 3D printing technology to be both lightweight and durable, providing comfort for extended wear.

A standout feature of the AIzuHand is its control mechanism, which utilizes both Artificial Neural Networks (ANN) and Spiking Neural Networks (SNN). ANN processes continuous data streams to manage the prosthetic's movements,

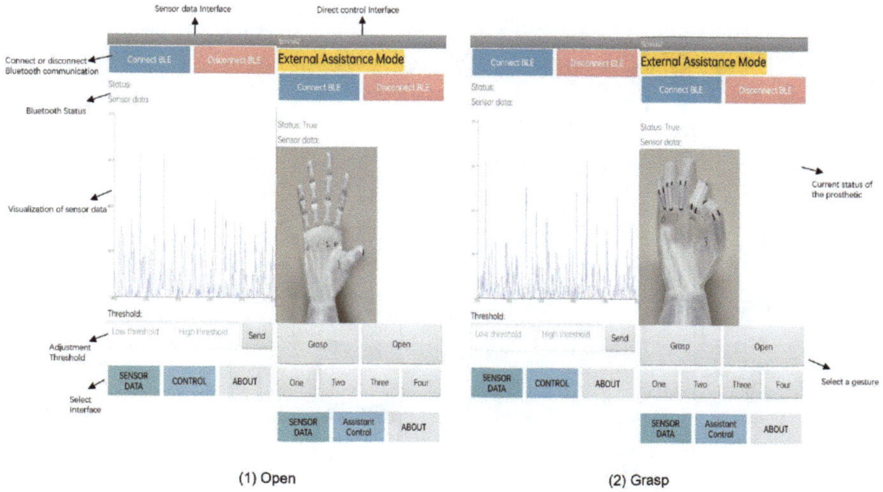

Fig. 9.6 A user-friendly GUI for AIzuHand calibration, real-time feedback, and other functional tasks. The GUI provides intuitive controls for adjusting the prosthetic settings to ensure optimal performance. This interface offers real-time feedback to the user, allowing for immediate adjustments and fine-tuning based on the prosthetic's response

offering adaptive and intelligent control. SNN, on the other hand, mimics the way biological neurons communicate, allowing for more efficient and low-power operation, particularly for real-time, sensory-motor tasks. This dual approach enables the AIzuHand to achieve high levels of dexterity and efficiency, making it a versatile tool for its users. Together, these components create a comprehensive and advanced system that restores functionality and enhances the user's quality of life through sophisticated, personalized control. The AIzuHand stands at the forefront of prosthetic technology, showcasing the potential of integrating AI-driven control with user-friendly smartphone interfaces. The developed application for AIzuHAnd prosthetic control is shown in Fig. 9.6. Using this user-friendly application, users can easily select and activate various hand gestures or predefined functions within the app, such as opening and closing the hand, gripping objects, or performing specific movements. Additionally, the app enables users to customize and configure these functions according to their preferences and needs, adapting the prosthetic hand's control to meet their specific requirements. The complete prototype with the different integrated components is shown in Fig. 9.7.

9.7 Virtual Reality Based Training System

Virtual Reality (VR) for prosthetic rehabilitation is revolutionizing how individuals with limb loss regain functionality and confidence. By immersing users in a controlled and interactive 3D environment, VR provides a safe space to practice

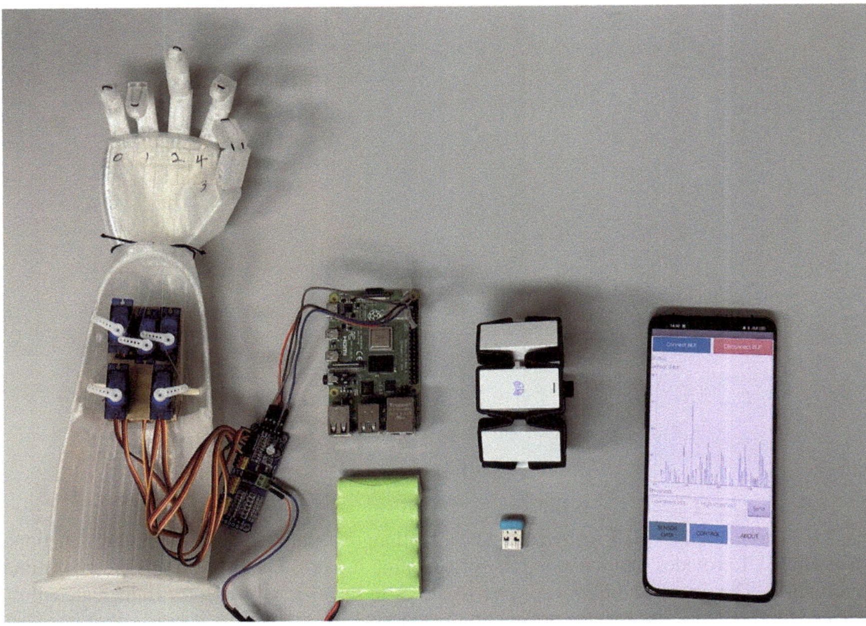

Fig. 9.7 AIzuHand prosthetic control with smartphone. AIzuHand Prosthetic Control with Smartphone, featuring seamless integration with mobile devices, allows users to easily adjust settings and monitor performance. This setup enables real-time control and customization of the prosthetic limb through a user-friendly app interface, providing instant feedback and making it convenient for users to tailor the prosthetic's functionality to their individual needs

and perfect the use of their prosthetic limbs. This immersive experience enhances motor learning and offers real-time feedback and adaptive exercises tailored to the user's progress. Users can engage in various simulated tasks that mimic everyday activities, improving their coordination, dexterity, and overall prosthetic control. Additionally, the engaging nature of VR makes the rehabilitation process more enjoyable and motivating, reducing the monotony often associated with traditional rehabilitation exercises. The combination of VR and prosthetics promotes a holistic approach to rehabilitation, addressing both physical and psychological aspects of recovery and empowering users to achieve greater independence and quality of life.

The AIzuHand, utilized for training, offers a groundbreaking and influential rehabilitation method for individuals with upper limb amputations, leveraging the immersive capabilities of Virtual Reality (VR). This innovative approach integrates the AIzuHand prosthetic with VR tools to create a realistic and engaging training environment, allowing users to practice and refine their motor skills in a controlled, virtual setting. The VR system provides real-time feedback and adaptive training scenarios tailored to the individual's progress and specific rehabilitation needs. Users can develop and enhance their muscle memory, coordination, and overall dexterity in a safe and supportive environment by simulating various everyday activities and tasks. The visual and sensory feedback from the VR tool helps bridge the gap between the virtual exercises and real-world applications, making the transition smoother and more effective. Additionally, this method promotes user engagement and motivation, as VR's interactive and gamified elements make the rehabilitation process more enjoyable and less monotonous. Overall, AIzuHand's integration with VR technology significantly advances prosthetic training, providing a comprehensive and user-centric rehabilitation experience that enhances the quality of life for individuals with upper limb amputations.

9.7.1 Interactive Virtual Scenarios: Kitchen and Workbench

The VR training system described in [8] offers an innovative and effective rehabilitation approach for individuals with upper limb amputations. The system integrates two main components: interactive virtual scenarios that simulate kitchen and workbench environments and incorporating VR games into rehabilitation. Users wear the Myo armband as an input device, enabling them to engage with the virtual scenes and participate in various open-source games tailored specifically for upper limb rehabilitation. This combination provides a comprehensive, immersive, and engaging way to enhance motor skills and support recovery.

The kitchen scene is designed to simulate a typical kitchen environment, allowing users to practice daily activities related to cooking and handling kitchen utensils. The scene consists of a kitchen counter, cabinets, shelves, and various interactable objects commonly found in a kitchen setting (Fig. 9.8). Users can use their prosthetic

Fig. 9.8 Kitchen scene in the VR environment. By simulating real-life scenarios, this VR kitchen environment aids rehabilitation and boosts confidence in managing everyday activities. The method features an immersive and interactive virtual kitchen where users with prosthetic hands can practice and enhance their daily living skills. The environment includes realistic appliances, utensils, and ingredients, allowing users to perform various kitchen tasks and activities in a controlled and safe setting

Fig. 9.9 Workbench scene in virtual environment, including books, pens, boxes of various sizes and other common tools. This virtual environment offers a realistic simulation to improve fine motor skills and dexterity, allowing users to engage in typical workbench activities such as writing, organizing, and manipulating different items

hand to pick up utensils, open cabinets, pour liquids, and perform other cooking and food preparation tasks. The scene offers a realistic and immersive experience that allows users to enhance their control and dexterity with their prosthetic hand in a familiar context.

The workbench scene shown in Fig. 9.9 is meticulously crafted to replicate a workshop or crafting area, allowing users to practice tasks requiring manual dexterity and object manipulation. It features a workbench with tools, materials, and objects commonly found in a workshop setting. Users can utilize their prosthetic hands to pick up and manipulate tools, assemble objects, and engage in craft-related activities. This immersive environment provides valuable opportunities for users to refine their fine motor skills, precision, and coordination, enhancing their ability to use their prosthetic hands in real-world workshop scenarios.

9.8 Chapter Summary

The AIzuHand prosthetic hand exemplifies remarkable advancements in prosthetic design and technology. Leveraging state-of-the-art 3D printing techniques, it offers a lightweight and durable structure that ensures both comfort and longevity. Integrating Artificial Neural Networks (ANN) and Spiking Neural Networks (SNN) into its control system provides sophisticated and responsive functionality, mimicking natural hand movements with exceptional precision and efficiency. This dual AI approach allows adaptive control, making the AIzuHand highly versatile and user-friendly.

Moreover, developing a smartphone-based application to control the AIzuHand has significantly enhanced its accessibility and customization. This app provides an intuitive interface, enabling users to fine-tune the prosthetic's functions to suit their preferences and needs, thus improving their overall user experience. The widespread availability of smartphones ensures that users can manage their prosthetic hands conveniently and in real-time.

Additionally, incorporating Virtual Reality (VR) in rehabilitation represents a revolutionary advancement in how individuals with limb loss regain functionality and confidence. The VR training system offers an immersive and interactive environment, allowing users to practice and refine their motor skills in a safe and engaging virtual setting. By simulating realistic scenarios, the VR tool bridges the gap between virtual exercises and real-world applications, making rehabilitation more effective and enjoyable.

In summary, the AIzuHand, with its innovative design, advanced AI control systems, and supportive technologies like the smartphone app and VR training, marks a significant milestone in prosthetic development. These advancements collectively enhance the functionality, accessibility, and overall quality of life for individuals with upper limb amputations, setting a new benchmark in prosthetics. This chapter underscores the transformative potential of integrating cutting-edge technology with human-centric design, paving the way for future innovations that will continue to improve the lives of those with limb loss.

9.9 Exercises

9.9.1 Exercise 1

How does integrating modern technologies, such as Artificial Neural Networks (ANN) and Spiking Neural Networks (SNN), enhance prosthetic hands' functionality and user experience in performing daily tasks? Discuss with examples.

9.9.2 Exercise 2

Explore how Spiking Neural Networks (SNN) and Artificial Neural Networks (ANN) enhance the control mechanisms of prosthetic hands. Describe the core principles of SNN and ANN, highlighting their differences in processing information and controlling movements. Discuss the advantages and limitations of each type of neural network in terms of responsiveness, power efficiency, and adaptability. Provide examples of specific tasks where these neural networks improve the functionality of prosthetic hands. Finally, future advancements and innovations could be considered to integrate SNN and ANN further into prosthetic technology, enhancing these devices' user experience and overall performance.

9.9.3 *Exercise 3*

Explore the critical considerations and innovative approaches in the design of modern prosthetic hands. Discuss the role of advanced materials, such as those used in 3D printing, and how they contribute to the durability and comfort of prosthetics. In integrating Artificial Neural Networks (ANN) and Spiking Neural Networks (SNN) for controlling prosthetic hands, explain how these technologies enhance functionality and user experience. Provide examples of successful prosthetic hand designs and the technologies that have driven their development.

9.9.4 *Exercise 4*

Evaluate the benefits and challenges of using Virtual Reality (VR) in the training and rehabilitation of prosthetic hand users. Discuss how VR environments can simulate real-world tasks and provide immersive, interactive experiences that enhance the user's learning process and motor skills development. Consider the technological requirements for integrating VR with prosthetic training, including hardware and software components. Reflect on any potential limitations or barriers to the widespread adoption of VR for this purpose. Provide examples of specific VR applications or scenarios successfully used in prosthetic hand training. How might future VR technology advancements improve prosthetic hand users' rehabilitation outcomes?

9.9.5 *Exercise 5*

Investigate the advantages and potential challenges of using a smartphone to control a prosthetic hand. Discuss how integrating smartphone technology can enhance the customization and real-time control of the prosthetic. Consider the implications of connectivity issues, user interface design, and battery life on the functionality and reliability of the prosthetic hand. Explore specific use cases where smartphone control might significantly improve the user experience, such as adjusting the grip strength for different tasks or switching between pre-set hand gestures. Reflect on future advancements in smartphone technology that could further enhance the interaction between users and their prosthetic devices.

9.9.6 Exercise 6

Explore the advantages and limitations of using Artificial Neural Networks (ANN) versus Spiking Neural Networks (SNN) for controlling prosthetic hands. Begin by discussing the basic principles of each type of neural network and how they process information. Compare their performance in terms of responsiveness, power efficiency, and adaptability in real-world scenarios. Provide examples of specific tasks or activities where one type of neural network might outperform the other. Consider the potential developments in ANN and SNN technology and how these advancements might influence the choice between them for prosthetic hand control. Reflect on which neural network currently offers users the best balance of efficiency and functionality.

9.9.7 Exercise 7

Investigate the various models of prosthetic hands and their unique features. Compare and contrast traditional body-powered prosthetics, myoelectric prosthetics, and advanced bionic models. Discuss how each model is designed to meet different needs and levels of activity. Evaluate the advantages and limitations of each type, considering factors such as cost, ease of use, functionality, and aesthetic appeal. Provide scenarios or tasks where one model might be preferable over another and reflect on how technological advancements, such as 3D printing and AI, influence the development of new prosthetic hand models and improve user experiences.

9.9.8 Exercise 8

Design a prosthetic hand that can lift and manipulate objects weighing up to 2 kg. Using the materials available, calculate the required torque for the motor at the prosthetic hand's wrist joint to lift the object. Assume the distance from the motor to the object (acting as a lever arm) is 15 cm. Additionally, determine the power consumption if the motor operates at an efficiency of 80% and the voltage supply is 7.4 V. This exercise aims to integrate practical design considerations with numerical calculations, providing a hands-on understanding of the engineering principles involved in prosthetic hand design. Ready to crunch some numbers? Design a prosthetic hand that can achieve a grip force of 10 N, controlled by both Spiking Neural Networks (SNN) and Artificial Neural Networks (ANN). Calculate the required torque if the distance from the center of the hand to the fingers is 8 cm using the formula below:

$$\text{Torque} = \text{Force} \times \text{Distance} \tag{9.1}$$

Compare the power consumption for controlling the prosthetic hand using ANN and SNN. Assume the ANN system consumes 6 W continuously while the SNN system consumes 4 W with intermittent spikes. Calculate the total energy consumption for each control method over 15 s. Based on your calculations, discuss the advantages and limitations of using SNN versus ANN for controlling the prosthetic hand, considering factors like energy efficiency, responsiveness, and overall performance.

9.9.9 Exercise 9

Design a prosthetic hand that incorporates pressure sensing feedback and uses Spiking Neural Networks (SNN) for control. Calculate the torque required to achieve a grip force of 6 N, given that the distance from the center of the hand to the fingertips is 12 cm. Additionally, assume the SNN control system consumes an average power of 5 W while actively managing the prosthetic hand. Calculate the total energy consumption in joules if the hand operates continuously for 25 s. Discuss the benefits and challenges of using SNN for controlling the prosthetic hand, particularly in responsiveness, power efficiency, and adaptability compared to traditional control methods.

9.9.10 Exercise 10

Design a prosthetic hand that incorporates temperature sensing feedback and utilizes Spiking Neural Networks (SNN) for control. Calculate the torque required to generate a grip force of 7 N, given that the distance from the center of the hand to the fingertips is 10 cm. Assume the SNN control system consumes an average power of 4.5 W while managing the prosthetic hand. Calculate the total energy consumption in joules if the hand operates continuously for 30 s. Discuss the advantages and challenges of incorporating temperature sensing feedback with SNN control in the prosthetic hand, mainly focusing on aspects such as responsiveness, power efficiency, and the potential for enhanced user experience compared to traditional control methods.

References

1. Ahsan MR, Ibrahimy MI, Khalifa OO et al (2009) EMG signal classification for human computer interaction: a review. Eur J Sci Res 33(3):480–501
2. Anonymous (2021) Design and analysis of EMG controlled anthropomorphic prosthetic hand. In: 2021 8th international conference on signal processing and integrated networks (SPIN), pp 1–5

3. Anonymous (2022) Design, manufacture and control of the prosthetic hand with 3D printing. In: 2022 international conference automatics and informatics (ICAI), pp 1–5
4. Anonymous (2023) Basics of hand prosthesis design. Springer, Berlin
5. Bouganis A, Shanahan M (2010) Training a spiking neural network to control a 4-DoF robotic ARM based on spike timing-dependent plasticity. In: The 2010 international joint conference on neural networks (IJCNN). IEEE, Piscataway, pp 1–8
6. Chen TY, Huang MB, Huang HP (2020) Comprehensive design of prosthetic hand with practical and reliable control. In: 2020 IEEE Eurasia conference on IOT, communication and engineering (ECICE), Yunlin, pp 1–6
7. Hochreiter S, Schmidhuber J (1997) Long short-term memory. Neural Comput 9(8):1735–1780
8. Hong C, Phea S, Dang KN, Ben Abdallah A (2023) The aizuhand neuromorphic prosthetic hand. In: ETLTC international conference on ICT integration in technical education (ETLTC2023), January 24–27
9. Lobo JL, Del Ser J, Bifet A, Kasabov N (2020) Spiking neural networks and online learning: an overview and perspectives. Neural Netw 121:88–100
10. Ogbodo M, Dang KN, Ben Abdallah A (2022) Study of a multi-modal neurorobotic prosthetic ARM control system based on recurrent spiking neural network. In: The 4th ETLTC international conference on ICT integration in technical education (ETLTC2022)
11. Phea S, Ben Abdallah A (2022) An affordable 3D-printed open-loop prosthetic hand prototype with neural network learning EMG-based manipulation for amputees. In: The 4th ETLTC international conference on ICT integration in technical education (ETLTC2022), January 25–28
12. Samadani A (2018) Gated recurrent neural networks for EMG-based hand gesture classification. A comparative study. In: 2018 40th annual international conference of the IEEE engineering in medicine and biology society (EMBC). IEEE, Piscataway, pp 1–4
13. Watanabe M, Ben Abdallah A (2022) A low-cost raspberry pi-based control system for upper limb prosthesis. In: The 4th ETLTC international conference on ICT integration in technical education (ETLTC2022), January 25–28

Chapter 10
Comprehensive Review of Neuromorphic Systems

Abstract This chapter provides a comprehensive overview of the field of neuromorphic systems, tracing its evolution from inception to its current state. The chapter begins with an introduction that outlines the motivations and goals driving neuromorphic computing. It shows the historical progression and milestones of neuromorphic engineering, highlighting key developments and influential research. The chapter is divided into three main sections, each focusing on different approaches to neuromorphic system implementation. The first section examines the software emulation approach, explicitly discussing the SpiNNaker project, which simulates spiking neural networks on a large scale. The second section explores digital hardware design approaches, featuring examples such as IBM's TrueNorth and Intel's Loihi, which represent significant advancements in digital neuromorphic computing. The final section covers analog and mixed-signal hardware approaches, with a detailed look at NeuroGrid, an innovative platform that integrates analog circuits to mimic neuronal behavior. This chapter compares and contrasts these varied approaches and identifies their strengths and limitations, thoroughly understanding neuromorphic systems' current landscape and future directions.

10.1 Introduction

In the 1980s, Carver Mead and his team at Caltech pioneered the concept of bio-inspired microelectronics, laying the foundation for neuromorphic engineering [17]. Mead's approach leveraged the intrinsic physics of transistors to mimic the behavior of neurons, providing a new direction for developing computing systems that emulate the brain's computational mechanisms. Since then, researchers have advanced neuromorphic architectures significantly, enhancing their scalability, learning capabilities, and energy efficiency.

The advent of semiconductor technology has allowed for the integration of a growing number of transistors onto single chips, enabling the development of increasingly large-scale neuromorphic systems. Moore's Law predicts the doubling of chip density every two years, which has played a crucial role in making large-scale neuromorphic systems feasible. Neuromorphic systems are typically classified

A. Ben Abdallah, K. N. Dang, *Neuromorphic Computing Principles and Organization*, https://doi.org/10.1007/978-3-031-83089-1_10

into three main design approaches: (1) software emulation, (2) digital hardware, and (3) analog and mixed-signal hardware implementations.

A prominent example of the software emulation approach is the SpiNNaker system, developed by the University of Manchester. SpiNNaker is a high-performance computing system that uses ARM cores to simulate neural models for neurons and synapses. Each SpiNNaker chip contains 18 cores, which communicate through an on-chip Network-on-Chip (NoC) that extends off-chip through dedicated wiring, allowing for scalable inter-chip communication. This approach enables flexible and large-scale neuron simulations, providing a valuable platform for studying brain-inspired computation.

Recent digital hardware implementations include IBM's TrueNorth and Intel's Loihi, both of which highlight the potential of digital circuits in neuromorphic systems. TrueNorth employs a multi-core NoC architecture where each core contains a 256×256 crossbar to route incoming spike events to post-synaptic neurons. The system uses a Leaky-Integrate-and-Fire (LIF) neuron model with fixed synaptic weights, making TrueNorth particularly effective for inference tasks. Training is performed off-chip, aligning TrueNorth with applications in pattern recognition and classification tasks rather than learning. Loihi, developed by Intel, introduces an asynchronous spiking neural network architecture where neurons can transmit spikes along active synapses. Loihi's neurons are programmable and support various models, allowing for flexibility in neuromorphic computation. Synaptic bit-widths are configurable from 1 to 9 bits, allowing designers to adjust precision based on application requirements.

Building on Mead's original work, the analog and mixed-signal approach continues to be explored in neuromorphic engineering. The BrainScaleS system employs wafer-scale analog circuits that operate up to 10,000 times faster than biological real-time. This system is well-suited for large-scale simulations where speed is critical, enabling accelerated testing of neural models. Meanwhile, Stanford University's Neurogrid leverages sub-threshold analog circuits for real-time operation. Its architecture includes an on-chip tree-based network topology optimized for efficient multicasting and high-speed communication among neurons. Each approach to neuromorphic system design offers distinct advantages and trade-offs in terms of energy efficiency, integration density, flexibility, analog vs. digital neurons, and hardware vs. software implementation.

Table 10.1 provides a comparative overview of prominent large-scale neuromorphic computing systems, highlighting the trade-offs among scalability, power efficiency, and flexibility. The SpiNNaker system, capable of simulating up to one million neurons, utilizes a high-performance computing architecture. However, its scalability is limited compared to other systems due to the challenges associated with maintaining efficiency as the scale increases. SpiNNaker's flexibility, however, offers unique advantages: it allows updates and enhancements to neuron operations, supports complex memory models, and accommodates a range of plasticity models, which makes it particularly valuable for research and prototyping. In contrast, chip-based solutions like TrueNorth, Neurogrid, and Loihi achieve higher scalability through multi-chip configurations enabled by 2D-NoC architectures, which natu-

Table 10.1 Comparison of large-scale neuromorphic computing systems

Platform	Neurogrid	BrainScaleS	SpiNNaker	TrueNorth	Loihi
Technology	Analog, sub-threshold	Analog, over-threshold	Digital, programmable	Digital, fixed	Digital, programmable
Feature size	180 nm	180 nm	130 nm	28 nm	14 nm
Die size	1.7 cm^2	0.5 cm^2	1 cm^2	4.3 cm^2	60 mm^2
# of transistors	23 M	15 M	100 M	5.4 B	2.07 B
# of neurons	65 K	512	16 K	1 M	131 K
# of synapses	100 M	100 K	16 M	256 M	16–128 M (8–1 bit/synapse)
Power consumption	150 mW	1.3 W	1 W	72 mW	–
Interconnect	Tree-multicast	Hierarchical	2D mesh-multicast	2D mesh-unicast	2D mesh-unicast
Neuron model	Adaptive quadratic IF	Adaptive exponential IF	Programmable	LIF	Programmable
Synapse model	Shared dendrite	4-bit digital	Programmable	Binary, 4 modes	1–8 bit
Run-time plasticity	No	STDP	Programmable	No	Programmable

rally support efficient scaling. Neurogrid and TrueNorth, for instance, can scale to one million neurons in their 16-chip configurations, achieving this scale without a significant increase in power consumption, making them energy-efficient options for large-scale applications.

Loihi stands out for its programmability, with its neuron models offering adjustable functionality to support a range of neural computations. This flexibility benefits applications requiring specialized neuron behavior; however, Loihi's design is the most complex among the systems, comprising 2.07 billion transistors to support approximately 131,000 neurons. This complexity enables advanced features and increases the system's design and integration overhead.

While hardware-accelerated neuromorphic systems such as TrueNorth and Neurogrid are highly energy-efficient, SpiNNaker and Loihi offer greater flexibility in neuron operation. These systems illustrate the trade-offs between flexibility, scalability, and power efficiency in neuromorphic design. As shown in Table 10.1, digital neuromorphic chips dominate recent designs. While analog neurons, such as those used in Neurogrid and BrainScaleS, can closely emulate the electrical behavior of biological neurons and are generally more power-efficient, they face several challenges in implementation. Fabrication of analog neurons is more complex compared to digital designs, which can leverage standard cells and commercial design tools. Additionally, the performance of analog neurons varies with process technology, temperature, and voltage fluctuations, leading to inconsistencies in neuron functionality. Although analog neurons offer high biological fidelity, their behavior is more challenging to control. Furthermore, limited simulation support for analog designs complicates the prototyping and debugging of large-scale analog neuromorphic systems, making digital approaches, like those in SpiNNaker, TrueNorth, and Loihi, more feasible for large-scale deployment.

10.2 Software Emulation Approaches

The concept of neuromorphic systems is rooted in neuroscience research that aims to replicate the operations of biological brains. Large-scale initiatives, such as the Human Brain Project [16], leverage exascale supercomputers to study the brain across various spatial and temporal scales, providing foundational insights for neuromorphic system design. Another notable project, SpiNNaker [12], utilizes a massively parallel processor architecture to emulate brain-like functions, offering a scalable platform for spiking neural network simulations.

There are several software emulation tools available for neuromorphic systems. For instance, Brian 2 [22] is a Python-based simulator for spiking neural networks, currently running on CPUs with a GPU-accelerated version under development as of 2021 [23]. Another prominent tool, NEST [13], supports over 50 neuron models, allowing detailed spiking neural network simulations. The SpiNNaker team has also developed a software package to run PyNN-based simulations directly on SpiNNaker hardware [20]. Additionally, GPU-accelerated platforms such as

PyCARL [5] and BindsNet [14] further enhance emulation performance, making them suitable for large-scale, high-speed neuromorphic computations.

10.2.1 SpiNNaker Platform

The SpiNNaker project [12] aims to develop a massively parallel supercomputer capable of real-time emulating biological brain functions. This system comprises over one million ARM9 processors and seven terabytes of distributed RAM across a 57,000-node configuration. Each SpiNNaker node contains 18 cores and 128 megabytes of SDRAM, with each core simulating around one thousand neurons. Although SpiNNaker uses general-purpose processors, it provides flexibility in implementing various neuron and synapse models, making it distinct from traditional supercomputer-based models in its dedicated computing and communication techniques designed to optimize brain emulation efficiency.

SpiNNaker's communication network is structured as a folded 2D triangular mesh, with a router on each node that manages packet flow from its 18 local cores and six inter-chip links. This network employs the Address-Event-Representation (AER) format to enable efficient, low-latency communication between cores, supporting the system's scalability and real-time requirements for neuron simulation and interaction. SpiNNaker employs the "point neural model" (refer to Fig. 10.1),

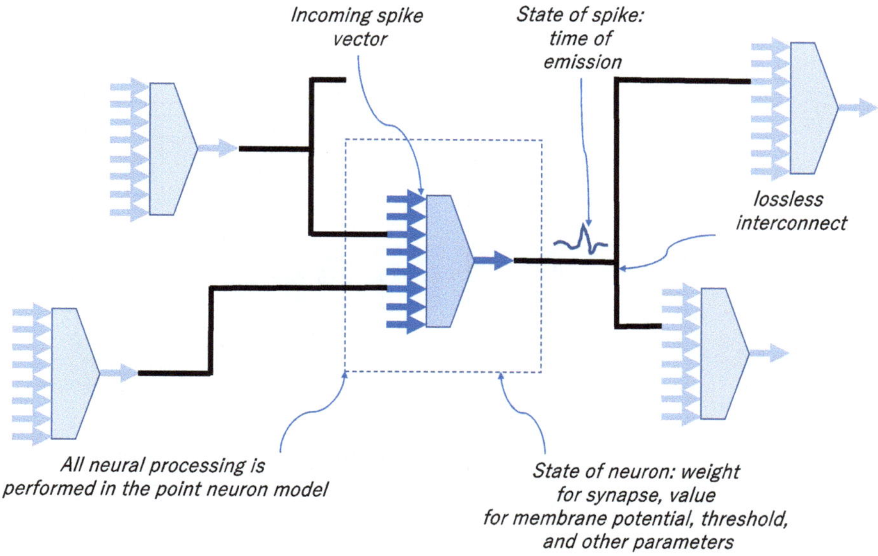

Fig. 10.1 The point neural model used in SpiNNaker: This model directs inputs to the soma without considering the dendritic structure. Learning updates only the *synapse* strength, with input spikes modified by *weights*

simplifying neuron functionality by disregarding the dendritic structure. In this model, all neuron inputs are directed to the *soma*, and only the *synapse* is updated to adjust connection strength. Input spikes that pass through the synapse are modulated according to the synaptic *weight*: a positive weight renders the synapse excitatory, while a negative weight renders it inhibitory.

10.2.1.1 SpiNNaker Architecture

The architecture of a SpiNNaker node is depicted in Fig. 10.2. Each node contains 18 ARM processors connected through an on-chip network. The packet router in each node handles communication, receiving packets from six neighboring nodes and each of the 18 local processors. Inside the router, packets are decoded and forwarded to one of the six external links or directly to a local processor. In addition to the processors and router, each node is equipped with internal RAM, ROM, Ethernet connectivity, a controller, and an external SRAM interface. SpiNNaker organizes its nodes in a triangular lattice topology, folded onto a toroidal surface, as shown in Fig. 10.2. The human brain contains approximately 10^{11} neurons. SpiNNaker aims to model 1% of this scale, equivalent to simulating the neural activity of ten entire mouse brains. Each neuron in the brain is typically connected to thousands of other neurons, with a mean firing rate of 10 Hz and a maximum firing rate in the hundreds of Hertz. In SpiNNaker, the target firing rate is set to 10 Hz, with each neuron receiving inputs from 1000 other neurons. The ARM processors

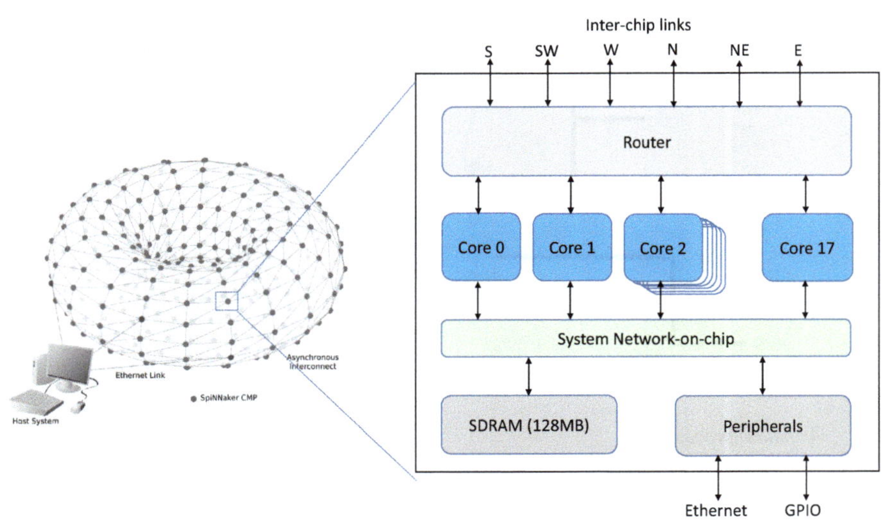

Fig. 10.2 SpiNNaker's architecture consists of a set of nodes interconnected through inter-chip links. Each node hosts a router facilitating communication between the inter-chip links and 18 ARM cores. In addition to the inter-chip links, the 18 ARM cores are also connected via a system Network-on-Chip (NoC) for efficient internal communication

in SpiNNaker operate at a clock frequency of 200 MHz, while the routers run at 100 MHz. These frequencies are selected to balance biological performance and power efficiency. SpiNNaker employs an interrupt-based wake-up mechanism to conserve energy, allowing the processor to enter a low-power sleep mode without activity, such as the absence of input spikes.

SpiNNaker employs the ARM968E-S processor [3], which belongs to the ARM9 family. This processor features a 32 KB instruction cache and a 64 KB data cache directly connected to the core. All core components are mapped and accessible through the AHB (Advanced High-Speed Bus), part of the ARM AMBA (Advanced Microcontroller Bus Architecture) interface standards. The processor has direct access to several key components, including the DMA (Direct Memory Access), the system NoC (Network-on-Chip) for intra-node communication, and the communication NoC for inter-node communication, as well as other peripherals such as interrupts and timers/counters. The DMA controller can also access the data cache directly, enabling the system NoC to deliver packets directly into the data cache memory.

In SpiNNaker, no conventional operating system runs on the cores. Instead, the system relies on an interrupt-driven mechanism. When an interrupt, in the form of a message, arrives, it triggers the core to wake up and handle the task. Initially, the packet is stored in a packet buffer, after which it activates the DMA (Direct Memory Access) to transfer the results and update the synaptic inputs (the spikes). Furthermore, the cores can also be awakened by external events.

Each node in SpiNNaker also includes timers and counters, which are managed and accessible via the AHB (Advanced High-Speed Bus) interface. These timers and counters provide real-time dynamics for biological spikes and other periodic timing controls.

Direct Memory Access (DMA) is used to access a core's data cache, facilitating the transfer of inter-neural connection data from SDRAM to the corresponding processor. DMA is also responsible for updating information such as states and outputs. Additionally, DMA enables the host ARM core to access the system NoC (Network-on-Chip), including SDRAM, in "bridge" mode. An error management module with interrupt capabilities is included to ensure crash recovery.

SpiNNaker connects to the host machine via Ethernet. Each node has an Ethernet interface, but only a few chips are directly connected to the host, which runs the software for programming and monitoring the SpiNNaker system. Each processor in SpiNNaker has cached memory, including ITCM (Instruction Tightly Coupled Memory) and DTCM (Data Tightly Coupled Memory), operating at 800 MBps. ITCM has a capacity of 32 KB, while DTCM is 64 KB. Additionally, there is a shared SRAM within the chip with a capacity of 32 KB and a speed of 25 MBps. Off-chip memory includes 128 MB of SDRAM, running at 64 MBps. Both SRAM and SDRAM are accessible at the node level.

As SpiNNaker is a 32-bit system, all memories are mapped into its 32-bit memory space, enabling processors within a node to access the data. However, nodes cannot access memory from other nodes directly. Instead, communication between nodes is achieved through packets delivered via 6-link interconnects, with no cache coherence between nodes.

10.2.1.2 Communication in SpiNNaker

A NoC (Network-on-Chip) system is employed to communicate between node processors. Since the memory space is visible at the node level, processes can access the necessary information. For inter-node communication, packets are used, and these packets come in two formats: 40-bit (5 bytes) or 72-bit (9 bytes). Each packet consists of 8 control bits and either one or two words, with the second word optional and indicating one bit in one of the eight control bits. Packets are transmitted to neighboring nodes and routed either to local cores or propagated to one neighbor. Depending on the routing protocol, they can be unicast or multicast. SpiNNaker employs Address Event Representation (AER) [21] for inter-neuron communication, where the address of neurons is sent instead of spikes. Compared to transmitting vectors of the neuron array's output, AER reduces complexity by sending fewer bits and exploiting the sparsity of firing events.

The SpiNNaker system consists of one million ARM cores, each emulating a thousand neurons, resulting in one billion neurons. Each neuron is assigned a unique address in AER format, represented by 32 bits. To transmit a spike, the system sends the 32-bit ID of the neuron, which is included as the optional payload in SpiNNaker packets, as shown in Fig. 10.3. There are four basic types of packets in the SpiNNaker system:

- *Nearest Neighbor*: This packet type facilitates communication between nodes and is primarily used for (1) initializing the system, (2) run-time flood-fill, and (3) debugging.
- *Point-to-Point*: This packet type includes the source node address and the destination node address (every 16 bits) in the first word. The router uses a look-up table to determine the correct output link for routing the packet.
- *Multi-cast*: This packet type is mainly used for inter-neural communication (i.e., spikes). The first word contains the AER of the firing neuron in 32-bit format. The router employs content-addressable memory (CAM) to determine the appropriate direction for routing this packet type.
- *Fixed-routing*: This packet type has a predefined routing path embedded in its content, offering a fast track from the launching node to the Ethernet-enabled node.

There are two types of interconnects in SpiNNaker: the system NoC and the communication NoC. The NoC system maintains the connectivity between the 18 processors and the SDRAM, while the NoC communication system handles input and output packets. The communication NoC follows a tree-based structure, where the input streams are merged into a single stream for routing. The output stream is then demultiplexed into six streams for distribution to neighbor nodes or local use. Figure 10.4 illustrates the flow of the input stream.

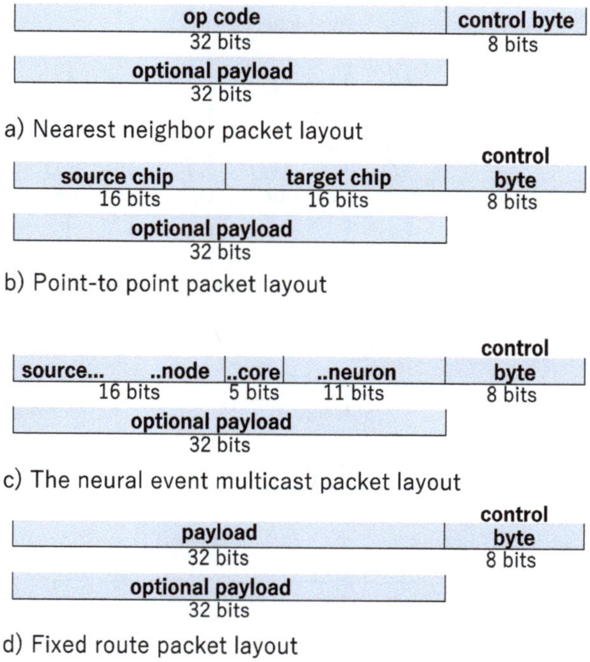

Fig. 10.3 Types of SpiNNaker packets: (**a**) Nearest neighbor, which facilitates communication with adjacent nodes; (**b**) Point-to-point, designed for direct communication between specific nodes; (**c**) Multicast, allowing data to be sent to multiple nodes simultaneously; and (**d**) Fixed route, which follows a predetermined path for efficient data transmission

The inter-chip links operate at 4 bits each and run at 60 MHz, while on-chip processor communication is 8 bits and operates at 200 MHz. Notably, there are 18 input streams from the 18 processors. When merged, the final stream is 72 bits at 100 MHz, resulting in one packet per cycle for routing. SpiNNaker also adopts the Address Event Representation (AER) protocol to establish connections between neurons. The AER format represents a spike with two critical pieces of information: (1) the time of the spike and (2) the neuron's identity. SpiNNaker uses packet-switched communication and broadcast/multicast routing to convey this information. Once a spike occurs, the AER signal is sent to the packet-switched communication fabric and delivered to the connected neurons.

Due to the electronic communication fabrics, spikes can reach their destinations almost instantaneously compared to biological signals in the brain. This capability allows SpiNNaker to map any neuron to any node (cluster of neurons) and effectively replicate the biological topology independent of the packet-switched communication topology. However, efficient mapping remains a significant challenge and has been extensively studied to minimize transmission time between neurons [4].

While electronic signals are delivered instantaneously, the "time" information of the spike must be preserved differently. In biological systems, spikes must occur at the right place and time, whereas in electronic systems, spikes are delivered without congestion. However, congestion or failures in the communication system can cause

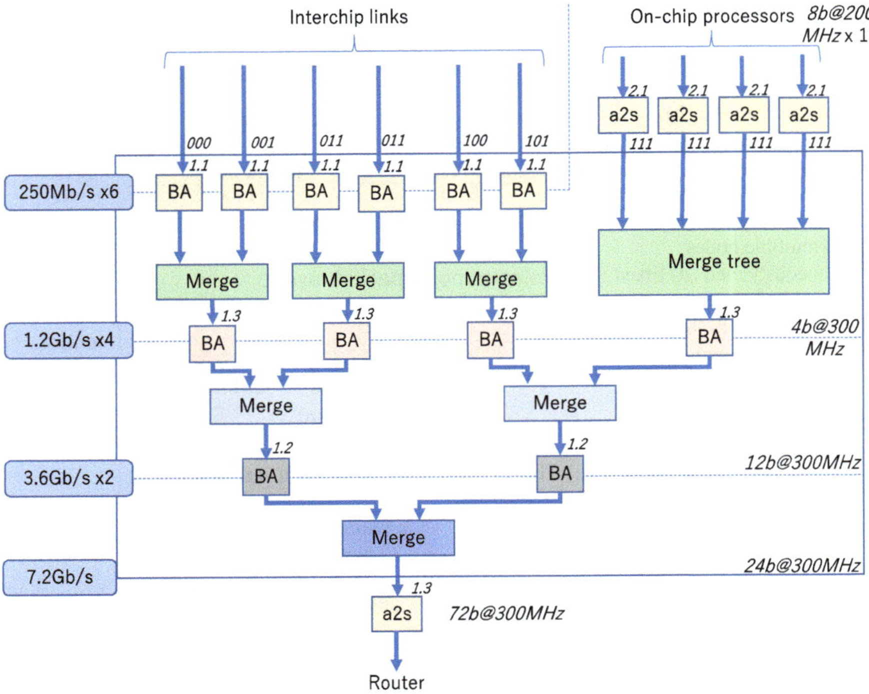

Fig. 10.4 The SpiNNaker input streams of the communication Network-on-Chip (NoC). This architecture features multiple levels of merge trees, where merging two streams effectively doubles the throughput. After merging, the inter-chip and on-chip links are directed to the router for efficient data routing

delays, drops, or misrouting of spikes. Therefore, scheduling methods and fault-tolerance mechanisms are necessary to ensure the reliability of the spiking system.

In SpiNNaker, each ARM processor is tasked with executing 1000 fixed-time-multiplexed neurons. With 18 ARM processors per node, each node handles 18,000 neurons. Consequently, SpiNNaker aims for a delivery time (spike window) of approximately 0.2 μs per hop to ensure that neurons respond to stimuli within the order of milliseconds, similar to biological systems. Communication between ARM cores in a SpiNNaker chip is initially managed by a Network-on-Chip (NoC). This communication is then converted to off-chip communication using packet-router modules. Six links are merged via a time-division multiplexer (TDM) into a local NoC stream. The output stream is subsequently split into six output links. In SpiNNaker, inter-node communication is facilitated through packets. Cores generate packets and transmit them to the local router, redirecting them to the target cores. If the destination neurons reside within the same node as the source, the local router sends the packets directly to the local cores. Otherwise, packets are forwarded to a neighboring node if the destination differs. As each node can only connect to six

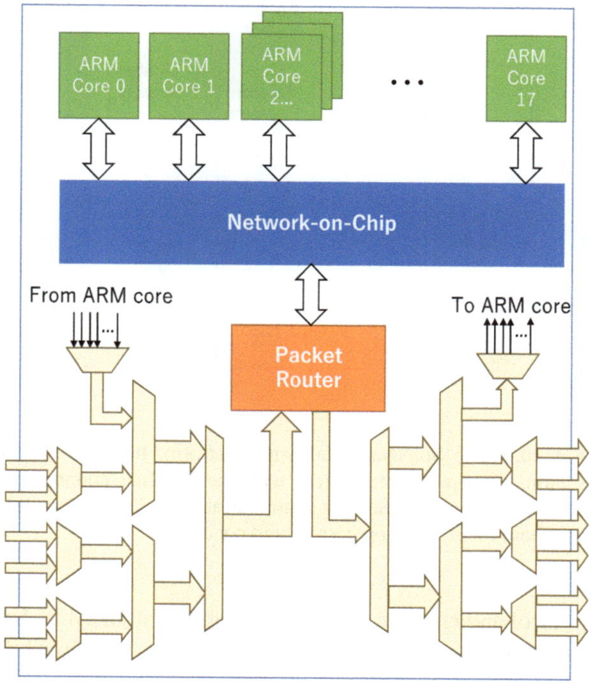

Fig. 10.5 Architecture of a SpiNNaker node featuring 18 ARM cores, each with a 32 KB instruction cache and a 64 KB data cache directly connected to the core. The node includes an on-chip Network-on-Chip (NoC) and an off-chip network for communication

other nodes, efficient routing techniques are essential for successful packet delivery (Fig. 10.5).

SpiNNaker packets are available in two formats: 40-bit and 72-bit, comprising eight control bits and either 4 or 8 bytes of data. Nearest neighbor packets are primarily used for system initialization, flood-fill communication (broadcast), and debugging. Point-to-point packets facilitate more detailed communications. Here, we focus on the *neural event multicast* packets, which are used for interneural communication. The AER format in SpiNNaker is summarized in Fig. 10.3, with the following fields: 16 bits for the node ID, 5 bits for the core ID (ARM core), and 11 bits for the neuron ID (neuron within the ARM core). Routing for AER packets is performed using the Content-Addressable Memory (CAM) method. First, the CAM is queried to locate the address in the output RAM. The output RAM then encodes the result in a one-hot format: the first 6 bits represent the inter-chip link, while the last 18 bits correspond to the internal core.

10.2.1.3 SpiNNaker Software Platform

The software platform of SpiNNaker is divided into two main components: the software running within the system and the software running on the host machine. For example, Fig. 10.6 illustrates the software platform for SpiNNaker. The software running on SpiNNaker is primarily written in C and operates at a low level to

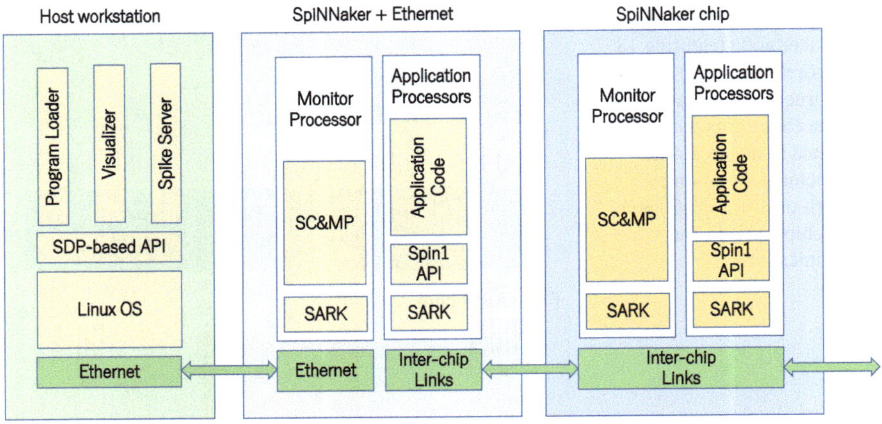

Fig. 10.6 The SpiNNaker Software platform: It comprises three components: the host workstation, the SpiNNaker system with the Ethernet connection, and the SpiNNaker chip. This architecture enables seamless communication and integration between the host and the SpiNNaker hardware for efficient processing and control

control and emulate the neuromorphic system. Most SpiNNaker applications utilize an event management library known as the Spin1 API. This library facilitates the association of interrupts with event-handling code. If no code is running, the processors enter a low-power sleep mode. When an event triggers an interrupt, the processor is activated. The software running on the host machine is responsible for downloading, monitoring, and visualizing data. It communicates with SpiNNaker through an Ethernet connection, as each node is equipped with one. SpiNNaker provides APIs that allow designers to develop applications in C, Perl, or Python on the host machine. Additionally, various visualizers are available to observe the system's inputs and outputs, including those of individual neurons. The host machine can also supply input spikes through a Spike Server application, which can either provide a data set or connect to input sensors that generate spiking inputs. SpiNNaker has been demonstrated with Negro—neuromorphic software platform—AER sensors and robotics.

10.3 Digital Hardware Design Approach

Hardware accelerators offer a more suitable solution to address this issue. The analog and mixed-signal approaches are discussed in the next section. Instead of relying on CPUs or GPUs for neuron operation and synaptic plasticity, the digital hardware approach uses specialized hardware designs for neurons and synapses. Typically, spikes are transmitted in Address-Event-Representation (AER) format and decoded at the receiver to obtain the weighted spike. This synapse operation can be performed using a resistive crossbar or memory.

Due to the complexity of other neuron models, most digital hardware implementations use a variation of the Integrate-and-Fire model (e.g., with leaky or stochastic inputs). This approach allows for low-cost and high-energy-efficient implementation, though flexibility in neural computation is limited. Several notable works in digital hardware include IBM's TrueNorth [18] (2014) and Intel's Loihi [8] (2018). Both chips follow similar principles: (1) neuron circuits serially emulate a group of neurons; (2) neurons are grouped into clusters; (3) clusters communicate via an asynchronous 2D mesh network-on-chip. The low complexity of these designs introduces new challenges for online learning.

In [10], a neuromorphic chip with 256 neurons and online learning capabilities is presented. An updated version in [11] features four Stochastic Spike-Driven Online Learning cores. NASH [15] represents another multi-core 3D Network-on-Chip design with STDP learning. A survey of neuro-inspired computing chips is also provided in [24]. In [2], Resparc is a collection of macro processing engines communicating between an internal switch network. The input is fed through a crossbar that implements the weight and accumulates at the neuron for computation. In [10], a neuro-processor with on-chip learning is proposed. The neuron is a simplified version of both Izhikevich and LIF neurons. Besides that, an SDSP learning mechanism is implemented in this chip.

On the other hand, a hybrid SNN/ANN chip is illustrated in [19]. It also follows the principle of multiple cores connected via an on-chip network. In each core, spikes arrive and are fed into a synapse memory, which transfers the weighted spikes into a soma for computation. While ANN uses the MAC and the ReLU activation function, the SNN uses integration and threshold comparison (similar to LIF). The following subsections will cover the design and operation of IBM TrueNorth and Intel Loihi, which are examples of digital hardware approaches.

10.3.1 IBM TrueNorth Architecture

IBM TrueNorth [18] aims to deliver a dense and energy-efficient platform for cognitive applications. The TrueNorth chip comprises 5.4 million transistors fabricated in 28 nm CMOS technology. Each chip houses 4096 neurosynaptic cores communicating in a 2D Mesh 64×64 asynchronous Network-on-Chip. Each core comprises 256 neurons and 256 inputs, resulting in 65,536 synapses. The chip operates asynchronously with a 1 kHz time-step clock [1]. It adopts the Integrate-and-Fire (IF) neuron model with a 1-bit synapse, fixed neuron-based weights, and 23 configurable parameters. Within each core, a single physical IF neuron performs the operations of 256 virtual neurons sequentially. TrueNorth is designed for offline training, and the chip only performs inference. Software is available for modeling, training, and mapping systems onto the TrueNorth architecture.

10.3.1.1 TrueNorth Neurosynaptic Architecture

TrueNorth chips can be connected to form larger systems. For instance, the NS16e circuit board hosts 16 IBM TrueNorth chips arranged in a 4×4 layout. The 2D Mesh Network-on-Chip (NoC) is naturally extended by connecting TrueNorth chips in 2D Mesh configurations. In TrueNorth, packets are routed based on the offset between nodes, determined by the difference in X and Y coordinates. This routing method theoretically allows TrueNorth to scale the size of its NoC efficiently. TrueNorth architecture is based on an asynchronous 2D Network-on-Chip (NoC). The chip layout and inter-chip communication are illustrated in Fig. 10.7 [1]. The neuron synaptic core (see Fig. 10.8), which consists of 256 neurons, is connected to a 2D-NoC router. Spikes are sent from pre-synaptic neurons to the network, where routers facilitate their delivery to the destination neurosynaptic core, housing the post-synaptic neurons. Spikes in Address-Event Representation (AER) format can traverse the chip periphery to off-chip wires and be routed to other chips. Figure 10.8 depicts the model for a single neurosynaptic core of TrueNorth. The input spikes arrive at axons and are sent to the neuron via a dendrite. The connections between axons and dendrites are represented as synapses. In the TrueNorth core, these connections are depicted in a synaptic crossbar where black dots signify synaptic connections. The synapses have only two modes: connected and unconnected, allowing the weight to be represented in binary. The output of the synaptic crossbar

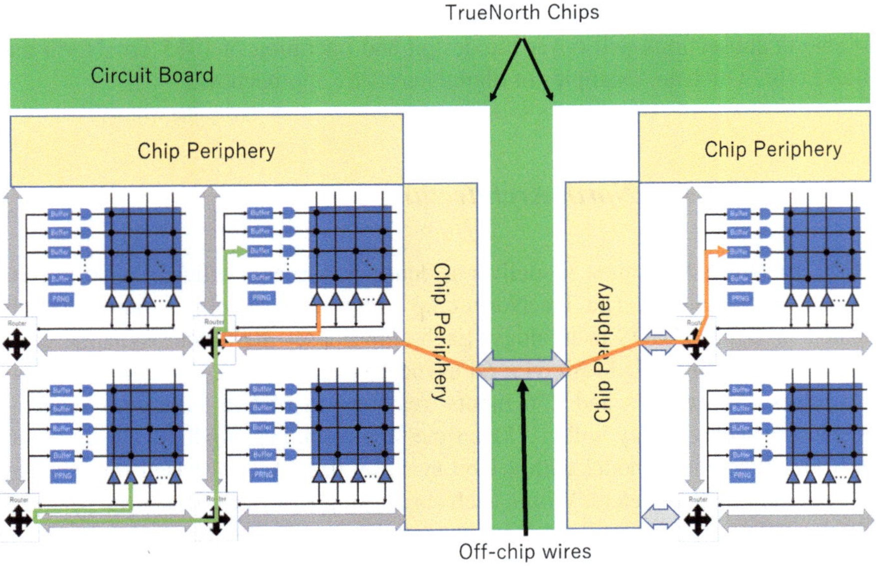

Fig. 10.7 Inter-chip communication in TrueNorth: The architecture illustrates how multiple chips exchange data and coordinate processing tasks. This system extends the Network-on-Chip (NoC) architecture, facilitating efficient collaboration among chips and enhancing overall performance for large-scale neural network implementations

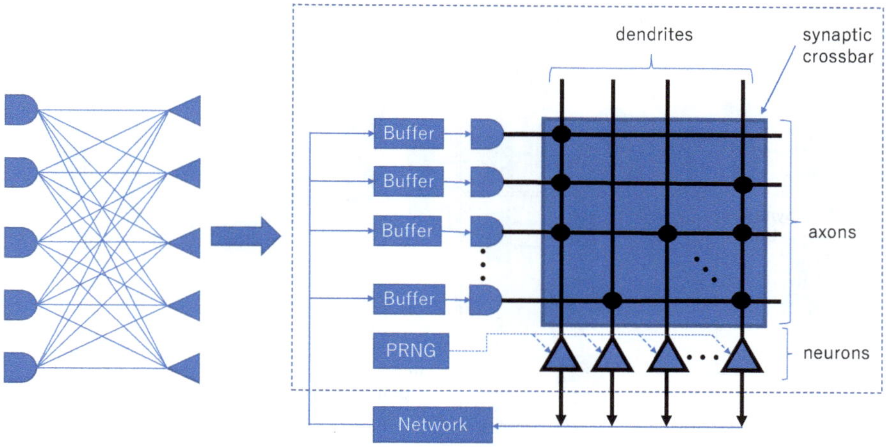

Fig. 10.8 Neural network model in the neurosynaptic core [1]: It includes a buffer for input spikes and a crossbar connecting dendrites to axons. The neuron integrates the incoming spikes and generates output signals to the network

is then multiplied by a fixed value, meaning the actual weights are not binary but fixed for each neuron (0 or a fixed value).

The neuron in TrueNorth operates based on synchronized 1 kHz global clocks. Meanwhile, the Network-on-Chip (NoC) is asynchronous, and the cores function independently. This implies that all neuron computations must be completed within 1 ms, regardless of variations in spike arrival times. This design helps TrueNorth to operate similarly to its software simulation, which is one of the advantages of using a fully digital neural implementation. The TrueNorth neuron follows the Leaky Integrate-and-Fire model, described by the following equation:

$$V_j(t) = V_j(t-1) + \sum_{i=0}^{N-1} A_i(t) w_{i,j} s_j^{G_i} - \lambda_j \tag{10.1}$$

Where $V_j(t)$ is the membrane potential of neuron j at the timestep t, $A_i(t)$ is the binary value representing the incoming spike from neuron i (1: has spike, 0: no spike), $w_{i,j}$ is the binary value representing the connectivity between axon i and dendrite j (1: connected, 0: unconnected), $s_j^{G_i}$ is the actual weight (synapse strength) between axon i and dendrite j and is classified into four types (G_i: 1 to 4), and λ_j is the leaky value of neuron j. The leaky and neuron equation can be adapted in several modes [7].

The TrueNorth processor uses a pseudo-random number generator, supporting stochastic spike integration, leak, and threshold. Both the leaky and reset mechanisms are also programmable. The architecture of the neuron is depicted in Fig. 10.9. The operation of a neuron is summarized in the following steps:

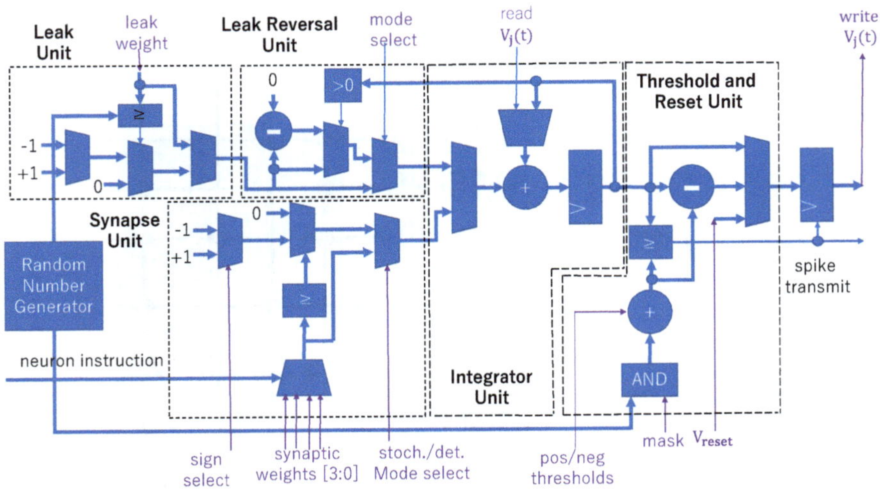

Fig. 10.9 The architecture of a TrueNorth neuron [1]. It comprises an integrator unit that accumulates input spikes, a threshold and reset mechanism for firing conditions, and two leak units to regulate the neuron's activity

- The neurosynaptic core receives spikes from the NoC and stores them in buffers.
- A 1 kHz global clock triggers the operation of all neurosynaptic cores.
- The spikes ($A_i(t)$) are sent from the buffers through the dendrites as depicted in Fig. 10.8.
- The neuron receives the spikes ($A_i(t)w_{i,j}$) and follows Eq. (10.1).
- At the end of the time step, a spike is generated and sent into the network if the membrane potential exceeds the threshold.
- After firing, the neuron's membrane potential is reset to a resting voltage.

As shown in Fig. 10.9, the synaptic weight is compared with a random number in stochastic mode, introducing randomness into the neuron model. Random leak mode and random threshold comparison can also be observed. The neuron operates according to the simplest LIF model in the deterministic model. In each neurosynaptic core of TrueNorth, only one physical neuron is used to simulate 256 neurons serially. Consequently, each neuron parameter and synaptic connection (in a 410-bit format) is loaded for computation. This approach is designed to run in biological real-time with a 1 kHz global synchronization clock, which does not require parallel neural computation. This design philosophy emphasizes that weights and parameters can be stored and reloaded, consistent with the goal of digital neuron implementation.

10.3.1.2 TrueNorth Synapses Design

The neuron's synaptic crossbar stores connections in binary format (1: connected, 0: unconnected). Since the neuron operates serially, the synaptic connections are embedded into a single SRAM with dimensions of 256 rows by 410 columns. Each row includes:

- 256 bits for synaptic connections,
- 124 bits for neuron parameters,
- 26 bits for spike destination (18-bit for network routing and 8-bit for axon index), and
- 4 bits for spike delivery tick.

The input spikes, formatted in 8-bit AER, serve as the index for the synaptic connection to determine the connection status (0 for unconnected, 1 for connected). If the axon and neuron are not connected, the returned weight is 0, indicating no incoming weighted spike.

10.3.1.3 Interconnect Design

Once a neuron fires, the spike is packaged and sent to the network to be delivered to a destination core. Inter-core connections are essential since neurons are clustered into neuro-synaptic cores with 256 neurons per core. TrueNorth utilizes a unicast-only 2D Mesh asynchronous network, which enables the architecture to be tiled at both the core and chip levels, as illustrated in Fig. 10.7. The scalability of the 2D Mesh topology allows TrueNorth chips to be arranged in a 2D mesh on the PCB. Off-chip wires connect two chips, extending the on-chip NoC to include the new chip, thereby continuing the asynchronous 2D NoC communication.

The routing process at each router comprises six phases: (1) from local, (2) forward east, (3) forward west, (4) forward north, (5) forward south, and (6) to local. To route a packet, an 18-bit value is used for dx and dy, representing the number of hops in the x- and y-directions. For example, a packet traveling from the node (1,3) to node (4,5) (formatted as (dy, dx)) starts with $dy = -3$ and $dx = -2$. The routing priority is east (increase dx), west (decrease dx), north (increase dy), and south (decrease dy). Thus, the packet will first move east to node (1,4), increasing dx by one. At node (1,4), dy and dx are updated to -3 and -1, respectively. The packet reaches its destination once both dx and dy are zero.

If multiple messages contend for the same router, they are serviced on a first-come, first-served basis. As TrueNorth operates on a unicast design, multicast packets are handled by sending them repetitively to a list of destinations. This is achieved by cloning the neuron within the same core (node).

10.3.1.4 TrueNorth Software

TrueNorth's hardware is supported by a software emulator, providing deterministic behavior comparable to the hardware. This allows for application development in software, which can then be mapped onto hardware. Similarly, training is performed in software before being implemented on TrueNorth chips.

The software model for TrueNorth involves modeling a network of neurosynaptic cores, which are indivisible building blocks [9]. The TrueNorth team developed a new programming paradigm called *Corelet*. This paradigm includes several components:

1. *Corelet*: An abstraction model that encapsulates the details of neurosynaptic cores.
2. *Corelet Language*: An object-oriented programming language for creating, composing, and decomposing Corelets.
3. *Corelet Library*: A library for reusing programs.
4. *Programming Environment*: Includes Compass, the TrueNorth architectural simulator, which provides results that closely match the TrueNorth system.

The Corelet abstraction model includes a *corelet seed*, representing a single neurosynaptic core that exposes only inputs and outputs while encapsulating its parameters and operations. The programming interface accesses only the input and output of the *corelet seed*. Multiple corelet seeds can be connected to form a corelet, and several corelets can be linked to create a new corelet. This modeling approach is illustrated in Fig. 10.10. Figure 10.10a shows a corelet consisting of neurons and input/output connectors. The corelet seed encapsulates the intra-core connections and exposes only external connections, resulting in a block as shown in Fig. 10.10b. If connected, two corelets can be combined into a single corelet, as illustrated by the

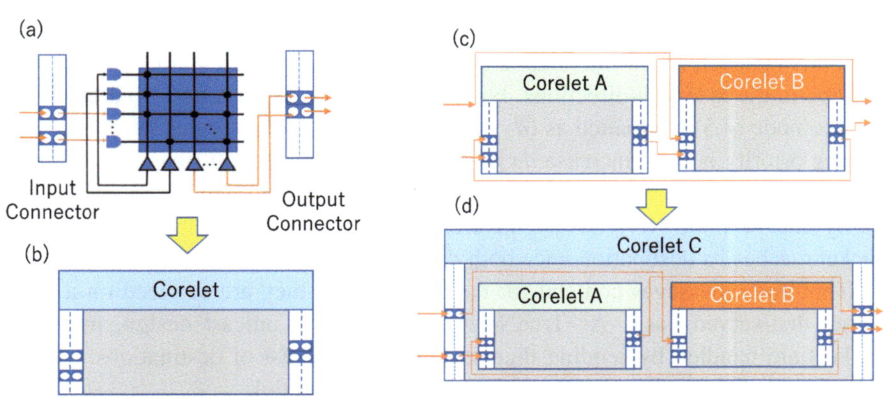

Fig. 10.10 The TrueNorth Corelet framework: (**a**) Neuro synaptic core with input and output connectors; (**b**) Corelet provides a wrapped model that only exposes the input-output; (**c**) Two connected corelets A and B; (**d**) Corelet C wraps two Corelets A and B and now exposes only the input and output connectors

connection between corelets A and B in Fig. 10.10c. Corelet C wraps both Corelets A and B, encapsulating their internal connections and exposing only the inputs and outputs.

The Compass simulator, written in C++ with MPI library calls and OpenMP threading primitives, has been scaled to support networks with up to 530 billion neurons and 137 trillion synapses. Applications of TrueNorth have demonstrated remarkably low power consumption [18], with uses including speaker recognition, composer recognition, digit recognition, eye detection, and multi-object recognition.

10.3.2 *Intel Loihi Processor*

The basic spiking neural units in Loihi are grouped into sets of trees. Each core also includes a programmable learning engine. Learning rules are microcode programmable, allowing for the implementation of various learning mechanisms, including simple pairwise STDP (Spike-Timing-Dependent Plasticity) as well as more complex schemes such as triplet STDP and reinforcement learning. Figure 10.11 shows the top-level architecture of Loihi. Incoming spikes carry information about the axon index, which the synapse unit uses to map the spike to the synaptic weight stored in memory. The dendrite unit then updates the neuron's internal values, while the axon unit generates the output spike based on the membrane potential. The learning unit updates the synaptic weight based on the dendrite output and the synaptic weight in memory. Both the weights and neurons in the Loihi core are variable (ranging from 1 to 8 bits), allowing the system to be programmed with different densities and resolutions.

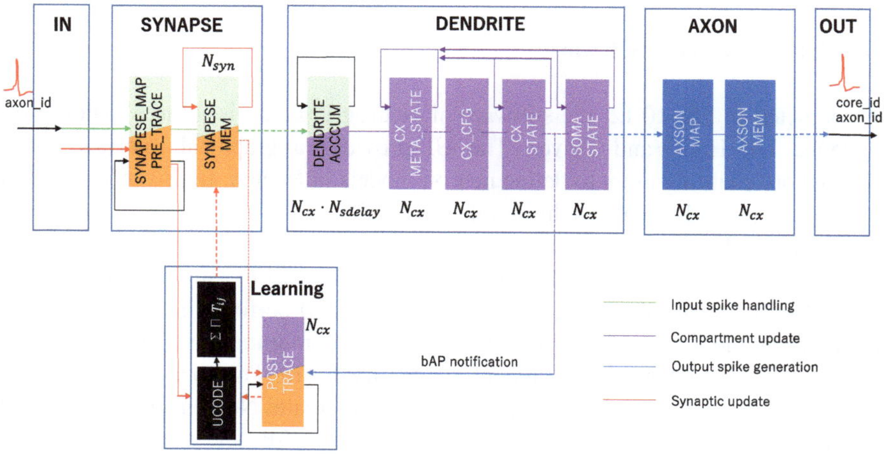

Fig. 10.11 Top-level architecture of Loihi core

The interconnect for Loihi is a 2D asynchronous network-on-chip, which can expand across multiple chips due to the scalability of the 2D mesh topology. When a neuron fires, a fan-out structure at the axon distributes spikes to all downstream neurons, which may be located within the same core or in other cores within the network. Each core supports up to 1024 neurons, and the maximum core-to-core fan-out is limited to 4096.

10.4 Analog and Mixed-Signal Hardware Approach

The original neuromorphic system, designed by Carver Mead and his team, has become the benchmark for developing and implementing neuromorphic systems using analog and mixed-signal approaches. Unlike digital emulation, which simulates neuron functions with varying levels of granularity, analog neurons aim to mimic the actual operations of biological neurons directly.

10.4.1 NeuroGrid Processor

The Neurogrid integrates software and hardware for real-time neuromorphic simulation. The software suite includes a user interface (UI), a hardware abstraction layer (HAL), and a driver for hardware interaction. Figure 10.12 illustrates the overall architecture of the Neurogrid system. The UI offers a programming model for the neural network, the HAL translates this model into the Neurogrid circuit, and the driver facilitates the download and deployment of the model via USB.

10.4.1.1 Neurogrid Software

As depicted in Fig. 10.12, the software of Neurogrid comprises three major components: UI, HAL, and Driver. The UI provides a graphical interface using NGPython, enabling users to define neuron models in Python. It also offers control functionalities and visualizes the simulation results.

The *HAL* (Hardware Abstraction Layer) manages network and filter configurations, connecting the graphical user interface (GUI) with the simulation platform. It handles the network's connectivity and activity, and performs network mapping to translate the Python environment into router configurations. Additionally, it manages data flow between the model and the hardware. The *Driver* generates the necessary configurations for routers and neurons. It creates Neurogrid packets based on the data flow, encodes them for transmission via USB, and translates received packets back into average data for visualization purposes.

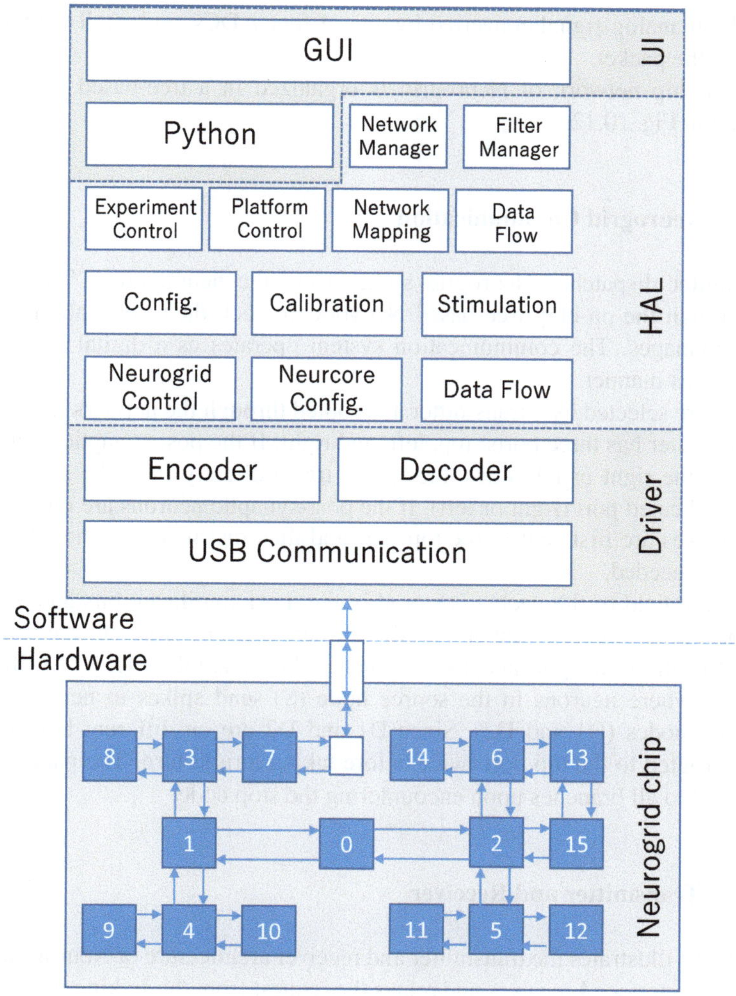

Fig. 10.12 Neurogrid system with both hardware and software [6]

10.4.1.2 Neurogrid Hardware Components

Neurogrid utilizes a sub-threshold analog circuit to model neurons and synapses in biological real-time. Due to the limitations of analog spikes traveling long distances, the communication of spikes is handled digitally using on-chip networks. A Neurogrid packet comprises a sequence of 12-bit words, including route, address, payload, and tail. The route information directs a core to forward the packet to the next node or consume it if it reaches its destination. The payload can contain various types of information: a spike index for the row in the neural array, data to be written to RAM, an analog signal converted by one of four ADCs, and a tail field to mark the end of the packet.

The on-chip network of Neurogrid is organized in a tree-based topology, as illustrated in Fig. 10.12.

10.4.1.3 Neurogrid Communication

A transmitter dispatches Neurogrid spikes from the neural array. These spikes travel through the on-chip tree-based Network to reach their destination, which a receiver manages. The communication system operates as a digital circuit in an asynchronous manner.

Spikes are selected by a transmitter and routed through the network. Neurogrid's tree NoC router has three ports: top, left, and right. If the post-synaptic neurons are located on the right or left sides, the spikes travel directly from the source to the router's dedicated port (right or left). If the post-synaptic neurons are on a different branch, spikes are first sent to the top port and then distributed to the left or right branches as needed.

The route field of the packet is stored in the most significant bits and is shifted as the packet is routed. If the stop code (all zeros) is encountered, the spikes are multicast to the left, right, and local branches. For example, Fig. 10.13 illustrates a scenario where neurons in the source node (S) send spikes to neurons in two destination nodes (D1 and D2). Since D1 and D2 are on different branches, the packet is routed to the top port twice before taking a right turn. The packet is then multicasted to all branches upon encountering the stop code.

10.4.1.4 Transmitter and Receiver

Figure 10.14 illustrates the transmitter and receiver architecture of Neurogrid. In the transmitter, interface **I** receives and relays the request from the spiking neuron (S) to the hierarchical row arbiters (J). Another interface and arbiter in the column select

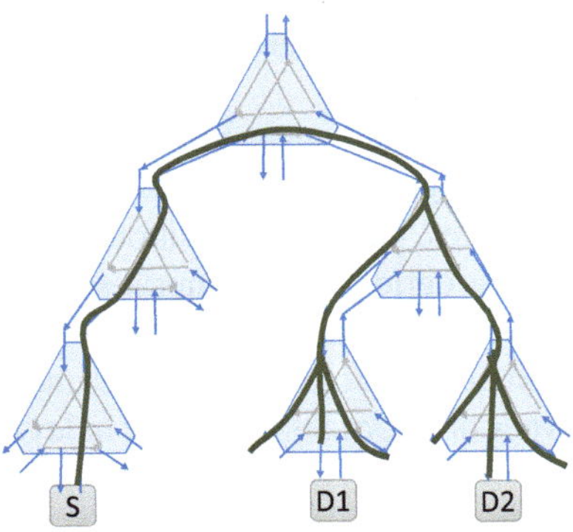

Fig. 10.13 Neurogrid packet transmission. (**a**) Transmitter. (**b**) Receiver

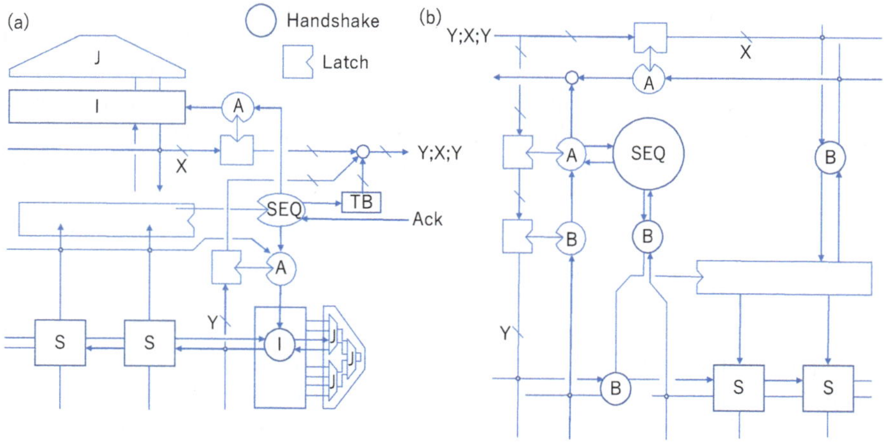

Fig. 10.14 Neurogrid transmitter and receiver architecture [6]: (**a**) Transmitter; (**b**) Receiver

the spiking neuron spikes. The spike packet includes the column address (X), row address (Y), and a tail word that concludes the packet. If the packet is acknowledged, it is forwarded to the sequencer (SEQ).

The receiver processes the row and column information of the packet as shown in Fig. 10.14b. It checks if the row and column indices match the packet's data. Once the packet is delivered to the correct row and column, it is forwarded to the spiking neuron (S), which issues an acknowledgment (ACK).

The routing in Neurogrid operates in two phases. The first phase is *point-to-point* routing, where the router directs the packet up/down or left/right based on the packet's initial word. The second phase is *branching* routing, where the router duplicates the packet to both the left and right ports for multicast distribution. These duplicated packets can be received by the local neuron array or filtered using information from a local SRAM of the core. The Neurogrid NoC is organized in a tree-based topology optimized for multicasting. In the first phase, packets are routed to the destination root router. From there, they are distributed across branches, regardless of the presence of a receipting neuron. The routing process is later simplified by filtering the packets, reducing complexity due to the low look-up table requirements.

10.5 Chapter Summary

Neuromorphic systems have made significant strides in recent years, driven by the need for more efficient and brain-like computing architectures. Recent advances include the development of hardware-based artificial neurons and synaptic devices that mimic the parallel and energy-efficient operations of biological neural networks. Notable progress has been made in spiking neural networks (SNNs), which offer more realistic and efficient neural computations than traditional artificial neural networks. Additionally, innovations in memristors and synaptic devices have enabled more compact and scalable neuromorphic systems. These systems are now being applied in diverse fields such as robotics, autonomous systems, and edge computing, showcasing their potential to revolutionize data processing and artificial intelligence.

This chapter provided a comprehensive overview of the field of neuromorphic engineering, tracing its evolution from inception to its current state. The chapter begins with an introduction that outlines the motivations and goals driving neuromorphic computing. It shows the historical progression and milestones of neuromorphic engineering, highlighting key developments and influential research. The chapter is divided into three main sections, each focusing on different approaches to neuromorphic system implementation. The first section examines the software emulation approach, specifically discussing the SpiNNaker project, which simulates spiking neural networks on a large scale. The second section explores digital hardware design approaches, featuring examples such as IBM's TrueNorth and Intel's Loihi, which represent significant advancements in digital neuromorphic computing. The final section covers analog and mixed-signal hardware approaches, with a detailed look at NeuroGrid, an innovative platform that integrates analog circuits to mimic neuronal behavior. This chapter compares and contrasts these varied approaches and identifies their strengths and limitations, thoroughly understanding neuromorphic systems' current landscape and future directions.

Future research focuses on improving scalability, fault tolerance, and energy efficiency to create more robust and sustainable neuromorphic computing solutions.

10.6 Exercises

10.6.1 Exercise 1

The IBM TrueNorth chip is a neuromorphic computing system designed to mimic the human brain's structure and function. It uses a network of digital neurons and synapses to perform parallel processing efficiently.

1. The TrueNorth chip comprises 1,000,000 neurons and 256,000,000 synapses. Given that the chip operates with a power consumption of 70 mW, calculate the energy consumption per neuron and per synapse.
2. If the TrueNorth chip encodes spike events using 9-bit words, how many unique spike patterns can the chip represent?
3. TrueNorth's architecture allows for simultaneous processing of up to 256 neurons per core. Assuming there are 4096 cores on the chip, calculate the maximum number of neurons that can be processed in parallel.

4. Provide two potential applications of the TrueNorth chip in real-world scenarios and discuss how its neuromorphic design contributes to these applications.

10.6.2 Exercise 2

Synchronous and asynchronous circuits represent two primary approaches to digital circuit design. Synchronous circuits depend on a global clock signal to coordinate the timing of all operations. Conversely, asynchronous circuits function without a clock signal, operating based on the availability of inputs. These principles lead to two distinct design choices for on-chip communication: asynchronous and synchronous. Explain the differences between these two design choices and discuss the significant advancements associated with each approach.

10.6.3 Exercise 3

In various systems, neurons or nodes can be addressed using different methods. TrueNorth, for instance, employs (dx, dy) for routing, representing the differences in address coordinate values between the source and destination. Assuming the address field is limited to a maximum of 8 bits, explain the primary difference between the TrueNorth approach and other conventional methods.

10.6.4 Exercise 4

Intel's Loihi chip is a neuromorphic computing system designed to mimic the structure and function of the human brain, using a network of digital neurons and synapses to perform parallel processing efficiently. Answer the following questions:

1. The Loihi chip comprises 128,000 neurons and 130,000,000 synapses. Given that the chip operates with a power consumption of 1 W calculate the energy consumption per neuron and per synapse.
2. If the Loihi chip encodes spike events using 32-bit words, how many unique spike patterns can the chip represent?
3. Loihi's architecture allows for simultaneous processing of up to 128 neurons per core. Assuming 6 embedded processor cores are on the chip, calculate the maximum number of neurons that can be processed in parallel.
4. Compare the energy efficiency of Loihi's 1 W power consumption with a conventional processor consuming 50 W. How many times more energy-efficient is Loihi?

5. Provide two potential applications of the Loihi chip in real-world scenarios and discuss how its neuromorphic design contributes to these applications.

10.6.5 Exercise 5

In Network-on-Chip (NoC) systems, there are several communication methods: unicast, multicast, and broadcast.

- Unicast: involves a one-to-one communication where data is sent from a single source to a single destination.
- Multicast: allows data to be sent from one source to multiple specific destinations simultaneously, without duplicating the data for each receiver.
- Broadcast: involves sending data from one source to all nodes in the network, ensuring that every node receives the same data.

Explain the differences between these communication methods. Additionally, discuss which method is most suitable for data transfer and spike communication in neuromorphic computing systems, considering efficiency, latency, and scalability factors.

10.6.6 Exercise 6

Scaling up neuromorphic systems often involves connecting multiple chips to work together, necessitating off-chip communication. What is off-chip communication, and how does it enhance the scalability of neuromorphic systems?

10.6.7 Exercise 7

The Intel Loihi chip employs an advanced Network-on-Chip (NoC) design to facilitate communication between its neuromorphic cores. Answer the following questions:

1. The Loihi chip consists of 128 neuromorphic cores, each connected to a router in a mesh topology. Calculate the network's total number of routers and direct connections (links), assuming each router has 4 neighboring connections.
2. If the Loihi chip uses data packets of size 128 bits for communication between cores, determine the total number of bits transmitted per second if the NoC operates at a frequency of 1 GHz and each core sends one packet per cycle.
3. Given that the average latency for data transfer across the NoC is 2 ns per hop, calculate the total latency for a data packet to travel across 10 hops in the network.

4. Each router in the NoC consumes 5 mW of power. Calculate the total power consumption of all routers in the chip. Additionally, discuss the energy efficiency benefits of using a NoC design in the Loihi chip.

10.6.8 Exercise 8

Biologically, the design and connections of neurons are complex. For example, a signal from an upstream neuron travels through an axon, crosses a synapse, and continues via a dendrite to reach the downstream neuron. Explain the concept of the neuron point model and discuss the reasons for its use.

10.6.9 Exercise 9

Given that the human brain contains approximately 10^{11} neurons, modeling it poses a significant challenge for current state-of-the-art designs. Using the IBM TrueNorth chip, calculate the number of chips required to model the human brain and estimate the scale of the on-chip and off-chip network necessary to support this model.

10.6.10 Exercise 10

The IBM TrueNorth and Intel Loihi chips are two pioneering examples of neuromorphic computing systems designed to emulate the human brain's structure and function. Both chips employ networks of digital neurons and synapses to perform parallel processing efficiently. Compare the two chips based on the following numerical values:

1. The TrueNorth chip comprises 1,000,000 neurons and 256,000,000 synapses, with a power consumption of 70 mW. The Loihi chip comprises 128,000 neurons and 130,000,000 synapses, with a power consumption of 1 W. Calculate the energy consumption per neuron and per synapse for each chip. Which chip is more energy-efficient in terms of neurons and synapses?
2. TrueNorth encodes spike events using 9-bit words, while Loihi uses 32-bit words. How many unique spike patterns can each chip represent?
3. TrueNorth's architecture allows for the simultaneous processing of up to 256 neurons per core, totaling 4096 cores. Loihi's architecture provides 128 neurons per core, with 6 embedded processor cores. Calculate the maximum number of neurons that can be processed in parallel for each chip. Compare their parallel processing capabilities.

4. Given that a conventional processor consumes 50 W, compare the energy efficiency of the TrueNorth and Loihi chips. How much more energy-efficient are these neuromorphic chips than a traditional processor?
5. Discuss two potential real-world applications for each chip and explain how their neuromorphic designs contribute to these applications.

References

1. Akopyan F, Sawada J, Cassidy A, Alvarez-Icaza R, Arthur J, Merolla P, Imam N, Nakamura Y, Datta P, Nam GJ et al (2015) Truenorth: design and tool flow of a 65 mw 1 million neuron programmable neurosynaptic chip. IEEE Trans Comput Aid Des Integr Circuits Syst 34(10):1537–1557
2. Ankit A, Sengupta A, Panda P, Roy K (2017) RESPARC: a reconfigurable and energy-efficient architecture with memristive crossbars for deep spiking neural networks. In: Proceedings of the 54th annual design automation conference 2017, pp 1–6
3. ARM (2004) ARM968E-S technical reference manual. ARM, arm ddi 0311c edition
4. Balaji A, Das A, Wu Y, Huynh K, Dell'Anna FG, Indiveri G, Krichmar JL, Dutt ND, Schaafsma S, Catthoor F (2019) Mapping spiking neural networks to neuromorphic hardware. IEEE Trans Very Large Scale Integr Syst 28(1):76–86
5. Balaji A, Adiraju P, Kashyap HJ, Das A, Krichmar JL, Dutt ND, Catthoor F (2020) PyCARL: a PyNN interface for hardware-software co-simulation of spiking neural network (2020). arXiv:2003.09696
6. Benjamin BV, Gao P, McQuinn E, Choudhary S, Chandrasekaran AR, Bussat JM, Alvarez-Icaza R, Arthur JV, Merolla PA, Boahen K (2014) Neurogrid: a mixed-analog-digital multichip system for large-scale neural simulations. Proc IEEE 102(5):699–716
7. Cassidy AS, Merolla P, Arthur JV, Esser SK, Jackson B, Alvarez-Icaza R, Datta P, Sawada J, Wong TM, Feldman V, et al (2013) Cognitive computing building block: a versatile and efficient digital neuron model for neurosynaptic cores. In: The 2013 international joint conference on neural networks (IJCNN). IEEE, Piscataway, pp 1–10
8. Davies M, Srinivasa N, Lin TH, Chinya G, Cao Y, Choday SH, Dimou G, Joshi P, Imam N, Jain S et al (2018) Loihi: a neuromorphic manycore processor with on-chip learning. IEEE Micro 38(1):82–99
9. Esser SK, Andreopoulos A, Appuswamy R, Datta P, Barch D, Amir A, Arthur JV, Cassidy A, Flickner M, Merolla P, Chandra S, Basilico N, Carpin S, Zimmerman T, Zee F, Alvarez-Icaza R, Kusnitz JA, Wong TM, Risk WP, McQuinn E, Nayak TK, Singh R, Modha DS (2013) Cognitive computing systems: algorithms and applications for networks of neurosynaptic cores. In: The 2013 international joint conference on neural networks, IJCNN 2013, Dallas, August 4–9, 2013. IEEE, Piscataway, pp 1–10
10. Frenkel C, Lefebvre M, Legat JD, Bol D (2018) A 0.086-mm2 12.7-pj/sop 64k-synapse 256-neuron online-learning digital spiking neuromorphic processor in 28-nm CMOS. IEEE Trans Biomed Circuits Syst 13(1):145–158
11. Frenkel C, Legat JD, Bol D (2019) Morphic: a 65-nm 738k-synapse/mm2 quad-core binary-weight digital neuromorphic processor with stochastic spike-driven online learning. IEEE Trans Biomed Circuits Syst 13(5):999–1010
12. Furber SB, Galluppi F, Temple S, Plana LA (2014) The spinnaker project. Proc IEEE 102(5):652–665
13. Gewaltig MO, Diesmann M (2007) Nest (neural simulation tool). Scholarpedia 2(4):1430
14. Hazan H, Saunders DJ, Khan H, Patel D, Sanghavi DT, Siegelmann HT, Kozma R (2018) Bindsnet: a machine learning-oriented spiking neural networks library in python. Front Neuroinf 12:89

15. Ikechukwu OM, Dang KN, Abdallah AB (2021) On the design of a fault-tolerant scalable three dimensional NoC-based digital neuromorphic system with on-chip learning. IEEE Access 9:64331–64345
16. Markram H, Meier K, Lippert T, Grillner S, Frackowiak R, Dehaene S, Knoll A, Sompolinsky H, Verstreken K, DeFelipe J et al (2011) Introducing the human brain project. Proc Comput Sci 7:39–42
17. Mead C (1989) Analog VLSI and neural systems. Addison-Wesley, New York
18. Merolla PA, Arthur JV, Alvarez-Icaza R, Cassidy AS, Sawada J, Akopyan F, Jackson BL, Imam N, Guo C, Nakamura Y et al (2014) A million spiking-neuron integrated circuit with a scalable communication network and interface. Science 345(6197):668–673
19. Pei J, Deng L, Song S, Zhao M, Zhang Y, Wu S, Wang G, Zou Z, Wu Z, He W et al (2019) Towards artificial general intelligence with hybrid Tianjic chip architecture. Nature 572(7767):106–111
20. Rhodes O, Bogdan PA, Brenninkmeijer C, Davidson S, Fellows D, Gait A, Lester DR, Mikaitis M, Plana LA, Rowley AGD, Stokes AB, Furber SB (2018) SPyNNaker: a software package for running PyNN simulations on spinnaker. Front Neurosci 12:816
21. Sivilotti MA (1991) Wiring considerations in analog VLSI systems, with application to field-programmable networks. Ph.D. Thesis, California Institute of Technology
22. Stimberg M, Brette R, Goodman DF (2019) Brian 2, an intuitive and efficient neural simulator. eLife 8:e47314
23. Stimberg M, Goodman DF, Nowotny T (2020) Brian2genn: accelerating spiking neural network simulations with graphics hardware. Sci Rep 10(1):1–12
24. Zhang W, Gao B, Tang J, Yao P, Yu S, Chang MF, Yoo HJ, Qian H, Wu H (2020) Neuro-inspired computing chips. Nat Electron 3(7):371–382

Index

A. Ben Abdallah, K. N. Dang, *Neuromorphic Computing Principles and Organization*, https://doi.org/10.1007/978-3-031-83089-1

MIX
Papier aus verantwortungsvollen Quellen
Paper from responsible sources
FSC® C105338

If you have any concerns about our products,
you can contact us on
ProductSafety@springernature.com

In case Publisher is established outside the EU,
the EU authorized representative is:
Springer Nature Customer Service Center GmbH
Europaplatz 3, 69115 Heidelberg, Germany

Printed by Libri Plureos GmbH
in Hamburg, Germany